PROSE MODELS

Fifth Edition

Gerald Levin

The University of Akron

Harcourt Brace Jovanovich, Inc.

New York   San Diego   Chicago   San Francisco   Atlanta

London   Sydney   Toronto

ISBN: 0-15-572280-8
Library of Congress Catalog Card Number: 80-82693
Printed in the United States of America

Copyrights and Acknowledgments

The author wishes to thank the copyright holders of the selections in this book, which
are listed below in order of their appearance in the Contents:

3 COUNTRY SUPERSTITIONS From *Wandering Through Winter* by Edwin Way Teale
(Dodd, Mead and Company, 1966). Reprinted by permission of the publisher. Selection
title by editor.   5 LOMA VISTA DRIVE From "People Start Running" by James
Stevenson (*The New Yorker*, January 28, 1980). Reprinted by permission; © 1980 The
New Yorker Magazine, Inc. Selection title by editor.   6 THE BLAST FUR-
NACE From *Home to the Wilderness* by Sally Carrighar. Copyright 1944 by Sally Car-
righar. Copyright © 1973 by I.C.E. Limited. Reprinted by permission of Houghton
Mifflin Company.   10 THE CORNER STORE Reprinted by permission of Russell
& Volkening, Inc., as agents for the author. Copyright © 1975 by Eudora Welty.
13 UNCLE MYERS From "Tin Butterfly," copyright 1951 by Mary McCarthy. Re-
printed from her volume *Memories of a Catholic Girlhood* by permission of Harcourt
Brace Jovanovich, Inc. Selection title by editor.   16 MY FIRST INTRODUCTION TO
THE CLASSICS From *My Early Life* by Winston S. Churchill. Reprinted by permission of
the Hamlyn Publishing Group Limited and Charles Scribner's Sons. Copyright 1930
Charles Scribner's Sons. Selection title by editor.   19 FITNESS IN THE MODERN
WORLD From *Man Adapting* by René Dubos (Yale University Press, 1964). Copyright
© 1965, 1980 by Yale University. Reprinted by permission.   21 QUEEN VICTO-
RIA AT THE END OF HER LIFE From *Queen Victoria* by Lytton Strachey. Copyright 1921
by Harcourt Brace Jovanovich, Inc.; renewed 1949 by James Strachey. Reprinted by
permission of the publisher. Selection title by editor.   23 THE BULLFIGHT From
"St. Augustine and the Bullfight" in *The Collected Essays and Occasional Writings of
Katherine Anne Porter* by Katherine Anne Porter. Copyright © 1970 by Katherine Anne
Porter. Reprinted by permission of Delacorte Press/Seymour Lawrence. Selection title
by editor.   26 CALCUTTA From *Calcutta*, copyright © 1971 by Geoffrey Moorhouse. Reprinted by permission of Harcourt Brace Jovanovich, Inc., and George Wei-
denfeld and Nicolson. Selection title by editor.   29 HALLEY'S COMET From
"The Cosmic Prison" in *The Invisible Pyramid* by Loren Eiseley. Copyright © 1970 by
Loren Eiseley. Reprinted by permission of Charles Scribner's Sons. Selection title by
editor.   32 EUPHEMISM Reprinted by permission from *Time*, The Weekly Newsmagazine; copyright Time Inc. 1969.   35 WORLD WAR ONE TRENCHES From *The
Great War and Modern Memory* by Paul Fussell. Copyright © 1975 by Oxford University Press, Inc. Reprinted by permission. Selection title by editor.   38 THE
AMERICAN WEDDING From *The Eternal Bliss Machine* by Marcia Seligson. Reprinted by

Continued on page 363

PREFACE

The Fifth Edition of *Prose Models* differs from the Fourth in several important ways: In Part One, the number of multiparagraph selections has been increased. In Part Two, the "Controversy" section has also been increased, with the addition of three contrasting essays on women and the draft. One section—"Variety of Paragraph Development"—has been dropped, and "Interpretation of Evidence" has been moved to bridge the sections on exposition and argument. The discussion of deductive reasoning has been shortened and simplified, and the new essays that illustrate this topic are briefer and more accessible. Throughout the book—particularly in the sections on the sentence and diction—there are more examples of expository writing and fewer of description and narration.

From the beginning I have been guided by the truth of James Sledd's statement that "nobody ever learned to write without reading." Accordingly, the 36 new selections are more than ever pertinent to the process of writing, both in style and in content. Instead of forcing student writers in a single direction by favoring the plain style thought by many to be appropriate to freshmen, I have sought to represent most of the important writing styles current today. In addition to looking for excellent writing models, I have sought selections that have something interesting and important to say to young adults. The new essays accordingly deal with issues and experiences of concern to them, for example, the changing status of American women. Among the writers new to the Fifth Edition are Renata Adler, Russell Baker, J. Bronowski, Joan Didion, René Dubos, Loren Eiseley, Frances FitzGerald, Ellen Goodman, John McPhee, James Stevenson, Calvin Trillin, and Larry Woiwode.

The plan of the book remains the same. Part One, on the elements of the essay, considers such topics as emphasis and the coordination and subordination of ideas in the paragraph and the sentence; Part

Two (which, with the exception of the Shaw, consists of complete essays or sections of books) considers many of these same topics in the context of the whole essay. Thus, the treatment of the topic sentence in the paragraph prepares for the treatment of the thesis in the whole essay. Throughout, the sections build on previous discussions, but they are sufficiently self-contained to be taught in a different order. A discussion of each rhetorical or logical topic follows the first selection in each of the 37 sections. Wherever possible, the questions and writing assignments are based on the rhetorical or logical topic of the selection as well as on its content. The Instructor's Manual provides suggestions for teaching each selection, alternative rhetorical topics for many, and answers to most of the questions.

I want to thank Alan Hart, The University of Akron, for his help in revising the logic discussion. And I am indebted to other colleagues at the University of Akron who made suggestions for this edition: William Francis, Bruce Holland, Robert Holland, Julia Hull, David L. Jones, Walter Lehrman, Alice J. MacDonald, Ruth Messenger, D'Orsay Pearson, John S. Phillipson, Sally K. Slocum, Frederik N. Smith, Cathryn C. Taliaferro, Arlene A. Toth, and Linda Weiner. Many other helpful suggestions came from instructors across the country, including Jay Farness, Northern Arizona University; Charles Fishman, State University of New York, Albany; A. G. Medlicott, Jr., University of Connecticut, Storrs; Stephen D. Reid, Colorado State University; and Margaret A. Strom, The George Washington University. My wife, Lillian Levin, and Elizabeth and Sylvia Levin helped me prepare the manuscript. And I am fortunate to have again had the advice and assistance of Natalie Bowen and Eben W. Ludlow, both of Harcourt Brace Jovanovich, at each stage of this revision.

Gerald Levin

CONTENTS

Antithesis

Length

Climax

DICTION   123

Usage

Tone

Concreteness

Imagery

Figurative Language

Faulty Diction

PART TWO

THE WHOLE ESSAY

EXPOSITION 183

Thesis

Main and Subordinate Ideas

Beginning and Ending

Analysis

Order of Ideas

Interpretation of Evidence

ARGUMENT AND PERSUASION   276

Deductive Reasoning

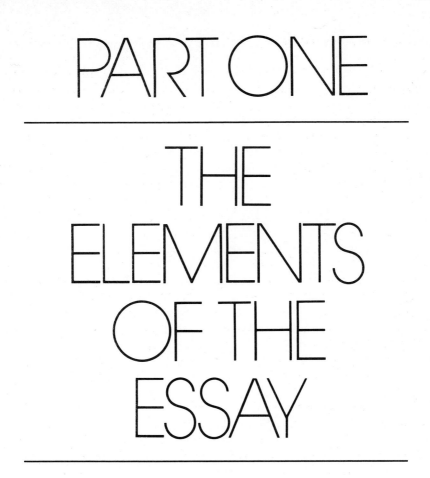

PART ONE

THE ELEMENTS OF THE ESSAY

THE PARAGRAPH: ORGANIZATION

Topic Sentence

EDWIN WAY TEALE
Country Superstitions

[1] In the folklore of the country, numerous superstitions relate to winter weather. [2] Back-country farmers examine their corn husks—the thicker the husk, the colder the winter. [3] They watch the acorn crop—the more acorns, the more severe the season. [4] They observe where white-faced hornets place their paper nests—the higher they are, the deeper will be the snow. [5] They examine the size and shape and color of the spleens of butchered hogs for clues to the severity of the season. [6] They keep track of the blooming of dogwood in the spring—the more abundant the blooms, the more bitter the cold in January. [7] When chipmunks carry their tails high and squirrels have heavier fur and mice come into country houses early in the fall, the superstitious gird themselves for a long, hard winter. [8] Without any scientific basis, a wider-than-usual black band on a woolly-bear caterpillar is accepted as a sign that winter will arrive early and stay late. [9] Even the way a cat sits beside the stove carries its message to the credulous. [10] According to a belief once widely held in the Ozarks, a cat sitting with its tail to the fire indicates very cold weather is on the way.

DISCUSSION: Topic Sentence

The *topic sentence* is a statement of the subject, or topic, of the paragraph, often found at the beginning of the paragraph. It may introduce an impression to be developed in specific detail, or a consideration to be examined, or a question to be answered:

> Now let us ask what are a child's rights, and what are the rights of society over the child. . . .—George Bernard Shaw, *Misalliance*

Sometimes the topic sentence is a complete statement of the main, or topic, idea:

> This country is in the process of discovering that it can no longer afford the big life. That is the downstream meaning of our present economic turmoil. From whatever area you approach the problem, be it resources, inflation, population or politics, the prospect remains the same. Solutions will necessarily require permanent alterations in the size and scope of our activities, possessions and dreams.—Leonard Gross, "Is Less More?"

As in this example, the topic idea may be repeated or restated at the end, following the details of the discussion.

Occasionally the topic sentence appears toward the middle of the paragraph, or even at the end, preceded by a series of details that build to it. The topic sentence is said to be *implied* when the details make the point without an explicit statement of the topic idea.

QUESTIONS

1. The topic sentence of Teale's paragraph—sentence 1—states the main or topic idea; sentences 2–10 illustrate it. What do these illustrations tell us about country life?
2. What later sentence in the paragraph reminds us of the topic idea?

WRITING ASSIGNMENTS

1. Describe a series of superstitions relating to another season of the year or to a particular activity. Build your paragraph to a conclusion about these superstitions.
2. Use one of the following statements as the topic sentence of a paragraph of your own. Provide a series of illustrations for the topic idea:
   a. Winter or summer sports make special demands on the participant.

b. Winter or summer sports make special demands on the spectator.

c. Winter or summer as a season has its special pleasures as well as hardships.

d. Riding the subway (or a similar activity) requires special skills.

JAMES STEVENSON

Loma Vista Drive

[1] Partway down the long, very steep slope of Loma Vista Drive, descending through Beverly Hills, with the city of Los Angeles spread out far below the houses of sparkling opulence on either side, there is a sign warning "Use Lowest Gear" and, shortly after that, a sign that says "Runaway Vehicle Escape Lane 600 Feet Ahead." [2] Just before Loma Vista crosses Doheny Road, it expands on the right into a third lane, composed of a succession of low, uneven piles of loose gravel nestled against cement block set in an embankment. [3] The operator of a runaway vehicle is apparently expected to steer his car into this soft and receptive lane and come to a halt like a baseball player sliding into third. [4] It seems a perfectly reasonable solution; the unsettling aspect is the underlying assumption that automobiles will so frequently go berserk hereabouts that some accommodation must be made for them. [5] Similarly, along the heavily populated canyon roads of Beverly Hills there are signs forbidding cigarettes and matches: these dry hills may burst into flame at any time. [6] The houses above Sunset Boulevard are stuck in the nearly vertical slopes like cloves in a ham; how they stay there is mysterious. [7] It seems likely that, if they do not catch fire first, a good rain will send them tumbling down the mountain; already, earth has slid out from under retaining walls, terraces, swimming pools, driveways, even roads. [8] In some places, tons of concrete have been poured like icing over a section of hillside to hold it back—and the concrete has even been painted green—but the earth has begun to slip away beneath that, too, leaving edges of concrete sticking out against the sky. [9] In addition, of course, the entire area sits close to the quiescent but menacing San Andreas Fault. [10] Gazing up the perilous roads at the plucky, high-risk homes perched in the tinderlike hills near the great rift, a visitor feels that this may be a community where desire and imagination automatically take precedence over danger, and even over reality.

QUESTIONS

1. Stevenson builds to his topic idea instead of beginning the paragraph with it. What is gained by ending the paragraph with it?
2. How do the details of the paragraph develop the topic idea? Which of them illustrate "desire" and which "imagination"?
3. How does the opening sentence introduce the subject and prepare the reader for the details that follow?
4. Did the topic idea have to be stated explicitly, or could Stevenson have depended on the details to state it implicitly?
5. This paragraph introduces a profile of a contemporary maker of horror films. Is the paragraph an appropriate introduction?

WRITING ASSIGNMENTS

1. Use Stevenson's paragraph as a model for a description of your own. Choose a street you know well, and describe it for a stranger—building through a series of details to a central idea that they illustrate.
2. Write a second paragraph, describing the street from the point of view of a person seeing it for the first time. Choose details that develop an idea; do not state this idea explicitly. Your details should be vivid enough and well enough organized to make the idea clear to your reader.

Main and Subordinate Ideas

SALLY CARRIGHAR

The Blast Furnace

1.   We were a father and his first-born, a four-year-old girl, setting out every Sunday afternoon to see the industrial marvels of Cleveland, Ohio. The young man had grown up in a smaller Canadian town and he was delighted with Cleveland, which hummed and clanged with the vast new developments steel had made possible. In temperament he was anything but an engineer; here however he was excited to feel that he had jumped into the very heart of the torrent of progress.

2.   Most often we walked on the banks of the Cuyahoga River to see the drawbridge come apart and rise up, like giant black jaws taking a bite of the sky, so that boats could go through: the long freighters that brought iron ore from Lake Superior, other large and small freighters, fishing boats, passenger steamers. My father's eyes never tired of watching them make their smooth way up and down the river. His father, born in Amsterdam of a seagoing family, had been a skipper on the Great Lakes. Perhaps my father too should have been a sailor, but he was something nearly as satisfying—he worked for a railroad.

3.   And so we went to the roundhouse where the steam engines stood when they were not pulling trains. They had all entered through the same door but inside their tracks spread apart, as gracefully as the ribs of a lady's fan. My father knew a great deal about engines, he knew the names of some of these and he walked among them with pride.

4.   On our way to the roundhouse we passed through the freight yards where long trains of boxcars lay on their sidings. My father said that the cars belonged to different railroads and came from various parts of the country, being coupled together here because all those in one train were bound for the same destination. This was getting too complicated but there was nothing complicated about my father's emotion when he said, "Working for a railroad is like living everywhere in the country at once!" A characteristic enchantment came into his eyes and voice, a contagious exhilaration which meant that anything it attached to was good. Living everywhere was something that even a child could grasp vaguely and pleasantly.

5.   My father and I made other trips and best were the ones to the blast furnaces. He explained how the iron ore from the boats was mixed with coal and carried in little cars to the top of the chimney above the furnace. It was dumped in, and as it fell down "a special kind of very hot air" was blown into it. The coal and iron ore caught fire, and below they fell into great tubs as melting metal, a pinkish gold liquid, incandescent as the sun is when it is starting to set. The man and child were allowed to go rather near the vats, to feel the scorching heat and to drown their gaze in the glowing boil. All the rest of the building was dark; the silhouettes of the men who worked at the vats were black shadows. Wearing long leather aprons, they moved about the vats ladling off the slag. That was very skilled work, my father said; the men had to know just how much of the worthless slag to remove. For years afterwards, when we could no longer spend Sunday afternoons on these expeditions, we used to go out of our house at night to see the pink reflections from the blast furnaces on the clouds over Cleveland. We could remember that we had watched

the vatfuls of heavily moving gold, and those events from the past were an unspoken bond between us.

6. Someone once said, "Your father must have been trying to turn you into a boy. He'd probably wanted his first child to be a son." Perhaps; but it was not strange to him to show a girl the achievements of men. He thought of women as human beings and assumed that they, even one very young, would be interested in anything that was interesting to him. He had absorbed that attitude from the women he'd grown up with, his mother and her four sisters, all of whom led adventurous lives. His favorite Aunt Chris had married a clipper captain and sailed with him all her life. When they retired, having seen the entire world, they chose to settle in Burma. Another aunt married one of the Morgan family, who established the famous breed of Morgan horses, and took up a homestead in Manitoba. Aunt Mary, a physician's wife, went with him out to San Francisco during the Gold Rush and stayed there. The fourth aunt had married the inspector of ships' chronometers at Quebec; and my father's mother, of course, had married her skipper from Holland. In the winter when he was not on his ship he ran a factory for making barrel staves that he had established in western Kentucky—all this and the fathering of five children by the time he was twenty-eight, when he lost his life in a notorious Lake Erie storm. His wife, a musician, brought up her five without complaint, just as her mother, also an early widow, had reared her five gallant girls. With his memories of women like these it was not surprising that my father would wish, even somewhat prematurely, to show his daughter the things that were thrilling to him. I did not comprehend all his family history at four but I did absorb the impression that girls and women reached out for life eagerly and that it was natural for them to be interested in absolutely everything.

DISCUSSION: Main and Subordinate Ideas

The *main* idea of a paragraph may be developed through a series of *subordinate* ideas that illustrate or develop it. Each of these ideas in turn may be illustrated or developed:

> Although the forest looks peaceful it supports incessant warfare, most of which is hidden and silent. [*topic sentence: main idea of paragraph*]
> [1] For thirty-five years the strong have been subduing the weak. [*subordinate idea: specific detail about the forest*]

²The blueberries that once flourished on the mountain have been destroyed. [*subordinate idea: a more specific detail—blueberries*]
³All the trees are individuals, as all human beings are individuals; and every tree poses a threat to every other tree. [*subordinate idea: another more specific detail—trees*]
⁴The competition is so fierce that you can hardly penetrate some of the thickets where the lower branches of neighboring trees are interlocked in a blind competition for survival. [*subordinate idea: development of sentence 3*]—Brooks Atkinson, "The Warfare in the Forest Is Not Wanton"

In longer paragraphs, the main idea may be distinguished by repeating or restating it, by opening the paragraph with it as Atkinson does, or by building the paragraph to a statement of it. When you organize a paragraph, keep in mind that the beginning and ending are usually the most emphatic parts because of their prominence.

QUESTIONS

1. In paragraph 1 Carrighar develops her opening sentence—the main idea of the paragraph—with specific detail about her father. What is the main idea of paragraph 2, and how does she use the detail of the paragraph to develop it?
2. Paragraph 4 moves from specific detail to the main idea. What is that idea, and how does the author give it prominence?
3. Which of the subordinate ideas in paragraph 5 are in turn illustrated or developed?
4. Paragraphs 1–5 are subordinate to paragraph 6, which draws a conclusion from the experiences described, and develops this conclusion through details of a different sort. What is this conclusion, and what new details develop it? How is this conclusion—the main idea of the paragraph—restated later in the paragraph and made prominent?

WRITING ASSIGNMENTS

1. Write several paragraphs describing childhood experiences with a parent or relative that taught you something about the adult world and about yourself. Begin with these truths, or build the paragraphs to them, as Carrighar does.
2. Write several paragraphs about the impressions you received as a child about girls and women, from information you received or impressions you developed about women in your family. If you wish,

contrast these impressions with those you received about boys and men.

3. Discuss how particular childhood experiences with friends led you to discoveries about yourself and the world that conflicted with values and ideas held by your parents and teachers. Use this discussion to draw a conclusion about growing up.

Unity

EUDORA WELTY

The Corner Store

1. Our Little Store rose right up from the sidewalk; standing in a street of family houses, it alone hadn't any yard in front, any tree or flower bed. It was a plain frame building covered over with brick. Above the door, a little railed porch ran across on an upstairs level and four windows with shades were looking out. But I didn't catch on to those.

2. Running in out of the sun, you met what seemed total obscurity inside. There were almost tangible smells—licorice recently sucked in a child's cheek, dill pickle brine that had leaked through a paper sack in a fresh trail across the wooden floor, ammonia-loaded ice that had been hoisted from wet croker sacks and slammed into the icebox with its sweet butter at the door, and perhaps the smell of still untrapped mice.

3. Then through the motes of cracker dust, cornmeal dust, the Gold Dust of the Gold Dust Twins that the floor had been swept out with, the realities emerged. Shelves climbed to high reach all the way around, set out with not too much of any one thing but a lot of things—lard, molasses, vinegar, starch, matches, kerosine, Octagon soap (about a year's worth of octagon-shaped coupons cut out and saved brought a signet ring addressed to you in the mail). It was up to you to remember what you came for, while your eye traveled from cans of sardines to tin whistles to ice cream salt to harmonicas to

flypaper (over your head, batting around on a thread beneath the blades of the ceiling fan, stuck with its testimonial catch).

4. Its confusion may have been in the eye of its beholder. Enchantment is cast upon you by all those things you weren't supposed to have need for, to lure you close to wooden tops you'd outgrown, boy's marbles and agates in little net pouches, small rubber balls that wouldn't bounce straight, frail, frazzly kite string, clay bubble pipes that would snap off in your teeth, the stiffest scissors. You could contemplate those long narrow boxes of sparklers gathering dust while you waited for it to be the Fourth of July or Christmas, and noisemakers in the shape of tin frogs for somebody's birthday party you hadn't been invited to yet, and see that they were all marvelous.

5. You might not have even looked for Mr. Sessions when he came around his store cheese (as big as a doll's house) and in front of the counter looking for you. When you'd finally asked him for, and received from him in its paper bag, whatever single thing it was that you had been sent for, the nickel that was left over was yours to spend.

6. Down at a child's eye level, inside those glass jars with mouths in their sides through which the grocer could run his scoop or a child's hand might be invited to reach for a choice, were wineballs, all-day suckers, gumdrops, peppermints. Making a row under the glass of a counter were the Tootsie Rolls, Hershey bars, Goo Goo Clusters, Baby Ruths. And whatever was the name of those pastilles that came stacked in a cardboard cylinder with a cardboard lid? They were thin and dry, about the size of tiddledy-winks, and in the shape of twisted rosettes. A kind of chocolate dust came out with them when you shook them out in your hand. Were they chocolate? I'd say, rather, they were brown. They didn't taste of anything at all, unless it was wood. Their attraction was the number you got for a nickel.

7. Making up your mind, you circled the store around and around, around the pickle barrel, around the tower of Crackerjack boxes; Mr. Sessions had built it for us himself on top of a packing case like a house of cards.

8. If it seemed too hot for Crackerjacks, I might get a cold drink. Mr. Sessions might have already stationed himself by the cold-drinks barrel, like a mind reader. Deep in ice water that looked black as ink, murky shapes—that would come up as Coca-Colas, Orange Crushes, and various flavors of pop—were all swimming around together. When you gave the word, Mr. Sessions plunged his bare arm in to the elbow and fished out your choice, first try. I favored a locally bottled concoction called Lake's Celery. (What else could it be called? It was

made by a Mr. Lake out of celery. It was a popular drink here for years but was not known universally, as I found out when I arrived in New York and ordered one in the Astor bar.) You drank on the premises, with feet set wide apart to miss the drip, and gave him back his bottle and your nickel.

9. But he didn't hurry you off. A standing scales was by the door, with a stack of iron weights and a brass slide on the balance arm, that would weigh you up to three hundred pounds. Mr. Sessions, whose hands were gentle and smelled of carbolic, would lift you up and set your feet on the platform, hold your loaf of bread for you, and, taking his time while you stood still for him, he would make certain of what you weighed today. He could even remember what you weighed the last time, so you could subtract and announce how much you'd gained. That was goody-bye.

DISCUSSION: Unity

A paragraph or essay will be *unified* if its writer deals with one idea at a time, without shifting abruptly from one to another. Writers must have clearly in mind their reason for proceeding from one idea to the next—what we will call the *principle of order*. The choice of principle is determined by the subject as well as by the audience. Thus, for a person learning to drive a car, the process is probably best presented chronologically, in the order in which each step usually occurs. For an audience of driving instructors, the steps of the process might be presented in the order of their difficulty, to single out those needing most explanation and practice.

The principles of order possible in the paragraph and essay are many: the writer may proceed from the easy to the difficult, as in the example just given; or from the least to the most interesting or most important idea; or from the general to the specific—from the theory of combustion to the details of that process; or from the specific to the general—from the details of how oxygen combines with the substance to the general theory of combustion; or from the simple to the complex—from simple effects of gravity, such as falling off a bicycle, to complex effects, such as the collapse of giant stars into "black holes" through their internal gravity.

QUESTIONS

1. The principles of order in Welty's paragraphs, taken from a longer essay, are chronological and spatial. What parts of the description are presented chronologically, and what parts are presented spatially?

2. What is the main idea of paragraph 8? How are subordinate ideas distinguished from the main idea?
3. What overall impression does Welty convey of the store? Does she state the impression directly, or does she let it emerge from the details of her description? What details most contribute to this impression?
4. Does Welty present each feature of the store and her experience one at a time without repetition, or does she return to earlier features and details?

WRITING ASSIGNMENTS

1. Describe some store or shop you remember from childhood. Decide on a dominant impression and make your details contribute to that impression. Organize each paragraph through one or more principles of order. Remember that your reader probably has not seen the store.
2. Welty states in paragraph 4: "Its confusion may have been in the eye of its beholder." Write a description of another kind of store or institution—a public library, a government office, a schoolroom or cafeteria—and show how a sense of confusion may arise from the feelings and attitude of the viewer.

MARY McCARTHY
Uncle Myers

¹And here was another strange thing about Myers. ²He not only did nothing for a living but he appeared to have no history. ³He came from Elkhart, Indiana, but beyond this fact nobody seemed to know anything about him—not even how he had met my aunt Margaret. ⁴Reconstructed from his conversation, a picture of Elkhart emerged for us that showed it as a flat place consisting chiefly of ball parks, poolrooms, and hardware stores. ⁵Aunt Margaret came from Chicago, which consisted of the Loop, Marshall Field's, assorted priests and monsignors, and the black-and-white problem. ⁶How had these two worlds impinged? ⁷Where our family spoke freely of its relations, real and imaginary, Myers spoke of no one, not even a parent. ⁸At the very beginning, when my father's old touring car, which had been shipped on, still remained in our garage, Myers had certain seedy

cronies whom he took riding in it or who simply sat in it in our drive-way, as if anchored in a houseboat; but when the car went, they went or were banished. [9] Uncle Myers and Aunt Margaret had no friends, no couples with whom they exchanged visits—only a middle-aged, black-haired, small, emaciated woman with a German name and a yellowed skin whom we were taken to see one afternoon because she was dying of cancer. [10] This protracted death had the aspect of a public execution, which was doubtless why Myers took us to it; that is, it was a spectacle and it was free, and it inspired restlessness and depression. [11] Myers was the perfect type of rootless or municipalized man who finds his pleasures in the handouts or overflow of an indus-trial civilization. [12] He enjoyed standing on a curbstone, watching parades, the more nondescript the better, the Labor Day parade being his favorite, and next to that a military parade, followed by the com-mercial parades with floats and girls dressed in costumes; he would even go to Lake Calhoun or Lake Harriet for doll-carriage parades and competitions of children dressed as Indians. [13] He liked bandstands, band concerts, public parks devoid of grass; sky writing attracted him; he was quick to hear of a department-store demonstration where colored bubbles were blown, advertising a soap, to the tune of "I'm Forever Blowing Bubbles," sung by a mellifluous soprano. [14] He col-lected coupons and tinfoil, bundles of newspaper for the old rag-and-bone man (thus interfering seriously with our school paper drives), free samples of cheese at Donaldson's, free tickets given out by a neighborhood movie house to the first installment of a serial—in all the years we lived with him, we never saw a full-length movie but only those truncated beginnings. [15] He was also fond of streetcar rides (could the system have been municipally owned?), soldiers' monu-ments, cemeteries, big, coarse flowers like cannas and cockscombs set in beds by city gardeners. [16] Museums did not appeal to him, though we did go one night with a large crowd to see Marshal Foch on the steps of the Art Institute. [17] He was always weighing himself on penny weighing machines. [18] He seldom left the house except on one of these purposeless errands, or else to go to a ball game, by himself. [19] In the winter, he spent the days at home in the den, or in the kitchen, mak-ing candy. [20] He often had enormous tin trays of decorated fondants cooling in the cellar, which leads my brother Kevin to think today that at one time in Myers' life he must have been a pastry cook or a confectioner. [21] He also liked to fashion those little figures made of pipe cleaners that were just then coming in as favors in the better candy shops, but Myers used *old* pipe cleaners, stained yellow and brown. [22] The bonbons, with their pecan or almond topping, that he laid out in such perfect rows were for his own use; we were permitted to watch him set them out, but never—and my brother Kevin confirms this—did we taste a single one.

QUESTIONS

1. At the beginning of the paragraph Mary McCarthy discusses Uncle Myers' history and proceeds to his friendships and interests. What are these interests?
2. Why is the information about the pipe cleaners and the candy saved for the end of the paragraph? How would the impression of Uncle Myers have been changed if the paragraph ended with the details of his cronies and his collections?
3. The paragraph is unified because McCarthy discusses one thing at a time, without returning haphazardly to earlier considerations. What is the principle of order in the whole paragraph? What is gained by not dividing the paragraph into several shorter ones?
4. Does McCarthy directly state her attitude toward Uncle Myers, or does she let it emerge through what she shows about him? What is that attitude?
5. How else might the paragraph have been organized to develop a different idea or impression?
6. Does Uncle Myers seem monstrous to you, or does McCarthy show his human side or give some explanation for his character?

WRITING ASSIGNMENTS

1. Build a paragraph around a central impression of an unusual person, selecting details from different areas of experience to develop this impression. Do not state your attitude toward the person; let your details reveal it.
2. Rewrite the paragraph on Uncle Myers, presenting the details in a different order, and providing a new topic sentence. In a short second paragraph explain your reasons for organizing the new paragraph as you did.

Transitions

WINSTON S. CHURCHILL

My First Introduction to the Classics

The school my parents had selected for my education was one of the most fashionable and expensive in the country. It modeled itself upon Eton and aimed at being preparatory for that Public School above all others. It was supposed to be the very last thing in schools. Only ten boys in a class; electric light (then a wonder); a swimming pond; spacious football and cricket grounds; two or three school treats, or "expeditions" as they were called, every term; the masters all M.A.'s in gowns and mortar-boards; a chapel of its own; no hampers allowed; everything provided by the authorities. It was a dark November afternoon when we arrived at this establishment. We had tea with the Headmaster, with whom my mother conversed in the most easy manner. I was preoccupied with the fear of spilling my cup and so making "a bad start." I was also miserable at the idea of being left alone among all these strangers in this great, fierce, formidable place. After all I was only seven, and I had been so happy in my nursery with all my toys. I had such wonderful toys: a real steam engine, a magic lantern, and a collection of soldiers already nearly a thousand strong. Now it was to be all lessons. Seven or eight hours of lessons every day except half-holidays, and football or cricket in addition.

When the last sound of my mother's departing wheels had died away, the Headmaster invited me to hand over any money I had in my possession. I produced my three half-crowns which were duly entered in a book, and I was told that from time to time there would be a "shop" at the school with all sorts of things which one would like to have, and that I could choose what I liked up to the limit of the seven and sixpence. Then we quitted the Headmaster's parlor and the comfortable private side of the house, and entered the more bleak apartments reserved for the instruction and accommodation of the pupils. I was taken into a Form Room and told to sit at a desk. All the other boys were out of doors, and I was alone with the Form Master. He produced a thin greeny-brown-covered book filled with words in different types of print.

"You have never done any Latin before, have you?" he said.

"No sir."

"This is a Latin grammar." He opened it at a well-thumbed page. "You must learn this," he said, pointing to a number of words in a frame of lines. "I will come back in half an hour and see what you know."

Behold me then on a gloomy evening, with an aching heart, seated in front of the First Declension.

Mensa	a table
Mensa	O table
Mensam	a table
Mensae	of a table
Mensae	to or for a table
Mensa	by, with or from a table

What on earth did it mean? Where was the sense of it? It seemed absolute rigmarole to me. However, there was one thing I could always do: I could learn by heart. And I thereupon proceeded, as far as my private sorrows would allow, to memorize the acrostic-looking task which had been set me.

In due course the Master returned.

"Have you learnt it?" he asked.

"I think I can *say* it, sir," I replied; and I gabbled it off.

He seemed so satisfied with this that I was emboldened to ask a question.

"What does it mean, sir?"

"It means what it says. Mensa, a table. Mensa is a noun of the First Declension. There are five declensions. You have learnt the singular of the First Declension."

"But," I repeated, "what does it mean?"

"Mensa means a table," he answered.

"Then why does mensa also mean O table," I enquired, "and what does O table mean?"

"Mensa, O table, is the vocative case," he replied.

"But why O table?" I persisted in genuine curiosity.

"O table,—you would use that in addressing a table, in invoking a table." And then seeing he was not carrying me with him, "You would use it in speaking to a table."

"But I never do," I blurted out in honest amazement.

"If you are impertinent you will be punished, and punished, let me tell you, very severely," was his conclusive rejoinder.

DISCUSSION: Transitions

Transitions can take the form of single words (*Thus*), or phrases (*Turning to the next question*), or whole sentences or questions that connect different ideas. The purpose of transitions is to show relationships of time (in narratives), of space (in descriptions), and of ideas when these relationships are not immediately clear. Here are a few important transitions that show the relationship of ideas:

qualification: however, nevertheless, nonetheless
illustration and explanation: for example, so, to explain
comparison: similarly, in the same way, by comparison, likewise
contrast: by contrast, on the one hand, on the other hand
consequence: thus, as a result, consequently, therefore, surely
concession: admittedly, nevertheless, at least
amplification: moreover, furthermore, also, in addition, indeed
summation: all in all, in summary, in conclusion, finally

Within sentences, punctuation shows some of these relationships: a colon indicates that an expansion, explanation, or illustration of the previous idea follows; a semicolon, that the connected ideas are equal in importance or closely related. Transitions are best kept brief and unobtrusive. In the paragraph as in the whole essay, the reader should be able to discover the relation of ideas at first reading.

QUESTIONS

1. In a chronological narrative, such as the Churchill, many of the transitions will refer to time: *It was a dark November afternoon when we arrived. . . . When the last sound of my mother's departing wheels had died away . . . Then we quitted. . . .* What other words and phrases refer to time and change of place?
2. What relation of ideas do the words *after all* and *now* establish in the first paragraph, and *behold me then* later on?
3. Where does Churchill use questions to make a transition to a new aspect of his experience?
4. Churchill states in his autobiography that this episode was "my first introduction to the classics." The selection of details—and in particular the conversation with the Form Master about the word *mensa*—reveals his attitude not only toward the school but toward children and education. What is that attitude?

5. Does Churchill the adult find humor in the episode, or does he write with bitterness and anger? Do you share his feelings?

WRITING ASSIGNMENT

Write a narrative of a similar experience of your own—your first day in a new school, your own first introduction to a forbidding subject, your discovery that adults could be different from what you had known them to be. Use transitions as Churchill does to mark changes in time and aspects of the experience. Try to make these transitions short.

RENÉ DUBOS
Fitness in the Modern World

[1] There is no such thing as fitness per se with regard to military service, because fitness must always be defined in terms of a particular combat situation. [2] In consequence, the armed forces find it necessary to revise the physical standards of health at frequent intervals, in order to keep them in tune with the changing requirements of military service. [3] With propeller-driven aircraft, for example, there were many situations in which survival depended on strength of arm and limb. [4] Moreover, the pilot of a fighter airplane in World War II had to watch for enemies in the sky by direct visual perception. [5] His head swiveled from side to side looking to the rear, and for this reason calisthenics to develop neck muscles were part of training.

[6] Today, power controls have lessened physical requirements of the aircraft operator, and with electronic vision the fighter pilot never needs to look to the rear. [7] In any case, direct vision would be of little help in modern air combat because of the terrific speeds at which aircraft approach each other. [8] At 600 miles per hour, and this is now moderate speed, half a mile means little more than a second, clearly not enough time for the pilot to see, to react, and to change the direction of his aircraft. [9] As a result, keenness of distant vision no longer means the difference between life and death for the fighter pilot; this attribute has been superseded by keenness in ability to detect slight changes on electronic dials and gauges. [10] More generally, strenuous physical conditioning programs are no longer as directly relevant to

performance in the armed forces as they used to be. [11]And in fact, recent tests indicate that pilots at the peak of physical form do not score any better in difficult operations than do those of comparable groups who are less well endowed physically.

[12]The changes in relevance of physical prowess to military performance have many counterparts in civilian life. [13]Effectiveness in modern technology depends to a large extent on dial-watching and on reading printed matter. [14]Whereas physical stamina and distant vision were once extremely important, muscles are now called into play chiefly during leisure time, and nearsightedness has become almost an asset in several professions. [15]The present trends of life seem to provide justification for the child who does not want to walk because he considers it old-fashioned and for his mother who dissuades him from engaging in physical exertion or exposing himself to inclemencies because modern existence is and will increasingly become air-conditioned and effortless. [16]And yet this attitude may have unfavorable consequences in the long run. [17]A state of adaptedness to the conditions of today is no guarantee of adaptability to the challenges of tomorrow.

QUESTIONS

1. What transitional words and phrases do you find in sentences 2–4? What relationships do these establish?
2. What relationships do the transitions in the second paragraph express? Could any of these be omitted without loss of coherence or clarity?
3. What other transitions might be substituted for those in sentences 2, 4, 9, and 11?
4. How does the whole discussion illustrate sentence 17—the thesis statement or main idea of the three paragraphs?

WRITING ASSIGNMENTS

1. Write a paragraph from your own experience that develops one of the following ideas. Restate the idea, qualifying or disagreeing with it, if you wish. Use transitional words and phrases where appropriate.
   a. Information we are given in school often is obsolete by the time we are ready to use it.
   b. Adults do not always tell us the whole truth about the world.
2. Illustrate sentence 17 from your own experience. You might show

how physical capabilities important to you in childhood are no longer important to you. Use transitional words and phrases where needed for coherence.

Climax

LYTTON STRACHEY

Queen Victoria at the End of Her Life

[1] She gave orders that nothing should be thrown away—and nothing was. [2] There, in drawer after drawer, in wardrobe after wardrobe, reposed the dresses of seventy years. [3] But not only the dresses—the furs and the mantles and subsidiary frills and the muffs and the parasols and the bonnets—all were ranged in chronological order, dated and complete. [4] A great cupboard was devoted to the dolls; in the china room at Windsor a special table held the mugs of her childhood, and her children's mugs as well. [5] Mementoes of the past surrounded her in serried accumulations. [6] In every room the tables were powdered thick with the photographs of relatives; their portraits, revealing them at all ages, covered the walls; their figures, in solid marble, rose up from pedestals, or gleamed from brackets in the form of gold and silver statuettes. [7] The dead, in every shape—in miniatures, in porcelain, in enormous life-size oil-paintings—were perpetually about her. [8] John Brown stood upon her writing-table in solid gold.* [9] Her favorite horses and dogs, endowed with a new durability, crowded round her footsteps. [10] Sharp, in silver gilt, dominated the dinner table; Boy and Boz lay together among unfading flowers, in bronze. [11] And it was not enough that each particle of the past should be given the stability of metal or of marble: the whole collection, in its arrangement, no less than its entity, should be immutably fixed. [12] There might be additions, but there might never be alterations. [13] No chintz might change, no carpet, no curtain, be replaced by another; or, if long use at last

---

* John Brown (1826–1883) was the Scottish attendant to Victoria's husband, Prince Albert, and after the death of the Prince in 1861, to the Queen herself. Ed.

made it necessary, the stuffs and the patterns must be so identically reproduced that the keenest eye might not detect the difference. [14] No new picture could be hung upon the walls at Windsor, for those already there had been put in their places by Albert, whose decisions were eternal. [15] So, indeed, were Victoria's. [16] To ensure that they should be the aid of the camera was called in. [17] Every single article in the Queen's possession was photographed from several points of view. [18] These photographs were submitted to Her Majesty, and when, after careful inspection, she had approved of them, they were placed in a series of albums, richly bound. [19] Then, opposite each photograph, an entry was made, indicating the number of the article, the number of the room in which it was kept, its exact position in the room and all its principal characteristics. [20] The fate of every object which had undergone this process was henceforth irrevocably sealed. [21] The whole multitude, once and for all, took up its steadfast station. [22] And Victoria, with a gigantic volume or two of the endless catalogue always beside her, to look through, to ponder upon, to expatiate over, could feel, with a double contentment, that the transitoriness of this world had been arrested by the amplitude of her might.

DISCUSSION: Climax

There is a natural order of climax in certain sentences and paragraphs, as in Julius Caesar's famous statement, "I came, I saw, I conquered." In the same way, the last two sentences of the following paragraph convey a sense of rising importance, as indeed the whole paragraph does:

It was something formidable and swift, like the sudden smashing of a vial of wrath. It seemed to explode all round the ship with an overpowering concussion and a rush of great waters, as if an immense dam had been blown up to windward. In an instant the men lost touch of each other. This is the disintegrating power of a great wind: it isolates one from one's kind. An earthquake, a landslip, an avalanche, overtake a man incidentally, as it were—without passion. A furious gale attacks him like a personal enemy, tries to grasp his limbs, fastens upon his mind, seeks to rout his very spirit out of him.—Joseph Conrad, *Typhoon*

As in this paragraph, climax can be achieved by making one idea seem to anticipate another, and by giving weight to the concluding idea. The terminal position—a position of natural emphasis in English sentences and paragraphs—is in part responsible for this effect. The writer is free to make one idea seem more important by virtue of the position given it.

QUESTIONS

1. Queen Victoria's husband, Prince Albert, died of a sudden illness in 1861, at the age of 42. Victoria, the same age as her husband, entered a long period of private mourning, and for the remainder of her life attempted to preserve her physical surroundings as they had existed in his lifetime. In this portrait of Victoria in her old age, Strachey develops and illustrates several major ideas that build to his thesis idea. What are these ideas?
2. Strachey states in sentence 2 that Victoria saved the dresses of seventy years; in sentence 3, that she saved her furs and bonnets, as well as other articles of clothing—and arranged and dated them chronologically. How does the formal transition between these sentences help to show that Strachey is moving from one surprising, even astonishing, fact to an even more surprising one?
3. Compare sentences 11 and 12 with those that follow. How does Strachey indicate that he is building the paragraph to even more surprising details?
4. What contributes to the climactic effect of the final sentence of the paragraph?
5. Has Strachey made Queen Victoria human to you? Or is she merely an eccentric?

WRITING ASSIGNMENTS

1. Write a character sketch of an unusual relative or friend or teacher, centering on a dominant trait and presenting related traits as Strachey does. Present these related traits in the order of rising importance—as illustrations of the dominant trait.
2. Rewrite Strachey's paragraph, beginning with his concluding sentence, and achieving a sense of climax in your reordering of ideas and details.

KATHERINE ANNE PORTER
The Bullfight

1. I took to the bullfights with my Mexican and Indian friends. I sat with them in the cafés where the bullfighters appeared; more than once went at two o'clock in the morning with a crowd to see the bulls

brought into the city; I visited the corral back of the ring where they could be seen before the corrida. Always, of course, I was in the company of impassioned adorers of the sport, with their special vocabulary and mannerisms and contempt for all others who did not belong to their charmed and chosen cult. Quite literally there were those among them I never heard speak of anything else; and I heard then all that can be said—the topic is limited, after all, like any other—in love and praise of bullfighting. But it can be tiresome, too. And I did not really live in that world, so narrow and so trivial, so cruel and so unconscious; I was a mere visitor. There was something deeply, irreparably wrong with my being there at all, something against the grain of my life; except for this (and here was the falseness I had finally to uncover): I loved the spectacle of the bullfights, I was drunk on it, I was in a strange, wild dream from which I did not want to be awakened. I was now drawn irresistibly to the bullring as before I had been drawn to the race tracks and the polo fields at home. But this had death in it, and it was the death in it that I loved. . . . And I was bitterly ashamed of this evil in me, and believed it to be in me only—no one had fallen so far into cruelty as this! These bullfight buffs I truly believed did not know what they were doing—but I did, and I knew better because I had once known better; so that spiritual pride got in and did its deadly work, too. How could I face the cold fact that at heart I was just a killer, like any other, that some deep corner of my soul consented not just willingly but with rapture? I still clung obstinately to my flattering view of myself as a unique case, as a humane, blood-avoiding civilized being, somehow a fallen angel, perhaps? Just the same, what was I doing there? And why was I beginning secretly to abhor Shelley as if he had done me a great injury, when in fact he had done me the terrible and dangerous favor of helping me to find myself out?★

2.   In the meantime I was reading St. Augustine; and if Shelley had helped me find myself out, St. Augustine helped me find myself again. I read for the first time then his story of a friend of his, a young man from the provinces who came to Rome and was taken up by the gang of clever, wellborn young hoodlums Augustine then ran with; and this young man, also wellborn but severely brought up, refused to go with the crowd to the gladiatorial combat; he was opposed to them on the simple grounds that they were cruel and criminal. His friends naturally ridiculed such dowdy sentiments; they nagged him slyly, be-

★ Shelley: A friend of the author's, who introduced her to bullfighting. Ed.

deviled him openly, and, of course, finally some part of him consented—but only to a degree. He would go with them, he said, but he
would not watch the games. And he did not, until the time for the
first slaughter, when the howling of the crowd brought him to his feet,
staring: and afterward he was more bloodthirsty than any.

3.   Why, of course: oh, it might be a commonplace of human nature,
it might be it could happen to anyone! I longed to be free of my
uniqueness, to be a fellow-sinner at least with someone: I could not
bear my guilt alone—and here was this student, this boy at Rome in
the fourth century, somebody I felt I knew well on sight, who had
been weak enough to be led into adventure but strong enough to turn
it into experience. For no matter how we both attempted to deceive
ourselves, our acts had all the earmarks of adventure: violence of motive, events taking place at top speed, at sustained intensity, under
powerful stimulus and a willful seeking for pure sensation; willful, I
say, because I was not kidnapped and forced, after all, nor was that
young friend of St. Augustine's. We both proceeded under the power
of our own weakness. When the time came to kill the splendid black
and white bull, I who had pitied him when he first came into the ring
stood straining on tiptoe to see everything, yet almost blinded with excitement, and crying out when the crowd roared, and kissing Shelley
on the cheekbone when he shook my elbow and shouted in the voice
of one justified: "Didn't I tell you? Didn't I?"

QUESTIONS

1. In this excerpt from a long essay, Porter describes her first experience with bullfighting. She describes also the effect of her reading
the *Confessions* of St. Augustine; the passage she refers to concerns his friend Alypius, a law student who was enticed to the
gladiatorial combats. The passage concludes:

For so soon as he saw that blood, he therewith drunk down
savageness; nor turned away, but fixed his eye, drinking in
frenzy, unawares, and was delighted with that guilty fight, and
intoxicated with the bloody pastime. Nor was he now the man he
came, but one of the throng he came unto, yea, a true associate
of theirs that brought him thither. Why say more? He beheld,
shouted, kindled, carried thence with him the madness which
should goad him to return not only with them who first drew
him thither, but also before them, yea and to draw in others.
(Book VI)

Notice that Porter's paragraphs end with a focus on similar ideas. What are these ideas, and how does this focus contribute to a sense of climax in the whole passage? Is the sense of climax greater at the end of the final pragraph?

2. How many blocks of ideas does paragraph 1 contain, and how is this division of ideas marked? Would the paragraph be more effective divided into several paragraphs? What is her main idea?

3. To what extent does Porter rely on formal transitions to convey rising excitement?

WRITING ASSIGNMENT

Write several paragraphs describing and analyzing an exciting experience about which you had mixed feelings. Explain how you resolved—or failed to resolve—these feelings. Arrange the sentences of one of your paragraphs in climactic order.

Point of View

GEOFFREY MOORHOUSE

Calcutta

1. When the international and jet-propelled traveler disembarks at Dum Dum he finds, if he has come by the right airline, that a highly polished limousine awaits his pleasure. It will be 6.30 or thereabouts in the morning, and the atmosphere will already be faintly sticky with heat and so unmistakably sweetened with a compound of mainly vegetable odors that the visitor can almost taste it. He need fear no discomfort at this stage, however, for he is to be transported into the city in air-conditioned splendor behind delicately tinted windows. From this smooth and relaxing position he can begin to observe how the other half of humanity lives. From the outset he notices some things which are reassuringly familiar. Along the first mile of this wide and tarmacadamed airport road are spaced the very same collection of gaudy hoardings that signal the way in and out of Heathrow or J. F.

Kennedy or Fiumicino; "Try a Little VC-10derness", says one—and some untidy idiot seems to have thrown up a collection of chicken coops in the shade of BOAC. Beside these homely reference points, however, the peculiarities of India are to be seen. The road is bordered by ditches and ponds, all brimming with water, in which women even at this hour are flogging garments clean, in which men are taking the first bath of the day. Beyond the spindle-elegant sodium lights, with buzzards and vultures perched on top, stand thickets of bamboo-and-thatch huts among avenues of palm. Along a canal, a large black barge top-heavy with hay is being poled inches at a time through a mass of pretty but choking mauve water hyacinth. And in the distance, lurking on the horizon, a range of tall factory chimneys is beginning to smoke.

2. Calcutta is announced with a pothole or two. Then a bus is overtaken, such a vehicle as the traveler has never seen before; its bodywork is battered with a thousand dents, as though an army of commuters had once tried to kick it to bits, and it is not only crammed with people, it has a score or so hanging off the platform and around the back like a cluster of grapes. It is lumbering and steaming into a suburban wasteland, stippled with blocks of dilapidated flats; and maybe Bishop Heber's imagery was not so far-fetched after all, for these are not at all unlike some of the homes for the workers you can see in Moscow today, though there they are not colored pink and they certainly haven't been decorated with the hammer and sickle in crude whitewash on the walls.* Swiftly, the outer Calcutta of these revolutionary symbols now coagulates into the inner Calcutta which is unlike anywhere else on earth. The limousine now lurches and rolls, for there are too many potholes to avoid. It rocks down cobblestoned roads lined with high factory walls which have an air of South Lancashire about them. It begins to thread its way through traffic along thoroughfares that have something of Bishopsgate or Holborn in their buildings.

3. It is the traffic that makes it all unique. A traffic in trams grinding round corners, a traffic in approximately London buses whose radiators seem ready to burst, in gypsy-green lorries with 'Ta-ta and By-by' and other slogans painted on the back, in taxis swerving all over the road with much blowing of horns, in rickshaws springing unexpectedly out of sidestreets, in bullock carts swaying ponderously along to

---

*Reginald Heber (1783–1826), who became bishop of Calcutta in 1823, compared the city to Moscow. He commented also on the large Greek-style houses and the city's hospitality. Ed.

the impediment of everyone, in sacred Brahmani cows and bulls non-chalantly strolling down the middle of the tram-tracks munching breakfast as they go. A traffic, too, in people who are hanging on to all forms of public transport, who are squatting cross-legged upon the counters of their shops, who are darting in and out of the roadways between the vehicles, who are staggering under enormous loads, who are walking briskly with briefcases, who are lying like dead things on the pavements, who are drenching themselves with muddy water in the gutters, who are arguing, laughing, gesticulating, defecating, and who are sometimes just standing still as though wondering what to do. There never were so many people in a city at seven o'clock in the morning. Patiently the driver of the limousine steers his passage between and around them, while they pause in mid-stride to let him through, or leap to get out of his way, or stare at him blankly, or curse him roundly, or occasionally spit in the path of his highly polished Cadillac. Presently, and quite remarkably, he comes to the end of the journey without collision and deposits the traveler and his luggage upon the pavement in front of an hotel. And here the traveler has his first encounter with a beggar. He had better make the best of it, for beggary is to be with him until the end of his days in Calcutta.

DISCUSSION: Point of View

The *physical* point of view of a descriptive paragraph or essay is the location or angle from which something is observed. If the location clarifies the experience, the writer may state this viewpoint explicitly. The writer may also state the *psychological* point of view—the dominant mood or attitude. We find both the physical and the psychological point of view stated in the following sentences:

> Once long ago as a child I can remember removing the cover from an old well. I was alone at the time and I can still anticipate, with a slight crawling of my scalp, the sight I inadvertently saw as I peered over the brink and followed a shaft of sunlight many feet down into the darkness.—Loren Eiseley, *The Immense Journey*

In writing of this kind, if we fail to clarify the point of view from which we are making the observation, or fail to indicate a change to another point of view, details will become blurred or seem out of proportion to those presented earlier. Abrupt or unexpected shifts in mood and attitude can also be confusing. Brief transitions that bridge these differences are the remedy.

QUESTIONS

1. The traveler to India might see Calcutta for the first time from a taxi or bus rather than from "a highly polished limousine." What is gained by seeing the city from the physical angle Moorhouse chooses?

2. The reference to the "very same collection of gaudy hoardings" leading in and out of Heathrow, J. F. Kennedy, and Fiumicino (the international airports of London, New York, and Rome, respectively) suggests that the traveler will at first think he is in a familiar world. He soon discovers that he is moving into an unfamiliar one. What other contrasts of this sort does Moorhouse imply?

3. How does Moorhouse establish the mental state of the typical traveler at the end of his journey to the hotel? Does he establish his own attitude toward Calcutta?

4. The reference to Bishopsgate and Holborn shows that Moorhouse is writing with a British audience in mind, people familiar with the architecture of these areas of London. What other statements call for knowledge of this kind?

5. Does Moorhouse succeed in capturing your attention and interest? Why or why not?

WRITING ASSIGNMENT

Use Moorhouse's description of Calcutta as a model for a description of a section of a college town or your home town. You may wish to portray the town as seen from a limousine, a Volkswagen, or a bicycle, but be careful to make the angle of vision contribute to the overall impression and the revelation of an attitude. Do not specify this attitude; let your selection of details reveal it.

LOREN EISELEY

Halley's Comet

1. To escape the cosmic prison man is poorly equipped. He has to drag portions of his environment with him, and his life span is that of a mayfly in terms of the distances he seeks to penetrate. There is no possible way to master such a universe by flight alone. Indeed such a dream is a dangerous illusion. This may seem a heretical statement, but its truth is self-evident if we try seriously to comprehend the na-

ture of time and space that I sought to grasp when held up to view the fiery messenger that flared across the zenith in 1910. "Seventy-five years," my father had whispered in my ear, "seventy-five years and it will be racing homeward. Perhaps you will live to see it again. Try to remember."

2. And so I remembered. I had gained a faint glimpse of the size of our prison house. Somewhere out there beyond a billion miles in space, an entity known as a comet had rounded on its track in the black darkness of the void. It was surging homeward toward the sun because it was an eccentric satellite of this solar system. If I lived to see it it would be but barely, and with the dimmed eyes of age. Yet it, too, in its long traverse, was but a flitting mayfly in terms of the universe the night sky revealed.

3. So relative is the cosmos we inhabit that, as we gaze upon the outer galaxies available to the reach of our telescopes, we are placed in about the position that a single white blood cell in our bodies would occupy, if it were intelligently capable of seeking to understand the nature of its own universe, the body it inhabits. The cell would encounter rivers ramifying into miles of distance seemingly leading nowhere. It would pass through gigantic structures whose meaning it could never grasp—the brain, for example. It could never know there was an outside, a vast being on a scale it could not conceive of and of which it formed an infinitesimal part. It would know only the pouring tumult of the creation it inhabited, but of the nature of that great beast, or even indeed that it was a beast, it could have no conception whatever. It might examine the liquid in which it floated and decide, as in the case of the fall of Lucretius's atoms, that the pouring of obscure torrents had created its world.

4. It might discover that creatures other than itself swam in the torrent. But that its universe was alive, had been born and was destined to perish, its own ephemeral existence would never allow it to perceive. It would never know the sun; it would explore only through dim tactile sensations and react to chemical stimuli that were borne to it along the mysterious conduits of the arteries and veins. Its universe would be centered upon a great arborescent tree of spouting blood. This, at best, generations of white blood cells by enormous labor and continuity might succeed, like astronomers, in charting.

5. They could never, by any conceivable stretch of the imagination, be aware that their so-called universe was, in actuality, the prowling body of a cat or the more time-enduring body of a philosopher, himself engaged upon the same quest in a more gigantic world and per-

haps deceived proportionately by greater vistas. What if, for example, the far galaxies man observes make up, across void spaces of which even we are atomically composed, some kind of enormous creature or cosmic snowflake whose exterior we will never see? We will know more than the phagocyte in our bodies, but no more than that limited creature can we climb out of our universe, or successfully enhance our size or longevity sufficiently to thrust our heads through the confines of the universe that terminates our vision.

QUESTIONS

1. Eiseley begins with the experience of seeing Halley's Comet in his youth. How does this physical point of view change in the course of his discussion?
2. The psychological point of view is developed through the physical: in telling us his feelings and in imagining those of the white cell or phagocyte, Eiseley reveals not only his feelings about comets and outer space but also his characteristic way of looking at the world. What is this characteristic way, and how do the details reveal it to us?
3. Eiseley states a thesis in his first sentence: "To escape the cosmic prison man is poorly equipped." How many restatements of this thesis do you find? How many explain and broaden the thesis?
4. Why is the dream of mastering the universe through flight alone "a heretical statement," one directly counter to established beliefs today? Can you cite other evidence of such beliefs?
5. Halley's Comet will return in 1985. Do you think the exploits of the Space Age will diminish interest in it?

WRITING ASSIGNMENTS

1. Develop Eiseley's thesis through a comparison of your own—one similar to that of the mayfly and the phagocyte.
2. Write a carefully organized paragraph on one of the following topics. Establish a clear physical or psychological point of view.
   a. a first view of a large city from an airplane or automobile
   b. meeting a relative or friend after a long absence
   c. revisiting a school you once attended
3. Write a description of your family from an imagined viewpoint, perhaps that of a household pet or a stranger. Notice that you will need to fix a time and a location. Let your reader discover the identity of the viewer through personal references and details.

THE PARAGRAPH: METHODS OF DEVELOPMENT

Definition

TIME

Euphemism

1.   From a Greek word meaning "to use words of good omen," euphemism is the substitution of a pleasant term for a blunt one—telling it like it isn't. Euphemism has probably existed since the beginning of language. As long as there have been things of which men thought the less said the better, there have been better ways of saying less. In everyday conversation the euphemism is, at worst, a necessary evil; at its best, it is a handy verbal tool to avoid making enemies needlessly, or shocking friends. Language purists and the blunt-spoken may wince when a young woman at a party coyly asks for direction to "the powder room," but to most people this kind of familiar euphemism is probably no more harmful or annoying than, say, a split infinitive.

2.   On a larger scale, though, the persistent growth of euphemism in a language represents a danger to thought and action, since its fundamental intent is to deceive. As linguist Benjamin Lee Whorf has pointed out, the structure of a given language determines, in part, how the society that speaks it views reality. If "substandard housing"

makes rotting slums appear more livable or inevitable to some people, then their view of American cities has been distorted and their ability to assess the significance of poverty has been reduced. Perhaps the most chilling example of euphemism's destructive power took place in Hitler's Germany. The wholesale corruption of the language under Nazism, notes critic George Steiner, is symbolized by the phrase *endgültige Lösung* (final solution), which "came to signify the death of 6,000,000 human beings in gas ovens."

DISCUSSION: Definition

Definition is the most fundamental way of developing and analyzing ideas. Readers must know the meaning of words essential to the discussion. How complete the definition is and what kind the writer uses depends on how much specific information is needed:

> One of the Greek inventions that Islam elaborated and spread was the astrolabe. As an observational device, it is primitive; it only measures the elevation of the sun or a star, and that crudely. But by coupling that single observation with one or more star maps, the astrolabe also carried out an elaborate scheme of computations that could determine latitude, sunrise and sunset, the time for prayer and the direction of Mecca for the traveler.—J. Bronowski, *The Ascent of Man*

Bronowski might have given us a detailed description of the astrolabe; he does not because we need only know what the astrolabe was used for.

The simplest kind of definition is to point to an object; in a museum I might merely point and say, "That's an astrolabe." But usually we want to know the characteristics of the object—or at least know as much as can be stated about it. To inform us of these characteristics, the author may begin with the original meaning of the word—that is, with its etymology. The word *gravity* comes from the Latin *gravitas*, meaning "weight" or "heaviness." These words help explain the word *gravity;* however, they are not the whole of its current meaning. The purpose of etymological definition is to illuminate the current meaning, and occasionally to argue that a word should return to its original meaning, if the two are different. The word *silly* originally meant "innocent" or "blessed"; its meanings today suggest simple-mindedness or thoughtlessness ("a silly question").

Most definitions are concerned with current meanings that people attach to words. The most common of these definitions are called *denotative* and *connotative. Denotative* definition singles out an object: it identifies the class (or *genus*) of objects to which the word belongs, then distinguishes the word by its specific difference from all other members of the class. The genus may be extremely broad or extremely narrow:

> **hero** A man [*genus*] distinguished for exceptional courage, fortitude, or bold enterprise, especially in time of war or danger [*specific difference*].
>
> **hero** U.S. A sandwich [*genus*] made with a loaf of bread cut lengthwise [*specific difference*].—*Standard College Dictionary*

For words as broad in meaning as *thing,* the dictionary usually lists synonyms: *inanimate object, matter, concern,* and so on.

Connotative definition presents ideas and impressions, the emotional aura we associate with a word. The word *rose* has a precise denotation—a particular flower with describable properties—and a range of connotations, some of which derive from the flower, as in the expression "a rosy future." Though both *inexpensive* and *cheap* mean low in price, *cheap* usually carries the connotation of poor quality or of something contemptible. *Inexpensive* is an emotionally neutral word; *cheap* is not.

Other kinds of definition should be briefly mentioned. *Precising* definitions fix meanings that are indefinite, overlapping, or confused in popular usage. *Stipulative* definitions propose a name for a newly discovered phenomenon, so that it can be referred to and talked about, such as the term *quasar* for "quasi-stellar" sources of light in the sky whose true nature is not yet known. *Theoretical* definitions, by contrast, propose an explanation or theory of the phenomenon—an account of its true nature. Most textbook definitions of democracy and other abstract concepts are theoretical.

QUESTIONS

1. The *Time* essay includes the etymology of *euphemism* in the first sentence. What help does the etymology give you in understanding its present meaning? What present meanings are not contained in the etymology?
2. What denotative definition of *euphemism* is given in the essay? How similar is this definition to the one in your dictionary?
3. What examples are given of negative connotations of the word? Does the word have a positive connotation, and is an example given of it?
4. How do the examples in the second paragraph help you understand Whorf's idea that "the structure of a given language determines, in part, how the society that speaks it views reality"?

WRITING ASSIGNMENTS

1. Write a paragraph illustrating the positive uses of euphemism. Distinguish these uses carefully through various examples, drawing them from several areas of experience.
2. Write a paragraph illustrating the negative uses of euphemism. Distinguish these uses, and vary your examples.
3. Illustrate Whorf's statement about language and reality through euphemisms relating to death or some other experience. Be careful to state what your examples reveal about the people who use them.
4. Use the *Oxford English Dictionary* and other reference books to investigate the etymology and properties of one of the following, and write an account of the word:
   a. gyroscope   d. sergeant
   b. alcohol   e. dirigible
   c. cotton gin   f. vaccine
5. Use the *Oxford English Dictionary* and other reference books to show how etymology sheds light on the current meanings of one of the words below. Indicate the extent to which original meanings of the word have been retained in current usage.
   a. ornery   d. jargon
   b. humorous   e. nice
   c. foolish   f. mediocre

PAUL FUSSELL

World War One Trenches

1.   The two main British sectors duplicated each other also in their almost symbolic road systems. Each had a staging town behind: for Ypres it was Poperinghe (to the men, "Pop"); for the Somme, Amiens. From these towns troops proceeded with augmenting but usually well-concealed terror up a sinister road to the town of operations, either Ypres itself or Albert. And running into the enemy lines out of Ypres and Albert were the most sinister roads of all, one leading to Menin, the other to Bapaume, both in enemy territory. These roads defined the direction of ultimate attack and the hoped-for breakout. They were the goals of the bizarre inverse quest on which the soldiers were ironically embarked.

But most of the time they were not questing. They were sitting or lying or squatting in place below the level of the ground. "When all is said and done," Sassoon notes, "the war was mainly a matter of holes and ditches."[1] And in these holes and ditches extending for ninety miles, continually, even in the quietest times, some 7000 British men and officers were killed and wounded daily, just as a matter of course. "Wastage," the Staff called it.

2.   There were normally three lines of trenches. The front-line trench was anywhere from fifty yards or so to a mile from its enemy counterpart. Several hundred yards behind it was the support trench line. And several hundred yards behind that was the reserve line. There were three kinds of trenches: firing trenches, like these; communication trenches, running roughly perpendicular to the line and connecting the three lines; and "saps," shallower ditches thrust out into No Man's Land, providing access to forward observation posts, listening posts, grenade-throwing posts, and machine gun positions. The end of a sap was usually not manned all the time: night was the favorite time for going out. Coming up from the rear, one reached the trenches by following a communication trench sometimes a mile or more long. It often began in a town and gradually deepened. By the time pedestrians reached the reserve line, they were well below ground level.

3.   A firing trench was supposed to be six to eight feet deep and four or five feet wide. On the enemy side a parapet of earth or sandbags rose about two or three feet above the ground. A corresponding "parados" a foot or so high was often found on top of the friendly side. Into the sides of trenches were dug one- or two-man holes ("funk-holes"), and there were deeper dugouts, reached by dirt stairs, for use as command posts and officers' quarters. On the enemy side of a trench was a fire-step two feet high on which the defenders were supposed to stand, firing and throwing grenades, when repelling attack. A well-built trench did not run straight for any distance: that would have been to invite enfilade fire. Every few yards a good trench zig-zagged. It had frequent traverses designed to contain damage within a limited space. Moving along a trench thus involved a great deal of weaving and turning. The floor of a proper trench was covered with wooden duckboards, beneath which were sumps a few feet deep designed to collect water. The walls, perpetually crumbling, were supported by sandbags, corrugated iron, or bundles of sticks or rushes. Except at night and in half-light, there was of course no looking over the top except through periscopes, which could be purchased in the "Trench Requisites" section of the main London department stores. The few snipers

---

[1] Siegfried Sassoon, *Memoirs of an Infantry Officer* (1930; New York, 1937), p. 228.

on duty during the day observed No Man's Land through loopholes cut in sheets of armor plate.

4. The entanglements of barbed wire had to be positioned far enough out in front of the trench to keep the enemy from sneaking up to grenade-throwing distance. Interestingly, the two novelties that contributed most to the personal menace of the war could be said to be American inventions. Barbed wire had first appeared on the American frontier in the late nineteenth century for use in restraining animals. And the machine gun was the brainchild of Hiram Stevens Maxim (1840–1916), an American who, disillusioned with native patent law, established his Maxim Gun Company in England and began manufacturing his guns in 1889. He was finally knighted for his efforts. At first the British regard for barbed wire was on a par with Sir Douglas Haig's understanding of the machine gun. In the autumn of 1914, the first wire Private Frank Richards saw emplaced before the British positions was a single strand of agricultural wire found in the vicinity.[2] Only later did the manufactured article begin to arrive from England in sufficient quantity to create the thickets of mock-organic rusty brown that helped give a look of eternal autumn to the front.

5. The whole British line was numbered by sections, neatly, from right to left. A section, normally occupied by a company, was roughly 300 yards wide. One might be occupying front-line trench section 51; or support trench S 51, behind it; or reserve trench SS 51, behind both. But a less formal way of identifying sections of trench was by place or street names with a distinctly London flavor. *Piccadilly* was a favorite; popular also were *Regent Street* and *Strand;* junctions were *Hyde Park Corner* and *Marble Arch.* Greater wit—and deeper homesickness—sometimes surfaced in the naming of the German trenches opposite. Sassoon remembers "Durley" 's account of the attack at Delville Wood in September, 1916: "Our objective was Pint Trench, taking Bitter and Beer and clearing Ale and Vat, and also Pilsen Lane."[3] Directional and traffic control signs were everywhere in the trenches, giving the whole system the air of a parody modern city, although one literally "underground."

QUESTIONS

1. How is the description of the trenches related to the points Fussell makes about them in paragraph 2?

[2] Frank Richards, *Old Soldiers Never Die* (1933), pp. 44–45.
[3] *Memoirs of an Infantry Officer,* p. 151.

2. What details convey the feeling of life in the trenches? How does Fussell remind the reader that a war is being fought?
3. Why does he mention the names of the trench sections? Is this information essential to the definition of the trenches?
4. How complete is the definition? Can you think of any essential information that you need to visualize or understand trenches?
5. What details if any surprised you, and why?

WRITING ASSIGNMENT

Write a definition of one of the following. Relate the details of your definition to an explanation of the uses of the object being defined.
a. the interchange of a city expressway
b. the playing board of a game like Monopoly
c. an important part of a musical instrument (trumpet keys, violin bow)
d. bicycle pedals
e. lawn mower
f. electric food mixer

MARCIA SELIGSON
The American Wedding

1. Every culture, in every time throughout history, has commemorated the transition of a human being from one state in life to another. Birth, the emergence into manhood, graduation from school at various levels, birthdays, marriage, death—each of these outstanding steps is acknowledged by a ceremony of some sort, always public, the guests in effect becoming witnesses to the statement of life's ongoingness, of the natural order of history. To insure the special significance of the rite of passage, its apartness from any other event of the day, these rituals usually require pageantry, costumed adornment, and are accompanied by gift-bearing and feasting. We wear black to funerals, bring presents to christenings and birthday parties, get loaded at wakes, eat ourselves sick at bar mitzvahs. Birth, marriage and death, to be sure, are the most elemental and major steps, and as there is only one of those ritual commemorations for which we are *actually*, fully present, the wedding becomes, for mankind, its most vital rite of passage. And for this reason it is anchored at the very core of civilization.

2.   For the rites of passage the ceremony itself is organic to the society for which the individual is being groomed, in his journey from one state to the next. In African hunting societies, for example, a boy at puberty is thrown naked into the jungle and required to kill a lion. His value as a man will be judged by how successful he can be in meeting the demands of his culture. In America, newlyweds are being prepared for their roles in a consumer society, so it is surely appropriate that all of the dynamics of wedding hoo-hah testify to these commercial, mercantile terms. Gifts are purchased not only by the "witnesses" but by bride for groom, groom for bride, bride for attendants, attendants for bride. Prenuptial parties, bachelor dinners, showers. The ever-mushrooming splash and flash circusness of the wedding itself. The American wedding is a ritual event of ferocious, gluttonous consuming, a debauch of intensified buying, never again to be repeated in the life of an American couple.

QUESTIONS

1. The first paragraph defines *rite of passage* denotatively. What theory of social reality does Seligson present in the second paragraph?
2. What is the principle of order in the first paragraph? Is the second paragraph developed in the same way?
3. Has Seligson exaggerated her characterization of the American wedding, or has she described it as it is?

WRITING ASSIGNMENTS

1. Describe a ceremony of high-school or college life—June graduation, the class play, the senior dance—and discuss the extent to which it is "organic" to the society of the institution.
2. Examine advertisements in magazines and newspapers that depict brides and festivities associated with weddings (bridal showers, the wedding ceremony, receptions, and the like). In a short essay describe these advertisements and discuss whether or not they support Seligson's statement that the American wedding is "a ritual event of ferocious, gluttonous consuming, a debauch of intensified buying."

JOSEPH WOOD KRUTCH

The Meaning of "Normal"

1.   The words we choose to define or suggest what we believe to be important facts exert a very powerful influence upon civilization. A mere name can persuade us to approve or disapprove, as it does, for example, when we describe certain attitudes as "cynical" on the one hand or "realistic" on the other. No one wants to be "unrealistic" and no one wants to be "snarling." Therefore his attitude toward the thing described may very well depend upon which designation is current among his contemporaries; and the less critical his mind, the more influential the most commonly used vocabulary will be.

2.   It is for this reason that, even as a mere verbal confusion, the use of "normal" to designate what ought to be called "average" is of tremendous importance and serves not only to indicate but actually to reinforce the belief that average ability, refinement, intellectuality, or even virtue is an ideal to be aimed at. Since we cannot do anything to the purpose until we think straight and since we cannot think straight without properly defined words it may be that the very first step toward an emancipation from the tyranny of "conformity" should be the attempt to substitute for "normal," as commonly used, a genuine synonym for "average."

3.   Fortunately, such a genuine and familiar synonym does exist. That which is "average" is also properly described as "mediocre." And if we were accustomed to call the average man, not "the common man" or still less "the normal man," but "the mediocre man" we should not be so easily hypnotized into believing that mediocrity is an ideal to be aimed at.

4.   A second step in the same direction would be to return to the word "normal" its original meaning. According to the Shorter Oxford Dictionary it derives from the Latin "norma," which has been Anglicized as "norm" and is, in turn, thus defined: "A rule or authoritative standard." The adjective "normative" is not commonly misused—no doubt because it is not part of that "vocabulary of the average man" by which educators now set so much store. It still generally means "establishing a norm or standard." But "normal" seldom means, as it should, "corresponding to the standard by which a thing is to be judged." If it did, "a normal man" would again mean, not what the average man *is* but what, in its fullest significance, the word "man"

should imply, even "what a man *ought* to be." And that is a very different thing from the "average" or "mediocre" man whom we have so perversely accustomed ourselves to regard as most worthy of admiration.

5.   Only by defining and then attempting to reach up toward the "normal" as properly defined can a democratic society save itself from those defects which the enemies of democracy have always maintained were the necessary consequences of such a society. Until "preparation for life" rather than "familiarity with the best that has been thought and said" became the aim of education every schoolboy knew that Emerson had bid us hitch our wagons to a star. We now hitch them to a mediocrity instead.

6.   Unless, then, normal is a useless and confusing synonym for average it should mean what the word normative suggests, namely, a *concept of what ought to be* rather than a *description of what is*. It should mean what at times it has meant—the fullest possible realization of what the human being is capable of—the complete, not the aborted human being. It is an *entelechy*, not a mean; something excellent, not something mediocre; something rare, not common; not what the majority are, but what few, if any, actually measure up to.

7.   Where, it will be asked, do we get this norm, upon what basis does it rest? Upon the answer to that question depends what a civilization will be like and especially in what direction it will move. At various times religion, philosophy, law, and custom have contributed to it in varying degrees. When none of these is available poetry and literature may do so. But unless we can say in one way or another, "I have some idea of what men ought to be as well as some knowledge of what they are," then civilization is lost.

QUESTIONS

1. Krutch's definition of *normal* is a precising definition: he is seeking to make an uncommon meaning of *normal* its common one. How does Krutch try to persuade us of the need for this other definition?
2. How does Krutch account for the present differences in the connotations of *normative* and *normal,* which derive from the same word? Does he state or imply why *normal* came to mean *average?*
3. Can the meaning of *entelechy* be determined from its context? What help does the etymology of the word provide?
4. Use the synonym listings in your dictionary to determine the exact difference in meaning between the following pairs of words. Write

sentences using ten of the italicized words to reflect their precise dictionary meanings.

a. *essential;* necessary
b. *predict;* prophesy
c. *mimic;* mock
d. sinister; *portentous*
e. fortitude; *forbearance*
f. phase; *facet*
g. agent; *factor*
h. recumbent; *prone*
i. adroit; *deft*
j. *dextrous;* handy
k. blended; *mingled*
l. *perturbed;* agitated

WRITING ASSIGNMENTS

1. Define one of the following words by stating what it is not as well as what it is. Comment on the significance of its etymology.

   a. tolerance   d. impeachment
   b. stinginess   e. tact
   c. contraband

2. Discuss the different meanings—denotative and connotative—of one of the following words, illustrating these meanings by your use of them.

   a. funny   d. crazy
   b. average   e. tacky
   c. cool   f. weird

Division and Classification

ALLAN NEVINS
The Newspaper

1. Obviously, it is futile to talk of accuracy or inaccuracy, authority or lack of authority, with reference to the newspaper as a whole. The newspaper cannot be dismissed with either a blanket endorsement or a blanket condemnation. It cannot be used as if all its parts had equal value or authenticity. The first duty of the historical student of the newspaper is to discriminate. He must weigh every separate department, every article, every writer, for what the department or article or writer seems to be worth. Clearly, a great part of what is printed in every newspaper is from official sources, and hence may be relied upon to be perfectly accurate. The weather report is accurate; so are court notices, election notices, building permits, lists of marriage licenses, bankruptcy lists. Though unofficial, other classes of news are almost totally free from error. The most complete precautions are taken to keep the stock market quotations minutely accurate, both by stock exchange authorities and by the newspaper staffs. An error in stock quotations may have the most disastrous consequences, and mistakes are hence excluded by every means within human power. So with shipping news, news of deaths, and a considerable body of similar matter—sports records, registers of Congressional or legislative votes, and so on.

2. Thus one great division of material in newspapers can be treated as completely authentic. There is another large division which may in general be treated as trustworthy and authoritative. This is the news which is prepared by experts under conditions exempt from hurry and favorable to the gathering of all the significant facts. The weekly review of a real estate expert is a case in point. The sporting news of the best newspapers, prepared by experts under conditions which make for accuracy, is singularly uniform, and this uniformity is the best evidence that it is truthful and well proportioned. Society news, industrial news, and similar intelligence, especially when it appears in the form of weekly surveys written by known specialists, is worthy of the utmost reliance.

3. But in dealing with news which contains a large subjective element, and which is prepared under conditions of hurry and strain, the critical faculty must be kept constantly alert. Every conscientious correspondent at an inauguration, or a battle, or a political rally, or in an interview, tries to report the facts. But not one of them can help reporting, in addition to the facts, the impression that he has personally received of them. The most honest and careful observer ordinarily sees a little of what he wishes to see. It is through failure to make critical allowance for this fact that the historical student of newspapers is most likely to be led astray. Beveridge in his life of Lincoln remarks upon the striking difference between the Democratic reports and the Republican reports of the Lincoln-Douglas debates. At Ottawa, Illinois, for example, these two great leaders held their first joint debate on August 21, 1858. Lincoln came on a special train of fourteen cars crowded with shouting Republicans. It arrived at Ottawa at noon and, according to the Republican papers, when Lincoln alighted a shout went up from a dense and enthusiastic crowd which made the bluffs of the Illinois River and the woods along it ring and ring again. Lincoln entered a carriage; according to the *Chicago Tribune* men with evergreens, mottoes, fair young ladies, bands of music, military companies, and a dense mass of cheering humanity followed him through the streets in a scene of tumultuous excitement. But according to the *Philadelphia Press* and other Douglas papers, Lincoln had only a chilly and lackadaisical reception. "As his procession passed," stated the *Philadelphia Press*, "scarcely a cheer went up. They marched along silently and sorrowfully, as if it were a funeral cortege following him to the grave." On the other hand, the Democratic papers declared that the reception of Douglas was perfectly tremendous; the cheers were so thundering, said the *Philadelphia Press*, that they seemed to rend the very air. But the *Chicago Tribune* said that Douglas had no reception of consequence; that the only cheers he got came from the Irish Catholics. Yet both reports were probably fairly honest. They saw what they wished to see.

DISCUSSION: Division and Classification

Division and *classification* are related methods of analysis. To classify is to create a grouping of objects, persons, or ideas that share significant qualities. Thus Chevrolets, Buicks, and Oldsmobiles belong to the class *American automobiles* and to other classes as well: *General Motors products, vehicles of transportation, gasoline-operated ma-*

chines. A given class—for example, *American automobiles*—can be divided in numerous ways: by manufacturer, engine size, kind of transmission, fuel economy, name, color. And any of the resulting divisions (or subclassifications) can in turn be treated as a class and divided by another principle:

> *class:* American automobiles
> *principle of division:* manufacturer
> *purpose of division:* to illustrate the variety of American automobiles
> *division according to manufacturer:* Ford, Chrysler, General Motors, American Motors, etc.

> *class:* General Motors automobiles
> *principle of subdivision:* names
> *purpose of division:* to illustrate the abundance of model names
> *division according to names:* Chevrolets, Buicks, Oldsmobiles, etc.

Chevrolets, in turn, can be divided by the same principle, or by another—engine size, for example. Each division and subdivision must be consistently worked out according to a single principle, and each should be as exhaustive as knowledge permits—if the division claims to be complete. If several principles of division are employed in an analysis, each division must be kept separate to avoid overlapping distinctions. Division can extend to ideas like discipline and justice, to people, to activities. The following paragraph employs division in a scientific definition:

purpose of analysis	For the investigator of meteorites the basic challenge is deducing the history of the *meteorites* from a bewildering abundance of evidence. The richness of the problem is
principle of division: types according to constituent material	indicated by the sheer variety of *types* of meteorite. The two main classes are the *stony meteorites* and the *iron meteorites.*
first type: stony meteorites	The stony meteorites consist mainly of silicates, with an admixture of nickel and iron.
second type: iron meteorites	The iron meteorites consist mainly of nickel and iron in various proportions. A smaller
third type: stony-iron meteorites	class is the stony-iron meteorites, which are intermediate in composition between the other two. Stony meteorites are in turn
subdivision of stony meteorites	divided into two groups: the chondrites and

principle of subdivision:
presence or absence
of chrondrules
principles of further
subdivisions

the achondrites, according to whether or not they contain chondrules, spherical aggregates of iron-magnesium silicate. Within each group there are further subdivisions based on mineralogical and chemical composition.

—i. R. Cameron,
"Meteorites and Cosmic Radiation"

(italics added)

QUESTIONS

1. Nevins divides materials in newspapers according to their degree of reliability: this is his principle of division. What are the three divisions he distinguishes?
2. What point is he making through these divisions?
3. In referring to the "large subjective element" of certain newspaper accounts, is Nevins referring to bias or prejudice? What does his example of the Lincoln-Douglas debates show?
4. What is the order of ideas in the three paragraphs? Why does Nevins save "news which contains a large subjective element" for last?
5. How many classes can you think of for newspapers?

WRITING ASSIGNMENTS

1. Divide materials in newspapers by another principle of division and use your division to make a point, as Nevins does.
2. Analyze the front-page stories of an issue of a newspaper according to the degree of their reliability. Discuss the "subjective element" of one of the stories, as Nevins discusses the account of the Lincoln-Douglas debates.

JOHN HOLT

Kinds of Discipline

1.   A child, in growing up, may meet and learn from three different kinds of disciplines. The first and most important is what we might call the Discipline of Nature or of Reality. When he is trying to do

something real, if he does the wrong thing or doesn't do the right one, he doesn't get the result he wants. If he doesn't pile one block right on top of another, or tries to build on a slanting surface, his tower falls down. If he hits the wrong key, he hears the wrong note. If he doesn't hit the nail squarely on the head, it bends, and he has to pull it out and start with another. If he doesn't measure properly what he is trying to build, it won't open, close, fit, stand up, fly, float, whistle, or do whatever he wants it to do. If he closes his eyes when he swings, he doesn't hit the ball. A child meets this kind of discipline every time he tries to *do* something, which is why it is so important in school to give children more chances to do things, instead of just reading or listening to someone talk (or pretending to). This discipline is a great teacher. The learner never has to wait long for his answer; it usually comes quickly, often instantly. Also it is clear, and very often points toward the needed correction; from what happened he can not only see that what he did was wrong, but also why, and what he needs to do instead. Finally, and most important, the giver of the answer, call it Nature, is impersonal, impartial, and indifferent. She does not give opinions, or make judgments; she cannot be wheedled, bullied, or fooled; she does not get angry or disappointed; she does not praise or blame; she does not remember past failures or hold grudges; with her one always gets a fresh start, this time is the one that counts.

2. The next discipline we might call the Discipline of Culture, of Society, of What People Really Do. Man is a social, a cultural animal. Children sense around them this culture, this network of agreements, cutoms, habits, and rules binding the adults together. They want to understand it and be a part of it. They watch very carefully what people around them are doing and want to do the same. They want to do right, unless they become convinced they can't do right. Thus children rarely misbehave seriously in church, but sit as quietly as they can. The example of all those grownups is contagious. Some mysterious ritual is going on, and children, who like rituals, want to be part of it. In the same way, the little children that I see at concerts or operas, though they may fidget a little, or perhaps take a nap now and then, rarely make any disturbance. With all those grownups sitting there, neither moving nor talking, it is the most natural thing in the world to imitate them. Children who live among adults who are habitually courteous to each other, and to them, will soon learn to be courteous. Children who live surrounded by people who speak a certain way will speak that way, however much we may try to tell them that speaking that way is bad or wrong.

3.   The third discipline is the one most people mean when they speak of discipline—the Discipline of Superior Force, of sergeant to private, of "you do what I tell you or I'll make you wish you had." There is bound to be some of this in a child's life. Living as we do surrounded by things that can hurt children, or that children can hurt, we cannot avoid it. We can't afford to let a small child find out from experience the danger of playing in a busy street, or of fooling with the pots on the top of a stove, or of eating up the pills in the medicine cabinet. So, along with other precautions, we say to him, "Don't play in the street, or touch things on the stove, or go into the medicine cabinet, or I'll punish you." Between him and the danger too great for him to imagine we put a lesser danger, but one he can imagine and maybe therefore want to avoid. He can have no idea of what it would be like to be hit by a car, but he can imagine being shouted at, or spanked, or sent to his room. He avoids these substitutes for the greater danger until he can understand it and avoid it for its own sake. But we ought to use this discipline only when it is necessary to protect the life, health, safety, or well-being of people or other living creatures, or to prevent destruction of things that people care about. We ought not to assume too long, as we usually do, that a child cannot understand the real nature of the danger from which we want to protect him. The sooner he avoids the danger, not to escape our punishment, but as a matter of good sense, the better. He can learn that faster than we think. In Mexico, for example, where people drive their cars with a good deal of spirit, I saw many children no older than five or four walking unattended on the streets. They understood about cars, they knew what to do. A child whose life is full of the threat and fear of punishment is locked into babyhood. There is no way for him to grow up, to learn to take responsibility for his life and acts. Most important of all, we should not assume that having to yield to the threat of our superior force is good for the child's character. It is never good for *anyone's* character. To bow to superior force makes us feel impotent and cowardly for not having had the strength or courage to resist. Worse, it makes us resentful and vengeful. We can hardly wait to make someone pay for our humiliation, yield to us as we were once made to yield. No, if we cannot always avoid using the Discipline of Superior Force, we should at least use it as seldom as we can.

4.   There are places where all three disciplines overlap. Any very demanding human activity combines in it the disciplines of Superior Force, of Culture, and of Nature. The novice will be told, "Do it this way, never mind asking why, just do it that way, that is the way we

always do it." But it probably *is* just the way they always do it, and usually for the very good reason that it is a way that has been found to work. Think, for example, of ballet training. The student in a class is told to do this exercise, or that; to stand so; to do this or that with his head, arms, shoulders, abdomen, hips, legs, feet. He is constantly corrected. There is no argument. But behind these seemingly autocratic demands by the teacher lie many decades of custom and tradition, and behind that, the necessities of dancing itself. You cannot make the moves of classical ballet unless over many years you have acquired, and renewed every day, the needed strength and suppleness in scores of muscles and joints. Nor can you do the difficult motions, making them look easy, unless you have learned hundreds of easier ones first. Dance teachers may not always agree on all the details of teaching these strengths and skills. But no novice could learn them all by himself. You could not go for a night or two to watch the ballet and then, without any other knowledge at all, teach yourself how to do it. In the same way, you would be unlikely to learn any complicated and difficult human activity without drawing heavily on the experience of those who know it better. But the point is that the authority of these experts or teachers stems from, grows out of their greater competence and experience, the fact that what they do *works*, not the fact that they happen to be the teacher and as such have the power to kick a student out of the class. And the further point is that children are always and everywhere attracted to that competence, and ready and eager to submit themselves to a discipline that grows out of it. We hear constantly that children will never do anything unless compelled to by bribes or threats. But in their private lives, or in extracurricular activities in school, in sports, music, drama, art, running a newspaper, and so on, they often submit themselves willingly and wholeheartedly to very intense disciplines, simply because they want to learn to do a given thing well. Our Little-Napoleon football coaches, of whom we have too many and hear far too much, blind us to the fact that millions of children work hard every year getting better at sports and games without coaches barking and yelling at them.

QUESTIONS

1. Does Holt divide discipline according to source or to the uses of discipline in education—or according to some other principle?
2. Is Holt's division exhaustive?
3. Holt states in paragraph 4 that the kinds of discipline distinguished

overlap. How do they? Does he show that they nevertheless remain distinct?

4. The principle of division might have been the effects of discipline on the personality of the young person. Is Holt concerned with effects in the course of his discussion?
5. What other principles of division might be employed in a discussion of discipline and to what purpose?
6. Do you agree with Holt that people learn best when they are not coerced? Do you agree with him about football coaches?

WRITING ASSIGNMENTS

1. Divide discipline according to a different principle from Holt's. Make your divisions exclusive of one another and indicate how exhaustive you think they are.
2. Write an essay on jobs or hobbies, developing the topic by division. If you divide by more than one principle, keep each breakdown and discussion separate and consistent.

CAROLINE BIRD

Queue

1. Queuing gets more things through a space-time bottleneck by lining them up in space or time. Schedules and appointment calendars line things and people up in time: queues, lists, or priority systems line them up in space. Like things can be lined up or queued to get more of them into a limited space. Canners do it when they line the anchovies up head by tail to get more into the can at a time (the anchovies *share* the time-space of the can when they are curled around something else, like a caper). You queue in space when you put all the tall books on one tall shelf so that you can get more shelves and hence more books on the wall at the same time.

2. Staggering is a form of queuing which lines things up in time to get them through a limited space. Billing is staggered through the month to get more bills through the time-space of the billing department. New York City welfare checks can no longer all be sent out on the same day. French resorts are overloaded and Parisian services understaffed because Frenchmen who get a vacation insist on taking the

whole month of August off at once. Staggering will be eventually necessary to avert breakdown of the French economy.

3. People and things can be lined up by the speed at which they move so that fast movers are not slowed to the pace of slow movers ahead of them. High-speed lanes for cars, toll lines reserved for those with exact change, and express check-out counters in supermarkets line up or queue the fast movers.

4. People react strongly, and variously to being queued. Russians line themselves up without being told. Moscow theater audiences file out, last row first, like school children marching out of assemblies. In America, on the contrary, theatrical performances break up like the Arctic ice in springtime. Commuters and the constitutionally impatient gather themselves for a dash up the aisle, while the rest of the audience is still applauding. Fidgeters and people who can't bear having anyone ahead of them sidle across rows to emergency exits, while placid souls who seem to enjoy the presence of others drift happily up the aisle with the crowd. In Moscow, the theater is emptied faster. In New York, you can get out fast if you're willing to work at it.

5. Even on a first-come, first-served basis, Americans don't like queues. Rather than put some people in front of other people, we prefer to row them up horizontally on the starting line and let the best man win, the way they did when they shot off a gun to open the Oklahoma land rush. West Indians like queuing even less. There were so many bus-boarding accidents in Bridgetown that the British-bred Barbados Assembly passed a law requiring passengers to form a line of not more than two abreast whenever six or more persons were waiting for a bus.

6. Whether they like it or not, Americans are spending more time in queues. We now expect to queue for library books, cabs, movies, ski lifts, tees, subway tokens, and even campsites in the wilds of our national parks. Doctors, dentists, barbers, and employment interviewers line us up. So do headwaiters, sales clerks, cashiers, bank tellers, income tax adjusters, and the few remaining meat cutters. Lawn services line our lawns up for mowing. Plumbers line our emergencies up for fixing.

7. The queue is standing operating procedure for any transaction which may not be free at the time it is demanded. Freight cars queue for unloading, telephone calls for circuits, and stacked airplanes for permission to land. In order to get through a big organization, decisions may have to wait in one line after another, as they are bucked from desk to desk. Traffic control problems frequently involve similar queues of queues.

8. "Queuing theory" describes how queues grow and shrink. It has become a hot branch of mathematics practiced by operations researchers studying complicated traffic and transportation systems.

QUESTIONS

1. The queue is the class—the general practice of lining people up—to which many kinds of queuing are fitted. "Staggering" is a kind of queuing, the author tells us. What other kinds does she discuss? How do the examples of queuing fit these kinds?
2. What does her analysis show about Americans? Is she singling out one quality of Americans, or does she illustrate several through attitudes toward queuing?
3. What do the contrasting examples of the problem of queuing in Moscow and Barbados show about Americans?
4. How do paragraphs 7 and 8 differ from earlier paragraphs in subject and focus? Why are these paragraphs saved for the end of the discussion?
5. Do you agree with Bird about the American attitude toward queuing?

WRITING ASSIGNMENT

Identify your attitude toward standing in line by discussing three or four different queuing situations and your behavior in them. Arrange these examples in the order of their importance to understanding or defining your general attitude.

Comparison and Contrast

MARIE WINN

Reading and Television

1. A comparison between reading and viewing may be made in respect to the pace of each experience, and the relative control a person has over that pace, for the pace may influence the ways one uses the material received in each experience. In addition, the pace of each experience may determine how much it intrudes upon other aspects of one's life.

2. The pace of reading, clearly, depends entirely upon the reader. He may read as slowly or as rapidly as he can or wishes to read. If he does not understand something, he may stop and reread it, or go in search of elucidation before continuing. The reader can accelerate his pace when the material is easy or less than interesting, and slow down when it is difficult or enthralling. If what he reads is moving, he can put down the book for a few moments and cope with his emotions without fear of losing anything.

3. The pace of the television experience cannot be controlled by the viewer; only its beginning and end are within his control as he clicks the knob on and off. He cannot slow down a delightful program or speed up a dreary one. He cannot "turn back" if a word or phrase is not understood. The program moves inexorably forward, and what is lost or misunderstood remains so.

4. Nor can the television viewer readily transform the material he receives into a form that might suit his particular emotional needs, as he invariably does with material he reads. The images move too quickly. He cannot use his own imagination to invest the people and events portrayed on television with the personal meanings that would help him understand and resolve relationships and conflicts in his own life; he is under the power of the imagination of the show's creators. In the television experience the eyes and ears are overwhelmed with the immediacy of sights and sounds. They flash from the television set just fast enough for the eyes and ears to take them in before moving

on quickly to the new pictures and sounds . . . so as *not to lose the thread.*

5. Not to lose the thread . . . it is this need, occasioned by the irreversible direction and relentless velocity of the television experience, that not only limits the workings of the viewer's imagination, but also causes television to intrude into human affairs far more than reading experiences can ever do. If someone enters the room while one is watching television—a friend, a relative, a child, someone, perhaps, one has not seen for some time—one must continue to watch or one will lose the thread. The greetings must wait, for the television program will not. A book, of course, can be set aside, with a pang of regret, perhaps, but with no sense of permanent loss.

DISCUSSION: Comparison and Contrast

Two or more people, objects, actions, or ideas may be compared and contrasted for the purpose of arriving at a relative estimate or evaluation:

> If Socrates was as innocent as this at the age of seventy, it may be imagined how innocent Joan was at the age of seventeen. Now Socrates was a man of argument, operating slowly and peacefully on men's minds, whereas Joan was a woman of action, operating with impetuous violence on their bodies. That, no doubt, is why the contemporaries of Socrates endured him so long, and why Joan was destroyed before she was fully grown. But both of them combined terrifying ability with a frankness, personal modesty, and benevolence which made the furious dislike to which they fell victims absolutely unreasonable, and therefore inapprehensible by themselves.—George Bernard Shaw, Preface to *St. Joan*

The opening comparison tells us something important through the differences in Socrates' and Joan's ages and ways of operating on minds and bodies; the concluding sentence moves to similarities between them. The evaluation of both Socrates and Joan is made *through* the comparison and contrast; light is shed on both of them, not on one only. The comparison and contrast could have been organized differently: Shaw could have presented all of Socrates' qualities first, then all of Joan's, instead of interweaving them.

In general, comparison is concerned with resemblance, contrast with difference (however, comparison is sometimes used to mean a concern with resemblance and difference). When comparison and contrast occur in the same passage, they must be carefully distinguished to avoid confusing the reader. They can, of course, be combined with other methods of analysis: important terms may be defined before being compared; or comparison and contrast may serve to define these terms.

QUESTIONS

1. What is the purpose of the comparison, according to paragraph 1?
2. What are the differences stressed by the writer? In what order are these presented?
3. Does Winn say that we should give up television, or is she making no recommendation?
4. Does her description of reading and watching television agree with your experience? Is reading ever as compelling an experience as television for you?
5. Is the experience of watching a sports event on television much the same as watching the news or a movie? If not, what are the differences? Do these similarities give support to Winn, or do they provide contrary evidence?

WRITING ASSIGNMENTS

1. In a few well-developed paragraphs, develop a comparison between one of the following pairs. State the purpose of your comparison somewhere in your essay, and draw conclusions as you discuss the similarities or differences.
   a. playing baseball (or another sport) and watching baseball
   b. listening to a particular kind of music and dancing to it
   c. reading a book and seeing the movie made from it
   d. riding a bicycle and driving a car on a busy highway
2. Compare the experience of reading a newspaper or newsmagazine with that of reading a novel or a textbook. Draw conclusions from your comparison at the end of your discussion.

J. BRONOWSKI

The Athlete and the Gazelle

1. Every human action goes back in some part to our animal origins; we should be cold and lonely creatures if we were cut off from that blood-stream of life. Nevertheless, it is right to ask for a distinction: What are the physical gifts that man must share with the animals, and

what are the gifts that make him different? Consider any example, the more straightforward the better—say, the simple action of an athlete when running or jumping. When he hears the gun, the starting response of the runner is the same as the flight response of the gazelle. He seems all animal in action. The heartbeat goes up; when he sprints at top speed the heart is pumping five times as much blood as normal, and ninety per cent of it is for the muscles. He needs twenty gallons of air a minute now to aerate his blood with the oxygen that it must carry to the muscles.

2.   The violent coursing of the blood and intake of air can be made visible, for they show up as heat on infra-red films which are sensitive to such radiation. (The blue or light zones are hottest; the red or dark zones are cooler.) The flush that we see and that the infra-red camera analyses is a by-product that signals the limit of muscular action. For the main chemical action is to get energy for the muscles by burning sugar there; but three-quarters of that is lost as heat. And there is another limit, on the runner and the gazelle equally, which is more severe. At this speed, the chemical burn-up in the muscles is too fast to be complete. The waste products of incomplete burning, chiefly lactic acid, now foul up the blood. This is what causes fatigue, and blocks the muscle action until the blood can be cleansed with fresh oxygen.

3.   So far, there is nothing to distinguish the athlete from the gazelle—all that, in one way or another, is the normal metabolism of an animal in flight. But there is a cardinal difference: the runner was not in flight. The shot that set him off was the starter's pistol, and what he was experiencing, deliberately, was not fear but exaltation. The runner is like a child at play; his actions are an adventure in freedom, and the only purpose of his breathless chemistry was to explore the limits of his own strength.

4.   Naturally there are physical differences between man and the other animals, even between man and the apes. In the act of vaulting, the athlete grasps his pole, for example, with an exact grip that no ape can quite match. Yet such differences are secondary by comparison with the overriding difference, which is that the athlete is an adult whose behavior is not driven by his immediate environment, as animal actions are. In themselves, his actions make no practical sense at all; they are an exercise that is not directed to the present. The athlete's mind is fixed ahead of him, building up his skill; and he vaults in imagination into the future.

5.   Poised for that leap, the pole-vaulter is a capsule of human abilities: the grasp of the hand, the arch of the foot, the muscles of the

shoulder and pelvis—the pole itself, in which energy is stored and released like a bow firing an arrow. The radical character in that complex is the sense of foresight, that is, the ability to fix an objective ahead and rigorously hold his attention on it. The athlete's performance unfolds a continuous plan; from one extreme to the other, it is the invention of the pole, the concentration of the mind at the moment before leaping, which give it the stamp of humanity.

QUESTIONS

1. What similarities between humans and animals does Bronowski develop through his example?
2. What are the differences between the pole vaulter and the gazelle and other animals discussed?
3. In general, what are the physical traits that humans share with animals, and what gifts make humans different?
4. What other comparison between humans and animals would have allowed Bronowski to distinguish human from animal qualities?

WRITING ASSIGNMENTS

1. Compare and contrast one of the following pairs of activities to arrive at a relative estimate of them and to make a point:
   a. softball and hardball
   b. football and touch football
   c. jogging and running
   d. tennis and badminton
   e. checkers and chess
2. Do the same for one of the following pairs of activities:
   a. studying for examinations in different subjects
   b. learning to drive a car and to ride a bicycle
   c. repairing or changing an automobile and a bicycle tire
   d. driving in a small town and in a large city

HANNAH ARENDT

The Concentration-Camp Inmate

Forced labor as a punishment is limited as to time and intensity. The convict retains his rights over his body; he is not absolutely tortured and he is not absolutely dominated. Banishment banishes only from one part of the world to another part of the world, also inhabited by human beings; it does not exclude from the human world altogether. Throughout history slavery has been an institution within a social order; slaves were not, like concentration-camp inmates, withdrawn from the sight and hence the protection of their fellow-men; as instruments of labor they had a definite price and as property a definite value. The concentration-camp inmate has no price, because he can always be replaced; nobody knows to whom he belongs, because he is never seen. From the point of view of normal society he is absolutely superfluous, although in times of acute labor shortage, as in Russia and in Germany during the war, he is used for work.

QUESTIONS

1. Arendt might simply have described the typical existence of the concentration-camp inmate. Instead she defines that existence through contrast with other forms of imprisonment and servitude: through a relative estimate. What is the advantage of this procedure—defining by means of contrast—over other methods?
2. What accounts for the order of ideas? Are they presented in the order of their importance?
3. What does the paragraph tell us about the values of a society in which concentration camps exist?

WRITING ASSIGNMENT

Make a list of significant similarities and differences between one of the following pairs and use it to write a paragraph. Use your comparison and contrast to arrive at a relative estimate—which is better or worse?—and to make a definite point.

a. streetcar or bus nuisance and back-seat driver
b. silent bore and talkative bore
c. classroom comic and dormitory comic
d. expectations of high-school and college English teachers

Analogy

MICHAEL COLLINS
Circling the Moon

1. My command module chores now include an extra task: finding the LM on the surface. If I can see it through my sextant, center my cross hairs on it, and mark the instant of superposition, then my computer will know something it doesn't know now: where the LM actually is, instead of where it is supposed to be. This is a valuable—not vital, but valuable—piece of information for "Hal" to have, especially as a starting reference point for the sequence of rendezvous maneuvers which will come tomorrow (or sooner?). Of course, the ground can take its measurements as well, but it really has no way of judging where the LM came down, except by comparing Neil and Buzz's description of their surrounding terrain (lurain?) with the rather crude maps which Houston has. But I am far past the landing site now, about to swing around behind the left edge of the moon, so it will be awhile before I get my first crack at looking for the LM. It takes me two hours to circle the moon once.

2. Meanwhile, the command module is purring along in grand shape. I have turned the lights up bright, and the cockpit reflects a cheeriness which I want very much to share. My concerns are exterior ones, having to do with the vicissitudes of my two friends on the moon and their uncertain return path to me, but inside, all is well as this familiar machine and I circle and watch and wait. I have removed the center couch and stored it underneath the left one, and this gives the place an entirely different aspect. It opens up a central aisle between the main instrument panel and the lower equipment bay, a pathway which allows me to zip from upper hatch window to lower sextant and return. The main reason for removing the couch is to provide adequate access for Neil and Buzz to enter the command module through the side hatch, in the event that the probe and drogue mechanism cannot be cleared from the tunnel. If such is the case, we would have to open the hatch to the vacuum of space, and Neil and Buzz would have to make an extravehicular transfer from the LM, dragging

their rock boxes behind them. All three of us would be in bulky pressurized suits, requiring a tremendous amount of space and a wide path into the lower equipment bay. In addition to providing more room, these preparations give me the feeling of being proprietor of a small resort hotel, about to receive the onrush of skiers coming in out of the cold. Everything is prepared for them; it is a happy place, and I couldn't make them more welcome unless I had a fireplace. I know from pre-flight press questions that I will be described as a lonely man ("Not since Adam has any man experienced such loneliness"), and I guess that the TV commentators must be reveling in my solitude and deriving all sorts of phony philosophy from it, but I hope not. Far from feeling lonely or abandoned, I feel very much a part of what is taking place on the lunar surface. I know that I would be a liar or a fool if I said that I have the best of the three Apollo 11 seats, but I can say with truth and equanimity that I am perfectly satisfied with the one I have. This venture has been structured for three men, and I consider my third to be as necessary as either of the other two.

3.   I don't mean to deny a feeling of solitude. It is there, reinforced by the fact that radio contact with the earth abruptly cuts off at the instant I disappear behind the moon. I am alone now, truly alone, and absolutely isolated from any known life. I am it. If a count were taken, the score would be three billion plus two over on the other side of the moon, and one plus God only knows what on this side. I feel this powerfully—not as fear or loneliness—but as awareness, anticipation, satisfaction, confidence, almost exultation. I like the feeling. Outside my window I can see stars—and that is all. Where I know the moon to be, there is simply a black void; the moon's presence is defined solely by the absence of stars. To compare the sensation with something terrestrial, perhaps being alone in a skiff in the middle of the Pacific Ocean on a pitchblack night would most nearly approximate my situation. In a skiff, one would see bright stars above and black sea below; I see the same stars, minus the twinkling, of course, and absolutely nothing below. In each case, time and distance are extremely important factors. In terms of distance, I am much more remote, but in terms of time, lunar orbit is much closer to civilized conversation than is the mid-Pacific. Although I may be nearly a quarter of a million miles away, I am cut off from human voices for only forty-eight minutes out of each two hours, while the man in the skiff—grazing the very surface of the planet—is not so privileged, or burdened. Of the two quantities, time and distance, time tends to be a much more personal one, so that I feel simultaneously closer to, and

farther away from, Houston than I would if I were on some remote spot on earth which would deny me conversation with other humans for months on end.

DISCUSSION: Analogy

Illustrative *analogy* is a special kind of example, a comparison between two quite different things or activities for the purpose of explanation: a child growing like a tender plant and needing sun, water, and a receptive soil as well as proper care from a skilled gardener. The comparison may be point by point. But there are differences also, and if there is danger of the analogy being carried too far (children are not so tender that they need as much protection as plants from the hazards of living), the writer may state these differences to limit the inferences that may be drawn. He or she has chosen the analogy for the sake of vivid illustration and nothing more. We will see later that analogy is often used in argument: children *should* be fully protected from various hazards because they are tender plants. The argument will stand or fall depending on how convinced we are of the similarities and of the unimportance of the differences.

Analogy is often used in explanations of scientific ideas. One of the most famous is the analogy between the moving apart of the galaxies in the universe and an expanding raisin cake:

> Suppose the cake swells uniformly as it cooks, but the raisins themselves remain of the same size. Let each raisin represent a cluster of galaxies, and imagine yourself inside one of them. As the cake swells, you will observe that all the other raisins move away from you. Moreover, the farther away the raisin, the faster it will seem to move. When the cake has swollen to twice its initial dimensions, the distance between all the raisins will have doubled itself—two raisins that were initially an inch apart will now be two inches apart; two raisins that were a foot apart will have moved two feet apart. Since the entire action takes place within the same time interval, obviously the more distant raisins must move apart faster than those close at hand. So it happens with the clusters of galaxies.—Fred Hoyle, "When Time Began"

And Hoyle draws a further conclusion from his analogy:

> No matter which raisin you happen to be inside, the others will always move away from you. Hence the fact that we observe all the other galaxies to be moving away from us does not mean that we are situated at the center of the universe. Indeed, it seems certain that the universe has no center.

In another explanation of the expanding galaxies, he compares the galaxies to dots marked on an expanding balloon. The dots remain the same size as the balloon expands—like the raisins in the expanding cake. Each analogy has its advantages and disadvantages. One advantage of the raisin analogy is the disparity of size between a raisin and a galaxy—a system of sometimes billions of stars occupying an enormous amount of space. The disparity in size provides a relative estimate of size in the universe.

QUESTIONS

1. Collins is describing the 1969 moon landing of Neil Armstrong and Buzz Aldrin. What are the points of similarity between the returning astronauts and the returning skiers? Are these points of similarity stated or implied? (The "LM" is the landing module.)
2. What other analogy might Collins have employed to describe the returning astronauts? What would have been gained or lost in descriptive power or explanation had he employed it?
3. What is the similarity, and what are the differences, in the analogy between the skiff and the command module? What point is Collins making through the differences?

WRITING ASSIGNMENT

Explain the sensation of being alone in a car in heavy traffic or a storm, or traveling away from home for the first time, through analogy to another kind of experience similar enough to help make your experience vivid. Comment on the differences and their significance at some point in your explanation.

J. ANTHONY LUKAS

Pinball

1.   Pinball is a metaphor for life, pitting man's skill, nerve, persistence, and luck against the perverse machinery of human existence. The playfield is rich with rewards: targets that bring huge scores, bright lights, chiming bells, free balls, and extra games. But it is replete with perils, too: culs-de-sac, traps, gutters, and gobble holes down which the ball may disappear forever.

2. Each pull of the plunger launches the ball into a miniature universe of incalculable possibilities. As the steel sphere hurtles into the ellipse at the top of the playfield, it hangs for a moment in exquisite tension between triumph and disaster. Down one lane lies a hole worth thousands, down another a sickening lurch to oblivion. The ball trembles on the lip, seeming to lean first one way, then the other.

3. A player is not powerless to control the ball's wild flight, any more than man is powerless to control his own life. He may nudge the machine with hands, arms, or hips, jogging it just enough to change the angle of the ball's descent. And he is armed with "flippers" which can propel the ball back up the playfield, aiming at the targets with the richest payoffs. But, just as man's boldest strokes and bravest ventures often boomerang, so an ill-timed flip can ricochet the ball straight down "death alley," and a too vigorous nudge will send the machine into "tilt." Winning pinball, like a rewarding life, requires delicate touch, fine calibrations, careful discrimination between boldness and folly.

QUESTIONS

1. What are the points of similarity between pinball and life?
2. In what order does Lukas present these points of similarity?
3. Given the purpose of the analogy, need Lukas have presented any points of dissimilarity between pinfall and life? Can you think of any that would weaken the analogy or qualify it?
4. To what extent would tennis or basketball or football present an analogy to a rewarding life?
5. Do you find the analogy to pinball effective?

WRITING ASSIGNMENTS

1. Describe a rewarding life through the analogy of another game or activity that presents a sufficient number of similarities. If there are significant points of dissimilarity that qualify or weaken the analogy, discuss these also.
2. Describe an unrewarding life through the analogy of another game or activity. Then contrast the points you have made with those Lukas makes about a rewarding life.

Example

E. B. WHITE

New York

It is a miracle that New York works at all. The whole thing is implausible. Every time the residents brush their teeth, millions of gallons of water must be drawn from the Catskills and the hills of Westchester. When a young man in Manhattan writes a letter to his girl in Brooklyn, the love message gets blown to her through a pneumatic tube—*pfft*—just like that. The subterranean system of telephone cables, power lines, steam pipes, gas mains and sewer pipes is reason enough to abandon the island to the gods and the weevils. Every time an incision is made in the pavement, the noisy surgeons expose ganglia that are tangled beyond belief. By rights New York should have destroyed itself long ago, from panic or fire or rioting or failure of some vital supply line in its circulatory system or from some deep labyrinthine short circuit. Long ago the city should have experienced an insoluble traffic snarl at some impossible bottleneck. It should have perished of hunger when food lines failed for a few days. It should have been wiped out by a plague starting in its slums or carried in by ships' rats. It should have been overwhelmed by the sea that licks at it on every side. The workers in its myriad cells should have succumbed to nerves, from the fearful pall of smoke-fog that drifts over every few days from Jersey, blotting out all light at noon and leaving the high offices suspended, men groping and depressed, and the sense of world's end. It should have been touched in the head by the August heat and gone off its rocker.

DISCUSSION: Example

An idea may be illustrated by a series of short examples or by a long example, if one is needed to make it clear. The word *example* originally referred to a sample or typical instance; the word still has this meaning, and for many writers it is an outstanding instance, even one essential to understanding the idea under discussion:

Example **65**

The world is full of things whose right-hand version is different from the left-hand version: a right-handed corkscrew as against a left-handed, a right snail as against a left one. Above all, the two hands; they can be mirrored one in the other, but they cannot be turned in such a way that the right hand and the left hand become interchangeable. That was known in Pasteur's time to be true also of some crystals, whose facets are so arranged that there are right-hand versions and left-hand versions.—J. Bronowski, *The Ascent of Man*

To write of right-hand and left-hand things in nature would be unclear to most readers without examples. In the same way, to write that New York is different today from the New York of fifty years ago would mean little without examples.

QUESTIONS

1. What examples does White give to show that "the whole thing is implausible"?
2. White explicitly compares New York City to a human being. What are the similarities, and how does the comparison help to emphasize the "miracle" he is describing?
3. What is the tone of the paragraph, and how does White achieve it?

WRITING ASSIGNMENTS

1. In a well-developed paragraph state an idea about your hometown or city and develop it by a series of short examples. Make your examples vivid and lively.
2. Develop one of the following statements by example:
   a. The insupportable labor of doing nothing.—Sir Richard Steele
   b. The first blow is half the battle.—Oliver Goldsmith
   c. Ask yourself whether you are happy, and you cease to be so.—John Stuart Mill
   d. Parentage is a very important profession; but no test of fitness for it is ever imposed in the interest of the children.—George Bernard Shaw

TOM WOLFE

Thursday Morning in a New York Subway Station

1. Love! Attar of libido in the air! It is 8:45 A.M. Thursday morning in the IRT subway station at 50th Street and Broadway and already two kids are hung up in a kind of herringbone weave of arms and legs, which proves, one has to admit, that love is not *confined* to Sunday in New York. Still, the odds! All the faces come popping in clots out of the Seventh Avenue local, past the King Size Ice Cream machine, and the turnstiles start whacking away as if the world were breaking up on the reefs. Four steps past the turnstiles everybody is already backed up haunch to paunch for the climb up the ramp and the stairs to the surface, a great funnel of flesh, wool, felt, leather, rubber and steaming alumicron, with the blood squeezing through everybody's old sclerotic arteries in hopped-up spurts from too much coffee and the effort of surfacing from the subway at the rush hour. Yet there on the landing are a boy and a girl, both about eighteen, in one of those utter, My Sin, backbreaking embraces.

2. He envelops her not only with his arms but with his chest, which has the American teen-ager concave shape to it. She has her head cocked at a 90-degree angle and they both have their eyes pressed shut for all they are worth and some incredibly feverish action going with each other's mouths. All round them, ten, scores, it seems like hundreds, of faces and bodies are perspiring, trooping and bellying up the stairs with arteriosclerotic grimaces past a showcase full of such novel items as Joy Buzzers, Squirting Nickels, Finger Rats, Scary Tarantulas and spoons with realistic dead flies on them, past Fred's barbershop, which is just off the landing and has glossy photographs of young men with the kind of baroque haircuts one can get in there, and up onto 50th Street into a madhouse of traffic and shops with weird lingerie and gray hair-dyeing displays in the windows, signs for free teacup readings and a pool-playing match between the Playboy Bunnies and Downey's Showgirls, and then everybody pounds on toward the Time-Life Building, the Brill Building or NBC.

3. The boy and the girl just keep on writhing in their embroilment. Her hand is sliding up the back of his neck, which he turns when her fingers wander into the intricate formal gardens of his Chicago Boxcar

Example 67

hairdo at the base of the skull. The turn causes his face to start to mash in the ciliated hull of her beehive hairdo, and so she rolls her head 180 degrees to the other side, using their mouths for the pivot. But aside from good hair grooming, they are oblivious to everything but each other. Everybody gives them a once-over. Disgusting! Amusing! How touching! A few kids pass by and say things like "Swing it, baby." But the great majority in that heaving funnel up the stairs seem to be as much astounded as anything else. The vision of love at rush hour cannot strike anyone exactly as romance. It is a feat, like a fat man crossing the English Channel in a barrel. It is an earnest accomplishment against the tide. It is a piece of slightly gross heroics, after the manner of those knobby, varicose old men who come out from some place in baggy shorts every year and run through the streets of Boston in the Marathon race. And somehow that is the gaffe against love all week long in New York, for everybody, not just two kids writhing under their coiffures in the 50th Street subway station; too hurried, too crowded, too hard, and no time for dalliance.

QUESTIONS

1. Wolfe illustrates "the gaffe against love all week long in New York." What precisely is the "gaffe"? What do the details suggest about the Thursday morning mood of New Yorkers?
2. What does the description of the showcase and of 50th Street imply about the world of the lovers? Would they seem comical in any setting?
3. How similar is Wolfe's view of New York to White's, in the quality of life or its pace?

WRITING ASSIGNMENTS

1. Every piece of writing suggests something about the personality, interests, and ideas of the author, even when he or she speaks to us through a narrator. Discuss the impression you receive of the author of this selection.
2. Describe one or two people in a situation made comical by the setting. Allow your reader to visualize the setting as well as the situation through your choice of examples.

Process

FLORENCE H. PETTIT

How to Sharpen Your Knife

If you have never done any whittling or wood carving before, the first skill to learn is how to sharpen your knife. You may be surprised to learn that even a brand-new knife needs sharpening. Knives are never sold honed (finely sharpened), although some gouges and chisels are. It is essential to learn the firm stroke on the stone that will keep your blades sharp. The sharpening stone must be fixed in place on the table, so that it will not move around. You can do this by placing a piece of rubber inner tube or a thin piece of foam rubber under it. Or you can tack four strips of wood, if you have a rough worktable, to frame the stone and hold it in place. Put a generous puddle of oil on the stone—this will soon disappear into the surface of a new stone, and you will need to keep adding more oil. Press the knife blade flat against the stone in the puddle of oil, using your index finger. Whichever way the cutting edge of the knife faces is the side of the blade that should get a little more pressure. Move the blade around three or four times in a narrow oval about the size of your fingernail, going *counterclockwise* when the sharp edge is facing right. Now turn the blade over in the same spot on the stone, press hard, and move it around the small oval *clockwise*, with more pressure on the cutting edge that faces left. Repeat the ovals, flipping the knife blade over six or seven times, and applying lighter pressure to the blade the last two times. Wipe the blade clean with a piece of rag or tissue and rub it flat on the piece of leather strop at least twice on each side. Stroke *away* from the cutting edge to remove the little burr of metal that may be left on the blade.

DISCUSSION: Process

An important method of paragraph development is that of tracing or analyzing a mechanical, natural, or historical process. In general, a *process* is a series of connected actions, each developing from the preceding one, that results in something: a decision, a product, an effect of some kind. Though the stages of a process are presented chronologically—that is, in the order in which they occur—the writer may interrupt the account to discuss the implicatons or details of a particular stage. In complex processes, various stages may individually contain a number of steps, each of which may be distinguished for the reader. Process analysis is often closely related to causal analysis, to be discussed in the next section, and may be combined with it.

QUESTIONS

1. What details help the reader to visualize the mechanical process described in the paragraph?
2. Are the stages of the process presented chronologically? If not, why not?
3. Are any terms defined in context—that is, in the description of how to sharpen a knife?

WRITING ASSIGNMENTS

1. Describe a mechanical process comparable to sharpening a knife—for example, sharpening the blades of a hand mower or pruning a tree or painting the exterior of a house.
2. Rewrite the paragraph on how to sharpen a knife, explaining the process to a child who is just beginning to learn how to carve wood.

JULIA M. SETON

Snow Houses

1.   The invention of the snow house by the Eskimo (or Innuit, as they call themselves) was one of the greatest triumphs over environment that man has ever accomplished. In the Arctic Circle, it is not that people lack ability or industry, but the surroundings restrict constructive effort to the barest necessities of existence. This effectually retards progress to higher development. Agriculture is impossible all along the thousands of miles of the north shore. The only wood is such as drifts in. Other than this driftwood, the only available building materials are snow, ice, stone, and bones of animals. All of these

have been used for dwellings and storage places, differing in various tribes according to the requirements and skill of the workers. The lack of necessary timbers to build walls and span wide spaces is probably one reason why these tribes construct their houses at least partly beneath the surface of the ground. This device also makes the houses more impervious to the cold.

2. Most of us are inclined to think that the Eskimo lives always in an igloo or snow house. This is not entirely true. After the long cold winter, the family is very apt to move, when the weather permits, into a tent of sealskin. The actual construction of such tent is similar to that used by other, more southerly tribes. The snow house, however, is an interesting and unique habitation. Our summer campers will not build with snow, but the ingeniousness of the art is worth recording, and some of our winter camps in the mountains might try to make snow houses. It is essential that the snow itself be of the right kind. It must be taken from a bank formed by a single storm, or the blocks will break when cut. The snow must be very fine-grained but not too hard to be cut with a snow knife. In the old days, these knives were made of ivory and had a slight curve.

3. A deep snowdrift is chosen. Two parallel cuts are made crosswise into the drift, about eight inches deep and two feet apart. With two vertical cuts, a small block is removed, making it easier to continue the work of sawing and taking out the blocks, which, when ready for use, measure three or four feet in length, two feet in height, and six to eight inches in thickness. As one man cuts the blocks, another starts building. On a level place, a row of blocks is set up in a circle, slanted inward slightly so as to fit closely together. Then starting at the top corner of one block, an oblique line is cut all around the top of this first row until it ends at the ground where it meets up with the first block, thus forming one thread of a spiral. Now, round and round the blocks are added, each inclined a little more inward than the previous one and each supported by the surrounding blocks. When the building has progressed to a considerable height, the builder does the work of fitting from the inside and the blocks are put in place by the man who cuts them outside. The key block and those directly next to it are irregular in shape, cut to fit the hole which is left. This must be very carefully done, or the whole structure is apt to cave in, especially in moderate weather. The joints between the blocks are closed with scraps and loose snow pressed into the spaces. A piece of thick clear ice from the lake is sometimes set into the side of the dome toward the sun. This admits light, yet keeps out cold.

4.   Lucien M. Turner has given us a short but graphic picture of the interior of an igloo.

The interior walls, in severe weather, become coated with frost films from the breath, etc., condensing and crystallizing on the inside of the dome, and often presenting by the lamplight a brilliant show of myriads of reflecting surfaces scintillating with greater luster than skillfully set gems.

A raised bed is made by piling blocks into a solid mass, then covering this with boughs of spruce or dry grass, if obtainable. Otherwise, fine twigs of willow or alder are used, and over these are thrown heavy skins of reindeer or bear. Softer skins of the same animals are used as covers.

5.   At Point Barrow, Alaska, houses of snow are used only temporarily; for example, the hunting grounds on the rivers, and occasionally by visitors at the village who prefer having their own quarters. These houses are not built in the dome or beehive shape. John Murdoch tells us that here the snow house consists of an oblong room about six feet by twelve feet. The walls are made of blocks of snow, high enough so that a person can stand up inside the rooms. Poles are laid across the top and over these is stretched a roof of canvas. Outside at the south end of a low, narrow, covered passage of snow about ten feet long leads to a low door. Above this is a window made of seal entrail. At the outer end of the passage there is an opening at the top, so that one climbs over a low wall of snow to enter the house. At the right of the passage close to the house is a small fireplace built of slabs of snow, with a smoke hole in the top and a stick stuck across at the proper height to hang a pot on. When the first fire is built in this fireplace, there is considerable melting of the surface of the snow, but as soon as the fire is allowed to go out, this freezes to a hard glaze of ice, which afterwards melts only to a trifling extent. The door of the house is protected by a curtain of canvas. At the other end, the floor is raised into a kind of settee on which are laid boards and skins.

QUESTIONS

1. What details must Seton provide about the world of the Eskimo so that we are able to understand the process she describes fully?
2. How many stages in the building of snow houses does she distinguish?
3. Which of these is the more complex, and how do you know? What steps seem to you the most ingenious?

4. How different is the process Seton describes from the one you pictured in your mind previously?

WRITING ASSIGNMENT

Each of the processes below has a number of stages. Describe one of them for someone who has never performed it. Keep each of the stages distinct as Seton does.

a. refinishing a piece of furniture
b. canning tomatoes or another food
c. replacing a muffler or another automobile part
d. assembling a stereo system

Cause and Effect

JOHN BROOKS

The Telephone

1. What has the telephone done to us, or for us, in the hundred years of its existence? A few effects suggest themselves at once. It has saved lives by getting rapid word of illness, injury, or famine from remote places. By joining with the elevator to make possible the multistory residence or office building, it has made possible—for better or worse—the modern city. By bringing about a quantum leap in the speed and ease with which information moves from place to place, it has greatly accelerated the rate of scientific and technological change and growth in industry. Beyond doubt it has crippled if not killed the ancient art of letter writing. It has made living alone possible for persons with normal social impulses; by so doing, it has played a role in one of the greatest social changes of this century, the breakup of the multigenerational household. It has made the waging of war chillingly more efficient than formerly. Perhaps (though not provably) it has prevented wars that might have arisen out of international misunderstanding caused by written communication. Or perhaps—again not provably—by magnifying and extending irrational personal conflicts

based on voice contact, it has caused wars. Certainly it has extended the scope of human conflicts, since it impartially disseminates the useful knowledge of scientists and the babble of bores, the affection of the affectionate and the malice of the malicious.

2. But the question remains unanswered. The obvious effects just cited seem inadequate, mechanistic; they only scratch the surface. Perhaps the crucial effects are evanescent and unmeasurable. Use of the telephone involves personal risk because it involves exposure; for some, to be "hung up on" is among the worst of fears; others dream of a ringing telephone and wake up with a pounding heart. The telephone's actual ring—more, perhaps, than any other sound in our daily lives—evokes hope, relief, fear, anxiety, joy, according to our expectations. The telephone is our nerve-end to society.

3. In some ways it is in itself a thing of paradox. In one sense a metaphor for the times it helped create, in another sense the telephone is their polar opposite. It is small and gentle—relying on low voltages and miniature parts—in times of hugeness and violence. It is basically simple in times of complexity. It is so nearly human, recreating voices so faithfully that friends or lovers need not identify themselves by name even when talking across oceans, that to ask its effects on human life may seem hardly more fruitful than to ask the effect of the hand or the foot. The Canadian philosopher Marshall McLuhan—one of the few who have addressed themselves to these questions—was perhaps not far from the mark when he spoke of the telephone creating "a kind of extra-sensory perception."

DISCUSSION: Cause and Effect

One familiar kind of causal analysis distinguishes four related causes of an object. The *material* cause of a dictionary, for example, is the paper, ink, and other materials used in its manufacture. The *formal* cause is its shape—the alphabetic arrangement of words, and the arrangement of definitions according to a plan. The *efficient* cause is the dictionary writer; the *final* cause is the use intended. The analysis of a chemical compound is more rigorous, demanding an account of the substances that form the compound and the process by which the formation occurs.

Process analysis *("how")* usually joins with causal analysis *("why")*, because we are interested in both the *how* and *why* of objects that come into being and of events that occur. The *why* of an event is sometimes more difficult to explain. One common form of analysis distinguishes the *immediate* cause—circumstances close in time to the event—from the *remote* cause—circumstances farther away. Consider this chain of events: a student does not study for an important exam, flunks the course, drops in grade average, loses a scholarship, and drops out of school. Not studying for the exam is the immediate cause of flunking the exam, and the remote cause of dropping out of school. At times we are more concerned with remote causes, at other times the immediate. The reasons for not studying are probably the most important to the student and to college officials deciding whether to renew the scholarship.

Historical processes, which trace a similar chain of events, are usually more complex. The Japanese attack on Pearl Harbor was the immediate cause of war between the United States and Japan, but a series of previous events—some quite remote in time—prepared for it. One of many was possibly the Immigration Act of 1924, which restricted Asian immigration into the United States. This legislation was in turn influenced by other circumstances and events. We will not understand the attack on Pearl Harbor if we do not consider remote causes as well as the immediate ones.

QUESTIONS

1. Why does Brooks consider the effects he discusses in paragraph 1 less significant than those in paragraph 2? What does he mean by the statement, "Perhaps the crucial effects are evanescent and unmeasurable?

2. In what ways is the telephone a paradox? Does the author show it to be a paradox in paragraphs 1 and 2?

3. Has Brooks stated all the effects of the telephone, or has he identified only a few? What central point is he making about the telephone?

WRITING ASSIGNMENTS

1. Develop one of the ideas in the essay from your personal experience. You might discuss your own positive and negative attitudes toward the telephone, and the reasons for them, or you might develop the statement, "In some ways it is in itself a thing of paradox."

2. Write an essay describing what it would be like to live without a telephone, or what a single day might be like without one.

3. Discuss the impact of the telephone on life in your home. Distinguish the various uses and effects of the telephone for various members of your family.

WILLIAM E. BURROWS
The American Vigilante

1. The American vigilante phenomenon has gone through three distinct phases, though with considerable overlapping. The first was classic vigilantism, which erupted initially in South Carolina's back country on the eve of the Revolution and concerned itself with punishing ordinary badmen—horse and cattle thieves, counterfeiters, and assorted gangs of desperadoes. Classic vigilantism had as its main target the killers and spoilers who infested the early frontier. The second, or neovigilante, phase started with the great San Francisco committee of 1856 and had as its target ethnic and religious minorities and political opponents, usually clustered in urban areas. Neovigilantism was essentially urban and had little or nothing to do with cactus, horses, and gunslingers. The current phase, pseudo-vigilantism, a less deadly but potentially volatile mixture of the first two, can be said to have started in response to the soaring crime and the racial upheavals of the 1960s. Both criminals and blacks have been the objects of pseudo-vigilante activities, and in a number of instances blacks themselves have organized vigilante-like groups to fight drug addiction among their own people.

2. The American vigilante may have turned mean while growing up, but he started out as a helpful child, and one born of necessity. He was conceived as the only feasible defense against the perils of a constantly expanding frontier that usually left effective law enforcement far behind. Settlers who abandoned the relative security of the urban footholds back east, with their stabilizing schools, churches, municipal governments, courts, constables, and familiar neighborhoods, and pushed across the Appalachians into the great wilderness beyond were taking serious chances. They were laying their lives on the line, against Indians, desperadoes, and the elements, in order to grab timber, land, gold, and other resources. It was perfectly natural, given such a situation, that they would want to bring with them as much of the old stability as possible. In effect, those people wanted the best of two worlds: to carve up virgin Kentucky or Ohio woodlands and mine unclaimed California and Montana gold, but to do so under the benevolent eyes of the Philadelphia or Boston police force and with the blessing of the New York or Baltimore political establishment. But that was obviously impossible. The price they had to pay in return for a

chance to get the frontier's resources often was acute social instability, which translated into almost constant danger. They all knew that the alternative to establishing some kind of stability was to be plundered by the predators—to have their communities ravaged and their hard-earned wealth taken away from them. That was intolerable. Do-it-yourself law enforcement seemed to be the only answer.

3. If the early pioneers took the law into their own hands begrudgingly—as was usually the case, since it was more profitable to plant crops or make chairs than it was to chase bandits—at least they were ideologically suited to it. The ideology of vigilantism, which began to take shape during the first few decades of the nineteenth century, had three basic components: popular sovereignty, the right of revolution, and the law of self-preservation. And those rested, like a tricorn, on a head of violence. As every nineteenth century American schoolchild knew, violence worked. It had been spectacularly successful in yanking the colonies out from under the Crown in the first place. As a crucial tool for survival, in fact, it could be traced all the way back to Plymouth and Jamestown, when all those bloodthirsty savages, wild animals, and even an occasional renegade white had had to be subdued or liquidated for the apparent good of the majority.

4. The concept of popular sovereignty—democracy—was the single most important political element contributing to the vigilante reaction. Obviously, no monarch would have allowed a bunch of armed subjects to ride around the countryside hanging the people they hated. If that kind of thing had caught on, the rabble might eventually have raised their sights, and then where would he have been? So one of the key reasons for vigilantism's taking hold in America was the belief that the rule of the people superseded all other rule. And from that followed the premise that they had the power to act in their own best interest in the absence of effective constituted authority. That's what Judge Henry Dow was getting at when he told Molly Wood that if people make the law they can and should be able to unmake it.

5. The right of revolution justified the overturn by force of any authority considered by the people to be ineffective or harmful to the maintenance of real law and order. It provided the philosophical basis for insurrection, as in the hackneyed but true-to-life scene in which the angry mob storms the jail, subdues the sheriff and deputies, and lynches the prisoner. In doing that, vigilantes and lynch mobs were perfectly aware of the fact that they were kicking the props out from under whatever lawful authority existed. But the vigilante credo had it that when lawful authorities contributed to injustice, either willingly

or out of helplessness, they almost deserved what the redcoats had
gotten in 1776.

6.   Finally, vigilante ideology rested on the ultimate argument of survival as the first law of nature—kill or be killed. If no one else was
going to protect a man's life and property, natural law dictated that he
had to do it himself or suffer the consequences. It was as simple as
that, or so vigilantes assured one another time and again.

QUESTIONS

1. How does Burrows divide vigilantism in the whole discussion? How
   does he divide the ideology of vigilantism in paragraph 3?
2. What examples does Burrows give for each of the three components or causes of vigilantism in paragraphs 3–6? In what order are
   these causes arranged?
3. What were the immediate and remote causes of vigilantism on the
   American frontier?
4. What understanding about our society did you gain from the discussion of the rise of "pseudo-vigilantism"?

WRITING ASSIGNMENT

Develop a short essay on one of the following topics, using causal
analysis and examples to develop a thesis.

a. cheating in high school
b. driving habits of teenagers
c. family arguments
d. television and family life
e. choosing a college
f. establishing strong friendships

THE SENTENCE

Addition and Modification

JANE JACOBS

Hudson Street

1.   Under the seeming disorder of the old city, wherever the old city is working successfully, is a marvelous order for maintaining the safety of the streets and the freedom of the city. It is a complex order. Its essence is intricacy of sidewalk use, bringing with it a constant succession of eyes. This order is all composed of movement and change, and although it is life, not art, we may fancifully call it the art form of the city and liken it to the dance—not to a simple-minded precision dance with everyone kicking up at the same time, twirling in unison and bowing off en masse, but to an intricate ballet in which the individual dancers and ensembles all have distinctive parts which miraculously reinforce each other and compose an orderly whole. The ballet of the good city sidewalk never repeats itself from place to place, and in any one place is always replete with new improvisations.

2.   The stretch of Hudson Street where I live is each day the scene of an intricate sidewalk ballet. I make my own first entrance into it a little after eight when I put out the garbage can, surely a prosaic occupation, but I enjoy my part, my little clang, as the droves of junior high school students walk by the center of the stage dropping candy wrappers. (How do they eat so much candy so early in the morning?)

3.   While I sweep up the wrappers I watch the other rituals of morning: Mr. Halpert unlocking the laundry's handcart from its mooring to a cellar door, Joe Cornacchia's son-in-law stacking out the empty

crates from the delicatessen, the barber bringing out his sidewalk folding chair, Mr. Goldstein arranging the coils of wire which proclaim
the hardware store is open, the wife of the tenement's superintendent
depositing her chunky three-year-old with a toy mandolin on the
stoop, the vantage point from which he is learning the English his
mother cannot speak. Now the primary children, heading for
St. Luke's, dribble through to the south; the children for St. Veronica's cross, heading to the west, and the children for P.S. 41, heading
toward the east. Two new entrances are being made from the wings:
well-dressed and even elegant women and men with brief cases emerge
from doorways and side streets. Most of these are heading for the bus
and subways, but some hover on the curbs, stopping taxis which have
miraculously appeared at the right moment, for the taxis are part of a
wider morning ritual: having dropped passengers from midtown in the
downtown financial district, they are now bringing downtowners up to
midtown. Simultaneously, numbers of women in housedresses have
emerged and as they crisscross with one another they pause for quick
conversations that sound with either laughter or joint indignation,
never, it seems, anything between. It is time for me to hurry to work
too, and I exchange my ritual farewell with Mr. Lofaro, the short,
thick-bodied, white-aproned fruit man who stands outside his doorway a little up the street, his arms folded, his feet planted, looking
solid as earth itself. We nod; we each glance quickly up and down the
street, then look back to each other and smile. We have done this
many a morning for more than ten years, and we both know what it
means: All is well.
4.   The heart-of-the-day ballet I seldom see, because part of the nature of it is that working people who live there, like me, are mostly
gone, filling the roles of strangers on other sidewalks. But from days
off, I know enough of it to know that it becomes more and more intricate. Longshoremen who are not working that day gather at the
White Horse or the Ideal or the International for beer and conversation. The executives and business lunchers from the industries just to
the west throng the Dorgene restaurant and the Lion's Head coffee
house; meat-market workers and communications scientists fill the
bakery lunchroom. Character dancers come on, a strange old man
with strings of old shoes over his shoulders, motor-scooter riders with
big beards and girl friends who bounce on the back of the scooters and
wear their hair long in front of their faces as well as behind, drunks
who follow the advice of the Hat Council and are always turned out in
hats, but not hats the Council would approve. Mr. Lacey, the lock-

smith, shuts up his shop for a while and goes to exchange the time of day with Mr. Slube at the cigar store. Mr. Koochagian, the tailor, waters the luxuriant jungle of plants in his window, gives them a critical look from the outside, accepts a compliment on them from two passersby, fingers the leaves on the plane tree in front of our house with a thoughtful gardener's appraisal, and crosses the street for a bite at the Ideal where he can keep an eye on customers and wigwag across the message that he is coming. The baby carriages come out, and clusters of everyone from toddlers with dolls to teen-agers with homework gather at the stoops.

5.   When I get home after work, the ballet is reaching its crescendo. This is the time of roller skates and stilts and tricycles, and games in the lee of the stoop with bottletops and plastic cowboys; this is the time of bundles and packages, zigzagging from the drug store to the fruit stand and back over to the butcher's; this is the time when teenagers, all dressed up, are pausing to ask if their slips show or their collars look right; this is the time when beautiful girls get out of MG's; this is the time when the fire engines go through; this is the time when anybody you know around Hudson Street will go by.

6.   As darkness thickens and Mr. Halpert moors the laundry cart to the cellar door again, the ballet goes on under lights, eddying back and forth but intensifying at the bright spotlight pools of Joe's sidewalk pizza dispensary, the bars, the delicatessen, the restaurant and the drug store. The night workers stop now at the delicatessen, to pick up salami and a container of milk. Things have settled down for the evening but the street and its ballet have not come to a stop.

7.   I know the deep night ballet and its seasons best from waking long after midnight to tend a baby and, sitting in the dark, seeing the shadows and hearing the sounds of the sidewalk. Mostly it is a sound like infinitely patterning snatches of party conversation and, about three in the morning, singing, very good singing. Sometimes there is sharpness and anger or sad, sad weeping, or a flurry of search for a string of beads broken. One night a young man came roaring along, bellowing terrible language at two girls whom he had apparently picked up and who were disappointing him. Doors opened, a wary semicircle formed around him, not too close, until the police came. Out came the heads, too, along Hudson Street, offering opinion, "Drunk . . . Crazy . . . A wild kid from the suburbs." *

8.   Deep in the night, I am almost unaware how many people are on

---

* He turned out to be a wild kid from the suburbs. Sometimes, on Hudson Street, we are tempted to believe the suburbs must be a difficult place to bring up children.

the street unless something calls them together, like the bagpipe. Who the piper was and why he favored our street I have no idea. The bagpipe just skirled out in the February night, and as if it were a signal the random, dwindled movements of the sidewalk took on direction. Swiftly, quietly, almost magically a little crowd was there, a crowd that evolved into a circle with a Highland fling inside it. The crowd could be seen on the shadowy sidewalk, the dancers could be seen, but the bagpiper himself was almost invisible because his bravura was all in his music. He was a very little man in a plain brown overcoat. When he finished and vanished, the dancers and watchers applauded, and applause came from the galleries too, half a dozen of the hundred windows on Hudson Street. Then the windows closed, and the little crowd dissolved into the random movements of the night street.

9. The strangers on Hudson Street, the allies whose eyes help us natives keep the peace of the street, are so many that they always seem to be different people from one day to the next. That does not matter. Whether they are so many always-different people as they seem to be, I do not know. Likely they are. When Jimmy Rogan fell through a plate-glass window (he was separating some scuffling friends) and almost lost his arm, a stranger in an old T shirt emerged from the Ideal bar, swiftly applied an expert tourniquet and, according to the hospital's emergency staff, saved Jimmy's life. Nobody remembered seeing the man before and no one has seen him since. The hospital was called in this way: a woman sitting on the steps next to the accident ran over to the bus stop, wordlessly snatched the dime from the hand of a stranger who was waiting with his fifteen-cent fare ready, and raced into the Ideal's phone booth. The stranger raced after her to offer the nickel too. Nobody remembered seeing him before, and no one has seen him since. When you see the same stranger three or four times on Hudson Street, you begin to nod. This is almost getting to be an acquaintance, a public acquaintance, of course.

10. I have made the daily ballet of Hudson Street sound more frenetic than it is, because writing it telescopes it. In real life, it is not that way. In real life, to be sure, something is always going on, the ballet is never at a halt, but the general effect is peaceful and the general tenor even leisurely. People who know well such animated city streets will know how it is. I am afraid people who do not will always have it a little wrong in their heads—like the old prints of rhinoceroses made from travelers' descriptions of rhinoceroses.

11. On Hudson Street, the same as in the North End of Boston or in any other animated neighborhoods of great cities, we are not innately

more competent at keeping the sidewalks safe than are the people who try to live off the hostile truce of Turf in a blind-eyed city. We are the lucky possessors of a city order that makes it relatively simple to keep the peace because there are plenty of eyes on the street. But there is nothing simple about that order itself, or the bewildering number of components that go into it. Most of those components are specialized in one way or another. They unite in their joint effect upon the sidewalk, which is not specialized in the least. That is its strength.

DISCUSSION: Addition and Modification

As a paragraph usually begins with a topic sentence that states the subject or central idea, so the sentence may begin with a main clause that performs a similar job:

> *Character dancers come on,*
>> *a strange old man* with strings of old shoes over his shoulders
>> *motor-scooter riders* with big beards and girl friends who bounce on the back of the scooters and wear their hair long in front of their faces as well as behind,
>> *drunks* who follow the advice of the Hat Council and are always turned out in hats,
>>> but not hats the Council would approve.

The three additions—*strange old man, motor-scooter riders, drunks*—make the main clause specific: they name the character dancers. Notice that these *appositives* (adjacent words or phrases that explain or identify another word) are considerably longer than the main clause. Notice, too, that the third appositive is itself modified. English sentences can be modified endlessly. They are not, however, because the reader would soon lose sight of the central idea. The length of a sentence often depends on how many ideas and details a reader can grasp.

QUESTIONS

1. In the Jacobs, the main clause in the first sentence of paragraph 3 is followed by a series of appositives explaining the *rituals of morning.* How many appositives do you find? Which of them is modified?
2. The colon in the following sentence introduces an addition that explains the main clause:

Two new entrances are being made from the wings: well-dressed and even elegant women and men with brief cases emerge from doorways and side streets.

Does the colon in the succeeding sentences, in paragraph 2, serve the same purpose? What about the colon in the concluding sentence of the paragraph?

3. The second sentence of paragraph 5 might have been divided into four separate sentences. What is gained by joining the main clauses through semicolons? Are the semicolons in paragraph 3 used in the same way?
4. Notice that the main clause of the first sentence of paragraph 6 is modified by the opening subordinate clause and by the phrases that follow, beginning with *eddying*. Try rewriting the sentence, beginning with the main clause. Can the opening subordinate clause be put elsewhere in the sentence without obscuring the meaning?
5. What point is Jacobs making about the "daily ballet" of Hudson Street? How do the various details illustrate her point?
6. Jacobs is defining what makes a New York street a neighborhood. How different is this neighborhood from yours?

WRITING ASSIGNMENTS

1. Explain in your own words why the specialization in each of the "bewildering number of components" that make up the street is the source of its strength. Show how several of the examples in the essay illustrate this strength.
2. Develop the following main clauses through addition. Use colons and semicolons if you wish:
   a. "Deep in the night, I am almost unaware how many people are on the street . . ."
   b. "The crowd could be seen on the shadowy sidewalk . . ."
   c. "People who know well such animated city streets will know how it is . . ."
3. Develop the following main clauses through appositives that explain the italicized word:
   a. "This is the time of roller skates and stilts and *tricycles* . . ."
   b. "The night workers stop now at the delicatessen, to pick up salami and a container of *milk* . . ."
   c. "He was a very little man in a plain brown overcoat . . ."

Emphasis

MARK TWAIN
The Steamboatman

[1] My father was a justice of the peace and I supposed he possessed the power of life and death over all men and could hang anybody that offended him. [2] This was distinction enough for me as a general thing, but the desire to be a steamboatman kept intruding nevertheless. [3] I first wanted to be a cabin-boy, so that I could come out with a white apron on and shake a table-cloth over the side, where all my old comrades could see me; later I thought I would rather be the deck-hand who stood on the end of the stage-plank with the coil of rope in his hand, because he was particularly conspicuous. [4] But these were only day-dreams—they were too heavenly to be contemplated as real possibilities. [5] By and by one of our boys went away. [6] He was not heard of for a long time. [7] At last he turned up as apprentice engineer or "striker" on a steamboat. [8] This thing shook the bottom out of all my Sunday-school teachings. [9] That boy had been notoriously worldly and I just the reverse; yet he was exalted to this eminence and I left in obscurity and misery. [10] There was nothing generous about this fellow in his greatness. [11] He would always manage to have a rusty bolt to scrub while his boat tarried at our town, and he would sit on the inside guard and scrub it, where we all could see him and envy him and loathe him. [12] And whenever his boat was laid up he would come home and swell around the town in his blackest and greasiest clothes, so that nobody could help remembering that he was a steamboatman; and he used all sorts of steamboat technicalities in his talk, as if he were so used to them that he forgot common people could not understand them. [13] He would speak of the "labboard" side of a horse in an easy, natural way that would make one wish he was dead. [14] And he was always talking about "St. Looy" like an old citizen; he would refer casually to occasions when he was "coming down Fourth Street," or when he was "passing by the Planter's House," or when there was a fire and he took a turn on the brakes of "the old Big Missouri"; and then he would go on and lie about how many towns the

size of ours were burned down there that day. [15] Two or three of the boys had long been persons of consideration among us because they had been to St. Louis once and had a vague general knowledge of its wonders, but the day of their glory was over now. [16] They lapsed into a humble silence and learned to disappear when the ruthless "cub"-engineer approached. [17] This fellow had money, too, and hair-oil. [18] Also an ignorant silver watch and a showy brass watch-chain. [19] He wore a leather belt and used no suspenders. [20] If ever a youth was cordially admired and hated by his comrades, this one was. [21] No girl could withstand his charms. [22] He "cut out" every boy in the village. [23] When his boat blew up at last, it diffused a tranquil contentment among us such as we had not known for months. [24] But when he came home the next week, alive, renowned, and appeared in church all battered up and bandaged, a shining hero, stared at and wondered over by everybody, it seemed to us that the partiality of Providence for an undeserving reptile had reached a point where it was open to criticism.

DISCUSSION: Emphasis

In speaking, we vary our sentences without much if any thought—interrupting the flow of ideas to emphasize a word or phrase, or to repeat an idea. The speaker of the following sentence, a witness before a congressional committee, repeats certain phrases and qualifies his ideas in a typical way:

> My experience is that we hold people sometimes in jail, young people in jail, for days at a time with a complete lack of concern of the parents, if they do live in homes where parents live together, a complete lack of concern in many instances on the part of the community or other agencies as to where these young people are or what they are doing.

Sentences as complex and disjointed as this one seems when transcribed and printed can be understood easily when they are spoken because the speaker is able to vary the vocal inflection to stress key words and phrases. Written punctuation can sometimes clarify the points of emphasis but in a limited way. Writers cannot depend directly on vocal inflection for clarity and emphasis; however, they can suggest these inflections by shaping the sentence in accord with ordinary speech patterns. Clear written sentences stay close to these patterns.

The core of English sentences, we said earlier, can be expanded, and at length, if each modifier is clearly connected to what precedes it. Any variation from the familiar subject-verb-complement pattern will emphasize particular words. In the following sentences the subject and predicate are given emphasis through their separation (italics added):

> When another night came *the columns,* changed to purple streaks, *filed across* two pontoon *bridges.* A glaring fire wine-tinted the waters of the river. *Its rays,* shining upon the moving masses of troops, *brought forth* here and there sudden *gleams* of silver or gold. Upon the other shore a dark and mysterious *range* of hills *was curved* against the sky.—Stephen Crane, *The Red Badge of Courage.*

These variations are natural to the way we speak; they need not have been planned. To achieve even greater emphasis the writer may vary the sentence even more, perhaps by making special use of the end of the sentence—the position that in English tends to be the most emphatic:

> The cold passed reluctantly from the earth, and the retiring fogs revealed an army stretched out on the hills, *resting.*—Crane

Or the writer may break up the sentence so that individual ideas and experiences receive separate emphasis:

> The youth stopped. He was transfixed by this terrific medley of all noises. It was as if worlds were being rended. There was the ripping sound of musketry and the breaking crash of the artillery.—Crane

These sentences might have been coordinated with words like *and, but, for, yet, nor,* and *or* (or with a semicolon)—with a corresponding distribution of emphasis.

The relation of subordinate clauses to other elements in a sentence is controlled largely by the requirements of English word order. The position of subordinate clauses that serve as nouns or adjectives (sometimes called noun clauses and adjective clauses) is rather fixed; the position of subordinate clauses that serve as adverbs (sometimes called adverb clauses) is not. The position of the adverb clause depends on its importance as an idea and on its length:

> I majored in zoology *because I like working with animals.*

> *Because I like working with animals* I majored in zoology.

The position of the subordinate clause determines what information is stressed: in the first sentence the subordinate clause seems to express the more important idea because it follows the main clause. In the second sentence, the main clause receives the emphasis. But the end of the sentence will not take the thrust of meaning if ideas appearing toward the beginning are given special emphasis, possibly through repetition.

Our informal spoken sentences show the least variation and depend heavily on coordination. The so-called *run-on sentence* in writing—a series of ideas strung together with *and* and other conjunctions—is a heavily coordinated sentence, without the usual vocal markers. The sentence *fragment* sometimes derives from the clipped sentences and phrases common in speech.

QUESTIONS

1. Rewrite Twain's first sentence, subordinating one of the clauses. How does the revision affect the emphasis of ideas in the original sentence?
2. Compare the following sentences:
   a. "But these were only day-dreams—they were too heavenly to be contemplated as real possibilities."
   b. Because these were only day-dreams, they were too heavenly to be contemplated as real possibilities.
   c. These were too heavenly to be contemplated as real possibilities, because they were only day-dreams.
   Which sentence puts the most emphasis on the idea, "they were too heavenly to be contemplated as real possibilities"? Which sentence puts the least emphasis on it, and why?
3. Combine sentences 17, 18, and 19 into a single sentence. What is gained or lost in emphasis in your revision?
4. How are coordinate conjunctions used for emphasis in sentence 12?
5. What does subordination contribute to emphasis in sentences 23 and 24?
6. What emotions does Twain convey, and how does the sentence construction help him to convey them and create a mood?
7. How well has Twain conveyed the sense of childhood aspiration and frustration?

WRITING ASSIGNMENTS

1. Rewrite Twain's paragraph, giving different emphasis to his ideas through a different coordination and subordination of sentence elements. You need not revise all of the sentences.

2. Twain says in his autobiography: "The truth is a person's memory has no more sense than his conscience and no appreciation whatever of values and proportions." Develop this idea from your own experience.

CARL SANDBURG
The Funeral of General Grant

[1] The Galesburg Marine Band marched past, men walking and their mouths blowing into their horns as they walked. [2] One man had a big horn that seemed to be wrapped around him and I was puzzled how he got into it. [3] They had on blue coats and pants and the stripe down the sides of the pants was either red or yellow and looked pretty. [4] Their music was slow and sad. [5] General Grant was dead and this was part of his funeral and the music should be sad. [6] It was only twenty years since the war ended and General Grant was the greatest general in the war and they wanted to show they were sad because he was dead. [7] That was the feeling I had and I could see there were many others had this same feeling. [8] Marching past came men wearing dark-blue coats and big black hats tied round with a little cord of what looked like gold with a knot and a little tassel. [9] They were the G.A.R., the Grand Army of the Republic, and I heard that some of these men had seen General Grant and had been in the war with him and could tell how he looked on a horse and what made him a great general. [10] Eight or ten of these G.A.R. men walked along the sides of a long black box on some kind of a black car pulled by eight black horses. [11] The body of General Grant wasn't in the box, but somewhere far away General Grant was being buried in a box like this one. [12] I could see everybody around was more quiet when this part of the parade passed.

QUESTIONS

1. What words are repeated in sentences 4–6? How does this repetition help establish a dominant mood?
2. Sentences 2–7 are mainly simple and compound—mostly main clauses, with almost no variation. How does this evenness also help establish a dominant mood?

3. What other repetitions do you notice in the paragraph, and what do they contribute to the dominant mood?
4. Is the point of view that of a child or of an adult remembering a childhood experience? How do you know?

WRITING ASSIGNMENTS

1. Rewrite Sandburg's paragraph, subordinating clauses wherever possible. Then discuss the effect of the changes you made on the original paragraph.
2. Describe a parade or celebration, and construct your sentences so that they convey the mood of the event.

NORMAN MAILER

The Death of Benny Paret

¹Paret was a Cuban, a proud club fighter who had become welterweight champion because of his unusual ability to take a punch. ²His style of fighting was to take three punches to the head in order to give back two. ³At the end of ten rounds, he would still be bouncing, his opponent would have a headache. ⁴But in the last two years, over the fifteen-round fights, he had started to take some bad maulings.

⁵This fight had its turns. ⁶Griffith won most of the early rounds, but Paret knocked Griffith down in the sixth. ⁷Griffith had trouble getting up, but made it, came alive and was dominating Paret again before the round was over. ⁸Then Paret began to wilt. ⁹In the middle of the eighth round, after a clubbing punch had turned his back to Griffith, Paret walked three disgusted steps away, showing his hindquarters. ¹⁰For a champion, he took much too long to turn back around. ¹¹It was the first hint of weakness Paret had ever shown, and it must have inspired a particular shame, because he fought the rest of the fight as if he were seeking to demonstrate that he could take more punishment than any man alive. ¹²In the twelfth, Griffith caught him. ¹³Paret got trapped in a corner. ¹⁴Trying to duck away, his left arm and his head became tangled on the wrong side of the top rope. ¹⁵Griffith was in like a cat ready to rip the life out of a huge boxed rat. ¹⁶He hit him eighteen right hands in a row, an act which took perhaps three or four seconds, Griffith making a pent-up whimpering sound all

the while he attacked, the right hand whipping like a piston rod which has broken through the crankcase, or like a baseball bat demolishing a pumpkin. [17] I was sitting in the second row of that corner—they were not ten feet away from me, and like everybody else, I was hypnotized. [18] I had never seen one man hit another so hard and so many times. [19] Over the referee's face came a look of woe as if some spasm had passed its way through him, and then he leaped on Griffith to pull him away. [20] It was the act of a brave man. [21] Griffith was uncontrollable. [22] His trainer leaped into the ring, his manager, his cut man, there were four people holding Griffith, but he was off on an orgy, he had left the Garden, he was back on a hoodlum's street. [23] If he had been able to break loose from his handlers and the referee, he would have jumped Paret to the floor and whaled on him there.

[24] And Paret? [25] Paret died on his feet. [26] As he took those eighteen punches something happened to everyone who was in psychic range of the event. [27] Some part of his death reached out to us. [28] One felt it hover in the air. [29] He was still standing in the ropes, trapped as he had been before, he gave some little half-smile of regret, as if he were saying, "I didn't know I was going to die just yet," and then, his head leaning back but still erect, his death came to breathe about him. [30] He began to pass away. [31] As he passed, so his limbs descended beneath him, and he sank slowly to the foor. [32] He went down more slowly than any fighter had ever gone down, he went down like a large ship which turns on end and slides second by second into its grave. [33] As he went down, the sound of Griffith's punches echoed in the mind like a heavy ax in the distance chopping into a wet log.

QUESTIONS

1. Each of the sentences in the second paragraph focuses on a distinct moment of the action. Could any of these sentences be combined without blurring the action?
2. Sentence 22 joins a number of actions occurring simultaneously. How does the sentence convey the jarring confusion of the moment?
3. Does sentence 29 describe a continuous action? Would the mood of the paragraph be changed if the sentence were broken up or punctuated differently?
4. How does repetition in sentence 32 reinforce the feeling Mailer is trying to communicate in the final paragraph?
5. Mailer's writing is closer to spoken patterns than the writing of others we have been studying. In how many of his sentences does

Mailer depart from the subject-verb-complement pattern—and to what effect?

6. Is Mailer concerned only with Paret, or is he making a statement about boxing as a sport?

WRITING ASSIGNMENT

Summarize what you think are the implications of the passage, including what the passage suggests about Mailer's attitude toward Benny Paret.

Loose and Periodic Sentences

JOHN STEINBECK

The Turtle

[1] The sun lay on the grass and warmed it, and in the shade under the grass the insects moved, ants and ant lions to set traps for them, grasshoppers to jump into the air and flick their yellow wings for a second, sow bugs like little armadillos, plodding restlessly on many tender feet. [2] And over the grass at the roadside a land turtle crawled, turning aside for nothing, dragging his highdomed shell over the grass. [3] His hard legs and yellow-nailed feet threshed slowly through the grass, not really walking, but boosting and dragging his shell along. [4] The barley beards slid off his shell, and the clover burrs fell on him and rolled to the ground. [5] His horny beak was partly open, and his fierce, humorous eyes, under brows like fingernails, stared straight ahead. [6] He came over the grass leaving a beaten trail behind him, and the hill, which was the highway embankment, reared up ahead of him. [7] For a moment he stopped, his head held high. [8] He blinked and looked up and down. [9] At last he started to climb the embankment. [10] Front clawed feet reached forward but did not touch. [11] The hind feet kicked his shell along, and it scraped on the grass, and on the gravel. [12] As the embankment grew steeper and steeper, the more frantic were the efforts of the land turtle. [13] Pushing hind

legs strained and slipped, boosting the shell along, and the horny head protruded as far as the neck could stretch. [14] Little by little the shell slid up the embankment until at last a parapet cut straight across its line of march, the shoulder of the road, a concrete wall four inches high. [15] As though they worked independently the hind legs pushed the shell against the wall. [16] The head upraised and peered over the wall to the broad smooth plain of cement. [17] Now the hands, braced on top of the wall, strained and lifted, and the shell came slowly up and rested its front end on the wall. [18] For a moment the turtle rested. [19] A red ant ran into the shell, into the soft skin inside the shell, and suddenly head and legs snapped in, and the armored tail clamped in sideways. [20] The red ant was crushed between body and legs. [21] And one head of wild oats was clamped into the shell by a front leg. [22] For a long moment the turtle lay still, and then the neck crept out and the old humorous frowning eyes looked about and the legs and tail came out. [23] The back legs went to work, straining like elephant legs, and the shell tipped to an angle so that the front legs could not reach the level cement plain. [24] But higher and higher the hind legs boosted it, until at last the center of balance was reached, the front tipped down, the front legs scratched at the pavement, and it was up. [25] But the head of wild oats was held by its stem around the front legs.

DISCUSSION: Loose and Periodic Sentences

Sentences are sometimes classified as loose or periodic to distinguish two important kinds of emphasis: the use made of the beginning or the end of the sentence. The loose sentence begins with the core idea, explanatory and qualifying phrases and causes trailing behind:

> It was not a screeching noise, only an intermittent hump-hump, as if the bird had to recall his grievance each time before he repeated it.—Flannery O'Connor

If the ideas that follow the core are afterthoughts, or inessential details, the sentence will seem "loose"—easy and relaxed in its movement perhaps even plodding if the content of the sentence permits:

> His eyes glittered like open pits of light as he moved across the sand, dragging his crushed shadow behind him.—O'Connor

A subordinate element, however, will not seem unemphatic or plodding if it expresses a strong action or idea:

He beat louder and louder, bamming at the same time with his free fist until he felt he was shaking the house.—O'Connor

Opening with modifiers or with a series of appositives, the periodic sentence ends with the core:

Living this way by the creek, where the light appears and vanishes on the water, where muskrats surface and dive, and redwings scatter, I have come to know a special side of nature.—Annie Dillard

The strongly periodic sentence is usually reserved for unusually strong emphasis:

To believe your own thought, to believe that what is true for you in your private heart is true for all men—that is *genius.*—Ralph Waldo Emerson

Most contemporary English sentences fall between the extremely loose and the extremely periodic. Compound sentences seem loose when succeeding clauses serve as afterthoughts or qualifications rather than as ideas equal in importance to the opening idea:

I was very conscious of the crowds at first, almost despairing to have to perform in front of them, and I never got used to it.—George Plimpton

Periodic sentences are used sparingly, with a distribution of emphasis more often through the whole sentence, as in Dillard's sentence above. Sometimes two moderately periodic sentences will be coordinated, with a corresponding distribution of emphasis:

Though reliable narration is by no means the only way of conveying to the audience the facts on which dramatic irony is based, it is a useful way, and in some works, works in which no one but the author can conceivably know what needs to be known, it may be indispensable.—Wayne C. Booth

QUESTIONS

1. In the Steinbeck paragraph, the essential element of sentence 2 is *a land turtle crawled.* If the concluding modifiers were moved toward the beginning of the sentence, would the shift in emphasis alter the meaning?

2. How does the moderately periodic construction of sentence 12 create a sense of action?

3. Convert sentence 3 into a periodic sentence. What is gained or lost by moving the phrase *dragging his shell along* to another part of the sentence?

4. Rewrite sentence 15 as a loose sentence. What effect is gained or lost by your revision?

5. Combine sentences 7, 8, and 9 into one sentence. Whis is more effective—your sentence or the original arrangement of sentences—and why?

6. Do the sentences in the passage, considered as a whole, seem predominantly loose or periodic? How does the dominant pattern affect the mood of the passage and contribute to its meaning? In general, what kind of sentence construction conveys a greater sense of anticipation and suspense, and why?

7. The following loose and periodic sentences are characteristic of some eighteenth- and nineteenth-century British and American prose. Rewrite them as loose or periodic sentences, changing the wording where necessary. Be ready to argue which is the more effective sentence and why.

   a. Considering that natural disposition in many men to lie, and in multitudes to believe, I have been perplexed what to do with that maxim so frequent in everybody's mouth, that truth will at last prevail.—Jonathan Swift.

   b. To this knowledge which all men carry about with them, and to these sympathies in which without any other discipline than that of our daily life, we are fitted to take delight, the poet principally directs his attention.—William Wordsworth

   c. Who first reduced lying into an art, and adapted it to politics, is not so clear from history, although I have made some diligent inquiries.—Swift

   d. Plants and animals, biding their time, closely followed the retiring ice, bestowing quick and joyous animation on the new-born landscape.—John Muir

8. Steinbeck's turtle has often been taken as *symbolic*—standing for more than itself. Do you agree?

WRITING ASSIGNMENT

Write an interpretation of the Steinbeck passage, with particular attention to how Steinbeck may be using the turtle to make a general statement about life. Analyze the detail with care.

JEFF GREENFIELD
Opening Day

[1] There are six of them not yet fifteen years old. [2] Their hair is short, sideburns ending at the top of the ear. [3] They wear tennis sneakers, T-shirts, nylon jackets, chinos. [4] Clutched in their hands are brown bags, one with the telltale spreading oil slick of a tunafish sandwich. [5] They are dancing the Rite of the Subway: shuffling up to the edge of the platform, leaning dangerously over to peer down into the tunnel, seeking to pull the train into the station by sheer force of will. [6] Nothing. [7] Just the echoes of tennis shoes slapping on the concrete platform of the Fifty-ninth Street IND station, as they pace impatiently from the rusting soft-drink machine to the overhead clock with the blinking bottle of Palo Vieja Rum, the Rum with the True-Flavor.

[8] Ronald and his friends are restless. [9] School is in session, but Ronald and his friends are not. [10] It is Opening Day at Yankee Stadium—1970. [11] And even though it is 10:45 A.M., even though it is four hours and fifteen minutes until game time, Ronald and his friends want to get the day started.

[12] A squeal far down the tracks; an echo that quickly becomes a rumble—a train is coming. [13] Ronald and his friends run up and down the platform, looking for a deserted space. [14] Suddenly, excitement turns to disgust. [15] The train is new, steel-shiny, and that is terrible, because that means it is an "A" train, and the "A" train does not go to Yankee Stadium. [16] Only the "D" train, always blackened by soot and dirt, its windows streaked with tracks of filthy rain, its bamboo-weave seats ripped out, scars of ink from day-old *Daily News* racing pages staining the floor, only this train goes to Yankee Stadium, cutting like an invisible wound underneath Harlem. [17] And when you are twelve years old, with a brown bag lunch and tennis sneakers, and $2.40 in your pocket—enough for admission, a hot dog, an orange drink, and two tokens—the first inevitable fact of life is that the "D" train never comes first.

[18] So Ronald and his friends groan and pace, and punch each other on the shoulder as two more "A" trains insolently rumble through the station. [19] Finally, a few minutes before 11 A.M., a blackened "D" train finally pulls into Fifty-ninth Street. [20] Ronald and his friends race on, bouncing from seat to seat, and watch the local stations speed by the windows as the express roars on to 125th Street. [21] As we pass

by 110th Street, one of Ronald's friends points out the window and yells: "Fifty-one blocks to go!"

QUESTIONS

1. Greenfield omits the verb (*are heard*) of the opening clause of sentence 7, turning it into a phrase, to which a series of modifiers are attached. How does the sentence convey the restless pacing of the boys waiting for the D train?
2. How does the loose construction of sentence 15 help to convey the feeling of disappointment:
3. How does sentence 16 differ from sentence 15 in construction? Is the sentence construction appropriate to the idea expressed?
4. Is sentence 17 loose or periodic? Is the construction appropriate to the idea the sentence expresses?
5. How loose are sentences 18, 19, and 20? Do you sense a build in excitement in these sentences, or do they express the same feelings through the same kind of sentence construction?
6. What qualities of youth has Greenfield captured in his description?

WRITING ASSIGNMENT

Describe an experience similar to the one Greenfield presents—for example, waiting for a date to arrive or for a basketball game to start. Combine periodic with loose sentences to convey a sense of waiting and rising excitement, as Greenfield does. You may wish to use some short sentences (like sentences 8–10) for special effect.

Parallelism

JOHN A. WILLIAMS

Driving Through Snowstorms

[1] Driving through snowstorms on icy roads for long distances is a most nerve-racking experience. [2] It is a paradox that the snow, coming down gently, blowing gleefully in a high wind, all the while lays down a treacherous carpet, freezes the windows, blocks the view. [3] The might of automated man is muted. [4] The horses, the powerful elec-

trical systems, the deep-tread tires, all go for nothing. [5] One minute the road feels firm, and the next the driver is sliding over it, light as a feather, in a panic, wondering what the heavy trailer trucks coming up from the rear are going to do. [6] The trucks are like giants when you have to pass them, not at sixty or seventy as you do when the road is dry, but at twenty-five and thirty. [7] Then their engines sound unnaturally loud. [8] Snow, slush and chips of ice spray from beneath the wheels, obscure the windshield, and rattle off your car. [9] Beneath the wheels there is plenty of room for you to skid and get mashed to a pulp. [10] Inch by inch you move up, past the rear wheels, the center wheels, the cab, the front wheels, all sliding too slowly by. [11] Straight ahead you continue, for to cut over sharply would send you into a skid, right in front of the vehicle. [12] At last, there is distance enough, and you creep back over, in front of the truck now, but with the sound of its engine still thundering in your ears.

DISCUSSION: Parallelism

The italicized words in the following sentence are parallel in structure, that is, they perform the same grammatical function in the sentence and are the same in form:

> So long as I remain alive and well I shall continue *to feel* strongly about prose style, *to love* the surface of the earth, and *to take* a pleasure in solid objects and scraps of useless information.— George Orwell

In speaking and writing, we naturally make elements such as these infinitives parallel. No matter how many words separate them, we continue the pattern we began. When a pattern is interrupted, we immediately know that something has gone wrong in the sentence:

> Then he drank a glass of water, his plate was pushed to one side, doubled the paper down before him between his elbows and read the paragraph over and over again.

Here is the sentence that the Irish novelist James Joyce actually wrote:

> Then he drank a glass of water, pushed his plate to one side, doubled the paper down before him between his elbows and read the paragraph over and over again.—*Dubliners*

Parallelism is an important means to concision and focus in sentences, as these examples show, and it permits considerable addition to the sentence without loss of coherence.

QUESTIONS

1. How does Williams make phrases parallel in sentence 2 to emphasize similar ideas?
2. In what other sentences do you find a similar use of parallelism?
3. How does Williams construct sentence 10 to imitate the action it describes?

WRITING ASSIGNMENT

Describe the experience of driving or walking on icy or wet streets or sidewalks, and contrast this experience with the experience that Williams describes.

ERNESTO GALARZA
Boyhood in a Sacramento Barrio

1. Our family conversations always occurred on our own kitchen porch, away from the gringos. One or the other of the adults would begin: *Se han fijado?* Had we noticed—that the Americans do not ask permission to leave the room; that they had no respectful way of addressing an elderly person; that they spit brown over the railing of the porch into the yard; that when they laughed they roared; that they never brought *saludos* to everyone in your family from everyone in their family when they visited; that *General Delibree* was only a clerk; that *zopilotes* were not allowed on the streets to collect garbage; that the policemen did not carry lanterns at night; that Americans didn't keep their feet on the floor when they were sitting; that there was a special automobile for going to jail; that a rancho was not a rancho at all but a very small hacienda; that the saloons served their customers free eggs, pickles, and sandwiches; that instead of bullfighting, the gringos for sport tried to kill each other with gloves?

2. I did not have nearly the strong feelings on these matters that Doña Henriqueta expressed. I felt a vague admiration for the way Mr. Brien could spit brown. Wayne, my classmate, laughed much better than the Mexicans, because he opened his big mouth wide and brayed like a donkey so he could be heard a block away. But it was the kind of laughter that made my mother tremble, and it was not permitted in our house.

3. Rules were laid down to keep me, as far as possible, *un muchacho bien educado.* If I had to spit I was to do it privately, or if in public, by the curb, with my head down and my back to people. I was never to wear my cap in the house and I was to take it off even on the porch if ladies or elderly gentlemen were sitting. If I wanted to scratch, under no circumstances was I to do it right then and there, in company, like the Americans, but I was to excuse myself. If Catfish or Russell yelled to me from across the street I was not to shout back. I was never to ask for tips for my errands or other services to the tenants of 418 L, for these were *atenciones* expected of me.

4. Above all I was never to fail in *respeto* to grownups, no matter who they were. It was an inflexible rule; I addressed myself to *Señor* Big Singh, *Señor* Big Ernie, *Señora* Dodson, *Señor* Cho-ree Lopez.

5. My standing in the family, but especially with my mother depended on my keeping these rules. I was not punished for breaking them. She simply reminded me that it gave her acute *vergüenza* to see me act thus, and that I would never grow up to be a correct *jefe de familia* if I did not know how to be a correct boy. I knew what *vergüenza* was from feeling it time and again; and the notion of growing up to keep a tight rein over a family of my own was somehow satisfying.

6. In our musty apartment in the basement of 418 L, ours remained a Mexican family. I never lost the sense that we were the same, from Jalco to Sacramento. There was the polished cedar box, taken out now and then from the closet to display our heirlooms. I had lost the rifle shells of the revolution, and Tio Tonche, too, was gone. But there was the butterfly sarape, the one I had worn through the Battle of Puebla; a black lace mantilla Doña Henriqueta modeled for us; bits of embroidery and lace she had made; the tin pictures of my grandparents; my report card signed by Señorita Bustamante and Don Salvador; letters from Aunt Esther; and the card with the address of the lady who had kept the Ajax for us. When our mementos were laid out on the bed I plunged my head into the empty box and took deep breaths of the aroma of *puro cedro,* pure Jalcocotán mixed with camphor.

7. We could have hung on the door of our apartment a sign like those we read in some store windows—*Aquí se habla español.* We not only spoke Spanish, we read it. From the *Librería Española,* two blocks up the street, Gustavo and I bought novels for my mother, like *Genoveva de Brabante,* a paperback with the poems of Amado Nervo and a handbook of the history of Mexico. The novels were never read aloud, the poems and the handbook were. Nervo was the famous poet from Tepic, close enough to Jalcocotáu to make him our own. And in

the history book I learned to read for myself, after many repetitions by my mother, about the deeds of the great Mexicans Don Salvador had recited so vividly to the class in Mazatlán. She refused to decide for me whether Abraham Lincoln was as great as Benito Juarez, or George Washington braver than the priest Don Miguel Hidalgo. At school there was no opportunity to settle these questions because nobody seemed to know about Juarez or Hidalgo; at least they were never mentioned and there were no pictures of them on the walls.

8.   The family talk I listened to with the greatest interest was about Jalco. Wherever the conversation began it always turned to the pueblo, our neighbors, anecdotes that were funny or sad, the folk tales and the witchcraft, and our kinfolk, who were still there. I usually lay on the floor those winter evenings, with my feet toward the kerosene heater, watching on the ceiling the flickering patterns of the light filtered through the scrollwork of the chimney. As I listened once again I chased the *zopilote* away from Coronel, or watched José take Nerón into the forest in a sack. Certain things became clear about the *rurales* and why the young men were taken away to kill Yaqui Indians, and about the Germans, the Englishmen, the Frenchmen, the Spaniards, and the Americans who owned the haciendas, the railroads, the ships, the big stores, the breweries. They owned Mexico because President Porfirio Díaz had let them steal it, José explained as I listened. Now Don Francisco Madero had been assassinated for trying to get it back. On such threads of family talk I followed my own recollection of the years from Jalco—the attack on Mazatlán, the captain of Acaponeta, the camp at El Nanchi and the arrival at Nogales on the flatcar.

9.   Only when we ventured uptown did we feel like aliens in a foreign land. Within the *barrio* we heard Spanish on the streets and in the alleys. On the railroad tracks, in the canneries, and along the riverfront there were more Mexicans than any other nationality. And except for the foremen, the work talk was in our language. In the secondhand shops, where the *barrio* people sold and bought furniture and clothing, there were Mexican clerks who knew the Mexican ways of making a sale. Families doubled up in decaying houses, cramping themselves so they could rent an extra room to *chicano* boarders, who accented the brown quality of our Mexican *colonia*.

VOCABULARY

barrio: neighborhood
Se jan fijado?: Did you notice?

saludos: greetings
zopilotes: vultures, buzzards
un muchacho bien educado: a well-bred boy
atenciones: duties
respeto: respect
vergüenza: shame, embarrassment
jefe de familia: head of the family
puro cedro: pure cedar
Aquí se habla español: Spanish spoken here
Librería Española: Spanish Bookstore
rurales: rural mounted police
chicano: American of Mexican descent
colonia: colony

QUESTIONS

1. How is parallelism used in the second sentence of paragraph 1 to give equal emphasis to the various ideas?
2. How is the same use made of parallelism in paragraph 6?
3. Whole sentences can be parallel to one another. How much parallelism of this kind do you find in paragraph 3?
4. In general, how loose or how strict do you find the parallelism of Galarza's sentences? How formal an effect do his sentences create?
5. How do you believe children are best taught to respect people different from them culturally? How different from Galarza's was your training in manners?

WRITING ASSIGNMENTS

1. Galarza uses his account to say something about Mexican and American folkways and the changes brought about in moving from one world to another. Discuss what Galarza is saying, and comment on his attitude toward the changes he experiences.
2. Discuss the increased importance manners have when you find yourself in a new environment, perhaps in a new school or neighborhood. You might want to discuss changes in speech habits as well as changes in behavior.

Balance

MAX LERNER

Sports in America

1. The psychic basis of American mass sports is tribal and feudal. Baseball is a good example of the modern totem symbols (Cubs, Tigers, Indians, Pirates, Dodgers, and Braves) and of sustained tribal animosities. The spectator is not *on* the team, but he can be *for* the team; he identifies himself with one team, sometimes with one player who becomes a jousting champion wearing his colors in a medieval tournament. Hence the hero symbolism in American sports and the impassioned hero worship which makes gods of mortals mediocre in every other respect, and gives them the place among the "Immortals" that the French reserve for their Academy intellectuals.

2. There is a stylized relation of artist to mass audience in the sports, especially in baseball. Each player develops a style of his own—the swagger as he steps to the plate, the unique windup a pitcher has, the clean-swinging and hard-driving hits, the precision quickness and grace of infield and outfield, the sense of surplus power behind whatever is done. There is the style of the spectator also: he becomes expert in the ritual of insult, provocation, and braggadocio; he boasts of the exaggerated prowess of his team and cries down the skill and courage of the other; he develops sustained feuds, carrying on a guerrilla war with the umpires and an organized badinage with the players, while he consumes mountains of ritual hot dogs and drinks oceans of ritual soda pop.

3. Each sport develops its own legendry, woven around the "stars" who become folk heroes. The figures in baseball's Hall of Fame have their sagas told and retold in newspapers and biographies, and the Plutarchs who recount exploits become themselves notable figures in the culture. Some of these sports writers later become political columnists, perhaps on the assumption that politics itself is only a sport riddled with greater hypocrisy and that it takes a salty and hard-hitting sports writer to expose the politicians. The sports heroes become national possessions, like the Grand Canyon and the gold in Fort

Knox. It is hard for a people who in their childhood have treasured the sports legendry as a cherished illusion to surrender it when they grow up.

DISCUSSION: Balance

A sentence is said to be balanced when parallel phrases or clauses, about the same length or weight, are used to stress similar ideas:

> The savage bows down to idols of wood and stone: the civilized man to idols of flesh and blood.—George Bernard Shaw

Exact balance extending to whole sentences, as well as to phrases and clauses, is found occasionally in writers of earlier centuries, as in Abraham Lincoln's description of the North and the South at war, in his Second Inaugural Address of 1865:

> Neither party expected for the war the magnitude or the duration which it has already attained. Neither anticipated that the cause of the conflict might cease with, or even before, the conflict itself should cease. Each looked for an easier triumph, and a result less fundamental and astounding. Both read the same Bible, and pray to the same God; and each invokes his aid against the other.

The marked rhythm of these sentences creates a highly formal effect by slowing the tempo. Exact balance interrupts the natural flow of the sentence, giving emphasis to most or all of its parts. For this reason writers today usually reserve exact sentence balance for speeches made on formal occasions. A moderate balance continues to be a useful way of achieving emphasis.

QUESTIONS

1. The longer the phrases that are parallel in structure and meaning, the greater the sense of balance in sentences and paragraphs. How does Lerner vary the length of phrases and clauses balanced in the second and third sentences of paragraph 2? How does this variation in length prevent the sentences from sounding too formal?
2. Is the balance of phrases in paragraph 1 tighter than in paragraph 2? How does this balance of phrases give emphasis to key ideas and promote concision?
3. How exactly are sentences balanced in paragraph 3?
4. Could Lerner's analysis be extended to country or rock music, or some other area of American life?

WRITING ASSIGNMENT

Discuss another American sport in light of one of the following statements:

a. "The psychic basis of American mass sports is tribal and feudal."

b. "There is a stylized relation of artist to mass audience in the sports."

c. "Each sport develops its own legendry, woven around the 'stars' who become folk heroes."

BRUCE CATTON

Trusting Ourselves

1.   We like to say that this is a skeptical age. The landscape is all littered with the sad fragments of things we no longer believe in, and we wear the resulting pessimism proudly, as a fashionable garment. We are too smart to be kidded.

2.   So we say. Actually, our age takes more things on faith than any previous age in history. It has to, because it believes (as our fathers understood the word) in nothing at all.

3.   The universe itself is entirely beyond our comprehension. It always was, of course, but our ancestors mused that God's plan is beyond human grasp and let it go at that. We try to thread our way through the mysteries of particles and quarks, of black holes and a constantly expanding universe, and of the great universal explosion that somehow created everything from our cloud-capped towers to the dreams of the people who inhabit them; and in sheer bewilderment we turn to our modern theologians, the physical scientists, for words of comfort. They peer beyond the limits of time and space, wrestle with the inadequacies of the language, and at last come forth with the answer: *the mystery is even bigger than we thought.*

4.   So we take things on faith, there being nothing else to do, and we feel that somehow we have thought our way through the whole tangle. Facing a world which has unfortunately come into possession of the fearful secrets of nuclear fission and at the same time has built an infinitely complicated society on the exploitation of boundless stores of energy which abruptly turn out not to be boundless at all, we pride

ourselves on the fact that at least we know the worst. And that, in the end, is what our modern creed comes down to; we know the worst, even if we don't do anything about it, and whatever happens, we won't be suckers.

5.   The trouble is that faith shapes life. Most faith makes one innocent, but we have the kind that makes one cynical. We have no heroes because we no longer believe in heroes. We suspect that man cannot rise above his average and that his average these days is pretty low. So we commit intellectual follies.

6.   We lead ourselves to think that there must not be an "imperial Presidency"—in other words, that the power of the office should be reduced—because the President is likely to be a mediocrity who shouldn't have so much authority. And we propose to remedy this by giving more power to Congress, apparently on the theory that it is easier to trust five hundred mediocrities than to trust one.

7.   We espouse the conspiracy theory of history. The assassinations of President Lincoln and President Kennedy, and the shooting of Martin Luther King and Robert Kennedy, had far-reaching consequences: one man couldn't have done such a momentous thing all by himself—not John Wilkes Booth, Lee Harvey Oswald, James Earl Ray, or Sirhan Sirhan. There had to be a plot and a lot of people, probably with some kind of protection.

8.   Behind the belief that the world is a mindless mechanism there hides a human loneliness which finds comfort somehow in the notion that the mechanism now and then strips its gears. So we have our Bermuda Triangles and our UFO's, and the fact that the most thoughtful students find no basis for these hair-raisers means nothing, because it is easier to trust in a tall tale than to trust in the fallible human who knocks it down. As cynics we find it easy to believe in anything but people.

9.   And this is where the real danger arises. We have lost our faith in mankind, and that is too bad, because the answer to today's fearful riddles is not going to come out of the skies. It is going to come out of mankind, and if we deride the source, we are bound to scoff at the answer.

10.   The next few generations are apt to be the most difficult in human history. If we are going to survive them, we have to begin by believing in ourselves once more. Everything else will follow. Whether faith really can move mountains may be open to question; but the faith that can move mankind can be defined quite simply—faith *in* mankind.

QUESTIONS

1. What phrases are balanced in the third sentence of paragraph 3? What elements are balanced in the fourth sentence? How does the sentence balance affect the emphasis given to these various elements?
2. What elements are balanced in the second sentence of paragraph 4?
3. What clauses are balanced in the second and third sentences of paragraph 5?
4. What sentence elements are balanced in paragraphs 7 and 10?
5. Though he depends on sentence balance in many of his paragraphs, Catton does not overuse this kind of construction. He varies his sentences to avoid too formal an effect. How much variation do you find in the sentences of paragraphs 2 and 8?
6. What other things do you think we take on faith? Do you agree that we do so for the reason Catton gives?

WRITING ASSIGNMENT

Develop one of the following statements from your own experience. Disagree with Catton if you wish:
a. "We are too smart to be kidded."
b. "So we take things on faith, there being nothing else to do, and we feel that somehow we have thought our way through the whole tangle."
c. "And that, in the end, is what our modern creed comes down to; we know the worst, even if we don't do anything about it, and whatever happens, we won't be suckers."
d. "We have no heroes because we no longer believe in heroes."

Antithesis

CASEY MILLER AND KATE SWIFT

"Manly" and "Womanly"

1. Webster's Third New International Dictionary (1966) defines *manly* as "having qualities appropriate to a man: not effeminate or timorous; bold, resolute, open in conduct or bearing." The definition goes on to include "belonging or appropriate in character to a man" (illustrated by "manly sports" and "beer is a manly drink"), "of undaunted courage: gallant, brave." The same dictionary's definition of *womanly* is less specific, relying heavily on phrases like "marked by qualities characteristic of a woman"; "possessed of the character or behavior befitting a grown woman"; "characteristic of, belonging to, or suitable to a woman's nature and attitudes rather than to a man's." Two of the examples provided are more informative: "convinced that drawing was a waste of time, if not downright womanly . . ." and "her usual womanly volubility."

2. In its definition of *manly* the Random House Dictionary of the English Language (1967) supplies the words "strong, brave, honorable, resolute, virile" as "qualities usually considered desirable in a man" and cites "feminine; weak, cowardly," as antonyms. Its definitions of *womanly* are "like or befitting a woman; feminine; not masculine or girlish" and "in the manner of, or befitting, a woman." The same dictionary's synonym essays for these words are worth quoting in full because of the contrasts they provide:

MANLY, MANFUL, MANNISH mean possessing the qualities of a man. MANLY implies possession of the most valuable or desirable qualities a man can have, as dignity, honesty, directness, etc., in opposition to servility, insincerity, underhandedness, etc.: *A manly foe is better than a weak friend*. It also connotes courage, strength, and fortitude: *manly determination to face what comes*. MANFUL stresses the reference to courage, strength, and industry: *manful resistance*. MANNISH applies to that which resembles man: *a boy with a mannish voice*. Applied to a woman, the term is derogatory, suggesting the aberrant possession of masculine characteristics: *a mannish girl; a mannish stride*.

WOMANLY, WOMANLIKE, WOMANISH, mean resembling a woman. WOMANLY implies resemblance in appropriate, fitting ways: *womanly decorum, modesty*. WOMANLIKE, a neutral synonym, may suggest mild disapproval or, more rarely, disgust: *Womanlike, she (he) burst into tears*. WOMANISH usually implies an inappropriate resemblance and suggests weakness or effeminacy: *womanish petulance*.

3. What are these parallel essays saying? That we perceive males in terms of human qualities, females in terms of qualities—often negative—assigned to them as females. The qualities males possess may be good or bad, but those that come to mind when we consider what makes "a man" are positive. Women are defined circularly, through characteristics seen to be appropriate or inappropriate to women—not to human beings. In fact, when women exhibit positive attributes considered typical of men—dignity, honesty, courage, strength, or fortitude—they are thought of as aberrant. A person who is "womanlike" may (although the term is said to be "neutral") prompt a feeling of disgust.

4. The broad range of positive characteristics used to define males could be used to define females too, of course, but they are not. The characteristics of women—weakness is among the most frequently cited—are something apart. At its entry for *woman* Webster's Third provides this list of "qualities considered distinctive of womanhood": "Gentleness, affection, and domesticity or on the other hand fickleness, superficiality, and folly." Among the "qualities considered distinctive of manhood" listed in the entry for *man*, no negative attributes detract from the "courage, strength, and vigor" the definers associate with males. According to this dictionary, *womanish* means "unsuitable to a man or to a strong character of either sex."

5. Lexicographers do not make up definitions out of thin air. Their task is to record how words are used, it is not to say how they should be used. The examples they choose to illustrate meanings can therefore be especially revealing of cultural expectations. The American Heritage Dictionary (1969), which provides "manly courage" and "masculine charm," also gives us "Woman is fickle," "brought out the woman in him," "womanly virtue," "feminine allure," "feminine wiles," and "womanish tears." The same dictionary defines *effeminate*, which comes from the Latin *effeminare*, meaning "to make a woman out of," as "having the qualities associated with women; not characteristic of a man; unmanly" and "characterized by softness, weakness, or lack of force; not dynamic or vigorous." For synonyms one is referred to *feminine*.

6. *Brother* and *sister* and their derivatives have acquired similar features. A columnist who wrote that "the political operatives known as 'Kennedy men' and 'Nixon men' have been sisters under their skins" could not possibly have called those adversaries "brothers," with all the mutual respect and loyalty that word implies. As the writer explained, "Like the colonel's lady and Judy O'Grady, their styles were different but their unwavering determination to win was strikingly similar." Other kinds of sisters for whom no comparable male siblings exist include the sob sister, the weak sister, and the plain ordinary sissy, whose counterpart in the brotherhood is the buddy, a real pal. Like *effeminate*, these female-related words and phrases are applied to males when a cutting insult is intended.

7. Masculine, manly, manlike, and other male-associated words used to compliment men are frequently also considered complimentary when applied to women: thus a woman may be said to have manly determination, to have a masculine mind, to take adversity like a man, or to struggle manfully against overwhelming odds. The one male-associated word sometimes used to insult her is mannish, which may suggest she is too strong or aggressive to be a true woman, or that she is homosexually oriented, in which case mannish can become a code word.

8. Female-associated words, on the other hand, must be hedged, as in "He has almost feminine intuition," if they are used to describe a man without insulting him. He may be praised for admirable qualities defined as peculiar to women, but he cannot be said to have womanly compassion or womanlike tenderness. In exceptions to this rule—for example, when a medic on the battlefield or a sports figure in some postgame situation of unusual drama is said to be "as gentle as a woman"—the life-and-death quality of the circumstances makes its own ironic and terrible commentary on the standards of "masculinity" ordinarily expected of men.

9. The role expectations compressed into our male-positive-important and female-negative-trivial words are extremely damaging, as we are beginning to find out. The female stereotypes they convey are obvious, but the harm doesn't stop there. The inflexible demands made on males, which allow neither for variation nor for human frailty, are dehumanizing. They put a premium on a kind of perfection that can be achieved only through strength, courage, industry, and fortitude. These are admirable qualities, but if they are associated only with males, and their opposites are associated only with females, they become sex-related demands that few individuals can fulfill.

DISCUSSION: Antithesis

When contrasting ideas are balanced in sentences and paragraphs, they are said to be in *antithesis:*

> History proves that dictatorships do not grow out of strong and successful governments, but out of weak and helpless ones.—Franklin D. Roosevelt

Whole sentences containing antithetical phrases may also be balanced:

> Rome did not invent education, but she developed it on a scale unknown before, gave it state support, and formed the curriculum that persisted till our harassed youth. She did not invent the arch, the vault, or the dome, but she used them with such audacity and magnificence that in some fields her architecture has remained unequaled.—Will Durant, *Caesar and Christ*

The balancing of phrases and of sentences heightens the contrast of ideas.

QUESTIONS

1. The Miller-Swift essay illustrates the use of moderate antithesis in ordinary exposition—antithesis arising naturally from a contrast of ideas. In how many ways do the writers contrast words and attitudes relating to assumed masculine and feminine qualities?
2. What elements in the second sentence of paragraph 3 are antithetical? What elements in later sentences of the same paragraph are also antithetical?
3. Identify antithetical phrases or clauses in the following:
   a. paragraph 5, sentence 2
   b. paragraph 6, sentence 3
   c. paragraph 8, sentence 2
   d. paragraph 9, sentence 1
   How does the antithesis sharpen the contrast of ideas in these sentences?
4. Do you agree that language today (and other influences like movies and television) make "sex-related demands that few individuals can fulfill"?

WRITING ASSIGNMENTS

1. Discuss the extent to which the attitudes toward men and women contained in the dictionary definitions discussed are reflected in prevailing attitudes toward work or recreation. Draw on your own

experience for examples. Disagree with Miller and Swift if your experience suggests attitudes different from those they identify.
2. Analyze your own conception of manliness and womanliness, contrasting ideas where possible, and using moderate antithesis in some of your sentences.

MARTIN LUTHER KING, JR.
Nonviolent Resistance

1.   Oppressed people deal with their oppression in three characteristic ways. One way is acquiescence: the oppressed resign themselves to their doom. They tacitly adjust themselves to oppression, and thereby become conditioned to it. In every movement toward freedom some of the oppressed prefer to remain oppressed. Almost 2800 years ago Moses set out to lead the children of Israel from the slavery of Egypt to the freedom of the promised land. He soon discovered that slaves do not always welcome their deliverers. They become accustomed to being slaves. They would rather bear those ills they have, as Shakespeare pointed out, than flee to others that they know not of. They prefer the "fleshpots of Egypt" to the ordeals of emancipation.

2.   There is such a thing as the freedom of exhaustion. Some people are so worn down by the yoke of oppression that they give up. A few years ago in the slum areas of Atlanta, a Negro guitarist used to sing almost daily: "Ben down so long that down don't bother me." This is the type of negative freedom and resignation that often engulfs the life of the oppressed.

3.   But this is not the way out. To accept passively an unjust system is to coöperate with that system; thereby the oppressed become as evil as the oppressor. Noncoöperation with evil is as much a moral obligation as is coöperation with good. The oppressed must never allow the conscience of the oppressor to slumber. Religion reminds every man that he is his brother's keeper. To accept injustice or segregation passively is to say to the oppressor that his actions are morally right. It is a way of allowing his conscience to fall asleep. At this moment the oppressed fails to be his brother's keeper. So acquiescence—while often the easier way—is not the moral way. It is the way of the coward. The Negro cannot win the respect of his oppressor by acquiescing; he merely increases the oppressor's arrogance and contempt. Acquiescence is interpreted as proof of the Negro's inferiority. The Negro cannot win the respect of the white people of the South or the

peoples of the world if he is willing to sell the future of his children for his personal and immediate comfort and safety.

4.   A second way that oppressed people sometimes deal with oppression is to resort to physical violence and corroding hatred. Violence often brings about momentary results. Nations have frequently won their independence in battle. But in spite of temporary victories, violence never brings permanent peace. It solves no social problem; it merely creates new and more complicated ones.

5.   Violence as a way of achieving racial justice is both impractical and immoral. It is impractical because it is a descending spiral ending in destruction for all. The old law of an eye for an eye leaves everybody blind. It is immoral because it seeks to humiliate the opponent rather than win his understanding; it seeks to annihilate rather than to convert. Violence is immoral because it thrives on hatred rather than love. It destroys community and makes brotherhood impossible. It leaves society in monologue rather than dialogue. Violence ends by defeating itself. It creates bitterness in the survivors and brutality in the destroyers. A voice echoes through time saying to every potential Peter, "Put up your sword." History is cluttered with the wreckage of nations that failed to follow this command.

6.   If the American Negro and other victims of oppression succumb to the temptation of using violence in the struggle for freedom, future generations will be the recipients of a desolate night of bitterness, and our chief legacy to them will be an endless reign of meaningless chaos. Violence is not the way.

7.   The third way open to oppressed people in their quest for freedom is the way of nonviolent resistance. Like the synthesis in Hegelian philosophy, the principle of nonviolent resistance seeks to reconcile the truths of two opposites—acquiescence and violence—while avoiding the extremes and immoralities of both. The nonviolent resister agrees with the person who acquiesces that one should not be physically aggressive toward his opponent; but he balances the equation by agreeing with the person of violence that evil must be resisted. He avoids the nonresistance of the former and the violent resistance of the latter. With nonviolent resistance, no individual or group need submit to any wrong, nor need anyone resort to violence in order to right a wrong.

8.   It seems to me that this is the method that must guide the actions of the Negro in the present crisis in race relations. Through nonviolent resistance the Negro will be able to rise to the noble height of opposing the unjust system while loving the perpetrators of the system. The Negro must work passionately and unrelentingly for full stature as a

citizen, but he must not use inferior methods to gain it. He must never come to terms with falsehood, malice, hate, or destruction.

9.   Nonviolent resistance makes it possible for the Negro to remain in the South and struggle for his rights. The Negro's problem will not be solved by running away. He cannot listen to the glib suggestion of those who would urge him to migrate en masse to other sections of the country. By grasping his great opportunity in the South he can make a lasting contribution to the moral strength of the nation and set a sublime example of courage for generations yet unborn.

10.   By nonviolent resistance, the Negro can also enlist all men of good will in his struggle for equality. The problem is not a purely racial one, with Negroes set against whites. In the end, it is not a struggle between people at all, but a tension between justice and injustice. Nonviolent resistance is not aimed against oppressors but against oppression. Under its banner consciences, not racial groups, are enlisted.

11.   If the Negro is to achieve the goal of integration, he must organize himself into a militant and nonviolent mass movement. All three elements are indispensable. The movement for equality and justice can only be a success if it has both a mass and militant character; the barriers to be overcome require both. Nonviolence is an imperative in order to bring about ultimate community.

12.   A mass movement of militant quality that is not at the same time committed to nonviolence tends to generate conflict, which in turn breeds anarchy. The support of the participants and the sympathy of the uncommitted are both inhibited by the threat that bloodshed will engulf the community. This reaction in turn encourages the opposition to threaten and resort to force. When, however, the mass movement repudiates violence while moving resolutely toward its goal, its opponents are revealed as the instigators and practitioners of violence if it occurs. Then public support is magnetically attracted to the advocates of nonviolence, while those who employ violence are literally disarmed by overwhelming sentiment against their stand.

QUESTIONS

1. A moderate balancing and antithetical arrangement of phrases with a minimum balancing and antithetical arrangement of clauses creates a formal effect and, at the same time, tempers the tension of the passage. In the King, note the sentences that conclude paragraph 1:

They would rather *bear those ills they have,* as Shakespeare pointed out, than *flee to others that they know not of.*

They prefer *the "fleshpots of Egypt"*
to *the ordeals of emancipation.*

What sentences in paragraph 5 contain antithetical elements? How exact is the antithesis? How many of these sentences are balanced to emphasize similar ideas?
2. How exact is the antithesis of ideas in paragraphs 8 and 10?
3. One way to moderate the tension of a passage containing considerable balance and antithesis is to vary the length of sentences. To what extent are the sentences of paragraphs 5, 8, and 10 varied in their length?
4. What ideas of King's do you find pertinent to America in the 1980s?

WRITING ASSIGNMENTS

1. Compare King's sentence style with that of another of his writings, for example, "Letter from Birmingham Jail." Discuss how the relative exactness of sentence balance and antithesis is used to moderate or increase the tension of the writing.
2. Compare a letter by Saint Paul in the King James version of the Bible with the rendering of the same letter in the Revised Standard Version. Comment on the differences you notice in the use of balance or antithesis.

Length

ERNEST HEMINGWAY
The Shooting of the Buffalo

¹ The car was going a wild forty-five miles an hour across the open and as Macomber watched, the buffalo got bigger and bigger until he could see the gray, hairless, scabby look of one huge bull and how his neck was a part of his shoulders and the shiny black of his horns as he galloped a little behind the others that were strung out in that steady plunging gait; and then, the car swaying as though it had just jumped a road, they drew up close and he could see the plunging hugeness of the bull, and the dust in his sparsely haired hide, the wide boss of

horn and his outstretched, wide-nostrilled muzzle, and he was raising his rifle when Wilson shouted, "Not from the car, you fool!" and he had no fear, only hatred of Wilson, while the brakes clamped on and the car skidded, plowing sideways to an almost stop and Wilson was out on one side and he on the other, stumbling as his feet hit the still speeding-by of the earth, and then he was shooting at the bull as he moved away, hearing the bullets whunk into him, emptying his rifle at him as he moved steadily away, finally remembering to get his shots forward into the shoulder, and as he fumbled to re-load, he saw the bull was down. [2] Down on his knees, his big head tossing, and seeing the other two still galloping he shot at the leader and hit him. [3] He shot again and missed and he heard the *carawonging* roar as Wilson shot and saw the leading bull slide forward onto his nose.

DISCUSSION: Length

There is nothing intrinsically effective or ineffective, superior or inferior, about long or short sentences, just as there is nothing intrinsically effective in a single note of the scale. Effectiveness depends on the use or function of sentence length in a given context.

Ordinary exposition often begins with the main idea and accumulates detail:

> She was a spirited-looking young woman, with dark curly hair cropped and parted on the side, a short oval face with straight eyebrows, and a large curved mouth.—Katherine Anne Porter

How much detail a writer can provide depends on how effectively the main idea can be kept before the reader: detail becomes excessive when the main idea seems to disappear into it. In prose that describes physical action, the sentence may depict one connected action:

> Morrall would duck his head in the huddle and if it was feasible he would call a play which took the ball laterally across the field—a pitchout, perhaps, and the play would eat up ground toward the girls, the ball carrier sprinting for the sidelines, with his running guards in front of him, running low, and behind them the linemen coming too, so that twenty-two men were converging on them at a fair clip.—George Plimpton

Sentences longer than this are rarely used, partly because of the difficulty of maintaining clarity.

By contrast, a paragraph may be constructed of very short, disconnected sentences, resulting in an effect that resembles "primer style." Hemingway uses such sentences in a short story to express the monotony felt by a veteran of the First World War on his return home:

He sat there on the porch reading a book on the war. It was a history and he was reading about all the engagements he had been in. It was the most interesting reading he had ever done. He wished there were more maps. He looked forward with a good feeling to reading all the really good histories when they would come out with good detail maps. Now he was really learning about the war. He had been a good soldier. That made a difference.—"Soldier's Home"

QUESTIONS

1. Read aloud the first sentence of Hemingway's "The Shooting of the Buffalo," noting the main clauses. In light of the considerable length of the sentence, how are these clauses given emphasis? Read the sentence aloud again, this time breaking it into shorter sentences. What change in effect do you notice? Is there an *equivalence* between the original sentence, particularly in its length, and the experience described?
2. Why does Hemingway end the sentence with *he saw the bull was down* rather than continue into the next sentence?
3. Change the subordinate elements in sentence 2 into main clauses and the first two main clauses of sentence 3 into subordinate clauses. How do these changes affect the passage?
4. Use your dictionary to determine whether there are synonyms for the following words: *scabby, plunging, hugeness, speeding-by, whunk, carawonging.* Would any synonyms you found be more suitable than Hemingway's words? How do you explain the absence of some of these words in the dictionary?

WRITING ASSIGNMENT

Rewrite the entire passage by breaking it into shorter sentences. In a second paragraph discuss the ways in which the revision alters the mood.

JOYCE MAYNARD

The Pressure of The Group

1.   The pressure of The Group is strong in any period. There was a new kind of pressure affecting us during the sixties though—not just the push toward conformity and the fear and distrust that people have by nature (and that public schools seem to reinforce) of anything

that's different. In the fifties, I think, groups pretty rigidly con-
formed, but they were indiscriminating too. A pair of bobby sox, a V-
necked sweater, and you were *in*. The sixties were a more critical-
minded, sophisticated time, full of more negative adjectives than lavish
superlatives, a time when it was easier to do things wrong than to do
them right. Products, ourselves, of hours spent listening to TV commercials, we had become comparative shoppers, suspicious and demanding, minutely analyzing one another's actions and appearances—new haircuts with unevenly trimmed sideburns, cowlicks,
unmatched socks, Band-Aids that, we suspected, concealed pimples,
new dresses, new shoes. We knew each other's faces and bodies and
wardrobes so well that any change was noticed at once, the fuel for
endless notes. That's why I dressed so carefully mornings—I was
about to face the scrutiny of fifteen gossip-seeking girls, ten only
slightly less observant boys ready to imitate my voice and walk, and
one stern, prune-faced teacher who would check my spelling and my
long division with the care my enemies gave to my hems. At every
moment—even at home, with no one but family there—I'd be conscious of what the other kids, The Group, would think if they could
see me now.

2.   They ruled over us all—and over each other—like a supreme
court. Their presence was frightening, their judgments quick and firm
and often damning, and the tightness of the circle when I was in it
only made the times when I was outside seem more miserable. The hierarchy was re-established a hundred times a day—in choosing
partners for science experiments, in study halls, when the exchange of
homework problems began, and at lunch. But most of all in note passing. We rarely needed to take notes, and so we passed them. We could
have whispered easily enough, of course, or remained silent. (It wasn't
ever that we had important things to say.) But note passing was far
more intriguing, spylike. (Those were "The Man from U.N.C.L.E."
days, all of us playing Illya Kuryakin.) Most of all, note passing was
exclusive. Whispers were impermanent and could be overheard. Notes
could be tightly sealed and folded, their journeys followed down the
rows to make sure none was intercepted along the way. Getting a note,
even an angry one, was always a compliment. Whenever I received
one, I was amazed and grateful that I had made some slight impression on the world, that I was worthy of someone's time and ink. There
were kids, I knew, whose letters died, like anonymous fan mail, unanswered and unread.

3.   I think it was in notes more than in conversations or Girl Scout

meetings or Saturday mornings together on our bikes, that friendships and hatreds were established. We committed ourselves on paper to things we never would have said out loud (this seems odd to me now) and we saved them all—round-lettered, backhand messages written on blue-lined loose-leaf paper, the corners of old workbook pages, candy wrappers, lunch bags; they circulated around the classroom from desk to desk and year to year (once, in the seventh grade, we even had a pulley between desks). These were, I think, the greatest writing practice we got in school. Sometimes the notes contained news, stretched out in soap opera-type installment doses, to last us through an uneventful day. Stories leaked slowly—"Guess what?" would travel down my row to Becky till, at last, the teacher's mind deep in another matter, my note would cross the hardest point along its course, the latitudinal gulch between our rows (not within them) and she would unwrap it, folded like an origami bird, and write her answer, "What?" and pass it back to me. We wrote about TV shows watched the night before, about how we hated math and what our weekend and after-school plans were ("Are you going to walk home or take the bus?" "Short cut or long way around?").

4. Great wars, or so they seemed to us, were waged in notes, based on elaborate strategies we worked out, like homework, the night before. If things were getting dull, I'd plan to pick a fight with accusations of two-facedness (talking about someone behind his back was the most common offense) or cruelty to an underdog. Realizing early that I wasn't going to be a leader among the *in*, and refusing to simply follow, I became the champion of the class failures. The boy with the harelip, the girl who lived in a trailer and smelled bad, the one who tended to drool a little on her collar, I defended (enjoying the image of myself as kind and gentle benefactress, protecting the sensitive, the poet soul) from the group I loved and envied—for their coolness—and hated for the fact that they had never quite admitted me. I lectured Margie in suffering, histrionic moralistic tones ("You, who have always been popular, cannot know what it's like not to be. Think, for a moment, what Franny feels like when you laugh at her or lead her on to make a fool of herself, because she thinks that then you'll be her friend. I *know*—I know what it's like on this side of the fence . . .") Margie, a genuinely friendly girl, would be first puzzled and defensive. And then, as her troops moved in on me, sarcastic and coldly vicious. She'd write back to deny the charges, and there would be the ghastly period I always forgot about, setting out on my battles, when I seemed to be sinking and friendless, and wished I'd never started the whole thing.

QUESTIONS

1. Maynard varies the length of the sentences of paragraph 2 for emphasis. Which sentences are the shortest? Do they convey greater emphasis than the longer ones?
2. What sentences in paragraph 1 might be broken up to gain emphasis in the same way?
3. What is gained in paragraph 3 by coordinating the two parts of the second sentence with a semicolon? What is gained through the extreme use of coordination in the fifth sentence?
4. How many sentences in paragraph 4 are moderately periodic? How many of them are loose? How close are these sentences to the sentences of ordinary speech?
5. Was "the pressure of The Group" strong in your high school?

WRITING ASSIGNMENTS

1. Rewrite one of Maynard's paragraphs, achieving different emphasis in some of the sentences by reducing or expanding their length.
2. Analyze the pressures exerted by The Group in your high school experience. In the course of this analysis, compare your experience with Maynard's.
3. Discuss the similarities and differences you observe between boys in a group and girls in a group, at a particular age. Draw a conclusion about boys and girls in the early 1980s.

Climax

JOHN UPDIKE

My Grandmother

¹When we were all still alive, the five of us in that kerosene-lit house, on Friday and Saturday nights, at an hour when in the spring and summer there was still abundant light in the air, I would set out in my father's car for town, where my friends lived. ²I had, by moving ten miles away, at last acquired friends: an illustration of that strange law whereby, like Orpheus leading Eurydice, we achieve our

desire by turning our back on it. [3] I had even gained a girl, so that the vibrations were as sexual as social that made me jangle with anticipation as I clowned in front of the mirror in our kitchen, shaving from a basin of stove-heated water, combing my hair with a dripping comb, adjusting my reflection in the mirror until I had achieved just that electric angle from which my face seemed beautiful and everlastingly, by the very volumes of air and sky and grass that lay mutely banked about our home, beloved. [4] My grandmother would hover near me, watching fearfully, as she had when I was a child, afraid that I would fall from a tree. [5] Delirious, humming, I would swoop and lift her, lift her like a child, crooking one arm under her knees and cupping the other behind her back. [6] Exultant in my height, my strength, I would lift that frail brittle body weighing perhaps a hundred pounds and twirl with it in my arms while the rest of the family watched with startled smiles of alarm. [7] Had I stumbled, or dropped her, I might have broken her back, but my joy always proved a secure cradle. [8] And whatever irony was in the impulse, whatever implicit contrast between this ancient husk, scarcely female, and the pliant, warm girl I would embrace before the evening was done, direct delight flooded away: I was carrying her who had carried me, I was giving my past a dance, I had lifted the anxious caretaker of my childhood from the floor, I was bringing her with my boldness to the edge of danger, from which she had always sought to guard me.

DISCUSSION: Climax

Our discussion of periodic sentences indicated one important way that climax can be achieved—by delaying the main idea or the completion of the main idea until the end of the sentence. We saw also that, even in loose sentences, modifying or qualifying phrases and clauses that follow the main idea can be arranged in the order of rising importance—as in *I came, I saw, I conquered.* A necessary condition of climax is a sense of anticipation, promoted chiefly through the ideas themselves. Obviously anticlimax will result if we make the culminating idea less significant than what has gone before. The letdown that results may be deliberately comic, as in this sentence by Thomas De Quincey:

> If once a man indulges himself in murder, very soon he comes to think little of robbery; and from robbing he next comes to drinking and Sabbath-breaking, and from that to incivility and procrastination.

QUESTIONS

1. In the Updike, how does the ending of sentence 3 vary the normal sentence pattern to take advantage of the strong terminal position? Is the double emphasis given to *beloved* justified by the context?
2. Sentence 3 develops through an accumulation of detail. Does the sentence develop a single idea? Could it be broken up without interrupting the meaning or disturbing the effect?
3. How is climax achieved in sentences 5 and 8? Is it achieved through the same kind of sentence construction?

WRITING ASSIGNMENTS

1. Describe an episode or a series of incidents involving a close relative or friend. Let your details reveal your attitude toward him or her; do not state the attitude directly.
2. Discuss how the sense of anticipation built into Updike's paragraph is conveyed through sentence climax.

ANNIE DILLARD

The Mystery of Beauty

1. Cruelty is a mystery, and the waste of pain. But if we describe a world to compass these things, a world that is a long, brute game, then we bump against another mystery: the inrush of power and light, the canary that sings on the skull. Unless all ages and races of men have been deluded by the same mass hypnotist (who?), there seems to be such a thing as beauty, a grace wholly gratuitous. About five years ago I saw a mockingbird make a straight vertical descent from the roof gutter of a four-story building. It was an act as careless and spontaneous as the curl of a stem or the kindling of a star.

2. The mockingbird took a single step into the air and dropped. His wings were still folded against his sides as though he were singing from a limb and not falling, accelerating thirty-two feet per second per second, through empty air. Just a breath before he would have been dashed to the ground, he unfurled his wings with exact, deliberate care, revealing the broad bars of white, spread his elegant, white-banded tail, and so floated onto the grass. I had just rounded a corner

when his insouciant step caught my eye; there was no one else in sight. The fact of his free fall was like the old philosophical conundrum about the tree that falls in the forest. The answer must be, I think, that beauty and grace are performed whether or not we will or sense them. The least we can do is try to be there.

3. Another time I saw another wonder: sharks off the Atlantic coast of Florida. There is a way a wave rises above the ocean horizon, a triangular wedge against the sky. If you stand where the ocean breaks on a shallow beach, you see the raised water in a wave is translucent, shot with lights. One late afternoon at low tide a hundred big sharks passed the beach near the mouth of a tidal river in a feeding frenzy. As each green wave rose from the churning water, it illuminated within itself the six- or eight-foot-long bodies of twisting sharks. The sharks disappeared as each wave rolled toward me; then a new wave would swell above the horizon, containing in it, like scorpions in amber, sharks that roiled and heaved. The sight held awesome wonders: power and beauty, grace tangled in a rapture with violence.

QUESTIONS

1. How does the colon help to create a sense of climax in the second sentence of paragraph 1? What use does Dillard make of the colon at the end of paragraph 3?
2. Notice that phrases such as *a grace wholly gratuitous* and *the kindling of a star* seem more important than phrases preceding them in their sentences by virtue of their position at the end. What similar uses does the author make of the end of sentences in paragraphs 2 and 3?
3. How does the author explain the phrase *a grace wholly gratuitous* later in the passage? What general point about cruelty and violence is she making?

WRITING ASSIGNMENT

Develop one of the author's ideas from your own observations. Let the reader see and feel the experience as you saw and felt it. Build one or two of your sentences to convey a sense of climax, and if possible one of your paragraphs.

DICTION

Usage

JONATHAN EVAN MASLOW

Street Sports

1. Upper West Side children almost always play handball and racquetball in boy-girl pairs, usually accompanied by pervasive disco music from stereo tape decks. The games now are more courting rituals than were the deadly confrontations of bygone years, when Jewish and Italian kids smashed unreturnable "killers" and the Big-Time meant playing four-wall handball at City College. The West Side has its share of former City handball aces. They used to play at the YMCA until, as one ace explains, "Raskin dropped dead of a heart attack right there on the court. So we all stopped playing." The kids today often play the sidewalk version of racquetball, in which the ball can bounce before hitting the wall. This reduces traffic incidents resulting from stray shots. But a thirteen-year-old on 107th Street tells me, "Only little creeps play on a bounce—hey, I'm serious, man." So, it seems, even the Small Time has its unyielding categories of excellence.

2. It should also be noted that the Small-Time runs on the proverb "Play faster, we need the court." Almost all sports here are under strict time pressures, either from people waiting to play or from the general mad pace of city life. One hallmark of the West Side athlete is that he or she manages to swim, run, or compete in a regular team game while also working 16 hours a day, nursing along a Great American Novel, carrying on love affairs, and going into the third year of

psychoanalysis. Perhaps it's a sense of someone gaining on us from behind that accounts for the fact that so many of our sports are thinly disguised modes of transporation—jogging, bicycling, and skateboarding.

3. Of these three locomotive sports, bicycling might actually have a chance of becoming the mass conveyance the city needs—that is, if it wasn't for New York's gangs of teen-age bicycle thieves, who operate in citywide rings. The question bicyclists on the Upper West Side most often ask each other is, "What kind of lock do you have?"

4. The skateboarders, mostly adolescent boys, congregate at a place in Riverside Park known as the Ramp. This consists of scraps of woebegone plywood fastened together at progressively steeper inclines so that the first piece of wood is actually on the ground and the last piece, some 15 feet above it, is *vertical* to the ground. "Getting vertical"—also called getting radical—involves driving toward the Ramp at full speed and scaling the incline in a surfer's crouch position until the skateboarder is heading straight up like a missile at takeoff. At the top of the Ramp, he executes a 180-degree "kickflip" and comes hurtling down the other way.

5. It takes two or three years of constant practice to get really radical, but our boys put out the effort with tremendous devotion, customizing their boards the way kids used to build soap box derby racers. When they're not testing their skill and balance on the Ramp, they're recklessly "tick tacking" through "slalom" courses marked off with beer cans.

6. "Yeah, that's dangerous," admits Noah Southall, a fetching spokeslad turned out in a brushed Afro and a powder-blue warm-up suit. "But it's fun, we enjoy it, and it's challenging. Out of forty kids in my class, I'd say twenty-five have skateboards and about eight are really good. We're trying to get skateboarding into the 1980 Olympics as an event. But right now, see, we have to start here. Like in California, they have public skateboard parks where the kids can ride huge pipes and tubes. Pipes and tubes are the best way to get radical. I wiped out plenty of times, but that was mostly before I knew what I was doing. I still get plenty of scrapes and bruises, but no broken bones so far. My mother, she just says, 'Be careful.' "

7. "He'll break his leg," butts in an elderly gent, watching the skateboarders from the park bench sidelines near the Ramp. "You'll see, he'll break his leg; it's only a matter of time." In the Small-Time, we also have our critics.

8. Certainly the outstanding sporting type in our neighborhood is

the basketball Whiz, knight-errant of the playgrounds. The obsession of every Small-Time Whiz is to shoot his way into the pros, but the competition is utterly fierce. If there are, say, 200 rims in the vicinity, each one will have hanging out under it a kid who by his sixteenth birthday can do almost everything Julius Erving does. The playground Whiz plays basketball relentlessly, morning till night, day after day, in summer as well as in winter, year in, year out. He may leave the court after a typical session having scored 300 or 400 points. He develops an endurance that makes Tarzan look whimpy.

9. After the other guys go home for dinner—or, more likely, off to their girl friends' houses—the Whiz sticks around to work on his jump shot. He practices his moves like a figure skater, instinctively aware that to make the Big-Time requires not just talent but also entertainment ability—a shtick! Whizzes develop moves like you've never seen—triple pumps, stutter steps, reverse-slam dunks, behind the back lay-ups. They can put the ball up a hundred different ways, and they're not bashful when it comes to going for the hoop.

10. If too many Whizzes play on the same court, the result can be a dreadful combination of ten simultaneous one-on-one games. For this reason, basketball Whizzes tend to spread themselves over the neighborhood. But once a Whiz has found his turf, he sticks to it; that playground becomes, in a sense, his home court. The kids who play with a legitimate Whiz defer to him on his turf, paying a kind of homage to his ambition. They recognize his special talent and, I think, encourage and protect it. If a Whiz hogs the ball, he does so not out of selfishness or pride but for a greater good: money. In our neighborhood, don't forget, they call former Knick Bill Bradley "Dollar Bill."

11. On occasion, colleges send scouts to have a look at the Whizzes. The scouts are the personnel agents of the Big-Time. They drive LTDs and other fine cars. But out of the thousands of street kids who are good enough, maybe one will make the pros. Maybe one! A Columbia University coach says that playground rules—such as keeping the ball after you score a basket and keeping the court if you win the game—shape a Whiz into playing the game in an aggressive, driving, survival-of-the-fittest style. The "pure shooters" of the Midwest run all over our kids in the Big-Time colleges, so most Whizzes will have spent every waking hour for ten years or more for naught. Imagine the bitterness of young lives collapsing so spectacularly—once a Whiz gets too old for the playground, he's just another nobody. Upper West Side cops say there's no one more self-destructive than a basketball

Whiz who doesn't make it, easy prey for the drug pushers waiting on every playground to relieve his pain.

12. Yet the possibility of failure—I should say, the remote chance of success—doesn't keep a single potential basketball star at home. Why should it? This may be the Small-Time, but every New Yorker believes in his heart of hearts that he has the stuff to make the Big-Time.

DISCUSSION: Usage

None of us speaks or writes in the same way on all occasions: the differences depend on how formal the occasion is. A letter of application for a job will be more formal than a letter to a friend; a graduation speech will sound different from a locker-room conversation.

Each of us has a formal and informal language and, whether we know it or not, standards for judging their effectiveness. These standards come from the different groups we belong to—each group with its special idioms and vocabulary. Teenagers share a common language, which sometimes they have to translate for their parents; teenagers of a particular racial or ethnic background share a special dialect or language. So do teenagers of a particular city or region of the country. Though teenagers in New York City share expressions and idioms with all other teenagers in the city, they may share a special dialect with their families and with their friends. At school they may share a language with their teachers different from the dialect they speak at home. Even a family may have its own private language—special words and expressions to describe acts and feelings.

Cutting across these difference is a standardized English we hear on television and read in newspapers—a language sometimes less colorful and personal than these other languages, but serving as a medium for communication among diverse groups of people, not only in the United States but in other English-speaking countries. This standard is of long growth and it changes less than the informal language and slang of particular groups. This standard, represented in the readings in this book, falls between two extremes—one formal and abstract in its content and sentences, the other informal and concrete:

[*Formal*] Musical experiences of suspense are very similar to those experienced in real life. Both in life and in music the emotions thus arising have essentially the same stimulus situation: the situation of ignorance, the awareness of the individual's impotence and inability to act where the future course of events is unknown. Because these musical experiences are so very similar to those existing in the drama and in life itself, they are often felt to be particularly powerful and effective.—Leonard B. Meyer, *Emotion and Meaning in Music*

[*Informal*] Bryant's specializes in barbecued spareribs and barbecued beef—the beef sliced from briskets of steer that have been cooked over a hickory fire for thirteen hours. When I'm away from Kansas City and depressed, I try to envision someone walking up to the counterman at Bryant's and ordering a beef sandwich to go—for me. The counterman tosses a couple of pieces of bread onto the counter, grabs a half-pound of beef from the pile next to him, slaps it onto the bread, brushes on some sauce in almost the same motion, and then wraps it all up in two thicknesses of butcher paper in a futile attempt to keep the customer's hand dry as he carries off his prize.—Calvin Trillin, *American Fried*

The abstract ideas of the first passage could be stated in the most informal language. But usage is a matter of convention as well as personal choice, and if we would not be surprised to find Meyer's ideas stated in various ways, we probably would be surprised to find barbecue described in highly formal language. As a rule, informal writing is closer to the patterns of ordinary speech; formal writing often seems impersonal because it departs widely from these patterns (few people routinely speak Meyer's sentences). Much standard writing today has both formal and informal characteristics: we may combine colloquialisms with an abstract vocabulary in rather formal sentences containing striking parallelism and balance. We may even introduce slang (racy, hybrid, usually short-lived expressions) into an abstract discussion. In the following sentences, the pauses suggest the stop-and-start way we speak:

It felt as I would have expected: wonderful. The lights went out; flickering matches transformed the Garden into a giant planetarium. Dylan and the Band came back for a reprise of "Most Likely You'll Go Your Way," left, came back again, and ended with a rousing electric version of "Blowin' in the Wind." I went home as high on Dylan as I'd ever been.—Ellen Willis (on Bob Dylan's Madison Square Garden concert)

QUESTIONS

1. In the Maslow, certain words like *little creeps* (paragraph 1) and *Whiz* (paragraph 10) are teenage slang. What other words do you recognize as teenage slang? Does Maslow identify these as slang for his reader?

2. What is the meaning of *radical* in paragraphs 4 and 6? Should it be classified with teenage slang?
3. What words or expressions belong to the jargon of particular sports? Does Maslow single out these words for the reader?
4. What words and expressions seem to be peculiar to New Yorkers, and how do you know?
5. *Shtick* is a Yiddish expression that means: "a prank, a piece of clowning," "a piece of misconduct," "a devious trick; a bit of cheating," "a studied, contrived or characteristic piece of 'business' employed by an actor or actress; overly used gestures, grimaces, or devices to steal attention" (Leo Rosten, *The Joys of Yiddish*). Which of these meanings are intended in paragraph 9?
6. How formal or informal is the language of Maslow? How close to the spoken idiom are his sentences? How would you characterize him on the basis of the language he employs?
7. What points is he making about New York street sports? What distinction is he developing between "Small-Time" and "Big-Time," and why does he emphasize it in his final paragraphs?
8. What does Maslow tell you about growing up in New York? How different is that world from yours?

WRITING ASSIGNMENTS

1. Analyze the language of two sports columnists, noting the degree of formality and informality that you find in each, and the extent to which each depends on sports jargon in description and commentary. State what makes the writing of each effective or ineffective.
2. Discuss a special jargon or slang that you share with friends or members of your family. Comment on the special meanings and values some of the words have for you.
3. Every profession and trade has a special language or jargon that provides a "shorthand" or concise means of communication. Examine a trade journal or popular magazine directed to a particular audience—*Popular Mechanics, Field and Stream,* a medical or sociological journal—and identify particular words and expressions that belong to such a language. Discuss the special meanings conveyed by several of these words and expressions.

DERECK WILLIAMSON
Tell It Like It Was

1. A browse through the Little League Baseball Official Rules indicates that times have changed since my sandlot baseball days. I'll tell it like it is now, and then try to tell it like it was then.

PLAYING EQUIPMENT—Each team must have at least twelve conventional baseball uniforms. The Official Little League Shoulder Patch must be affixed to the upper left sleeve of the uniform blouse. Games may not be played except in uniforms. These uniforms are the property of the League, and are to be loaned to the players for such period as the League may determine.

2. Playing equipment—Each guy came out to the ballfield looking like a bum. Shirts were optional. Patches went on pants because they were torn up sliding. Anybody wearing a clean or neat garment was jumped on, and rubbed around in the dirt.

Each League must provide in each dugout at least six (6) protective helmets approved by Little League Headquarters. The wearing of such approved helmets by the batter, all base runners, and coaches is mandatory. Shoes with metal spikes or cleats are prohibited. Catchers must wear masks during practice, pitcher warm-up, and regular games.

3. There were no dugouts—only the ditch that ran across the field just behind second base. In the ditch were at least sixty (60) frogs. Headgear was optional. The most popular were brimless caps and capless brims. There was only one helmet in the league—a leather aviator's helmet, with goggles, owned by Spike Snyder. Shoes with metal spikes or cleats could not be worn, because they all belonged to big brothers in high school and didn't fit. Catchers didn't wear masks. To avoid being hit in the head they stood eight feet behind the plate and let the ball bounce once.

PITCHERS—Any player on the team roster may pitch. A player shall not pitch in more than six (6) innings in a calendar week. Delivery of a single pitch shall constitute having pitched in an inning.

4. Pitchers—Any player who owned the ball pitched. A player could not pitch on more than seven (7) days in a calendar week, or more

than one hundred (100) innings a day, because it got too dark. Delivery of a pitch straight down and the pitcher falling senseless beside the ball constituted exhaustion.

EQUIPMENT—The ball shall weigh not less than five ounces or more than five and one-quarter (5¼) ounces avoirdupois. It shall measure not less than nine (9) inches nor more than nine and one-quarter (9¼) inches in circumference. The bat shall be round and made of wood. It shall not be more than thirty-three (33) inches in length. Bats may be taped for a distance not exceeding sixteen (16) inches from the small end. The first baseman is the only fielder who may wear a mitt. All other fielders must use fielder's gloves.

5. Equipment—The ball could be of any weight, and anybody stupid enough to say "avoirdupois" out loud deserved what he got. Circumferences of the ball depended on the amount of tape wrapped around it. Sometimes the tape came loose when you hit the ball, and the circumference changed rapidly. Sometimes it was just tape by the time it reached the fielder, and the circumference was zero (0).
6. Bats were made of wood and were round unless they had been used for hitting rocks. After bats were broken they were taped for their entire length and it was hard to tell which was the small end. The first baseman was lucky if he got either a mitt or a glove. The only mitt belonged to the fat right fielder, who wore it even when he was at bat.

PROTESTS—Protests shall be considered only when based on the violation or interpretation of a playing rule or the use of an ineligible player. No protest shall be considered on a decision involving an umpire's judgment.

7. Protests—A protest was considered only when you were awfully sure you could lick the other guy. There was no umpire, unless some kid was on crutches and couldn't play. Nobody paid any attention to his calls, because he was just another kid.

FIELD DECORUM—The actions of players, managers, coaches, umpires, and League officials must be above reproach.

8. Field decorum—There were no managers, or coaches, or any of those big people. Only players who swore and spat. Anyone caught being above reproach got clobbered.

QUESTIONS

1. Williamson contrasts two kinds of baseball through two attitudes toward it—attitudes expressed not only in the details of the games but in ways of talking or writing about it. What is the chief difference between the language of Little League Baseball Official Rules and that of his account of sandlot baseball?
2. Is Williamson approving of Little League baseball, critical of it, or merely amused? Or is his feeling neutral? Do you share his attitude?

WRITING ASSIGNMENTS

1. Rewrite the Little League Baseball Official Rules for the information of children playing the game. Then analyze the changes that you made in vocabulary and sentence construction and the reasons for these changes.
2. Write a one-paragraph letter to a former high-school teacher asking for advice about a present course or a possible future career. Write a second one-paragraph letter to a friend who has taken the course or embarked on such a career, asking the same advice. In a third paragraph discuss the adjustments in usage you made and the reasons for them.

Tone

CALVIN TRILLIN

At the Annual Meeting
of the American Dietetic Association

1. At the annual meeting of the American Dietetic Association in New Orleans, I lived in constant fear that the dietitians would find out what I had been eating all week. The discovery would be made, I figured, by an undercover operative—some strict diet-balancer who normally worked as the nutritionist in a state home for the aged but was

posing as a raving glutton in order to trap me. "How were the oyster loaves at the Acme today?" she would ask casually, chewing on a Baby Ruth bar and fixing me with a look of pure food envy.

2. "Not bad at all," I would say, thrown off my guard by having met an apparent soulmate in an exhibition hall that included displays for such items as "textured protein granules with beeflike flavor" and some evil-looking powdered substance for which the most appetizing boast was that it was rapidly absorbed in the upper intestine. "I had to have two oyster loaves, in fact, which left room for only an ordinary-sized platter of red beans and rice and homemade sausage at Buster Holmes's place on Burgundy Street. I think if I hadn't had so much beer at the Acme, I might have been able to go a few pieces of Buster's garlic chicken, but—"

3. "Get him, girls!" the agent would shout, whereupon a gang of dietitians would fall upon me and hold me down while the chairman of the public-policy committee crammed carrot-and-raisin salad down my throat.

4. "Oysters are extremely high in cholesterol," a lecturer would say while the force-feeding was going on. "If one must eat oysters, oysters on the half shell rather than the fried oysters in the oyster loaf would be a better choice. Buster Holmes's homemade sausage defies scientific analysis."

5. "There were some good carbohydrates in the beer," I reply weakly between bites. Nobody is listening to me. A line is forming behind the dietitian who is dishing out the carrot-and-raisin salad—a dozen determined-looking ladies holding plates of green vegetables and gray meat. I spot the dietitian from Southwest High School in Kansas City, standing patiently with some broccoli I left on my plate in 1952.

6. My fears, as it turned out, were without foundation. I should have realized that on the first day of the meeting, when I was having breakfast at the Four Seasons, a pastry shop on Royal Street that has made me happy to be awake on a number of mornings in the past. I had figured that a week during which not only the dietitians but also the franchise operators of Roy Rogers Family Restaurants were meeting would be a good time for someone who is interested in both eating habits and conventions to be in New Orleans, but I had no intention of permitting an inquiry into other people's eating habits to interfere with my own. When I'm in New Orleans, my habit has always been to eat as much as I possibly can—partly, of course, as a precaution against developing some serious nutritional problem like rémoulade-

sauce deficiency in the event I don't make it back to town for a while. On that first day of the dietitians' meeting, I was demonstrating my usual lack of restraint with Four Seasons *croissants*. After the first few bites, I was in no mood to worry about being observed by some special agent in the pay of the American Dietetic Association. The dietitians, after all, did not have the only game in town for a convention buff. The Independent Oil Compounders were having their annual meeting at the Royal Orleans, right across the street. The National Screw Machine Product Association was meeting at the Royal Sonesta and the Louisiana Nursing Home Association was meeting at the Fontainebleau. The Roosevelt was harboring a slew of narcotics-control agents. I looked around at the other breakfasters defiantly. I was astonished to find myself surrounded by women carrying the program of the annual meeting of the American Dietetic Association. Some of them were even wearing their identification badges. None of them were spying on me, because they were all too busy eating. The woman at the table next to me was attacking not merely a *croissant* but a *croissant* filled with cream and covered with chocolate. Tortes and sweet rolls were disappearing all around me. A lady across the room was wolfing down a huge piece of cheesecake. At nine o'clock in the morning! I should have known then that I had nothing to fear from the dietitians. They are obviously just folks.

DISCUSSION: Tone

We have referred to the *tone* of a piece of writing, and we can define it now as the reflection of the writer's attitude toward his or her subject or reader. Writers may be mildly or strongly sarcastic, bitter, angry, mocking, whimsical, facetious, admiring, joyful, awe-struck—perhaps indifferent. They will reveal their attitude in one or more ways, depending on what they assume about their audience and on the effect they want to produce. If they do not state their attitude directly, they will indicate it indirectly: they may exaggerate to the point of absurdity for a humorous effect; or understate so that there is an obvious discrepancy between what is shown or what is said, producing an ironic effect; or they may present the facts without deliberate exaggeration or understatement, so that their attitude emerges gradually but unmistakably from their selection of detail. They will be aware that the tone of a statement can *qualify* meaning—in the way a sarcastic tone of voice indicates that we intend our words to be caustic.

In short, the tone of a paragraph or an essay is to be found in the voice we hear as we read. Whether or not they intend to do so, all writers express themselves in a voice that conveys an impression—if nothing else, an impression of unreflecting, dull people whose monotonous sentences indicate that they take little interest in what they say or how they say it. Writers interested in their subject and their audience are not likely to be dull; their positive attitude will be obvious. Occasionally, in the course of writing, writers will discover something about themselves or their subject—perhaps even that they have made a false start and need to begin again. False starts in writing are often failures to discover the voice—that is, the proper tone—to use in expressing an idea or developing an impression. And just as our ideas and attitudes will change from one piece of writing to another, the tone of an essay may change in response to shifts in attitude and emphasis. For an essay need not reveal one dominant tone: the voice of the writer may take on the nuances we hear in speech. In writing, these shifts in voice will be reflected in the modulations and rhythms of the sentences and paragraphs, which in turn reflect something of the rhythms and stresses of speech.

QUESTIONS

1. How would you describe Trillin's attitude toward the dietitians? Is he admiring of them, as well as amused? Is he saying or implying that they should not or cannot be taken seriously?
2. What does the description of the foods on display contribute to the tone of the passage? What is the contribution of the comment in paragraph 6, "They are obviously just folks"?
3. How informal is the writing of the passage? How close to the spoken idiom are Trillin's sentences?
4. What similar contradictions in ideas and behavior can you cite?

WRITING ASSIGNMENTS

1. Describe one of the following, establishing a dominant tone through the details you select. Express your feelings about the event, if you wish.
   a. a meeting of a school organization
   b. a meeting of a social club or sports organization
   c. an exhibition of automobiles or motorcycles (or a similar product)
   d. a country fair or amusement park
2. Describe the same event from another point of view. Establish a different tone through a different selection of details.

LIANE ELLISON NORMAN

Pedestrian Students and High-Flying Squirrels

1. The squirrel is curious. He darts and edges, profile first, one bright black eye on me, the other alert for enemies on the other side. Like a fencer, he faces both ways, for every impulse toward me, an impulse away. His tail is airy. He flicks and flourishes it, taking readings of some subtle kind.

2. I am enjoying a reprieve of warm sun in a season of rain and impending frost. Around me today is the wine of the garden's final ripening. On the zucchini, planted late, the flagrant blossoms flare and decline in a day's time.

3. I am sitting on the front porch thinking about my students. Many of them earnestly and ardently want me to teach them to be hacks. Give us ten tricks, they plead, ten nifty fail-safe ways to write a news story. Don't make us think our way through these problems, they storm (and when I am insistent that thinking *is* the trick, "You never listen to us," they complain.) Who cares about the First Amendment? they sneer. What are John Peter Zenger and Hugo Black to us? Teach us how to earn a living. They will be content, they explain, with know-how and jobs, satisfied to do no more than cover the tedium of school board and weather.

4. Under the rebellion, there is a plaintive panic. What if, on the job—assuming there is a job to be on—they fearlessly defend the free press against government, grand jury, and media monopoly, but don't know how to write an obituary. Shouldn't obituaries come first?

5. I hope not, but even obituaries need good information and firm prose, and both, I say, require clear thought.

6. The squirrel does not share my meditation. He grows tired of inquiring into me. His dismissive tail floats out behind as he takes a running leap into the tree. Up the bark he goes and onto a branch, where he crashes through the leaves. He soars from slender perch to slender perch, shaking up the tree as if he were the west wind. What a madcap he is, to go racing from one twig that dips under him to another at those heights!

7. His acrobatic clamor loosens buckeyes in their prickly armor. They drop, break open, and he is down the tree in a twinkling, picking, choosing. He finds what he wants and carries it, an outsize nut

which is burnished like a fine cello, across the lawn, up a pole, and across the tightrope telephone line to the other side, where he disappears in maple foliage.

8.   Some inner clock or calendar tells him to stock his larder against the deep snows and hard times that are coming. I have heard that squirrels are fuzzy-minded, that they collect their winter groceries and store them, and then forget where they are cached. But this squirrel is purposeful; he appears to know he'd better look ahead. Faced with necessity, he is prudent, but not fearful. He prances and flies as he goes about his task of preparation, and he never fails to look into whatever startles his attention.

9.   Though he is not an ordinary pedestrian, crossing the street far above, I sometimes see the mangled fur of a squirrel on the street, with no flirtation left. Even a high-flying squirrel may zap himself on an aerial live wire. His days are dangerous and his winters are lean, but still he lays in provisions the way a trapeze artist goes about his work, with daring and dash.

10.   For the squirrel, there is no work but living. He gathers food, reproduces, tends the children for a while, and stays out of danger. Doing these things with style is what distinguishes him. But for my students, unemployment looms as large as the horizon itself. Their anxiety has cause. And yet, what good is it? Ten tricks or no ten tricks, there are not enough jobs. The well-trained, well-educated stand in line for unemployment checks with the unfortunates and the drifters. Neither skill nor virtue holds certain promise. This being so, I wonder, why should these students, not demand, for the well-being of their souls, the liberation of their minds?

11.   It grieves me that they want to be pedestrians, earthbound and always careful. You ask too much, they say. What you want is painful and unfair. There are a multitude of pressures that instruct them to train, not free, themselves.

12.   Many of them are the first generation to go to college; family aspirations are in their trust. Advisers and models tell them to be doctors, lawyers, engineers, cops, and public-relations people; no one ever tells them they can be poets, philosophers, farmers, inventors, or wizards. Their elders are anxious too; they reject the eccentric and the novel. And, realism notwithstanding, they cling to talismanic determination; play it safe and do things right and I, each one thinks, will get a job even though others won't.

13.   I tell them fondly of my college days, which were a dizzy time (as I think the squrrel's time must be), as I let loose and pitched from fairly firm stands into the space of intellect and imagination, never

quite sure what solid branch I would light on. That was the most useful thing I learned, the practical advantage (not to mention the exhilaration) of launching out to find where my propellant mind could take me.

14. A luxury? one student ponders, a little wistfully.

15. Yes, luxury, and yet necessity, and it aroused that flight, a fierce unappeasable appetite to know and to essay. The luxury I speak of is not like other privileges of wealth and power that must be hoarded to be had. If jobs are scarce, the heady regions of treetop adventure are not. Flight and gaiety cost nothing, though of course they may cost everything.

16. The squirrel, my frisky analogue, is not perfectly free. He must go on all fours, however nimbly he does it. Dogs are always after him, and when he barely escapes, they rant up the tree as he dodges among the branches that give under his small weight. He feeds on summer's plenty and pays the price of strontium in his bones. He is no freer of industrial ordure than I am. He lives, mates, and dies (no obituary, first or last, for him), but still he plunges and balances, risking his neck because it is his nature.

17. I like the little squirrel for his simplicity and bravery. He will never get ahead in life, never find a good job, never settle down, never be safe. There are no sure-fire tricks to make it as a squirrel.

QUESTIONS

1. What is the difference in Norman's attitude toward the squirrel and toward the students she teaches? Do you hear a different tone of voice in the paragraphs dealing with each?
2. Does the essay end in the same tone in which it begins?
3. In what ways does the writer resemble the squirrel? How does she establish these points of resemblance?
4. Do you agree with Norman's characterization of college students today? Are the students you know different from the journalism students she is describing?
5. What point is the writer making in her final sentence, "There are no sure-fire tricks to make it as a squirrel"? Could this sentence be taken as the central idea or thesis of the essay?

WRITING ASSIGNMENT

Discuss your own goals in life, what you hope to gain from a college education, and what experiences and circumstances have shaped you as a student. In the course of your essay, discuss the extent to which you fit the characterization of college students in the essay.

JAMES BALDWIN

Fifth Avenue, Uptown

1. There is a housing project standing now where the house in which we grew up once stood, and one of those stunted city trees is snarling where our doorway used to be. This is on the rehabilitated side of the avenue. The other side of the avenue—for progress takes time—has not been rehabilitated yet and it looks exactly as it looked in the days when we sat with our noses pressed against the windowpane, longing to be allowed to go "across the street." The grocery store which gave us credit is still there, and there can be no doubt that it is still giving credit. The people in the project certainly need it—far more, indeed, than they ever needed the project. The last time I passed by, the Jewish proprietor was still standing among his shelves, looking sadder and heavier but scarcely any older. Farther down the block stands the shoe-repair store in which our shoes were repaired until reparation became impossible and in which, then, we bought all our "new" ones. The Negro proprietor is still in the window, head down, working at the leather.
2. These two, I imagine, could tell a long tale if they would (perhaps they would be glad to if they could), having watched so many, for so long, struggling in the fishhooks, the barbed wire, of this avenue.
3. The avenue is elsewhere the renowned and elegant Fifth. The area I am describing, which, in today's gang parlance, would be called "the turf," is bounded by Lenox Avenue on the west, the Harlem River on the east, 135th Street on the north, and 130th Street on the south. We never lived beyond these boundaries; this is where we grew up. Walking along 145th Street—for example—familiar as it is, and similar, does not have the same impact because I do not know any of the people on the block. But when I turn east on 131st Street and Lenox Avenue, there is first a soda-pop joint, then a shoeshine "parlor," then a grocery store, then a dry cleaners', then the houses. All along the street there are people who watched me grow up, people who grew up with me, people I watched grow up along with my

brothers and sisters; and, sometimes in my arms, sometimes under-foot, sometimes at my shoulder—or on it—their children, a riot, a forest of children, who include my nieces and nephews.

4.   When we reach the end of this long block, we find ourselves on wide, filthy, hostile Fifth Avenue, facing that project which hangs over the avenue like a monument to the folly, and the cowardice, of good intentions. All along the block, for anyone who knows it, are immense human gaps, like craters. These gaps are not created merely by those who have moved away, inevitably into some other ghetto; or by those who have risen, almost always into a greater capacity for self-loathing and self-delusion; or yet by those who, by whatever means—War II, the Korean war, a policeman's gun or billy, a gang war, a brawl, madness, an overdose of heroin, or, simply, unnatural exhaustion—are dead. I am talking about those who are left, and I am talking principally about the young. What are they doing? Well, some, a minority, are fanatical churchgoers, members of the more extreme of the Holy Roller sects. Many, many more are "moslems," by affiliation or sympathy, that is to say that they are united by nothing more—and nothing less—than a hatred of the white world and all its works. They are present, for example, at every Buy Black street-corner meeting—meetings in which the speaker urges his hearers to cease trading with white men and establish a separate economy. Neither the speaker nor his hearers can possibly do this, of course, since Negroes do not own General Motors or RCA or the A & P, nor, indeed, do they own more than a wholly insufficient fraction of anything else in Harlem (those who *do* own anything are more interested in their profits than in their fellows). But these meetings nevertheless keep alive in the partici-pators a certain pride of bitterness without which, however futile this bitterness may be, they could scarcely remain alive at all. Many have given up. They stay home and watch the TV screen, living on the earnings of their parents, cousins, brothers, or uncles, and only leave the house to go to the movies or to the nearest bar. "How're you making it?" one may ask, running into them along the block, or in the bar. "Oh, I'm TV-ing it"; with the saddest, sweetest, most shame-faced of smiles, and from a great distance. This distance one is compelled to respect; anyone who has traveled so far will not easily be dragged again into the world. There are further retreats, of course, than the TV screen or the bar. There are those who are simply sitting on their stoops, "stoned," animated for a moment only, and hideously, by the approach of someone who may lend them the money for a "fix." Or by the approach of someone from whom they can

purchase it, one of the shrewd ones, on the way to prison or just coming out.

5.   And the others, who have avoided all of these deaths, get up in the morning and go downtown to meet "the man." They work in the white man's world all day and come home in the evening to this fetid block. They struggle to instill in their children some private sense of honor or dignity which will help the child to survive. This means, of course, that they must struggle, stolidly, incessantly, to keep this sense alive in themelves, in spite of the insults, the indifference, and the cruelty they are certain to encounter in their working day. They patiently browbeat the landlord into fixing the heat, the plaster, the plumbing; this demands prodigious patience; nor is patience usually enough. In trying to make their hovels habitable, they are perpetually throwing good money after bad. Such frustration, so long endured, is driving many strong, admirable men and women whose only crime is color to the very gates of paranoia.

6.   One remembers them from another time—playing handball in the playground, going to church, wondering if they were going to be promoted at school. One remembers them going off to war—gladly, to escape this block. One remembers their return. Perhaps one remembers their wedding day. And one sees where the girl is now—vainly looking for salvation from some other embittered, trussed, and struggling boy—and sees the all-but-abandoned children in the streets.

QUESTIONS

1. What is Baldwin's general attitude toward upper Fifth Avenue and the Harlem of the late 1950s, when this description was written? Is his attitude toward the inhabitants of the street markedly different from his attitude toward the street itself? Does he state his attitude directly, or instead imply it in his details?

2. Does Baldwin maintain an overall tone in these paragraphs, or does his tone shift at some point?

3. Is he writing to persuade the reader to take action on the social evils suffered by the people on the street, or is he merely describing a street he knows well?

4. What impression do you get of Baldwin? What seem to be his most prominent qualities as an observer and writer?

WRITING ASSIGNMENTS

1. Analyze three paragraphs from different articles in an issue of a newspaper or newsmagazine to show how usage varies according to subject, attitude, and the approach of individual writers. You might compare the diction of two reports of the same event—in two newsmagazines or newspapers—to illustrate the possible variations.
2. Describe a street you remember well from your high-school days. Establish a dominant tone as you write. If you shift your tone, do so without being abrupt.

Concreteness

CLAUDE BROWN

A Building in Upper Harlem

[1] There is a building in upper Harlem on a shabby side street with several other buildings that resemble it in both appearance and condition. [2] "This building" is in an advanced state of deterioration; only cold water runs through the water pipes, the rats here are as large as cats. [3] The saving grace of this building might very well be the erratic patterns of the varied and brilliant colors of the graffiti which adorn it internally and externally from basement to roof. [4] This building has no electricity in the apartments, but the electricity in the hallway lamp fixtures is still on. [5] Some of the apartments have garbage piled up in them five feet high and that makes opening the door a very difficult task for those whose nasal passages are sufficiently insensitive to permit entry. [6] In some of the apartments and on the rooftop, the garbage and assorted debris are piled only one or two feet high. and the trash has been there so long that plant life has generated. [7] The most rapid tour possible through this building will necessitate boiling oneself in a hot tub of strong disinfectant for a couple of hours, and even then this astonishingly formidable breed of lice will continue to make its presence felt throughout a long itchy night, [8] This building is adjacent to a fully occupied tenement whose inhabitants are families, some of which include several children. [9] This building has a few steps missing from

the staircase above the second floor and there are no lightbulbs in the hallway; it's a very unsafe place for trespassers, even during the day. [10] This building's last family tenants was emancipated several weeks ago; they hit the numbers and moved to the Bronx, shouting, "Free at last, free at last; thank God for the number man." [11] Prior to their liberation, the "last family" had lived a most unusual existence. [12] Somebody had to be at home at all times to protect the family's second-hand-hot television from becoming a third-hand-hot television; there were too many junkies in and out who used the vacant apartments to stash their loot until they could "down" it and who also used some of the apartments for sleeping and as "shooting galleries." [13] For protection, the last family had a large, vicious German shepherd. [14] This dog was needed for the rats as well as the junkies. [15] A cat would be no help at all. [16] The sight of the rats in this building would give any cat smaller than a mountain lion instant heart failure. [17] The last family considered itself fortunate, despite the many unpleasant, unhealthy and unsafe aspects of its residence. [18] "We ain't paid no rent in two years. [19] I guess the city just forgot that we was here or they was just too embarrassed to ask for it," said the head of the last family. [20] This building has holes in the walls large enough for a man to walk through two adjacent apartments. [21] This building has holes in the ceilings on the fourth and fifth floors, and when it rains, the rain settles on the floor of a fourth-story apartment. [22] This building is not unique, there are many others like it in the ghettos of New York City; and like many others . . . this building is owned by the City of New York.

DISCUSSION: Concreteness

Writing is *concrete* when it makes an observation or impression perceptible to the senses. Eric Sevareid makes concrete the changes that occurred in his hometown in North Dakota:

> Sounds have changed; I heard not once the clopping of a horse's hoof, nor the mourn of a coyote. I heard instead the shriek of brakes, the heavy throbbing of the once-a-day Braniff airliner into Minot, the shattering sirens born of war, the honk of a diesel locomotive which surely cannot call to faraway places the heart of a wakeful boy like the old steam whistle in the night.—"Velva, North Dakota"

Complex ideas can be made concrete with vivid examples; indeed, examples are essential to our understanding:

I have described the hand when it uses a tool as an instrument of discovery. . . . We see this every time a child learns to couple hand and tool together—to lace its shoes, to thread a needle, to fly a kite or to play a penny whistle. With the practical action there goes another, namely finding pleasure in the action for its own sake—in the skill that one perfects, and perfects by being pleased with it. This at bottom is responsible for every work of art, and science too: our poetic delight in what human beings do because they can do it.—J. Bronowski, *The Ascent of Man*

We will see later how imagery and figurative language can increase the vividness of specific details.

   Whatever the purpose of the writer, excessive detail will blur the focus and perhaps make the writing incoherent. Voltaire said, "The secret of being a bore is to tell everything." A boring movie may show everything in what seems like an endless stream of detail; a boring paragraph or essay does the same thing. To develop an idea or impression effectively detail must be *selected.* Good writing is economical.

QUESTIONS

1. Brown's description of a Harlem slum building depends on an accretion of detail. From what physical angle of vision is the building described in sentences 1–9? Are we given an overall view from a single point of observation?
2. What is gained by reserving the information about the adjacent building for the middle of the paragraph—following the description of the deserted building? What is gained in the whole paragraph by saving the information about the owner of the building for the end? What is the principle of order in the whole paragraph?
3. The final sentence indicates that the author is making the building representative or symbolic of an *attitude,* reflected in a particular environment. What is that attitude and how does the selection of detail help us to understand it?
4. Did Brown succeed in shocking you about the Harlem building? How else might he have done so?

WRITING ASSIGNMENT

Discuss the implications of the details of the paragraph: what the building reveals about the city that owns it and what it suggests about the lives of its inhabitants.

JOHN UPDIKE

Central Park

On the afternoon of the first day of spring, when the gutters were still heaped high with Monday's snow but the sky itself was swept clean, we put on our galoshes and walked up the sunny side of Fifth Avenue to Central Park. There we saw:

Great black rocks emerging from the melting drifts, their craggy skins glistening like the backs of resurrected brontosaurs.

A pigeon on the half-frozen pond strutting to the edge of the ice and looking a duck in the face.

A policeman getting his shoe wet testing the ice.

Three elderly relatives trying to coax a little boy to accompany his father on a sled ride down a short but steep slope. After much balking, the boy did, and, sure enough, the sled tipped over and the father got his collar full of snow. Everybody laughed except the boy, who sniffled.

Four boys in black leather jackets throwing snowballs at each other. (The snow was ideally soggy, and packed hard with one squeeze.)

Seven men without hats.

Twelve snowmen, none of them intact.

Two men listening to the radio in a car parked outside the Zoo; Mel Allen was broadcasting the Yanks-Cardinals game from St. Petersburg.

A tahr (*Hemitragus jemlaicus*) pleasantly squinting in the sunlight.

An aoudad absently pawing the mud and chewing.

A yak with its back turned.

Empty cages labeled "Coati," "Orang-outang," "Ocelot."

A father saying to his little boy, who was annoyed almost to tears by the inactivity of the seals, "Father [Father Seal, we assumed] is very tired; he worked hard all day."

Most of the cafeteria's out-of-doors tables occupied.

A pretty girl in black pants falling on them at the Wollman Memorial Rink.

"BILL & DORIS" carved on a tree. "REX & RITA" written in the snow.

Two old men playing, and six supervising, a checkers game.

The Michael Friedsam Foundation Merry-Go-Round, nearly empty of children but overflowing with calliope music.

A man on a bench near the carrousel reading, through sunglasses, a book on economics.

Crews of shinglers repairing the roof of the Tavern-on-the-Green.

A woman dropping a camera she was trying to load, the film unrolling in the slush and exposing itself.

A little colored boy in aviator goggles rubbing his ears and saying, "He really hurt me." "No, he didn't," his nursemaid told him.

The green head of Giuseppe Mazzini staring across the white softball field, unblinking, though the sun was in its eyes.

Water murmuring down walks and rocks and steps. A grown man trying to block one rivulet with snow.

Things like brown sticks nosing through a plot of cleared soil.

A tire track in a piece of mud far removed from where any automobiles could be.

Footprints around a KEEP OFF sign.

Two pigeons feeding each other.

Two showgirls, whose faces had not yet thawed the frost of their makeup, treading indignantly through the slush.

A plump old man saying "Chick, chick" and feeding peanuts to squirrels.

Many solitary men throwing snowballs at tree trunks.

Many birds calling to each other about how little the Ramble has changed.

One red mitten lying lost under a poplar tree.

An airplane, very bright and distant, slowly moving through the branches of a sycamore.

QUESTIONS

1. Has Updike described what he saw at random, or do you see a principle of order in the essay—spatial perhaps, or climactic?
2. How do Updike's details create a dominant impression, or is he trying to avoid creating a dominant impression?
3. What is gained by presenting these impressions in phrases—actually shortened sentences?
4. What impression do you get of Updike from the essay—particularly from what he notices and chooses to describe?

WRITING ASSIGNMENT

Describe an afternoon in a park or athletic field, as Updike does. Make your details as vivid as you can, without developing each impression.

RENATA ADLER

WABC

1. Let's assume that a former radio addict who kicked the habit in 1954 now switches to WABC, 770 on the AM dial. If he is under thirty and has tuned in during news time, he may think for a moment that nothing has changed: Fred Foy, one of the newscasters, used to be the announcer for "The Lone Ranger," and another, George Ansboro, used to be the announcer for "Young Widder Brown." In a few minutes, however, he will hear one of the disc jockeys—Herb Oscar Anderson, Bob Dayton, Dan Ingram, Bruce Morrow, Charlie Greer, or Bob Lewis—and then, the chances are, his mood and Weltanschauung will change entirely. To begin with, he is likely to be addressed at once, familiarly, as "cousin," for it is customary, on jukebox-music stations, to enlist disc jockeys and fans in some sort of group or family. At WABC, listeners are "cousins" and disc jockeys are "All Americans"; at WMCA, listeners are simply listeners, but disc jockeys are "Good Guys"; and at WINS, where disc jockeys are simply disc jockeys and listeners are simply listeners, the disc jockeys show their solidarity by playing basketball as a team and challenging all comers.

2. However that may be, in any given quarter hour, our hypothetical WABC listener will be joining a chronologically mixed but aesthetically unified new generation of about a quarter of a million child cousins, teenage cousins, and perennially young adult cousins who are listening to the new music—the New Sound—over what has become, according to The Pulse Inc., a rating service, the most popular radio station in New York. (WOR, its nearest competitor, is a relatively non-generational "talk" station.) Our listener can hear WABC in most of New England and at least as far south as the United States Naval Base at Guantanamo. (Later at night, according to Station KOB, which is bringing suit, he can also hear it as far west as Albuquerque, New Mexico, where it allegedly interferes with local stations.)

3. Our listener will probably begin by turning the volume down, for, depending on the hour, he may be greeted by astral screams of "*Swing*, Charlie, *swing!*" "All the *way* with HOA!" "*More* music and *much* more *excitement, here* at *Day*ton *Place!*" "Boba*loo*, the big fat *Daddy Poo!*" or "Cousin *Bru*cie!" *Cou*sin Brucie! Cousin Bru*cie! Cou*sin *Bru*cie! *Cousin Brucie!*" There may also be voices—apparently

submerged in several feet of water—gurgling "Your music authority, seventy-seven, WA-BeatleC!" and conversation thereafter always proceeds at fever pitch. The listener may be urgently invited to vote in the "Principal of the Year Contest" (sixteen million handwritten votes were received last year), to send in for a "Kissin' Cousin Card" or a "Kemosabe Card" (a hundred and fifty thousand requests have been filled in a single week), to participate in a "Beatle Drawing Contest" (seventy-five thousand entries have been received, the winning entries to be exhibited in Huntington Hartford's Gallery of Modern Art), or to send in a box top—any old box top—"just as a whim!" (A few days later, he may be asked whether he knows anyone who can use a warehouseful of box tops.)

4.   If he has tuned in during the early morning, our listener will hear Herb Oscar Anderson crooning his theme song. "Hello Again," and reading notices about dogs and persons who have disappeared during the night. ("Dear Nancy, eighteen years old. We're sorry you left. Please come back and we'll forget all about it. Love, Mom and Dad." Nancy usually hears it and comes back; the lost dogs are usually found and returned, also.) In the late morning, he will hear Bob Dayton welcoming his listeners to "Dayton Place" and wishing a happy birthday to many of them. In the early afternoon, there is Dan Ingram, on "Your Ingram Singram" or "Your Ingram Flingram," announcing that he is there "laughing and biting, and scratching." Now and then, Dan will shout "Charge!" or announce a weather report as having come to him from "Peter the Meter Reader and our weather girl Fat Pontoon and her Soggy Stockings." In the evening, there is Bruce Morrow announcing, with terrific intensity, that it is or will soon be "Date Night," and giving all his girl listeners a big kiss (pronounced "mmmwa") as he asks all fans in cars to blow their horns at once. (If our listener has his window open, he will doubtless hear horns blowing all up and down the street.) Bruce Morrow may recount some recent escapade, like a breaking down of his car that forced him to buy a horse from the owner of an applecart and to ride it at full gallop through the Lincoln Tunnel on his way to a record hop in Palisades Park.

5.   Then it is time for Bob Lewis, "the big fat Daddy Poo," making weird choking noises to introduce a commercial for an exam cram book ("Kids, have exams got you by the throat?") and announcing record hops as far away as Galesburg, Michigan ("I don't think many of you will be able to attend this one, but . . ."). Finally, there is Charlie Greer, on "Your All Night Office Party," who repeatedly

warns the listener, "Don't be a dial twister or I'll give you a Charlie Greer blister," until it is morning and time for Herb Oscar Anderson to sing "Hello Again" again. All the disc jockeys will keep up this continuous stream of chatter, singing with or answering back to records, relaying personal messages to fans, reading traffic reports phoned on by regular "cousins" (like Eddie Schmeltz, a construction worker in Passaic, and Joe Firmata, a hearse driver in Brooklyn), coughing, sneezing, groaning, chortling, or laughing wildly, until our listener is more than likely to be stunned into becoming a non-generational cousin himself.

QUESTIONS

1. What qualities of the radio station is Adler trying to convey? What aspects of the broadcast does she focus on?
2. How different are the disc jockeys in personality and style? What point is Adler making in noting these differences?
3. What point is she making about the audience of the station?
4. What is the dominant tone of the description? Does the tone shift from paragraph to paragraph?
5. In what order are the details presented?
6. How different are disc jockeys today from those described?

WRITING ASSIGNMENTS

1. Describe a radio station you listen to. Do not comment directly on the qualities of the station. Let your details reveal these qualities, and your attitude toward the station.
2. Write one or two paragraphs that develop one of the following ideas in specific detail. Draw your details from several areas of experience if you can—home, school, place of recreation, place of work:
   a. "I have known people to stop and buy an apple on the corner and then walk away as if they had solved the unemployment problem."—Heywood Broun
   b. "Heroes are created by popular demand, sometimes out of the scantiest materials."—Gerald Johnson
   c. "Everything is funny as long as it is happening to somebody else."—Will Rogers

Imagery

RACHEL CARSON

Walking to the Seacoast

1. One of my own favorite approaches to a rocky seacoast is by a rough path through an evergreen forest that has its own peculiar enchantment. It is usually an early morning tide that takes me along that forest path, so that the light is still pale and fog drifts in from the sea beyond. It is almost a ghost forest, for among the living spruce and balsam are many dead trees—some still erect, some sagging earthward, some lying on the floor of the forest. All the trees, the living and the dead, are clothed with green and silver crusts of lichens. Tufts of the bearded lichen or old man's beard hang from the branches like bits of sea mist tangled there. Green woodland mosses and a yielding carpet of reindeer moss cover the ground. In the quiet of that place even the voice of the surf is reduced to a whispered echo and the sounds of the forest are but the ghosts of sound—the faint sighing of evergreen needles in the moving air; the creaks and heavier groans of half-fallen trees resting against their neighbors and rubbing bark against bark; the light rattling fall of a dead branch broken under the feet of a squirrel and sent bouncing and ricocheting earthward.

2. But finally the path emerges from the dimness of the deeper forest and comes to a place where the sound of surf rises above the forest sounds—the hollow boom of the sea, rhythmic and insistent, striking against the rocks, falling away, rising again.

3. Up and down the coast the line of the forest is drawn sharp and clean on the edge of a seascape of surf and sky and rocks. The softness of the sea fog blurs the contours of the rocks; gray water and gray mists merge offshore in a dim and vaporous world that might be a world of creation, stirring with new life.

DISCUSSION: Imagery

Images convey sensory impressions: impressions of sight, hearing, smell, taste, or touch. The following passage from a story by James Joyce illustrates most of these:

The cold air stung us and we played till our bodies glowed. Our shouts echoed in the silent street. The career of our play brought us through the dark muddy lanes behind the houses where we ran the gauntlet of the rough tribes from the cottages, to the back doors of the dark dripping gardens where odors arose from the ashpits, to the dark odorous stables where a coachman smoothed and combed the horse or shook music from the buckled harness.—"Araby"

We think in images constantly. Joyce could not have expressed his sense of a particular street on a particular night in abstract language. The more evocative our imagery, when the situation calls for vivid impressions, the more directly will our words express experience. A passage will seem overwritten if a vivid representation of experience is not needed; so-called fine writing tries to be too evocative of sense experience. In the passage quoted above, Joyce selects only those details that will give the reader an impression of the physical sensations experienced in the darkness. The imagery suggests the vitality of imagination with which the story is concerned; that vitality could not have been conveyed without it.

QUESTIONS

1. Carson appeals to our senses of sight and sound in describing her walk to the seacoast. At what point do sounds become important? How many sounds does she describe? What contrasts does she develop, and why are these important to her dominant impression?
2. How does sight reinforce sound in the passage? Does Carson appeal to other senses for reinforcement?

WRITING ASSIGNMENT

Describe a walk you have taken, selecting details to create a dominant impression, and appealing to two or more of the senses as Carson does.

TRUMAN CAPOTE
A Christmas Memory

1.   Morning. Frozen rime lusters the grass; the sun, round as an
orange and orange as hot-weather moons, balances on the horizon,
burnishes the silvered winter woods. A wild turkey calls. A renegade
hog grunts in the undergrowth. Soon, by the edge of knee-deep,
rapid-running water, we have to abandon the buggy. Queenie wades
the stream first, paddles across barking complaints at the swiftness of
the current, the pneumonia-making coldness of it. We follow, holding
our shoes and equipment (a hatchet, a burlap sack) above our heads.
A mile more: of chastising thorns, burs and briers that catch at our
clothes; of rusty pine needles brilliant with gaudy fungus and molted
feathers. Here, there, a flash, a flutter, an ecstasy of shrillings remind
us that not all the birds have flown south. Always, the path unwinds
through lemony sun pools and pitch vine tunnels. Another creek to
cross: a disturbed armada of speckled trout froths the water round us,
and frogs the size of plates practice belly flops; beaver workmen are
building a dam. On the farther shore, Queenie shakes herself and
trembles. My friend shivers, too: not with cold but enthusiasm. One
of her hat's ragged roses sheds a petal as she lifts her head and inhales
the pine-heavy air. "We're almost there; can you smell it, Buddy?"
she says, as though we were approaching an ocean.
2.   And, indeed, it is a kind of ocean. Scented acres of holiday trees,
prickly leafed holly. Red berries shiny as Chinese bells: black crows
swoop upon them screaming. Having stuffed our burlap sacks with
enough greenery and crimson to garland a dozen windows, we set
about choosing a tree. "It should be," muses my friend, "twice as tall
as a boy. So a boy can't steal the star." The one we pick is twice as tall
as me. A brave handsome brute that survives thirty hatchet strokes
before it keels with a creaking rending cry. Lugging it like a kill, we
commence the long trek out. Every few yards we abandon the
struggle, sit down and pant. But we have the strength of triumphant
huntsmen; that and the tree's virile, icy perfume revive us, goad us
on. Many compliments accompany our sunset return along the red
clay road to town; but my friend is sly and noncommittal when pas-
sers-by praise the treasure perched on our buggy: what a fine tree and
where did it come from? "Yonderways," she murmurs vaguely. Once
a car stops and the rich mill owner's lazy wife leans out and whines:

"Giveya two-bits cash for that ol tree." Ordinarily my friend is afraid of saying no; but on this occasion she promptly shakes her head: "We wouldn't take a dollar." The mill owner's wife persists. "A dollar, my foot! Fifty cents. That's my last offer. Goodness, woman, you can get another one." In answer, my friend gently reflects: "I doubt it. There's never two of anything."

QUESTIONS

1. "There's never two of anything," the woman of "sixty-something" and a distant cousin of the seven-year-old boy says, and the details of the passage show us why. What aspects of the scene does the speaker focus on? To what senses does he appeal in his description of the morning?
2. At various points the speaker refers to the distance he and his friend had to travel and to the vastness of the field where they cut the tree. How different would the experience seem if they had cut the tree in a nearby wood?
3. How has Capote transformed an ordinary event—the cutting of a Christmas tree—into an experience that seems epic to the boy?
4. How does Capote convey the importance of odor to the total experience? Notice that smells, like taste, are difficult to describe. But we can be reminded of objects we associate with vivid odors, and this reminder makes the odors alive to us.
5. What impressions do you get of the character of the friend? How does Capote convey that impression?

WRITING ASSIGNMENT

Describe a Christmas morning or another holiday that stands apart from other such mornings in your memory. Try to render the sights and smells of the morning through images that you think will convey the experience to others.

LARRY WOIWODE

Killing a Deer

1. Once in the middle of a Wisconsin winter I shot a deer, my only one, while my wife and daughter watched. It had been hit by a delivery truck along a country road a few miles from where we lived and

one of its rear legs was torn off at the hock; a shattered shin and hoof lay steaming in the red-beaded snow. The driver of the truck and I stood and watched as it tried to leap a fence, kicked a while at the top wire it was entangled in, flailing the area with fresh ropes of blood, and then went hobbling across a pasture toward a wooded hill. Placid cows followed it with a curious awe. "Do you have a rifle with you?" the driver asked. "No, not with me. At home." He looked once more at the deer, then got in his truck and drove off.

2.   I went back to our Jeep where my wife and daughter were waiting, pale and withdrawn, and told them what I was about to do, and suggested that they'd better stay at home. No, they wanted to be with me, they said; they wanted to watch. My daughter was three and a half at the time. I got my rifle, a .22, a foolishly puny weapon to use on a deer but the only one I had, and we came back and saw that the deer was lying in some low brush near the base of the hill; no need to trail its blatant spoor. When I got about a hundred yards off, marveling at how it could have made it so far in its condition through snow that came over my boot tops, the deer tried to push itself up with its front legs, then collapsed. I aimed at the center of its skull, thinking, *This will be the quickest,* and heard the bullet ricochet off and go singing through the woods.

3.   The deer was on its feet, shaking its head as though stung, and I fired again at the same spot, quickly, and apparently missed. It was now moving at its fastest hobble up the hill, broadside to me, and I took my time to sight a heart shot. Before the report even registered in my mind, the deer went down in an explosion of snow and lay struggling there, spouting blood from its stump and a chest wound. I was shaking by now. Deer are color-blind as far as science can say, and as I went toward its quieting body to deliver the coup de grace, I realized I was being seen in black and white, and then the deer's eye seemed to home in on me, and I was struck with the understanding that I was its vision of approaching death. And then I seemed to enter its realm through its eye and saw the countryside and myself in shades of white and grey. *But I see the deer in color,* I thought.

4.   A few yards away, I aimed at its head once more, and there was the crack of a shot, the next-to-last round left in the magazine. The deer's head came up, and I could see its eye clearly now, dark, placid, filled with an appeal, it seemed, and then felt the surge of black and white surround and subsume me again. The second shot, or one of them, had pierced its neck; a grey-blue tongue hung out over its jaw; urine was trickling from below its tail; a doe. I held the rifle barrel

inches from its forehead, conscious of my wife's and daughter's eyes on me from behind, and as I fired off the final and fatal shot, felt myself drawn by them back into my multicolored, many-faceted world again.

QUESTIONS

1. To what senses does Woiwode appeal in describing the killing of the doe?
2. What emotions does he convey through the specific details he gives us?
3. The killing of the doe is a necessary one, a fact Woiwode emphasizes through details of the suffering of the wounded animal. What are his other details meant to show?
4. Why does he stress the difference between his view of the doe and what he imagines is the doe's view of him?

WRITING ASSIGNMENTS

1. Rewrite the description from the viewpoint of the wounded doe—beginning with the circumstances of the wounding, and ending with her death. Let your details make the point of the essay.
2. Narrate an experience in which you learned something unexpected about the world of nature. Let your reader see that world and undergo the experience as you did. Choose images that appeal to several of the senses, not just to one.

Figurative Language

JOHN McPHEE
Running the Rapids

[1] There is something quite deceptive in the sense of acceleration that comes just before a rapid. [2] The word "rapid" itself is, in a way, a misnomer. [3] It refers only to the speed of the white river relative to the speed of the smooth water that leads into and away from the rapid. [4] The white water is faster, but it is hardly "rapid." [5] The Colorado,

smooth, flows about seven miles per hour, and, white, it goes perhaps fifteen or, at its whitest and wildest, twenty miles per hour—not very rapid by the standards of the twentieth century. [6]Force of suggestion creates a false expectation. [7]The mere appearance of the river going over those boulders—the smoky spray, the scissoring waves—is enough to imply a rush to fatality, and this endorses the word used to describe it. [8]You feel as if you were about to be sucked into some sort of invisible pneumatic tube and shot like a bullet into the dim beyond. [9]But the white water, though faster than the rest of the river, is categorically slow. [10]Running the rapids in the Colorado is a series of brief experiences, because the rapids themselves are short. [11]In them, with the raft folding and bending—sudden hills of water filling the immediate skyline—things happen in slow motion. [12]The projector of your own existence slows way down, and you dive as in a dream, and gradually rise, and fall again. [13]The raft shudders across the ridgelines of water cordilleras to crash softly into the valleys beyond. [14]Space and time in there are something other than they are out here. [15]Tents of water form overhead, to break apart in rags. [16]Elapsed stopwatch time has no meaning at all.

DISCUSSION: Figurative Language

A simile is an explicit comparison (using *like* or *as*) that usually develops or implies one or more simple points of resemblance:

> Will Brangwen ducked his head and looked at his uncle with swift, mistrustful eyes, like a caged hawk.—D. H. Lawrence

A metaphor is an implicit comparison in which an object is presented as if it were something else:

> Some people are molded by their admirations, others by their hostilities.—Elizabeth Bowen

Personification is the attribution of human qualities to abstract ideas or objects:

> So some random light directing them with its pale footfall upon stair and mat, from some uncovered star, or wandering ship, or the Lighthouse even, the little airs mounted the staircase and nosed round bedroom doors.—Virginia Woolf

Simile, metaphor, and personification unite in the following passage:

Then Sunday light raced over the farm as fast as the chickens were flying. Immediately the first straight shaft of heat, solid as a hickory stick, was laid on the ridge.—Eudora Welty

One purpose of figures of speech is to evoke the qualities of experience and give shape or substance to an emotion or awareness that up to the moment of its expression may be indefinite. In exposition a writer will depend on metaphor because of its property of expressing an attitude as well as representing an idea:

England is not the jewelled isle of Shakespeare's much-quoted passage, nor is it the inferno depicted by Dr. Goebbels. More than either it resembles a family, a rather stuffy Victorian family, with not many black sheep in it but with all its cupboards bursting with skeletons. It has rich relations who have to be kowtowed to and poor relations who are horribly sat upon, and there is a deep conspiracy of silence about the source of the family income. It is a family in which the young are generally thwarted and most of the power is in the hands of irresponsible uncles and bedridden aunts.—George Orwell, "England, Your England"

QUESTIONS

1. Why does McPhee explain that the word *rapid* is a misnomer? Would the experience he describes seem different if he had not given this information?
2. What images do the metaphors *smoky* and *scissoring* create in sentence 7? How many similes do you find in sentence 8, and what do they add to the sentence?
3. What metaphors convey the "slow motion" of the experience described in sentences 12–16?
4. Are the words *folding* and *bending* used literally or metaphorically in sentence 11?
5. What use of personification do you find in sentence 13?

WRITING ASSIGNMENTS

1. Rewrite McPhee's paragraph, eliminating the metaphors, similes, and personification. Then write a second version, supplying metaphors and similes of your own.
2. Describe an experience similar to McPhee's—trying to keep your balance on an icy street, descending a steep hill—and use meta-

phors, similes, and personification to heighten the vividness of your details.

JESSAMYN WEST

Water in California

1.   I would never, if I could choose, live beside a pond or a pool or a lake or a reservoir. Thoreau was never tempted at Walden's edge to shake his fist and say, "Don't just sit there. Do something." Still waters, especially the waters of the great man-made lakes, so-called, which are really reservoirs, make me feel that way. I know the good that reservoirs do, but I don't really care to look at them. They are caged animals; a zoo where the animal is a dead river; a snake of enormous sinuosity of muscle, stripped of its rippling skin, bunched up, pegged down, movable only when man lets gravity take hold of his captive.

2.   The river I write by was once a dangerous animal. I am living in the midst of reminders of the Colorado's strength—mountains moved by it; canyons dug by it. It has been tamed, if not killed. It can no longer move mountains and houses, kill people and animals. Instead, properly chlorinated, it will quench the thirst, fill the swimming pools, and cool the radiators of Los Angeles County's millions. Would I have Angelenos parched, their pools empty, their engines hot? No. But I don't have to admire the look of what that quenching, filling, and cooling has done to the river that flows past my window.

3.   I don't know why the names of the great winds of the world move me so much more than the names of the great rivers. Astrologically this is wrong. My element is water, not air. Perhaps I am a true Californian in this respect. There is so much more wind than water in California that I have decided to live in the element that I possess.

4.   All Californians *should* be river lovers. Without our rivers we would all die. As it is, our rivers are all—because we love them so much—dying. We will not let them run away from us into the sea. We cage them behind our mile-high dams. We build dams the way the Aztecs built pyramids; then we flock to them for weekend devotions, which are almost religious and *are* sacrificial. Each Saturday and Sunday, as on the steps of the pyramids, youths and maidens are sacri-

ficed on the sacred dam waters: beheaded by outboard motors; knocked cuckoo by blows from flying water skis; drowned when stamina proves weaker than ambition. Even the no-longer-young are sacrificial victims: dead from a surfeit of beer and pizza, in six feet of intended drinking water.

5. Water in California has become a superhighway (the superhighway is our true sacrificial altar). It is a surface upon which a vehicle can be propelled at high speed. It has become in many ways a super-superhighway. The surface of water is not worn by travel and does not have to be repaired, so you pay no highway taxes for the gas you put in your Chris-Craft. Water is cooler than asphalt in summer and not much wetter than asphalt in winter, so as a year-round roadbed it has great advantages, to say nothing of the novelty: going fast on land is an old story to everyone in California; going fast on water is a new sensation, because the recently built dams now make it possible. The superhighways that lead us to the lakes are clogged on weekends as people with boats hasten to the super-superhighways to experience the sensation of (and perhaps become one of the sacrificial volunteers to) speed on water.

6. There are no laws against the explosive noises of water vehicles. Water encourages and justifies a minimum of clothing. And water travel, provided you can swim and are not decapitated or mangled by flying solid objects, does have another distinct advantage over asphalt: it opens up in case your craft turns over.

7. Yesterday afternoon I saw a boat on the river that made me stare: motorless, silent; a rowboat, with two middle-aged men, fully clothed, sitting in it and using oars. They were not fishing. They were just ahead of the mud hens. Perhaps they were helping the hens in their job of rolling up the sheen of the westering sun? They appeared to be watching the sunset. They were out of the past. They were stranger on the river than a horse and buggy on the road.

QUESTIONS

1. What central point is West making about water in California—in particular, the quality of life and the impact of technology on the Colorado River?

2. How does the opening discussion of reservoirs provide a lead into her discussion of this point in later paragraphs? What use does West make of metaphor in paragraphs 1–2 in developing her thoughts about reservoirs and the Colorado River? How is personification joined with metaphor?

3. How does the analogy with the Aztec pyramids help West to develop her point further? In what sense are modern youths sacrificed to the river? Are they being sacrificed for the same reason Aztec youths were?
4. What use does West make of metaphor in paragraph 4?
5. What statement in paragraph 7 is metaphorical? How does the episode described here intensify the idea West has been developing?
6. Informal reflections such as these require careful transitions since West lets her thoughts range widely, as may occur in conversation. What transitions does West use?
7. West uses water to characterize life in California. What facts of nature best characterize your city, state, or neighborhood?

WRITING ASSIGNMENT

West uses the Colorado River and the changes that technology has produced to describe one aspect of California life. Use a similar natural object—a park, a mountain, one of the Great Lakes, another great river like the Ohio or the Mississippi—to describe the culture of its region. Use figurative language to intensify your ideas and impressions.

Faulty Diction

GEORGE ORWELL

Politics and the English Language

1.   Most people who bother with the matter at all would admit that the English language is in a bad way, but it is generally assumed that we cannot by conscious action do anything about it. Our civilization is decadent and our language—so the argument runs—must inevitably share in the general collapse. It follows that any struggle against the abuse of language is a sentimental archaism, like preferring candles to electric light or hansom cabs to aeroplanes. Underneath this lies the half-conscious belief that language is a natural growth and not an instrument which we shape for our own purposes.

2. Now, it is clear that the decline of a language must ultimately have political and economic causes: it is not due simply to the bad influence of this or that individual writer. But an effect can become a cause, reinforcing the original cause and producing the same effect in an intensified form, and so on indefinitely. A man may take to drink because he feels himself to be a failure, and then fail all the more completely because he drinks. It is rather the same thing that is happening to the English language. It becomes ugly and inaccurate because our thoughts are foolish, but the slovenliness of our language makes it easier for us to have foolish thoughts. The point is that the process is reversible. Modern English, especially written English, is full of bad habits which spread by imitation and which can be avoided if one is willing to take the necessary trouble. If one gets rid of these habits one can think more clearly, and to think clearly is a necessary first step toward political regeneration: so that the fight against bad English is not frivolous and is not the exclusive concern of professional writers. I will come back to this presently, and I hope that by that time the meaning of what I have said here will have become clearer. Meanwhile, here are five specimens of the English language as it is now habitually written.

3. These five passages have not been picked out because they are especially bad—I could have quoted far worse if I had chosen—but because they illustrate various of the mental vices from which we now suffer. They are a little below the average, but are fairly representative samples. I number them so that I can refer back to them when necessary:

(1) I am not, indeed, sure whether it is not true to say that the Milton who once seemed not unlike a seventeenth-century Shelley had not become, out of an experience ever more bitter in each year, more alien [sic] to the founder of that Jesuit sect which nothing could induce him to tolerate.

Professor Harold Laski (Essay in *Freedom of Expression*)

(2) Above all, we cannot play ducks and drakes with a native battery of idioms which prescribes such egregious collocations of vocables as the Basic *put up with* for *tolerate* or *put at a loss* for *bewilder*.

Professor Lancelot Hogben (*Interglossa*)

(3) On the one side we have the free personality: by definition it is not neurotic, for it has neither conflict nor dream. Its desires, such as they are, are transparent, for they are just what institutional approval keeps in the forefront of consciousness; another institutional pattern would alter their number and intensity; there is little in them that is natural, irreducible, or

culturally dangerous. But *on the other side*, the social bond itself is nothing but the mutual reflection of these self-secure integrities. Recall the definition of love. Is not this the very picture of a small academic? Where is there a place in this hall of mirrors for either personality or fraternity?

Essay on psychology in *Politics* (New York)

(4) All the "best people" from the gentlemen's clubs, and all the frantic fascist captains, united in common hatred of Socialism and bestial horror of the rising tide of the mass revolutionary movement, have turned to acts of provocation, to foul incendiarism, to medieval legends of poisoned wells, to legalize their own destruction of proletarian organizations, and rouse the agitated petty-bourgeoisie to chauvinistic fervor on behalf of the fight against the revolutionary way out of the crisis.

Communist pamphlet

(5) If a new spirit *is* to be infused into this old country, there is one thorny and contentious reform which must be tackled, and that is the humanization and galvanization of the B.B.C. Timidity here will bespeak canker and atrophy of the soul. The heart of Britain may be sound and of strong beat, for instance, but the British lion's roar at present is like that of Bottom in Shakespeare's *Midsummer Night's Dream*—as gentle as any sucking dove. A virile new Britain cannot continue indefinitely to be traduced in the eyes or rather ears, of the world by the effete languors of Langham Place, brazenly masquerading as "standard English." When the Voice of Britain is heard at nine o'clock, better far and infinitely less ludicrous to hear aitches honestly dropped than the present priggish, inflated, inhibited, school-ma'amish arch braying of blameless bashful mewing maidens!

Letter in *Tribune*

4.   Each of these passages has faults of its own, but, quite apart from avoidable ugliness, two qualities are common to all of them. The first is staleness of imagery; the other is lack of precision. The writer either has a meaning and cannot express it, or he inadvertently says something else, or he is almost indifferent as to whether his words mean anything or not. This mixture of vagueness and sheer incompetence is the most marked characteristic of modern English prose, and especially of any kind of political writing. As soon as certain topics are raised, the concrete melts into the abstract and no one seems able to think of turns of speech that are not hackneyed: prose consists less and less of *words* chosen for the sake of their meaning, and more and more of *phrases* tacked together like the sections of a prefabricated henhouse. I list below, with notes and examples, various of the tricks by means of which the work of prose-construction is habitually dodged:

5.   *Dying metaphors.* A newly invented metaphor assists thought by

evoking a visual image, while on the other hand a metaphor which is technically "dead" (e.g. *iron resolution*) has in effect reverted to being an ordinary word and can generally be used without loss of vividness. But in between these two classes there is a huge dump of worn-out metaphors which have lost all evocative power and are merely used because they save people the trouble of inventing phrases for themselves. Examples are: *Ring the changes on, take up the cudgels for, toe the line, ride roughshod over, stand shoulder to shoulder with, play into the hands of, no axe to grind, grist to the mill, fishing in troubled waters, on the order of the day, Achilles' heel, swan song, hotbed.* Many of these are used without knowledge of their meaning (what is a "rift," for instance?), and incompatible metaphors are frequently mixed, a sure sign that the writer is not interested in what he is saying. Some metaphors now current have been twisted out of their original meaning without those who use them even being aware of the fact. For example, *toe the line* is sometimes written *tow the line.* Another example is *the hammer and the anvil,* now always used with the implication that the anvil gets the worst of it. In real life it is always the anvil that breaks the hammer, never the other way about: a writer who stopped to think what he was saying would be aware of this, and would avoid perverting the original phrase.

6. *Operators* or *verbal false limbs.* These save the trouble of picking out appropriate verbs and nouns, and at the same time pad each sentence with extra syllables which give it an appearance of symmetry. Characteristic phrases are *render inoperative, militate against, make contact with, be subjected to, give rise to, give grounds for, have the effect of, play a leading part (role) in, make itself felt, take effect, exhibit a tendency to, serve the purpose of, etc., etc.* The keynote is the elimination of simple verbs. Instead of being a single word, such as *break, stop, spoil, mend, kill,* a verb becomes a *phrase,* made up of a noun or adjective tacked on to some general-purpose verb such as *prove, serve, form, play, render.* In addition, the passive voice is wherever possible used in preference to the active, and noun constructions are used instead of gerunds (*by examination of* instead of *by examining*). The range of verbs is further cut down by means of the *-ize* and *de-* formations, and the banal statements are given an appearance of profundity by means of the *not un-* formation. Simple conjunctions and prepositions are replaced by such phrases as *with respect to, having regard to, the fact that, by dint of, in view of, in the interests of, on the hypothesis that;* and the ends of sentences are saved from anticlimax by such resounding commonplaces as *greatly to be desired, cannot be left out of account, a devel-*

opment to be expected in the near future, deserving of serious consideration, brought to a satisfying conclusion, and so on and so forth.

7. *Pretentious diction.* Words like *phenomenon, element, individual* (as noun), *objective, categorical, effective, virtual, basic, primary, promote, constitute, exhibit, exploit, utilize, eliminate, liquidate,* are used to dress up simple statement and give an air of scientific impartiality to biased judgments. Adjectives like *epoch-making, epic, historic, unforgettable, triumphant, age-old, inevitable, inexorable, veritable,* are used to dignify the sordid processes of international politics, while writing that aims at glorifying war usually takes on an archaic color, its characteristic words being: *realm, throne, chariot, mailed fist, trident, sword, shield, buckler, banner, jackboot, clarion.* Foreign words and expressions such as *cul de sac, ancien régime, deus ex machina, mutatis mutandis, status quo, gleichschaltung, weltanschauung,* are used to give an air of culture and elegance. Except for the useful abbreviations *i.e., e.g.,* and *etc.,* there is no real need for any of the hundreds of foreign phrases now current in English. Bad writers, and especially scientific, political, and sociological writers, are nearly always haunted by the notion that Latin or Greek words are grander than Saxon ones, and unnecessary words like *expedite, ameliorate, predict, extraneous, deracinated, clandestine, subaqueous,* and hundreds of others constantly gain ground from their Anglo-Saxon opposite numbers.* The jargon peculiar to Marxist writing (*hyena, hangman, cannibal, petty bourgeois, these gentry, lackey, flunkey, mad dog, White Guard,* etc.) consists largely of words and phrases translated from Russian, German, or French; but the normal way of coining a new word is to use a Latin or Greek root with the appropiate affix and, where necessary, the size formation. It is often easier to make up words of this kind (*deregionalize, impermissible, extramarital, nonfragmentary* and so forth) than to think up the English words that will cover one's meaning. The result, in general, is an increase in slovenliness and vagueness.

8. *Meaningless words.* In certain kinds of writing, particularly in art criticism and literary criticism, it is normal to come across long passages which are almost completely lacking in meaning.† Words like

---

* An interesting illustration of this is the way in which the English flower names which were in use till very recently are being ousted by Greek ones, *snapdragon* becoming *antirrhinum, forget-me-not* becoming *myosotis,* etc. It is hard to see any practical reason for this change of fashion: it is probably due to an instinctive turning away from the more homely word and a vague feeling that the Greek word is scientific.

† Example: "Comfort's catholicity of perception and image, strangely Whitmanesque in range, almost the exact opposite in aesthetic compulsion, continues to evoke that trembling atmospheric accumulative hinting at a cruel, an inexorably serene timeless-

romantic, plastic, values, human, dead, sentimental, natural, vitality, as used in art criticism, are strictly meaningless, in the sense that they not only do not point to any discoverable object, but are hardly ever expected to do so by the reader. When one critic writes, "The outstanding feature of Mr. X's work is its living quality," while another writes, "The immediately striking thing about Mr. X's work is its peculiar deadness," the reader accepts this as a simple difference of opinion. If words like *black* and *white* were involved, instead of the jargon words *dead* and *living*, he would see at once that language was being used in an improper way. Many political words are similarly abused. The word *Fascism* has now no meaning except in so far as it signifies "something not desirable." The words *democracy, socialism, freedom, patriotic, realistic, justice,* have each of them several different meanings which cannot be reconciled with one another. In the case of a word like *democracy,* not only is there no agreed definition, but the attempt to make one is resisted from all sides. It is almost universally felt that when we call a country democratic we are praising it: consequently the defenders of every kind of régime claim that it is a democracy, and fear that they might have to stop using the word if it were tied down to any one meaning. Words of this kind are often used in a consciously dishonest way. That is, the person who uses them has his own private definition, but allows his hearer to think he means something quite different. Statements like *Marshal Pétain was a true patriot, The Soviet press is the freest in the world, The Catholic Church is opposed to persecution,* are almost always made with intent to deceive. Other words used in variable meanings, in most cases more or less dishonestly, are: *class, totalitarian, science, progressive, reactionary, bourgeois, equality.*

9. Now that I have made this catalogue of swindles and perversions, let me give another example of the kind of writing that they lead to. This time it must of its nature be an imaginary one. I am going to translate a passage of good English into modern English of the worst sort. Here is a well-known verse from *Ecclesiastes:*

I returned and saw under the sun, that the race is not to the swift, nor the battle to the strong, neither yet bread to the wise, nor yet riches to men of understanding, nor yet favour to men of skill; but time and chance happeneth to them all.

---

ness. . . . Wrey Gardiner scores by aiming at simple bull's-eyes with precision. Only they are not so simple, and through this contented sadness runs more than the surface bittersweet of resignation." (*Poetry Quarterly.*)

Here it is in modern English:

Objective consideration of contemporary phenomena compels the conclusion that success or failure in competitive activities exhibits no tendency to be commensurate with innate capacity, but that a considerable element of the unpredictable must invariably be taken into account.

10.   This is a parody, but not a very gross one. Exhibit (3), above, for instance, contains several patches of the same kind of English. It will be seen that I have not made a full translation. The beginning and ending of the sentence follow the original meaning fairly closely, but in the middle the concrete illustrations—race, battle, bread—dissolve into the vague phrase "success or failure in competitive activities." This had to be so, because no modern writer of the kind I am discussing—no one capable of using phrases like "objective consideration of contemporary phenomena"—would ever tabulate his thoughts in that precise and detailed way. The whole tendency of modern prose is away from concreteness. Now analyze these two sentences a little more closely. The first contains forty-nine words but only sixty syllables, and all its words are those of everyday life. The second contains thirty-eight words of ninety syllables: eighteen of its words are from Latin roots, and one from Greek. The first sentence contains six vivid images, and only one phrase ("time and chance") that could be called vague. The second contains not a single fresh, arresting phrase, and in spite of its ninety syllables it gives only a shortened version of the meaning contained in the first. Yet without a doubt it is the second kind of sentence that is gaining ground in modern English. I do not want to exaggerate. This kind of writing is not yet universal, and outcrops of simplicity will occur here and there in the worst-written page. Still, if you or I were told to write a few lines on the uncertainty of human fortunes, we should probably come much nearer to my imaginary sentence than to the one from *Ecclesiastes*.
11.   As I have tried to show, modern writing at its worst does not consist in picking out words for the sake of their meaning and inventing images in order to make the meaning clearer. It consists in gumming together long strips of words which have already been set in order by someone else, and making the results presentable by sheer humbug. The attraction of this way of writing is that it is easy. It is easier—even quicker, once you have the habit—to say *In my opinion it is not an unjustifiable assumption that* than to say *I think*. If you use ready-made phrases, you not only don't have to hunt about for words;

you also don't have to bother with the rhythms of your sentences, since these phrases are generally so arranged as to be more or less euphonious. When you are composing in a hurry—when you are dictating to a stenographer, for instance, or making a public speech—it is natural to fall into a pretentious, Latinized style. Tags like *a consideration which we should do well to bear in mind* or *a conclusion to which all of us would readily assent* will save many a sentence from coming down with a bump. By using stale metaphors, similes, and idioms, you save much mental effort, at the cost of leaving your meaning vague, not only for your reader but for yourself. This is the significance of mixed metaphors. The sole aim of a metaphor is to call up a visual image. When these images clash—as in *The Fascist octopus has sung its swan song, the jackboot is thrown into the melting pot*—it can be taken as certain that the writer is not seeing a mental image of the objects he is naming; in other words he is not really thinking. Look again at the examples I gave at the beginning of this essay. Professor Laski (1) uses five negatives in fifty-three words. One of these is superfluous, making nonsense of the whole passage, and in addition there is the slip—*alien* for akin—making further nonsense, and several avoidable pieces of clumsiness which increase the general vaguenes. Professor Hogben (2) plays ducks and drakes with a battery which is able to write prescriptions, and, while disapproving of the everyday phrase *put up with,* is unwilling to look *egregious* up in the dictionary and see what it means; (3), if one takes an uncharitable attitude towards it, is simply meaningless: probably one could work out its intended meaning by reading the whole of the article in which it occurs. In (4), the writer knows more or less what he wants to say, but an accumulation of stale phrases chokes him like tea leaves blocking a sink. In (5), words and meaning have almost parted company. People who write in this manner usually have a general emotional meaning—they dislike one thing and want to express solidarity with another—but they are not interested in the detail of what they are saying. A scrupulous writer, in every sentence that he writes, will ask himself at least four questions, thus: What am I trying to say? What words will express it? What image or idiom will make it clearer? Is this image fresh enough to have an effect? And he will probably ask himself two more: Could I put it more shortly? Have I said anything that is avoidable ugly? But you are not obliged to go to all this trouble. You can shirk it by simply throwing your mind open and letting the ready-made phrases come crowding in. They will construct your sentences for you—even think your thoughts for you, to a certain extent—and at need they will perform the important service of partially concealing your meaning even from yourself. It is at this point that the special connection between politics and the debasement of language becomes clear.

12. In our time it is broadly true that political writing is bad writing. Where it is not true, it will generally be found that the writer is some kind of rebel, expressing his private opinions and not a "party line." Orthodoxy, of whatever color, seems to demand a lifeless, imitative style. The political dialects to be found in pamphlets, leading articles, manifestoes, White Papers and the speeches of undersecretaries do, of course, vary from party to party, but they are all alike in that one almost never finds in them a fresh, vivid, homemade turn of speech. When one watches some tired hack on the platform mechanically repeating the familiar phrases—*bestial atrocities, iron heel, bloodstained tyranny, free peoples of the world, stand shoulder to shoulder*—one often has a curious feeling that one is not watching a live human being but some kind of dummy: a feeling which suddenly becomes stronger at moments when the light catches the speaker's spectacles and turns them into blank discs which seem to have no eyes behind them. And this is not altogether fanciful. A speaker who uses that kind of phraseology has gone some distance toward turning himself into a machine. The appropriate noises are coming out of his larynx, but his brain is not involved as it would be if he were choosing his words for himself. If the speech he is making is one that he is accustomed to make over and over again, he may be almost unconscious of what he is saying, as one is when one utters the responses in church. And this reduced state of consciousness, if not indispensable, is at any rate favorable to political conformity.

13. In our time, political speech and writing are largely the defense of the indefensible. Things like the continuance of British rule in India, the Russian purges and deportations, the dropping of the atom bombs on Japan, can indeed be defended, but only by arguments which are too brutal for most people to face, and which do not square with the professed aims of political parties. This political language has to consist largely of euphemism, question-begging and sheer cloudy vagueness. Defenseless villages are bombarded from the air, the inhabitants driven out into the countryside, the cattle machine-gunned, the huts set on fire with incendiary bullets: this is called *pacification*. Millions of peasants are robbed of their farms and sent trudging along the roads with no more than they can carry: this is called *transfer of population* or *rectification of frontiers*. People are imprisoned for years without trial, or shot in the back of the neck or sent to die of scurvy in

Arctic lumber camps: this is called *elimination of unreliable elements.*
Such phraseology is needed if one wants to name things without calling up mental pictures of them. Consider for instance some comfortable English professor defending Russian totalitarianism. He cannot
say outright, "I believe in killing off your opponents when you can get
good results by doing so." Probably, therefore, he will say something
like this:

"While freely conceding that the Soviet régime exhibits certain features which the humanitarian may be inclined to deplore, we must, I
think, agree that a certain curtailment of the right to political opposition is an unavoidable concomitant of transitional periods, and that
the rigors which the Russian people have been called upon to undergo
have been amply justified in the sphere of concrete achievement."

14.   The inflated style is itself a kind of euphemism. A mass of Latin
words falls upon the facts like soft snow, blurring the outlines and
covering up all the details. The great enemy of clear language is insincerity. When there is a gap between one's real and one's declared
aims, one turns as it were instinctively to long words and exhausted
idioms, like a cuttlefish squirting out ink. In our age there is no such
thing as "keeping out of politics." All issues are political issues, and
politics itself is a mass of lies, evasions, folly, hatred, and schizo-
phrenia. When the general atmosphere is bad, language must suffer. I
should expect to find—this is a guess which I have not sufficient
knowledge to verify—that the German, Russian and Italian languages
have all deteriorated in the last ten or fifteen years, as a result of dicta-
torship.

15.   But if thought corrupts language, language can also corrupt
thought. A bad usage can spread by tradition and imitation, even
among people who should and do know better. The debased language
that I have been discussing is in some ways very convenient. Phrases
like *a not unjustifiable assumption, leaves much to be desired, would serve
no good purpose, a consideration which we should do well to bear in mind,*
are a continuous temptation, a packet of aspirins always at one's
elbow. Look back through this essay, and for certain you will find that
I have again and again committed the very faults I am protesting
against. By this morning's post I have received a pamphlet dealing
with conditions in Germany. The author tells me that he "felt impelled" to write it. I open it at random, and here is almost the first
sentence that I see:"[The Allies] have an opportunity not only of
achieving a radical transformation of Germany's social and political
structure in such a way as to avoid a nationalistic reaction in Germany

itself, but at the same time of laying the foundations of a co-operative and unified Europe." You see, he "feels impelled" to write—feels, presumably, that he has something new to say—and yet his words, like cavalry horses answering the bugle, group themselves automatically into the familiar dreary pattern. This invasion of one's mind by ready-made phrases (*lay the foundations, achieve a radical transformation*) can only be prevented if one is constantly on guard against them, and every such phrase anaesthetizes a portion of one's brain.

16.   I said earlier that the decadence of our language is probably curable. Those who deny this would argue, if they produced an argument at all, that language merely reflects existing social conditions, and that we cannot influence its development by any direct tinkering with words and constructions. So far as the general tone or spirit of a language goes, this may be true, but it is not true in detail. Silly words and expressions have often disappeared, not through any evolutionary process but owing to the conscious action of a minority. Two recent examples were *explore every avenue* and *leave no stone unturned,* which were killed by the jeers of a few journalists. There is a long list of flyblown metaphors which could similarly be got rid of if enough people would interest themselves in the job; and it should also be possible to laugh the *not un-* formation out of existence,★ to reduce the amount of Latin and Greek in the average sentence, to drive out foreign phrases and strayed scientific words, and, in general, to make pretentiousness unfashionable. But all these are minor points. The defense of the English language implies more than this, and perhaps it is best to start by saying what it does *not* imply.

17.   To begin with it has nothing to do with archaism, with the salvaging of obsolete words and turns of speech, or with the setting up of a "standard English" which must never be departed from. On the contrary, it is especially concerned with the scrapping of every word or idiom which has outworn its usefulness. It has nothing to do with correct grammar and syntax, which are of no importance so long as one makes one's meaning clear, or with the avoidance of Americanisms, or with having what is called a "good prose style." On the other hand it is not concerned with fake simplicity and the attempt to make written English colloquial. Nor does it even imply in every case preferring the Saxon word to the Latin one, though it does imply using the fewest and shortest words that will cover one's meaning. What is above all needed is to let the meaning choose the word, and not the

---

★One can cure oneself of the *not un-* formation by memorizing this sentence: *A not unblack dog was chasing a not unsmall rabbit across a not ungreen field.*

other way about. In prose, the worst thing one can do with words is to surrender to them. When you think of a concrete object, you think wordlessly, and then, if you want to describe the thing you have been visualizing you probably hunt about till you find the exact words that seem to fit it. When you think of something abstract you are more inclined to use words from the start, and unless you make a conscious effort to prevent it, the existing dialect will come rushing in and do the job for you, at the expense of blurring or even changing your meaning. Probably it is better to put off using words as long as possible and get one's meaning as clear as one can through pictures or sensations. Afterward one can choose—not simply *accept*—the phrases that will best cover the meaning, and then switch round and decide what impression one's words are likely to make on another person. This last effort of the mind cuts out all stale or mixed images, all prefabricated phrases, needless repetitions, and humbug and vagueness generally. But one can often be in doubt about the effect of a word or a phrase, and one needs rules that one can rely on when instinct fails. I think the following rules will cover most cases:

(i) Never use a metaphor, simile, or other figure of speech which you are used to seeing in print.

(ii) Never use a long word where a short one will do.

(ii) If it is possible to cut a word out, always cut it out.

(iv) Never use the passive where you can use the active.

(v) Never use a foreign phrase, a scientific word, or a jargon word if you can think of an everyday English equivalent.

(vi) Break any of these rules sooner than say anything outright barbarous.

These rules sound elementary, and so they are, but they demand a deep change of attitude in anyone who has grown used to writing in the style now fashionable. One could keep all of them and still write bad English, but one could not write the kind of stuff that I quoted in those five specimens at the beginning of this article.

18.   I have not here been considering the literary use of language, but merely language as an instrument for expressing and not for concealing or preventing thought. Stuart Chase and others have come near to claiming that all abstract words are meaningless, and have used this as a pretext for advocating a kind of political quietism. Since you don't know what Fascism is, how can you struggle against Fascism? One need not swallow such absurdities as this, but one ought to recognize that the present political chaos is connected with the decay

of language, and that one can probably bring about some improvement by starting at the verbal end. If you simplify your English, you are freed from the worst follies of orthodoxy. You cannot speak any of the necessary dialects, and when you make a stupid remark its stupidity will be obvious, even to yourself. Political language—and with variations this is true of all political parties, from Conservatives to Anarchists—is designed to make lies sound truthful and murder respectable, and to give an appearance of solidity to pure wind. One cannot change this all in a moment, but one can at least change one's own habits, and from time to time one can even, if one jeers loudly enough, send some worn-out and useless phrase—some *jackboot, Achilles' heel, hotbed, melting pot, acid test, veritable inferno,* or other lump of verbal refuse—into the dustbin where it belongs.

DISCUSSION: Faulty Diction

Diction can be faulty for the same reasons sentences are: imprecision, inflation, inappropriateness. These faults sometimes arise, as Orwell points out, because writers wish to disguise their thoughts and intentions. Faults also arise when, in seeking to avoid the looseness that can be found in speech, we depart too far from the usual speech patterns. The following suggestions may help you avoid awkward, monotonous, or overloaded sentences:

1. Avoid repeating a word if it is used to express a different meaning each time it occurs:

   We were present when the presentation was made.

2. Avoid repeating a word when the repetition can cause confusion or misunderstanding:

   The person who entered the room was not the individual we were expecting.

   Individual is a common synonym for *person,* but there is no reason to avoid using *person* a second time. Since *individual* has other meanings, the reader may think we intend one of these. In *Modern English Usage,* H. W. Fowler calls needless substitution of this kind "elegant variation."

3. Avoid deadwood—needless repetition and words and phrases for which there are simple, precise equivalents:

There are necessary skills writers need to make their ideas easy to grasp and comprehensible to each and every reader.

4. Avoid unnecessary euphemism, a mild substitute for a possibly shocking or offensive or blunt expression. Readers of Victorian novels routinely decipher such euphemisms as *ruined* and *betrayed* as descriptions of certain women; these readers, in turn, employ euphemisms that people fifty years from now will have to decipher. (We still use *limbs* to refer to a person's legs without realizing that the word was originally a euphemism.) We may employ euphemism to avoid giving offense. In a film about a young widow and her family living in New York City, offended children complain, "Momma! You went out with a *garbage man?*" This useful, but often despised, occupation may seem a little more desirable if any of the standard, and sometimes absurd, euphemisms are substituted for garbage man: *janitor, custodian, sanitary engineer.* The last of these can be confused with other occupations. And confusion and pain may result when unspecified qualities are made to seem sinister or contemptible by being left unnamed, as in the widely-used term *exceptional* to describe certain kinds of children. But are the words *slow* and *retarded* kinder to the less intelligent child or to the mentally deficient? What words should be used in speaking to them or about them? There is no easy advice to give: writers must be as honest, and at the same time as considerate of feelings, as they can.

5. Avoid clichés and bromides, which rob prose of conviction and vigor. A cliché is a phrase or saying that once may have been original and startling but has become trite through overuse: *honey of a girl, sweet as sugar, conspicuous by his absence, more sinned against than sinning.* A bromide is a dull platitude thought to be comforting: *It's the effort that counts, not the winning.*

6. Avoid mixed metaphors, which can make sentences unintentionally comic:

Blows to one's pride stick in the craw.

7. Avoid overlapping words, which obscure the meaning of a sentence. H. W. Fowler cites this example:

The *effect* of the tax is not likely to be *productive* of much real damage.

The italicized words mean the same thing.

8. Avoid the awkwardness that may result from too strict an adherence to the "rule" about ending sentences with prepositions. The following sentence came about because the writer wishes not to break this rule:

That's the ladder up which I climbed.

No one would speak such a sentence, but sentences like it are written in a mistaken effort to be correct.

QUESTIONS

1. How does the third example in Orwell's paragraph 3 help to explain the statement in paragraph 4 that "the concrete melts into the abstract"?
2. What visual image did *iron resolution* in paragraph 5 originally convey? What other dead metaphors can you cite, and what was the original significance?
3. Among the characteristic phrases cited in paragraph 6, Orwell might have included *in terms of.* Compare the following:

He explained his failure in terms of his attitude toward school.

Einstein was a creative thinker in physics because he thought in terms of mathematics instead of mystical concepts.

In which sentence is the phrase used less awkwardly, and why?
4. Why is the passage cited in the footnote to paragraph 8 "almost completely lacking in meaning"? Given Orwell's criticisms in paragraph 8, what would be the proper use of language in art criticism?
5. Compare the passage from Ecclesiastes quoted in paragraph 9 (King James Version) with modern renderings of it. Do you think these modern renderings are superior to Orwell's parody or to the King James version? Why?
6. "If you or I were told to write a few lines on the uncertainty of human fortunes," why would the writing come nearer to Orwell's parody than to the sentence from Ecclesiastes?
7. Given the assumptions Orwell makes in the whole essay, why are all issues "political issues"?
8. Orwell says in paragraph 17 that his concern has not been to promote a "standard English" or "to make written English colloquial." Explain what he means here. Has he not recommended the use of plain English words? What exceptions would he allow?
9. Rewrite the following sentences to eliminate the faults in diction:
   a. Her version of the story was not the rendering we had heard a week before.

b. He has more regard for his honor than he has respect for money.
c. There is a not uncommon way of expressing that idea.
d. She had unfortunate luck in dealing with the man who owned the premises where she lived and to whom she paid rent.
e. There is no candy in the jar there.
f. He is the man with whom she came with.
g. A free economy is the linchpin on which a progressive tariff policy must be built.
h. The result of the conference is certain to effect a change in the present tariff policy.

WRITING ASSIGNMENTS

1. Analyze a paragraph from the catalog of your college or university to discover its tone and judge the writing according to the criteria Orwell proposes.
2. Analyze a letter to the editor of a newspaper or magazine and indicate the self-impression the writer wishes to create, the qualities of the prose, and the virtues or defects of the letter.
3. Analyze three paragraphs from a current textbook in one of your courses to determine how much needless jargon is employed and how well the writing meets the standard of good writing Orwell proposes.
4. Analyze a published speech of a major political figure (see *The New York Times, Vital Speeches,* or *Congressional Record*). How honest is the use of language? Compare this speech with another by the same person. How consistent is he or she in use of language?

THOMAS H. MIDDLETON
Yay, Team?

1.   During the hearings concerning the confirmation of Representative Gerald Ford as Vice President in 1973, Ford commented, "You don't go out and tackle your quarterback once he has called the play," to which Senator Harrison A. Williams, Jr., countered, "If your quarterback was running toward the wrong goal line, wouldn't you tackle him?"

2.   "Yes," said Ford, "but that would be the exception rather than the rule."

3.   The football metaphor has become an accepted commonplace in recent years. In my opinion, it's a bad one. It's simply inept.

4.   Literate people are sensitive to jumbled metaphors. "The arms of the American Minuteman will be the scourge that stems the rising tide of vermin swooping down on the sleeping giant of outraged citizenry" collapses of its own disharmony, but "You don't go out and tackle your quarterback" may sound okay but it doesn't do the job.

5.   The trouble is that football, though it's big business, is still basically a game. It is not comparable to government. To use football as a metaphor for government—and particularly for war—is to over-simplify, perhaps with deadly results. It's easy to see why football terminology is seized upon by politicians. It has a simple, pragmatic, virile ring to it. And I suppose everyone who makes money from football, with the exception of some of the players, has in one way or another fostered the idea that football is contained warfare. "He hasn't used the bomb yet" means merely that the quarterback or the coach or whoever really calls the plays has not yet called for a long forward pass. And have you ever watched those films of the glorious moments from the preceding week's games?—slow-motion pictures of enormous bodies hurtling high in the air and landing on their heads to the ac-companiment of tympani and Götterdämmerung-oriented music. The narrator, with a deeply resonant voice, sounds like the same one who used to say, "But France's military might crumbled rapidly before the invincible onslaught of Hitler's Wehrmacht" over shots of thundering panzer divisions. During the Vietnam war, there were constant refer-ences to "our team" and "our quarterback," and I once heard a man urging a hawkish policy say, "When you're on your opponent's five-yard line, you don't punt!" He didn't mention that, in football, nei-ther do you saturate your opponent's city with high explosives from five miles in the air. Killing is equated with a game in this metaphor, and now there are a lot of people who deal with the fortunes of the American political system in the same terms.

6.   The hackneyed, timeworn old Ship of State works much better. There is a real matter of life and death in the fortunes of a ship. I'd feel more comfortable with a man who said, "You don't get rid of your captain once he's set his course" than with one who used quar-terbacks calling plays. If it's discovered that the captain's chosen course leads to Suicide Shoals, or that he and some of his fellow officers have been hacking holes in the hull below the waterline, it will occasion a greater sense of urgency than if the quarterback chooses to try for a field goal instead of a first down.

7.   I think we have a tendency to think of the world in terms of win-

ning, losing, happy endings, unhappy endings, and that sort of thing, as though the world were a game or a stage and all the men and women merely players. I'm a frequent listener to listener-response radio, as well as an ardent Letters-to-the-Editor fan. The other day I heard a woman who called in to one of the local talk stations say she'd like to live to be at least 100 "because I want to see how it all turns out."

8. World without end is a tough conception, but it doesn't help to picture the world in terms of opening kickoffs and final guns. In fact, thinking in terms of final guns, we just might *get* final guns.

QUESTIONS

1. Is Middleton saying that the football metaphor is inappropriate to the situations it has been applied to, or that it is dangerous to think about these situations in metaphorical terms?
2. Are there situations to which the football metaphor is applicable, in your opinion? How about a selling situation—for example selling shoes or used cars? Isn't the relationship between customer and salesman often an adversary relationship?

WRITING ASSIGNMENT

Analyze the use of metaphor in letters to the editor or in columns of your daily newspaper. Comment on their appropriateness, giving attention to points of similarity and dissimilarity.

RUSSELL BAKER
Little Red Riding Hood Revisited

In an effort to make the classics accessible to contemporary readers, I am translating them into the modern American language. Here is the translation of "Little Red Riding Hood":

Once upon a point in time, a small person named Little Red Riding Hood initiated plans for the preparation, delivery and transportation of foodstuffs to her grandmother, a senior citizen residing at a place of residence in a forest of indeterminate dimension.

In the process of implementing this program, her incursion into the forest was in mid-transportation process when it attained interface with an alleged perpetrator. This individual, a wolf, made inquiry as to the whereabouts of Little Red Riding Hood's goal as well as inferring that he was desirous of ascertaining the contents of Little Red Riding Hood's foodstuffs basket, and all that.

"It would be inappropriate to lie to me," the wolf said, displaying his huge jaw capability. Sensing that he was a mass of repressed hostility intertwined with acute alienation, she indicated.

"I see you indicating," the wolf said, "but what I don't see is whatever it is you're indicating at, you dig?"

Little Red Riding Hood indicated more fully, making one thing perfectly clear—to wit, that it was to her grandmother's residence and with a consignment of foodstuffs that her mission consisted of taking her to and with.

At this point in time the wolf moderated his rhetoric and proceeded to grandmother's residence. The elderly person was then subjected to the disadvantages of total consumption and transferred to residence in the perpetrator's stomach.

"That will raise the old woman's consciousness, the wolf said to himself. He was not a bad wolf, but only a victim of an oppressive society, a society that not only denied wolves' rights, but actually boasted of its capacity for keeping the wolf from the door. An interior malaise made itself manifest inside the wolf.

"Is that the national malaise I sense within my digestive tract?" wondered the wolf. "Or is it the old person seeking to retaliate for her consumption by telling wolf jokes to my duodenum?" It was time to make a judgment. The time was now, the hour had struck, the body lupine cried out for decision. The wolf was up to the challenge. He took two stomach powders right away and got into bed.

The wolf had adopted the abdominal-distress recovery posture when Little Red Riding Hood achieved his presence.

"Grandmother," she said, "your ocular implements are of an extraordinary order of magnitude."

"The purpose of this enlarged viewing capability," said the wolf "is to enable your image to register a more precise impression upon my sight systems."

"In reference to your ears," said Little Red Riding Hood, "it is noted with the deepest respect that far from being underprivileged, their elongation and enlargement appear to qualify you for unparalleled distinction."

"I hear you loud and clear, kid," said the wolf, "but what about these new choppers?"

"If it is not inappropriate," said Little Red Riding Hood, "it might be observed that with your new miracle masticating products you may even be able to chew taffy again."

This observation was followed by the adoption of an aggressive posture on the part of the wolf and the assertion that it was also possible for him, due to the high efficiency ratio of his jaw, to consume little persons, plus, as he stated, his firm determination to do so at once without delay and with all due process and propriety, notwithstanding the fact that the ingestion of one entire grandmother had already provided twice his daily recommended cholesterol intake.

There ensued flight by Little Red Riding Hood accompanied by pursuit in respect to the wolf and a subsequent intervention on the part of a third party, heretofore unnoted in the record.

Due to the firmness of the intervention, the wolf's stomach underwent ax-assisted aperture with the result that Red Riding Hood's grandmother was enabled to be removed with only minor discomfort.

The wolf's indigestion was immediately alleviated with such effectiveness that he signed a contract with the intervening third party to perform with grandmother in a television commercial demonstrating the swiftness of this dramatic relief for stomach discontent.

"I'm going to be on television," cried grandmother.

And they all joined her happily in crying, "What a phenomena!"

QUESTIONS

1. The faddish language Baker parodies reflects faddish ideas. Here is one example: "An interior malaise made itself manifest inside the wolf." What current attitude toward human predators is Baker satirizing? How does the language help him to satirize the idea?
2. Red Riding Hood prefers the farfetched to the simple, as in the expression "ocular implements." What other examples can you cite in the essay?
3. What examples of repetitious phrasing and sentence padding do you find?
4. What kind of advertising language is Baker satirizing toward the end of his version?
5. What is the difference between the wolf's language and Red Riding Hood's? What does the wolf's language tell you about his personality and view of the world?

6. What other ideas is Baker satirizing in the course of his telling of the story?

WRITING ASSIGNMENT

Rewrite another fairy tale in the modish language of advertising or other contemporary jargons and styles. Let your choice of jargon and style make a point—or several points—as Baker's telling of "Little Red Riding Hood" does.

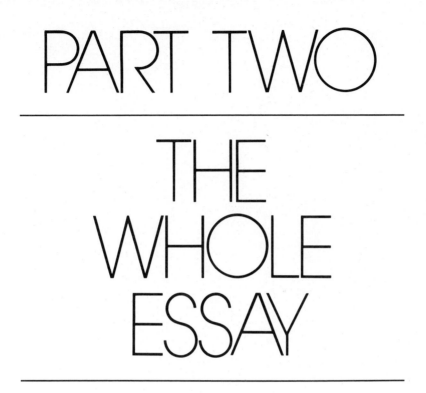

PART TWO

THE WHOLE ESSAY

EXPOSITION

Thesis

PEGGY AND PIERRE STREIT
A Well in India

1. The hot dry season in India. . . . A corrosive wind drives rivulets of sand across the land; torpid animals stand at the edge of dried-up water holes. The earth is cracked and in the rivers the sluggish, falling waters have exposed the sludge of the mud flats. Throughout the land the thoughts of men turn to water. And in the village of Rampura these thoughts are focused on the village well.

2. It is a simple concrete affair, built upon the hard earth worn by the feet of five hundred villagers. It is surmounted by a wooden structure over which ropes, tied to buckets, are lowered to the black, placid depths twenty feet below. Fanning out from the well are the huts of the villagers—their walls white from sun, their thatched roofs thick with dust blown in from the fields.

3. At the edge of the well is a semi-circle of earthen pots and, crouched at some distance behind them, a woman. She is an untouchable—a sweeper in Indian parlance—a scavenger of the village. She cleans latrines, disposes of dead animals and washes drains. She also delivers village babies, for this—like all her work—is considered unclean by most of village India.

4. Her work—indeed, her very presence—is considered polluting, and since there is no well for untouchables in Rampura, her water jars must be filled by upper-caste villagers.

5. There are dark shadows under her eyes and the flesh has fallen

away from her neck, for she, like her fellow outcastes, is at the end of a bitter struggle. And if, in her narrow world, shackled by tradition and hemmed in by poverty, she had been unaware of the power of the water of the well at whose edge she waits—she knows it now.

6.   Shanti, 30 years old, has been deserted by her husband, and supports her three children. Like her ancestors almost as far back as history records, she has cleaned the refuse from village huts and lanes. Hers is a life of inherited duties as well as inherited rights. She serves, and her work calls for payment of one chapatty—a thin wafer of unleavened bread—a day from each of the thirty families she cares for.

7.   But this is the hiatus between harvests; the oppressive lull before the burst of monsoon rains; the season of flies and dust, heat and disease, querulous voices and frayed tempers—and the season of want. There is little food in Rampura for anyone, and though Shanti's chores have continued as before, she has received only six chapatties a day for her family—starvation wages.

8.   Ten days ago she revolted. Driven by desperation, she defied an elemental law of village India. She refused to make her sweeper's rounds—refused to do the work tradition and religion had assigned her. Shocked at her audacity, but united in desperation, the village's six other sweeper families joined in her protest.

9.   Word of her action spread quickly across the invisible line that separates the untouchables' huts from the rest of the village. As the day wore on and the men returned from the fields, they gathered at the well—the heart of the village—and their voices rose, shrill with outrage: a *sweeper* defying them all! Shanti, a sweeper *and* a woman challenging a system that had prevailed unquestioned for centuries! Their indignation spilled over. It was true, perhaps, that the sweepers had not had their due. But that was no fault of the upper caste. No fault of theirs that sun and earth and water had failed to produce the food by which they could fulfill their obligations. So, to bring the insurgents to heel, they employed their ultimate weapon; the earthen water jars of the village untouchables would remain empty until they returned to work. For the sweepers of Rampura the well had run dry.

10.   No water: thirst, in the heat, went unslaked. The embers of the hearth were dead, for there was no water for cooking. The crumbling walls of outcaste huts went untended, for there was no water for repairs. There was no fuel, for the fires of the village were fed with dung mixed with water and dried. The dust and the sweat and the filth of their lives congealed on their skins and there it stayed, while life in the rest of the village—within sight of the sweepers—flowed on.

11. The day began and ended at the well. The men, their dhotis wrapped about their loins, congregated at the water's edge in the hushed post-dawn, their small brass water jugs in hand, their voices mingling in quiet conversation as they rinsed their bodies and brushed their teeth. The buffaloes were watered, their soft muzzles lingering in the buckets before they were driven off to the fields. Then came the women, their brass pots atop their heads, to begin the ritual of water drawing: the careful lowering of the bucket in the well, lest it come loose from the rope; the gratifying splash as it touched the water; the maneuvering to make it sink; the squeal of rope against wooden pulley as it ascended. The sun rose higher. Clothes were beaten clean on the rocks surrounding the well as the women gossiped. A traveler from a near-by road quenched his thirst from a villager's urn. Two little boys, hot and bored, dropped pebbles into the water and waited for their hollow splash, far below.

12. As the afternoon wore on and the sun turned orange through the dust, the men came back from the fields. They doused the parched, cracked hides of their water buffaloes and murmured contentedly, themselves, as the water coursed over their own shoulders and arms. And finally, as twilight closed in, came the evening procession of women, stately, graceful, their bare feet moving smoothly over the earth, their full skirts swinging about their ankles, the heavy brass pots once again balanced on their heads.

13. The day was ended and life was as it always was—almost. Only the fetid odor of accumulated refuse and the assertive buzz of flies attested to strife in the village. For, while tradition and religion decreed that sweepers must clean, it also ordained that the socially blessed must not. Refuse lay where it fell and rotted.

14. The strain of the water boycott was beginning to tell on the untouchables. For two days they had held their own. But on the third their thin reserve of flesh had fallen away. Movements were slower; voices softer; minds dull. More and more the desultory conversation turned to the ordinary; the delicious memory of sliding from the back of a wallowing buffalo into a pond; the feel of bare feet in wet mud; the touch of fresh water on parched lips; the anticipation of monsoon rains.

15. One by one the few tools they owned were sold for food. A week passed, and on the ninth day two sweeper children were down with fever. On the tenth day Shanti crossed the path that separated outcaste from upper caste and walked through familiar, winding alleyways to one of the huts she served.

16. "Your time is near," she told the young, expectant mother. "Tell your man to leave his sickle home when he goes to the fields. I've had to sell mine." (It is the field sickle that cuts the cord of newborn babies in much of village India.) Shanti, the instigator of the insurrection, had resumed her ancestral duties; the strike was broken. Next morning, as ever, she waited at the well. Silently, the procession of upper-caste women approached. They filled their jars to the brim and without a word they filled hers.

17. She lifted the urns to her head, steadied them, and started back to her quarters—back to a life ruled by the powers that still rule most of the world: not the power of atoms or electricity, nor the power of alliances or power blocs, but the elemental powers of hunger, of disease, of tradition—and of water.

DISCUSSION: Thesis

The *thesis* of an essay is its central or controlling idea, the proposition or chief argument—the point of the essay. The topic sentence of a paragraph may be a full or partial statement of the controlling idea: the thesis is always a full statement of it. Where the thesis appears in an essay depends on what writers assume about their audience. If they know the audience well and believe no introduction to the thesis is necessary, they may state it in the very first sentence. The Federalist papers of Hamilton, Jay, and Madison often start in this way:

> A firm Union will be of the utmost moment of the peace and liberty of the States, as a barrier against domestic faction and insurrection.—Alexander Hamilton, *The Federalist* No. 9

So do many newspaper editorials. Most writers, however, prefer to build to the thesis, stating it partially or fully later in the introductory paragraphs. If the thesis needs background and extended discussion to be understood, or perhaps is so controversial that it is preferable to build to it slowly, the writer may position it at the end of the essay. The following opening sentences of an essay state the subject only—the topics to be explored:

> Saints should always be judged guilty until they are proved innocent, but the tests that have to be applied to them are not, of course, the same in all cases. In Gandhi's case the questions one feels inclined to ask are: to what extent was Gandhi moved by vanity—by the consciousness of himself as a humble, naked old man, sitting on a praying mat and shaking empires by sheer spir-

itual power—and to what extent did he compromise his own principles by entering politics, which of their nature are inseparable from coercion and fraud?—George Orwell, "Reflections on Gandhi"

Important terms need to be defined, attitudes clarified, and a climate of opinion and the world of Gandhi portrayed before Orwell can state his thesis fully.

In some essays the writer leads the reader to draw conclusions from the details provided and their presentation. In these instances the thesis is said to be *implicit.*

Considerations of audience have much to do with where the thesis appears in the essay. Such rhetorical considerations also influence the uses made of the beginning and the ending of the essay, its tone and transitions, its order of ideas, and its unity and style.

QUESTIONS

1. The Streits build to a statement of their thesis at the end of paragraph 5. Why is it necessary to portray the world of the untouchable before stating the thesis?
2. Where in the essay is the thesis restated? Is the restatement more informative or detailed than the original statement of it?
3. What is the attitude of the authors toward the world they portray and the fate of Shanti? Do they seem to be taking sides?
4. Is it important to the thesis that Shanti is a woman? Are the authors concerned with her as a woman, in addition to their concern for her as an untouchable?
5. Is the concern of the essay equally with the power of water and the power of tradition? Or are these considerations subordinate to the portrayal of the untouchable and the courage shown?
6. Are we given a motive directly for what Shanti does—or is the motive implied?
7. How are transitions made through the seventeen short paragraphs?

WRITING ASSIGNMENTS

1. Develop an idea relating to the power of tradition and illustrate it from personal experience and observation. Provide enough background so that your reader understands why the tradition is important to the people who observe it.
2. Describe a conflict between you and your parents or school officials or between a person and a group of some sort. Explain how the conflict arises from a basic difference in attitude, ideas, or feel-

ings—a difference that reveals something important about you and the other people involved.

GEORGE ORWELL

Shooting an Elephant

1.   In Moulmein, in lower Burma, I was hated by large numbers of people—the only time in my life that I have been important enough for this to happen to me. I was sub-divisional police officer of the town, and in an aimless, petty kind of way anti-European feeling was very bitter. No one had the guts to raise a riot, but if a European woman went through the bazaars alone somebody would probably spit betel juice over her dress. As a police officer I was an obvious target and was baited whenever it seemed safe to do so. When a nimble Burman tripped me up on the football field and the referee (another Burman) looked the other way, the crowd yelled with hideous laughter. This happened more than once. In the end the sneering yellow faces of young men that met me everywhere, the insults hooted after me when I was at a safe distance, got badly on my nerves. The young Buddhist priests were the worst of all. There were several thousands of them in the town and none of them seemed to have anything to do except stand on street corners and jeer at Europeans.

2.   All this was perplexing and upsetting. For at that time I had already made up my mind that imperialism was an evil thing and the sooner I chucked up my job and got out of it the better. Theoretically—and secretly, of course—I was all for the Burmese and all against their oppressors, the British. As for the job I was doing, I hated it more bitterly than I can perhaps make clear. In a job like that you see the dirty work of Empire at close quarters. The wretched prisoners huddling in the stinking cages of the lock-ups, the gray, cowed faces of the long-term convicts, the scarred buttocks of the men who had been flogged with bamboos—all these oppressed me with an intolerable sense of guilt. But I could get nothing into perspective. I was young and ill educated and I had had to think out my problems in the utter silence that is imposed on every Englishman in the East. I did not even know that the British Empire is dying, still less did I know that it is a great deal better than the younger empires that are going to

supplant it. All I knew was that I was stuck between my hatred of the empire I served and my rage against the evil-spirited little beasts who tried to make my job impossible. With one part of my mind I thought of the British Raj as an unbreakable tyranny, as something clamped down, in *saecula saeculorum*, upon the will of prostrate peoples; with another part I thought that the greatest joy in the world would be to drive a bayonet into a Buddhist priest's guts. Feelings like these are the normal by-products of imperialism; ask any Anglo-Indian official, if you can catch him off duty.

3. One day something happened which in a roundabout way was enlightening. It was a tiny incident in itself, but it gave me a better glimpse than I had had before of the real nature of imperialism—the real motives for which despotic governments act. Early one morning the sub-inspector at a police station the other end of the town rang me up on the 'phone and said that an elephant was ravaging the bazaar. Would I please come and do something about it? I did not know what I could do, but I wanted to see what was happening and I got on to a pony and started out. I took my rifle, an old .44 Winchester and much too small to kill an elephant, but I thought the noise might be useful *in terrorem*. Various Burmans stopped me on the way and told me about the elephant's doings. It was not, of course, a wild elephant, but a tame one which had gone "must." It had been chained up, as tame elephants always are when their attack of "must" is due, but on the previous night it had broken its chain and escaped. Its mahout, the only person who could manage it when it was in that state, had set out in pursuit, but had taken the wrong direction and was now twelve hours' journey away, and in the morning the elephant had suddenly reappeared in the town. The Burmese population had no weapons and were quite helpless against it. It had already destroyed somebody's bamboo hut, killed a cow and raided some fruit-stalls and devoured the stock; also it had met the municipal rubbish van and, when the driver jumped out and took to his heels, had turned the van over and inflicted violences upon it.

4. The Burmese sub-inspector and some Indian constables were waiting for me in the quarter where the elephant had been seen. It was a very poor quarter, a labyrinth of squalid bamboo huts, thatched with palm-leaf, winding all over a steep hillside. I remember that it was a cloudy, stuffy morning at the beginning of the rains. We began questioning the people as to where the elephant had gone and, as usual, failed to get any definite information. That is invariably the case in the East; a story always sounds clear enough at a distance, but

the nearer you get to the scene of events the vaguer it becomes. Some of the people said that the elephant had gone in one direction, some said that he had gone in another, some professed not even to have heard of any elephant. I had almost made up my mind that the whole story was a pack of lies, when we heard yells a little distance away. There was a loud, scandalized cry of "Go away, child! Go away this instant!" and an old woman with a switch in her hand came round the corner of a hut, violently shooing away a crowd of naked children. Some more women followed, clicking their tongues and exclaiming; evidently there was something that the children ought not to have seen. I rounded the hut and saw a man's dead body sprawling in the mud. He was an Indian, a black Dravidian coolie, almost naked, and he could not have been dead many minutes. The people said that the elephant had come suddenly upon him round the corner of the hut, caught him with its trunk, put its foot on his back and ground him into the earth. This was the rainy season and the ground was soft, and his face had scored a trench a foot deep and a couple of yards long. He was lying on his belly with arms crucified and head sharply twisted to one side. His face was coated with mud, the eyes wide open, the teeth bared and grinning with an expression of unendurable agony. (Never tell me, by the way, that the dead look peaceful. Most of the corpses I have seen looked devilish.) The friction of the great beast's foot had stripped the skin from his back as neatly as one skins a rabbit. As soon as I saw the dead man I sent an orderly to a friend's house nearby to borrow an elephant rifle. I had already sent back the pony, not wanting it to go mad with fright and throw me if it smelt the elephant.

5.   The orderly came back in a few minutes with a rifle and five cartridges, and meanwhile some Burmans had arrived and told us that the elephant was in the paddy fields below, only a few hundred yards away. As I started forward practically the whole population of the quarter flocked out of the houses and followed me. They had seen the rifle and were all shouting excitedly that I was going to shoot the elephant. They had not shown much interest in the elephant when he was merely ravaging their homes, but it was different now that he was going to be shot. It was a bit of fun to them, as it would be to an English crowd; besides they wanted the meat. It made me vaguely uneasy. I had no intention of shooting the elephant—I had merely sent for the rifle to defend myself if necessary—and it is always unnerving to have a crowd following you. I marched down the hill, looking and feeling a fool, with the rifle over my shoulder and an ever-growing

army of people jostling at my heels. At the bottom, when you got away from the huts, there was a metalled road and beyond that a miry waste of paddy fields a thousand yards across, not yet ploughed but soggy from the first rains and dotted with coarse grass. The elephant was standing eight yards from the road, his left side toward us. He took not the slightest notice of the crowd's approach. He was tearing up bunches of grass, beating them against his knees to clean them, and stuffing them into his mouth.

6.   I had halted on the road. As soon as I saw the elephant I knew with perfect certainty that I ought not to shoot him. It is a serious matter to shoot a working elephant—it is comparable to destroying a huge and costly piece of machinery—and obviously one ought not to do it if it can possibly be avoided. And at that distance, peacefully eating, the elephant looked no more dangerous than a cow. I thought then and I think now that his attack of "must" was already passing off; in which case he would merely wander harmlessly about until the mahout came back and caught him. Moreover, I did not in the least want to shoot him. I decided that I would watch him for a little while to make sure that he did not turn savage again, and then go home.

7.   But at that moment I glanced round at the crowd that had followed me. It was an immense crowd, two thousand at the least and growing every minute. It blocked the road for a long distance on either side. I looked at the sea of yellow faces above the garish clothes—faces all happy and excited over this bit of fun, all certain that the elephant was going to be shot. They were watching me as they would watch a conjurer about to perform a trick. They did not like me, but with the magical rifle in my hands I was momentarily worth watching. And suddenly I realized that I should have to shoot the elephant after all. The people expected it of me and I had got to do it; I could feel their two thousand wills pressing me forward, irresistibly. And it was at this moment, as I stood there with the rifle in my hands, that I first grasped the hollowness, the futility of the white man's dominion in the East. Here was I, the white man with his gun, standing in front of the unarmed native crowd—seemingly the leading actor of the piece; but in reality I was only an absurd puppet pushed to and fro by the will of those yellow faces behind. I perceived in this moment that when the white man turns tyrant it is his own freedom that he destroys. He becomes a sort of hollow, posing dummy, the conventionalized figure of a sahib. For it is the condition of his rule that he shall spend his life in trying to impress the "natives," and so in every crisis he has got to do what the "natives" expect of him. He wears a

mask, and his face grows to fit it. I had got to shoot the elephant. I had committed myself to ding it when I sent for the rifle. A sahib has got to act like a sahib; he has got to appear resolute, to know his own mind and do definite things. To come all that way, rifle in hand, with two thousand people marching at my heels, and then to trail feebly away, having done nothing—no, that was impossible. The crowd would laugh at me. And my whole life, every white man's life in the East, was one long struggle not to be laughed at.

8.   But I did not want to shoot the elephant. I watched him beating his bunch of grass against his knees with that preoccupied grandmotherly air that elephants have. It seemed to me that it would be murder to shoot him. At that age I was not squeamish about killing animals, but I had never shot an elephant and never wanted to. (Somehow it always seems worse to kill a *large* animal.) Besides, there was the beast's owner to be considered. Alive, the elephant was worth at least a hundred pounds; dead, he would only be worth the value of his tusks, five pounds, possibly. But I had got to act quickly. I turned to some experienced-looking Burmans who had been there when we arrived, and asked them how the elephant had been behaving. They all said the same thing: he took no notice of you if you left him alone, but he might charge if you went too close to him.

9.   It was perfectly clear to me what I ought to do. I ought to walk up to within, say, twenty-five yards of the elephant and test his behavior. If he charged, I could shoot; if he took no notice of me, it would be safe to leave him until the mahout came back. But also I knew that I was going to do no such thing. I was a poor shot with a rifle and the ground was soft mud into which one would sink at every step. If the elephant charged and I missed him, I should have about as much chance as a toad under a steam-roller. But even then I was not thinking particularly of my own skin, only of the watchful yellow faces behind. For at that moment, with the crowd watching me, I was not afraid in the ordinary sense, as I would have been if I had been alone. A white man mustn't be frightened in front of "natives"; and so, in general, he isn't frightened. The sole thought in my mind was that if anything went wrong those two thousand Burmans would see me pursued, caught, trampled on, and reduced to a grinning corpse like that Indian up the hill. And if that happened it was quite probable that some of them would laugh. That would never do. There was only one alternative. I shoved the cartridges into the magazine and lay down on the road to get a better aim.

10.   The crowd grew very still, and a deep, low, happy sigh, as of peo-

ple who see the theater curtain go up at last, breathed from innumer-
able throats. They were going to have their bit of fun after all. The rifle
was a beautiful German thing with crosshair sights. I did not then
know that in shooting an elephant one would shoot to cut an imaginary bar running from ear-hole to ear-hole. I ought, therefore, as the
elephant was sideways on, to have aimed straight at his ear-hole; actually I aimed several inches in front of this, thinking the brain would
be further forward.

11.   When I pulled the trigger I did not hear the bang or feel the
kick—one never does when a shot goes home—but I heard the devilish roar of glee that went up from the crowd. In that instant, in too
short a time, one would have thought, even for the bullet to get there,
a mysterious, terrible change had come over the elephant. He neither
stirred nor fell, but every line of his body had altered. He looked suddenly stricken, shrunken, immensely old, as though the frightful impact of the bullet had paralyzed him without knocking him down. At
last, after what seemed a long time—it might have been five seconds, I
dare say—he sagged flabbily to his knees. His mouth slobbered. An
enormous senility seemed to have settled upon him. One could have
imagined him thousands of years old. I fired again into the same spot.
At the second shot he did not collapse but climbed with desperate
slowness to his feet and stood weakly upright, with legs sagging and
head drooping. I fired a third time. That was the shot that did for
him. You could see the agony of it jolt his whole body and knock the
last remnant of strength from his legs. But in falling he seemed for a
moment to rise, for as his hind legs collapsed beneath him he seemed
to tower upward like a huge rock toppling, his trunk reaching sky-
ward like a tree. He trumpeted, for the first and only time. And then
down he came, his belly toward me, with a crash that seemed to shake
the ground even where I lay.

12.   I got up. The Burmans were already racing past me across the
mud. It was obvious that the elephant would never rise again, but he
was not dead. He was breathing very rhythmically with long rattling
gasps, his great mound of a side painfully rising and falling. His
mouth was wide open—I could see far down into caverns of pale pink
throat. I waited a long time for him to die, but his breathing did not
weaken. Finally I fired my two remaining shots into the spot where I
thought his heart must be. The thick blood welled out of him like red
velvet, but still he did not die. His body did not even jerk when the
shots hit him, the tortured breathing continued without a pause. He
was dying, very slowly and in great agony, but in some world remote

from me where not even a bullet could damage him further. I felt that I had got to put an end to that dreadful noise. It seemed dreadful to see the great beast lying there, powerless to move and yet powerless to die, and not even to be able to finish him. I sent back for my small rifle and poured shot after shot into his heart and down his throat. They seemed to make no impression. The tortured gasps continued as steadily as the ticking of a clock.

13. In the end I could not stand it any longer and went away. I heard later that it took him half an hour to die. Burmans were bringing dahs and baskets even before I left, and I was told they had stripped his body almost to the bones by the afternoon.

14. Afterward, of course, there were endless discussions about the shooting of the elephant. The owner was furious, but he was only an Indian and could do nothing. Besides, legally I had done the right thing, for a mad elephant has to be killed, like a mad dog, if its owner fails to control it. Among the Europeans opinion was divided. The older men said I was right, the younger men said it was a damn shame to shoot an elephant for killing a coolie, because an elephant was worth more than any damn Coringhee coolie. And afterward I was very glad that the coolie had been killed; it put me legally in the right and it gave me a sufficient pretext for shooting the elephant. I often wondered whether any of the others grasped that I had done it solely to avoid looking a fool.

QUESTIONS

1. Orwell states in paragraph 3: "One day something happened which in a roundabout way was enlightening. It was a tiny incident in itself, but it gave me a better glimpse than I had had before of the real nature of imperialism—the real motives for which despotic governments act." The incident, in all its particularity, reveals the psychology of the imperialist ruler. What effect do the atmosphere (the stuffy, cloudy weather) and the behavior of the Burmans and their attitude toward the elephant have on this psychology? Why is the dead coolie described in detail in paragraph 4? Why is the shooting of the elephant described in detail in paragraph 11? In general, how does the incident reveal the motives Orwell mentions?

2. The incident reveals more than just the motives of the imperialist ruler: it reveals much about mob and crisis psychology and the man in the middle. What does it reveal specifically?

3. Where in the essay is the thesis stated, and how do you account for its placement?

4. The exactness of the diction contributes greatly to the development of the thesis, for Orwell does not merely *tell us,* he makes us see. In paragraph 11, for example, he states: ". . . I heard the devilish roar of *glee* that went up from the crowd." He might have chosen *laughter, hilarity,* or *mirth* to describe the behavior of the crowd, but *glee* is the exact word because it connotes something that the other three words do not—malice. And the elephant *"sagged* flabbily to his knees," not *dropped* or *sank,* because *sagged* connotes weight and, in the context of the passage, age. What does Orwell mean in the same paragraph by "His mouth slobbered" and "An enormous senility seemed to have settled upon him"? In paragraph 12 why *"caverns* of pale pink throat" rather than *depths?* In paragraph 4 why is the corpse *grinning* rather than *smiling?* (Consult the synonym listings in your dictionary, or compare definitions.)

WRITING ASSIGNMENTS

1. Illustrate the last sentence of the essay from your own experience. Build the essay to the moment when you acted to avoid looking like a fool. Make your reader see and feel what you saw and felt.
2. Orwell states: "And my whole life, every white man's life in the East, was one long struggle not to be laughed at." Drawing on your experience and observation, discuss what you see as the feelings and motives of people charged with enforcing rules of some sort— perhaps hall monitors in high school, or lifeguards at a swimming pool, or supervisors at a playground, or babysitters. Use your discussion to draw a conclusion, as Orwell does.

ERIC SEVAREID

Velva, North Dakota

1. My home town has changed in these thirty years of the American story. It is changing now, will go on changing as America changes. Its biography, I suspect, would read much the same as that of all other home towns. Depression and war and prosperity have all left their marks; modern science, modern tastes, manners, philosophies, fears and ambitions have touched my town as indelibly as they have touched New York or Panama City.

2.   Sights have changed: there is a new precision about street and home, a clearing away of chicken yards, cow barns, pigeon-crested cupolas, weed lots and coulees, the dim and secret adult-free rendez-vous of boys. An intricate metal "jungle gym" is a common backyard sight, the sack swing uncommon. There are wide expanses of clear windows, designed to let in the parlor light, fewer ornamental windows of colored glass designed to keep it out. Attic and screen porch are slowly vanishing and lovely shades of pastel are painted upon new houses, tints that once would have embarrassed farmer and merchant alike.

3.   Sounds have changed; I heard not once the clopping of a horse's hoof, nor the mourn of a coyote. I heard instead the shriek of brakes, the heavy throbbing of the once-a-day Braniff airliner into Minot, the shattering sirens born of war, the honk of a diesel locomotive which surely cannot call to faraway places the heart of a wakeful boy like the old steam whistle in the night. You can walk down the streets of my town now and hear from open windows the intimate voices of the Washington commentators in casual converse on the great affairs of state; but you cannot hear on Sunday morning the singing in Nor-wegian of the Lutheran hymns; the old country seems now part of a world left long behind and the old-country accents grow fainter in the speech of my Velva neighbors.

4.   The people have not changed, but the *kinds* of people have changed: there is no longer an official, certified town drunk, no longer a "Crazy John," spitting his worst epithet, "rotten chicken legs," as you hurriedly passed him by. People so sick are now sent to places of proper care. No longer is there an official town joker, like the druggist MacKnight, who would spot a customer in the front of the store, have him called to the phone, then slip to the phone behind the prescription case, and imitate the man's wife to perfection with orders to bring home more bread and sausage and Cream of Wheat. No longer anyone like the early attorney J. L. Lee, who sent fabulous dispatches to that fabulous tabloid, the *Chicago Blade,* such as his story of the wild man captured on the prairie and chained to the wall in the drugstore base-ment. (This, surely, was Velva's first notoriety; inquiries came from anthropologists all over the world.)

5.   No, the "characters" are vanishing in Velva, just as they are vanishing in our cities, in business, in politics. The "well-rounded, socially integrated" personality that the progressive schoolteachers are so obsessed with is increasing rapidly, and I am not at all sure that this is good. Maybe we need more personalities with knobs and handles

and rugged lumps of individuality. They may not make life more smooth; more interesting they surely make it.

6. They eat differently in Velva now; there are frozen fruits and sea food and exotic delicacies we only read about in novels in those meat-and-potato days. They dress differently. The hard white collars of the businessmen are gone with the shiny alpaca coats. There are comfortable tweeds now, and casual blazers with a touch in their colors of California, which seems so close in time and distance.

7. It is distance and time that have changed the most and worked the deepest changes in Velva's life. The telephone, the car, the smooth highway, radio and television are consolidating the entities of our country. The county seat of Towner now seems no closer than the state capital of Bismarck; the voices and concerns of Presidents, French premiers and Moroccan pashas are no farther away than the portable radio on Aunt Jessey's kitchen table. The national news magazines are stacked each week in Harold Anderson's drugstore beside the new soda fountain, and the excellent *Minot Daily News* smells hot from the press each afternoon.

8. Consolidation. The nearby hamlets of Sawyer and Logan and Voltaire had their own separate banks and papers and schools in my days of dusty buggies and Model Ts marooned in the snowdrifts. Now these hamlets are dying. A bright yellow bus takes the Voltaire kids to Velva each day for high school. Velva has grown—from 800 to 1,300—because the miners from the Truax coal mine can commute to their labors each morning and the nearby farmers can live in town if they choose. Minot has tripled in size to 30,000. Once the "Magic City" was a distant and splendid Baghdad, visited on special occasions long prepared for. Now it is a twenty-five minute commuter's jump away. So P. W. Miller and Jay Louis Monicken run their businesses in Minot but live on in their old family homes in Velva. So Ray Michelson's two girls on his farm to the west drive up each morning to their jobs as maids in Minot homes. Aunt Jessey said, "Why, Saturday night I counted sixty-five cars just between here and Sawyer, all going up to the show in Minot."

9. The hills are prison battlements no longer; the prairies no heart-sinking barrier, but a passageway free as the swelling ocean, inviting you to sail home and away at your whim and your leisure. (John and Helen made an easy little jaunt of 700 miles that week-end to see their eldest daughter in Wyoming.)

10. Consolidation. Art Kumm's bank serves a big region now; its assets are $2,000,000 to $3,000,000 instead of the $200,000 or

$300,000 in my father's day. Eighteen farms near Velva are under three ownerships now. They calculate in sections; "acres" is an almost forgotten term. Aunt Jessey owns a couple of farms, and she knows they are much better run. "It's no longer all take out and no put in," she said. "Folks strip farm now; they know all about fertilizers. They care for it and they'll hand on the land in good shape." The farmers gripe about their cash income, and not without reason at the moment, but they will admit that life is good compared with those days of drought and foreclosure, manure banked against the house for warmth, the hand pump frozen at 30 below and the fitful kerosene lamp on the kitchen table. Electrification has done much of this, eased back-breaking chores that made their wives old as parchment at forty, brought life and music and the sound of human voices into their parlors at night.

11.   And light upon the prairie. "From the hilltop," said Aunt Jessey, "the farms look like stars at night."

12.   Many politicians deplore the passing of the old family-size farm, but I am not so sure. I saw around Velva a release from what was like slavery to the tyrannical soil, release from the ignorance that darkens the soul and from the loneliness that corrodes it. In this generation my Velva friends have rejoined the general American society that their pioneering fathers left behind when they first made the barren trek in the days of the wheat rush. As I sit here in Washington writing this, I can feel their nearness. I never felt it before save in my dreams.

13.   But now I must ask myself: Are they nearer to one another? And the answer is no; yet I am certain that this is good. The shrinking of time and distance has made contrast and relief available to their daily lives. They do not know one another quite so well because they are not so much obliged to. I know that democracy rests upon social discipline, which in turn rests upon personal discipline; passions checked, hard words withheld, civic tasks accepted, work well done, accountings honestly rendered. The old-fashioned small town was this discipline in its starkest, most primitive form; without this discipline the small town would have blown itself apart.

14.   For personal and social neuroses festered under this hard scab of conformity. There was no place to go, no place to let off steam; few dared to voice unorthodox ideas, read strange books, admire esoteric art or publicly write or speak of their dreams and their soul's longings. The world was not "too much with us," the world was too little with us and we were too much with one another.

15.   The door to the world stands open now, inviting them to leave anytime they wish. It is the simple fact of the open door that makes all

the difference; with its opening the stale air rushed out. So, of course, the people themselves do not have to leave, because, as the stale air went out, the fresh air came in.

16.   Human nature is everywhere the same. He who is not forced to help his neighbor for his own existence will not only give him help, but his true good will as well. Minot and its hospital are now close at hand, but the people of Velva put their purses together, built their own clinic and homes for the two young doctors they persuaded to come and live among them. Velva has no organized charity, but when a farmer falls ill, his neighbors get in his crop; if a townsman has a financial catastrophe his personal friends raise a fund to help him out. When Bill's wife, Ethel, lay dying so long in the Minot hospital and nurses were not available, Helen and others took their turns driving up there just to sit with her so she would know in her gathering dark that friends were at hand.

17.   It is personal freedom that makes us better persons, and they are freer in Velva now. There is no real freedom without privacy, and a resident of my home town can be a private person much more than he could before. People are able to draw at least a little apart from one another. In drawing apart, they gave their best human instincts room for expansion.

QUESTIONS

1. Where does Sevareid indicate his attitude toward his home town? What is his thesis?
2. How does the selection of detail in the whole essay support the dominating impression Sevareid creates of the town in his opening paragraph? Is any of this detail unrelated to this impression?
3. What is the tone of the comment on the story of the wild man, and how is the comment related to the thesis?
4. How does Sevareid emphasize the causes of the change in life in Velva? Does he indicate a main cause?
5. What does Sevareid mean by the statement in paragraph 13, "without this discipline the small town would have blown itself apart"?
6. Sevareid points up a series of paradoxes toward the end. What are these, and what do they contribute to the tone of the conclusion?

WRITING ASSIGNMENTS

1. Analyze the shifts in tone and relate these to Sevareid's thesis. Analyze also how Sevareid introduces his thesis and keeps it before the reader.

2. Describe the changes that have occurred in the neighborhood in which you grew up and discuss the reasons for these changes.

TRACEY EARLY

Sounds That Bring Us Closer Together

1. Why is that woman laughing so early in the morning? I keep trying to put myself in her place, but she always surprises me. From somewhere else in the building, sound waves echoing around the courtyard to disguise their origin, comes a brutal argument. So I must wonder what makes that couple fight so furiously and, even more, what makes them continue living together despite their rage.

2. I live in an apartment, but not totally apart. I can tell a body not to enter my space, but I cannot command the sound waves. They enter as they will. And not only that, but they force their way into my head and, with no regard for my own volition, tie me into the lives of my neighbors.

3. Accosted also by sounds from the street, I am pulled into the activity there. A youngster tries to call his friend down from a high floor, and calls and calls his name, unaffected by lack of response. Soon I yearn for Henry to come down as much as the caller does. A transistor blares with a volume that bothers my ears. Drawn to the window, I marvel that the teenage boy, dancing alone on a stoop, can stand it right beside him. The sound must anesthetize like a drug. Now someone double parked is blocking a man who wants his car out. He honks, and makes me turn from whatever I'm thinking about to share his frustration, which is intense.

4. Back inside, I hear a young woman in an apartment next to mine practicing her clarinet. She is pretty good, beginning a professional career, I've learned, getting jobs with an orchestra here and there. Her practice hours give the building a cool, classical sound. I'm also brought into the anxieties of her young career. I hear the answering machine she has installed, asking whoever it is please to leave a message. Maybe it will mean another break for her.

5. From the apartment under me comes disco, with a beat that sends vibrations up the walls. And sometimes sends me up the walls. Excited dancers add their yelps. What world is that?

6. Then I remember that I, too, am making waves and forcing peo-

ple to live in my world. They must hear my radio, records I play, the noise of my coming and going and of my visitors. Living so close in city apartments, we are careful to acknowledge each other's privacy, and may astonish small towners by making our circle of friends elsewhere than among those most closely at hand. But as fellow residents we become neighbors nonetheless.

7.   I hear a phone ringing in some middle distance, on and on, and I begin thinking that one of my neighbors missed a call. I wonder if it was important.

QUESTIONS

1. Early builds to her thesis, instead of beginning with it. How late in the essay does the thesis appear? What is gained by building to it?
2. How do the opening two paragraphs prepare us for the experiences that follow, and for the thesis later in the essay?
3. If Early had begun with the thesis, how might it be connected to the ideas of the opening paragraphs?
4. What does the concluding paragraph contribute to our understanding of the thesis? Do you consider it an effective ending?
5. How are the details of the essay organized? More specifically, what is the principle of order?

WRITING ASSIGNMENTS

1. Develop the thesis of the essay from a different point of view, drawing on different experiences and describing a different world. You need not build to the thesis; put it where you think it will be most effective.
2. Write an essay suggested by one of the following topics. Build to your thesis as Early does. Select details that give it strong support:
   a. the anxieties of beginning a career
   b. sounds or statements that send me up the wall
   c. friends and neighbors—similarities and differences

ART BUCHWALD

Clean Your Room

You don't really feel the generation gap in this country until a son or daughter comes home from college for Christmas. Then it strikes you how out of it you really are.

This dialogue probably took place all over America last Christmas week:

"Nancy, you've been home from school for three days now. Why don't you clean up your room?"

"We don't have to clean up our rooms at college, Mother."

"That's very nice, Nancy, and I'm happy you're going to such a freewheeling institution. But while you're in the house, your father and I would like you to clean up your room."

"What difference does it make? It's *my* room."

"I know, dear, and it really doesn't mean that much to me. But your father has a great fear of the plague. He said this morning if it is going to start anywhere in this country, it's going to start in your room."

"Mother, you people aren't interested in anything that's relevant. Do you realize how the major corporations are polluting our environment?"

"Your father and I are very worried about it. But right now we're more concerned with the pollution in your bedroom. You haven't made your bed since you came home."

"I never make it up at the dorm."

"Of course you don't, and I'm sure the time you save goes toward your education. But we still have these old-fashioned ideas about making beds in the morning, and we can't shake them. Since you're home for such a short time, why don't you do it to humor us?"

"For heaven's sake, Mother, I'm grown up now. Why do you have to treat me like a child?"

"We're not treating you like a child. But it's very hard for us to realize you're an adult when you throw all your clothes on the floor."

"I haven't thrown all my clothes on the floor. Those are just the clothes I wore yesterday."

"Forgive me. I exaggerated. Well, how about the dirty dishes and empty soft-drink cans on your desk? Are you collecting them for a science project?"

"Mother, you don't understand us. You people were brought up to have clean rooms. But our generation doesn't care about things like that. It's what you have in your head that counts."

"No one respects education more than your father and I do, particularly at the prices they're charging. But we can't see how living in squalor can improve your mind."

"That's because of your priorities. You would rather have me make up my bed and pick up my clothes than become a free spirit who thinks for myself."

"We're not trying to stifle your free spirit. It's just that our Blue Cross has run out, and we have no protection in case anybody in the family catches typhoid."

"All right, I'll clean up my room if it means that much to you. But I want you to know you've ruined my vacation."

"It was a calculated risk I had to take. Oh, by the way, I know this is a terrible thing to ask of you, but would you mind helping me wash the dinner dishes?"

"Wash dishes? Nobody washes dishes at school."

"Your father and I were afraid of that."

QUESTIONS

1. Do you think Buchwald is making some real point, or is his purpose merely to amuse the reader? Is he successful in what he tries to do?
2. Is he poking fun at both Nancy and her parents—or at one of them only?
3. What is gained by presenting the parents and daughter through dialogue rather than through a summary of what happened?

WRITING ASSIGNMENT

Write a dialogue or an essay on a humorous situation involving teenagers and parents that reveals something about both of them—perhaps an attitude typical of these groups. Let the reader discover this truth through your details; don't state the truth directly.

W. S. MERWIN

Unchopping a Tree

1. Start with the leaves, the small twigs, and the nests that have been shaken, ripped, or broken off by the fall; these must be gathered and attached once again to their respective places. It is not arduous work, unless major limbs have been smashed or mutilated. If the fall was carefully and correctly planned, the chances of anything of the kind happening will have been reduced. Again, much depends upon the size, age, shape, and species of the tree. Still, you will be lucky if you

can get through this stage without having to use machinery. Even in the best of circumstances it is a labor that will make you wish often that you had won the favor of the universe of ants, the empire of mice, or at least a local tribe of squirrels, and could enlist their labors and their talents. But no, they leave you to it. They have learned, with time. This is men's work. It goes without saying that if the tree was hollow in whole or in part, and contained old nests of bird or mammal or insect, or hoards of nuts or such structures as wasps or bees build for their survival, the contents will have to be repaired where necessary, and reassembled, insofar as possible, in their original order, including the shells of nuts already opened. With spiders' webs you must simply do the best you can. We do not have the spider's weaving equipment, nor any substitute for the leaf's living bond with its point of attachment and nourishment. It is even harder to simulate the latter when the leaves have once become dry—as they are bound to do, for this is not the labor of a moment. Also it hardly needs saying that this is the time for repairing any neighboring trees or bushes or other growth that may have been damaged by the fall. The same rules apply. Where neighboring trees were of the same species it is difficult not to waste time conveying a detached leaf back to the wrong tree. Practice, practice. Put your hope in that.

2.   Now the tackle must be put into place or the scaffolding, depending on the surroundings and the dimensions of the tree. It is ticklish work. Almost always it involves, in itself, further damage to the area, which will have to be corrected later. But as you've heard, it can't be helped. And care now is likely to save you considerable trouble later. Be careful to grind nothing into the ground.

3.   At last the time comes for the erecting of the trunk. By now it will scarcely be necessary to remind you of the delicacy of this huge skeleton. Every motion of the tackle, every slight upward heave of the trunk, the branches, their elaborately reassembled panoply of leaves (now dead) will draw from you an involuntary gasp. You will watch for a leaf or a twig to be snapped off yet again. You will listen for the nuts to shift in the hollow limb and you will hear whether they are indeed falling into place or are spilling in disorder—in which case, or in the event of anything else of the kind—operations will have to cease, of course, while you correct the matter. The raising itself is no small enterprise, from the moment when the chains tighten around the old bandages until the bole hangs vertical above the stump, splinter above splinter. Now the final straightening of the splinters themselves can take place (the preliminary work is best done while the

wood is still green and soft, but at times when the splinters are not badly twisted most of the straightening is left until now, when the torn ends are face to face with each other). When the splinters are perfectly complementary the appropriate fixative is applied. Again we have no duplicate of the original substance. Ours is extremely strong, but it is rigid. It is limited to surfaces, and there is no play in it. However the core is not the part of the trunk that conducted life from the roots up into the branches and back again. It was relatively inert. The fixative for this part is not the same as the one for the outer layers and the bark, and if either of these is involved in the splintered section they must receive applications of the appropriate adhesives. Apart from being incorrect and probably ineffective, the core fixative would leave a scar on the bark.

4.   When all is ready the splintered trunk is lowered onto the splinters of the stump. This, one might say, is only the skeleton of the resurrection. Now the chips must be gathered, and the sawdust, and returned to their former positions. The fixative for the wood layers will be applied to chips and sawdust consisting only of wood. Chips and sawdust consisting of several substances will receive applications of the correct adhesives. It is as well, where possible, to shelter the materials from the elements while working. Weathering makes it harder to identify the smaller fragments. Bark sawdust in particular the earth lays claim to very quickly. You must find your own ways of coping with this problem. There is a certain beauty, you will notice at moments, in the pattern of the chips as they are fitted back into place. You will wonder to what extent it should be described as natural, to what extent manmade. It will lead you on to speculations about the parentage of beauty itself, to which you will return.

5.   The adhesive for the chips is translucent, and not so rigid as that for the splinters. That for the bark and its subcutaneous layers is transparent and runs into the fibers on either side, partially dissolving them into each other. It does not set the sap flowing again but it does pay a kind of tribute to the preoccupations of the ancient thoroughfares. You could not roll an egg over the joints but some of the mineshafts would still be passable, no doubt. For the first exploring insect who raises its head in the tight echoless passages. The day comes when it is all restored, even to the moss (now dead) over the wound. You will sleep badly, thinking of the removal of the scaffolding that must begin the next morning. How you will hope for sun and a still day!

6.   The removal of the scaffolding or tackle is not so dangerous,

perhaps, to the surroundings, as its installation, but it presents problems. It should be taken from the spot piece by piece as it is detached, and stored at a distance. You have come to accept it there, around the tree. The sky begins to look naked as the chains and struts one by one vacate their positions. Finally the moment arrives when the last sustaining piece is removed and the tree stands again on its own. It is as though its weight for a moment stood on your heart. You listen for a thud of settlement, a warning creak deep in the intricate joinery. You cannot believe it will hold. How like something dreamed it is, standing there all by itself. How long will it stand there now? The first breeze that touches its dead leaves all seems to flow into your mouth. You are afraid the motion of the clouds will be enough to push it over. What more can you do? What more can you do?

7.   But there is nothing more you can do.

8.   Others are waiting.

9.   Everything is going to have to be put back.

QUESTIONS

1. What are the chief indications of Merwin's purpose in this essay? Does he state that purpose directly?

2. Examine the following statement from paragraph 4 carefully: "You will wonder to what extent it should be described as natural, to what extent man-made. It will lead you on to speculations about the parentage of beauty itself, to which you will return." What is the tone of the statement—that is, what seems to be the writer's attitude toward his reader as well as toward the act of unchopping a tree? Is an attitude *implied* in the whole essay that no single statement expresses? Could you accept such an implication as embodying the thesis?

3. The writer has chosen a strategy to deal with his idea—that is, he approaches his reader in a particular way to achieve a particular effect. What does he want his reader to think and feel at the end of the essay, and what is his strategy in realizing these aims?

4. The essay ends with three single-sentence paragraphs. To what effect? What is Merwin saying?

WRITING ASSIGNMENT

Write an essay on a similar topic, for example, undoing an insult. Be consistent in conveying a tone and in building to your conclusion. Do not state your thesis directly; let the reader discover it in your tone and details.

Main and Subordinate Ideas

IRWIN EDMAN
Sincerity as a Fine Art

1. I remember often during my early adolescence listening to older
people making conversation. I vowed I would never willingly be a
conspirator at such transparent hypocrisies. When *I* went out to dinner, I found myself saying, I should speak only when I felt like it, and
I should say only what was on my mind. I used to listen while my
elders pretended to have a fascinated interest in visitors with whom I
knew they had only the most remote concern, and hear them discuss
with affected animation matters that I knew bored them to pain. I
remember having had it explained to me that this was the least that
good manners demanded. It was at this moment that I came to the
conclusion that good manners and dubious morals had much in common.
2. In these matters, I have become subdued to the general color of
civilized society. It has long ago been brought home to me that a guest
has obligations in addition to that of eating the food provided by his
host. It is fair enough that one should, if not sing, at least converse for
one's supper. I have even come to believe that my elders of long ago
were more interested in their visitors than I had supposed. I have
lighted upon the fact that questions asked out of politeness may elicit
answers that are fascinating on their own. An enchanting story may be
the unearned increment of a conventional inquiry.
3. And yet I have not ceased to be troubled at the momentum with
which on a social occasion one is embarked on a brief career of insincerity. I have found myself expressing opinions on Russia or on psy-
chiatry that I had not known I possessed. I have sometimes, out of
sheer inability to get out of it, maintained a position on old-age security, or on old age itself, that, save for some impulsive remark I had
let fall, I should not have considered it a point of honor to defend as
my considered philosophy on the subject. On shamefully numerous
occasions, I have repeated an anecdote by which I was myself bored to
death. I have talked with dowagers about literature, art, and educa-

tion, at moments when all three of these lofty themes seemed to me insufferably tedious and stuffy.

4.   I have come to admire those sturdy individualists who say—as I once planned to say—only whatever comes into their minds, and speak only when they are spoken to, and perhaps not even then. But I must admit I find them difficult socially, these high-minded boors who can be pricked into only the most minimal of replies, these dedicated roughnecks who find a savage pleasure in telling you without compromise what they think of everything, including your loyalties and your enthusiasms—and possibly yourself.

5.   There must be some way of acting both agreeably and sincerely. It is a fine art, practiced, one is told, by a few witty eighteenth-century courtiers. But wits today are rather celebrated for their malignity. It is a difficult alternative, that between truth and charm, and I confess that I am tempted to seek the easier and more genial path. If one plumped for sincerity, one would get to be known simply as a bear, a bear who would soon be walking alone, a boorish bear who at any rate would seldom be invited out to dinner. As Santayana remarks somewhere, "For a man of sluggish mind and bad manners, there is decidedly no place like home."

DISCUSSION: Main and Subordinate Ideas

The thesis is the most important idea in an essay, and restatements of it are equally important. When the thesis unfolds through details and discussion, we sometimes have a sense of rising importance, even perhaps one of climax. We know that subordinate ideas are building to this main one. When the essay opens with the thesis, we know that the ideas that develop it are subordinate. It is the logical relationship of ideas that gives us this sense of relative importance. An essay in which all ideas seemed to have the same importance would be extremely hard to read.

We can illustrate this logical relationship through the opening and concluding paragraphs of Eric Sevareid's "Velva, North Dakota." The indentation here symbolizes the relative weight of the ideas in the essay. Here are the opening sentences of the first seven paragraphs:

"My home town has changed in these thirty years of the American story."

   "Sights have changed . . ."
   "Sounds have changed . . ."
   "The people have not changed, but the *kinds* of people have changed . . ."

"No, the 'characters' are vanishing in Velva . . ."
"They eat differently in Velva now . . ."

"It is distance and time that have changed the most and worked the deepest changes in Velva's life."

Severeid builds to his thesis, as his increasingly broad generalizations show. Here are the opening sentences of the last five paragraphs:

"Many politicians deplore the passing of the old family-size farm, but I am not so sure."
"But now I must ask myself: Are they nearer to one another? And the answer is no; yet I am certain that this is good."
"For personal and social neuroses festered under this hard scab of conformity."
"Human nature is everywhere the same."
"It is personal freedom that makes us better persons, and they are freer in Velva now" (thesis).

As Severeid's sentences show, we do not always need formal transitions to tell us which ideas are main and which subordinate. The clear logical relationship of these ideas makes their relative importance evident. But as in the paragraph, formal transitions are sometimes necessary. Having a sense of this relative importance as we write—having our thesis in mind and the details and subordinate ideas that develop it—is essential to the coherence of the essay.

QUESTIONS

1. In the Edman, the main idea of paragraph 1 may be stated as follows: In my youth I was disturbed by the hypocrisy of adults. What subordinate ideas develop it in the paragraph?
2. The main idea of paragraph 2 may be stated as follows: As an adult I see the matter somewhat differently. What subordinate ideas develop it in the paragraph?
3. What are the main ideas of paragraphs 3–5?
4. Which of these ideas would you select as the thesis, and why?
5. To what extent does Edman depend on transitions to distinguish the main and subordinate ideas?
6. Does Edman offer a solution to the problem discussed in paragraphs 1–4? Is he suggesting, for example, that he found a middle course between two extremes? Can you offer a better solution?

WRITING ASSIGNMENTS

1. Edman's essay is organized in a traditional form: statement of a problem (paragraphs 1–4), discussion of a solution (paragraph 5). Write an essay in which you explore a similar problem and, like

Edman, explore a solution, examining the difficulties of finding one.

2. Write an essay on one of the following topics. Give your thesis emphasis by putting it in a prominent place in the essay—perhaps at the end of your opening paragraph, or in the final paragraph. If you begin the essay with your thesis, you may want to give it emphasis by repeating or restating it at key points:
   a. the art of keeping friends
   b. on not giving advice
   c. the art of persuading children
   d. on getting along with neighbors or roommates
   e. on living away from home

MARGARET MEAD AND RHODA METRAUX
The Gift of Autonomy

1. Every gift we give carries with it our idea of what a present is. Perhaps it expresses our personality; perhaps, on the contrary, it is what we believe the recipient really wants, a choice based on careful listening for the slightest hint of what he longs for or needs or should have, even though he may not realize it.

2. Gifts from parents to children always carry the most meaningful messages. The way parents think about presents goes one step beyond the objects themselves—the ties, dolls, sleds, record players, kerchiefs, bicycles and model airplanes that wait by the Christmas tree. The gifts are, in effect, one way of telling boys and girls, "We love you even though you have been a bad boy all month" or, "We love having a daughter" or, "We treat all our children alike" or, "It is all right for girls to have some toys made for boys" or, "This alarm clock will help you get started in the morning all by yourself." Throughout all the centuries since the invention of a Santa Claus figure who represented a special recognition of children's behavior, good and bad, presents have given parents a way of telling children about their love and hopes and expectations for them.

3. When I was a child, my parents used to give me a pair of books each Christmas. One was "light," easy reading; the other was "heavy," a book I had to think about if I was to enjoy it. This combination carried with it the message that there are different kinds of

pleasure to be gained through reading and that I should discover each kind for myself.

4.   If we think about all the presents we have given our children over the years, we will see how they fit into the hopes we have for each child. I do not mean this in the simple sense that we delight in a little girl's femininity, and so give her dolls, or that we implement a boy's masculinity by giving him model planes and boxing gloves. We do, of course, speak to our children in this simplest form of symbolism. And we do, of course, personalize what we say when we give our outdoors son a fishing rod and his experiment-minded brother a microscope.

5.   However, our giving also carries more subtle and complex messages. For example, we can ask ourselves: "What am I saying to my children about growing up to be independent, autonomous people?" An abstract question of this kind can be posed in relation to a whole range of presents for children of both sexes and of different ages. Where the choice to be made is between a simple toy engine that the child himself can wind up and a more complicated one that I shall have to wind up for him, which one do I give him? Choosing a doll for a little girl, do I buy her a perishable costume doll with one beautiful dress, a washable doll with a wardrobe or a doll for which she will make dresses out of the materials I also give her? The costume doll can perhaps be dressed and undressed, but that is all. A bath would be ruinous. A sturdy doll with a ready-made wardrobe places choice in the child's own hands. She herself can dress and undress it, bathe it safely and decide whether her "little girl" will wear pink or blue, plaid or plain. Giving my child materials out of which to fashion doll dresses is a lovely idea, and may perhaps encourage her to learn how to sew. But choice and autonomy both are reduced because now I must help her at every step.

6.   We can ask questions of this kind also about the presents of money that are given our children by grandparents and godparents, aunts and uncles and family friends. What do we tell our children about the bright silver dollar tucked into the toe of a Christmas stocking or the grown-up looking check that is made out in the child's own name? Is the money meant to be used now for some specific purpose—for the charm bracelet a little girl has admired or the radio a boy wants for his own room? Or is it an inducement, perhaps, to begin saving for the car a teen-ager must wait five years to own? Is the child told, directly or indirectly: "This is your money to do with as you like"? Or is the child asked: "Would you rather spend it or put it in the bank?"

7.   By defining the alternatives so sharply, we are, in effect, robbing the child of choice. In fact, when you tell him that the money is his and then give directions, hint at alternatives or reproach him for spending it in one way instead of another, the gift carries a very definite message: "I don't really trust your choices. I don't really want you to choose." If, on the other hand, the message is simple and direct ("This is your money, yours, to dispose of as you like"), then the child may even solicit your advice. But there is no real turning back once you have said, "This is your money."

8.   Over the years, there are always new ways of reinforcing or detracting from our children's growing sense of independence. For example, if you give a boy a box of stationery imprinted with his name and a supply of postage stamps, you are showing him that you expect him to write, address and mail his own letters. This means, of course, that you may never see the letters he writes, or you may become a consultant on appropriate terms of address or the correct abbreviations of names of states. At this point you can give him an almanac in which he himself can look up the answers to his questions—or you can keep the almanac on your own desk and become the mediator between his questions and the information he needs.

9.   Giving a girl a diary with a key is a way in which a mother can tell her daughter (boys, on the whole, do not keep diaries) that she respects her child's growing sense of identity and independence. Giving a boy a desk is one way of fostering his sense of personal privacy; but if we continually tidy it up or complain about its untidiness, as we see it, the original message miscarries.

10.   In many families the climax, and in some the crisis, of their individual pattern of giving comes as the children approach college, when their parents prepare to give them the most expensive "gift" of all—a college education. Of course, parents are not, as a rule, literally "giving" their children an education. What they are giving them is the opportunity to become educated.

11.   Many parents today meet the responsibility of supporting their children through the college years, wholly or in part, by taking out insurance policies for this special purpose. Usually such policies, whatever their specific form, are payable to the parents. Then the choice of a college and the course of study remains firmly in the parents' hands. Americans believe very strongly that he who pays the piper calls the tune.

12.   This is the *customary* way of doing things. It carries with it the message that our children, although approaching adulthood, are still

children in our eyes. But this need not be. The money instead can be set up as a fund available to the boy or girl. Its purpose can be specified: This is not money for just anything. It is money for higher education, intended to give you freedom and choice within this area of your life.

13.   For children who have grown up with an ever-enlarging sense of their own autonomy and independence, intelligent handling of the opportunity for further education will come naturally and easily. They are free, if they like, to postpone going to college for a year. Or they can drop out for a semester or a year without fearing that the tuition money will have vanished when they want to go back. A girl can marry before she goes to college, or while she is still a student, knowing that the choice of when and where she will continue her education remains open to her. Next year or ten years from now the money will be there, waiting, ready for her when she wants and needs it.

14.   Like the small presents of early childhood that carry the message "You need my help," the educational insurance policy in the parents' name places responsibility in the parents' hands. In many cases parents are not even required to spend the money on the education of the child in whose interest the policy was acquired. But when money is placed in the child's own name, a trust for a special purpose, the parents are saying: "This is what I hope to give you—the right of choice. I respect your right to choose. My gift is intended to underwrite your freedom to be a person. Long ago I gave you stamps so you could mail your own letters. I gave you an allowance so you could move more freely in your own world. Now, as then, I want you to be an autonomous, self-starting person, someone who enjoys interdependence with other people because instead of fighting for your independence, you have grown into it."

15.   All our giving carries with it messages about ourselves, our feelings about those to whom we give, how we see them as people and how we phrase the ties of relationship. Christmas giving, in which love and hope and trust play such an intrinsic part, can be an annual way of telling our children that we think of each of them as a person, as we also hope they will come to think of us.

QUESTIONS

1. If the statement in paragraph 11—"Americans believe very strongly that he who pays the piper calls the tune"—were the thesis of the essay, how might the essay have been organized to develop it? What parts of the present essay would you omit?

2. Where does the thesis of the essay first appear, and how is it restated later?
3. In what order are the various problems of giving presents discussed in paragraphs 4–10?
4. Why do the authors devote a considerable part of the essay to the educational insurance policy?
5. Is the purpose of the essay to analyze the practice of gift giving, or to give advice to parents and others on this matter? Do the authors address their readers as colleagues, or clients seeking advice, or merely as general readers?

WRITING ASSIGNMENTS

1. Analyze the gifts you gave members of your family last Christmas or Chanukah, and discuss the reasons for your choices. Give particular attention to your expectations in choosing the gift for each person.
2. Discuss the ways high school teachers can encourage or discourage students from doing their best work. Distinguish the problems that arise in two different subjects like English and mathematics.

WILLIAM ZINSSER
The Right to Fail

1. I like "dropout" as an addition to the American language because it's brief and it's clear. What I don't like is that we use it almost entirely as a dirty word.
2. We only apply it to people under twenty-one. Yet an adult who spends his days and nights watching mindless TV programs is more of a dropout than an eighteen-year-old who quits college, with its frequently mindless courses, to become, say, a VISTA volunteer. For the young, dropping out is often a way of dropping in.
3. To hold this opinion, however, is little short of treason in America. A boy or girl who leaves college is branded a failure—and the right to fail is one of the few freedoms that this country does not grant its citizens. The American dream is a dream of "getting ahead," painted in strokes of gold wherever we look. Our advertisements and TV commercials are a hymn to material success, our magazine articles

a toast to people who made it to the top. Smoke the right cigarette or drive the right car—so the ads imply—and girls will be swooning into your deodorized arms or caressing your expensive lapels. Happiness goes to the man who has the sweet smell of achievement. He is our national idol, and everybody else is our national fink.

4. I want to put in a word for the fink, especially the teen-age fink, because if we give him time to get through his finkdom—if we release him from the pressure of attaining certain goals by a certain age—he has a good chance of becoming our national idol, a Jefferson or a Thoreau, a Buckminster Fuller or an Adlai Stevenson, a man with a mind of his own. We need mavericks and dissenters and dreamers far more than we need junior vice-presidents, but we paralyze them by insisting that every step be a step up to the next rung of the ladder. Yet in the fluid years of youth, the only way for boys and girls to find their proper road is often to take a hundred side trips, poking out in different directions, faltering, drawing back, and starting again.

5. "But what if we fail?" they ask, whispering the dreadful word across the Generation Gap to their parents, who are back home at the Establishment, nursing their "middle-class values" and cultivating their "goal-oriented society." The parents whisper back: "Don't!"

6. What they should say is "Don't be afraid to fail!" Failure isn't fatal. Countless people have had a bout with it and come out stronger as a result. Many have even come out famous. History is strewn with eminent dropouts, "loners" who followed their own trail, not worrying about its odd twists and turns because they had faith in their own sense of direction. To read their biographies is always exhilarating, not only because they beat the system, but because their system was better than the one that they beat.

7. Luckily, such rebels still turn up often enough to prove that individualism, though badly threatened, is not extinct. Much has been written, for instance, about the fitful scholastic career of Thomas P. F. Hoving, New York's former Parks Commissioner and now director of the Metropolitan Museum of Art. Hoving was a dropout's dropout, entering and leaving schools as if they were motels, often at the request of the management. Still, he must have learned something during those unorthodox years, for he dropped in again at the top of his profession.

8. His case reminds me of another boyhood—that of Holden Caulfield in J. D. Salinger's *The Catcher in the Rye*, the most popular literary hero of the postwar period. There is nothing accidental about the grip that this dropout continues to hold on the affections of an entire

American generation. Nobody else, real or invented, has made such an engaging shambles of our "goal-oriented society," so gratified our secret belief that the "phonies" are in power and the good guys up the creek. Whether Holden has also reached the top of his chosen field today is one of those speculations that delight fanciers of good fiction. I speculate that he has. Holden Caulfield, incidentally, is now thirty-six.

9.   I'm not urging everyone to go out and fail just for the sheer therapy of it, or to quit college just to coddle some vague discontent. Obviously it's better to succeed than to flop, and in general a long education is more helpful than a short one. (Thanks to my own education, for example, I can tell George Eliot from T. S. Eliot, I can handle the pluperfect tense in French, and I know that Caesar beat the Helvetii because he had enough frumentum.) I only mean that failure isn't bad in itself, or success automatically good.

10.   Fred Zinnemann, who has directed some of Hollywood's most honored movies, was asked by a reporter, when *A Man for All Seasons* won every prize, about his previous film *Behold a Pale Horse*, which was a box-office disaster. "I don't feel any obligation to be successful," Zinnemann replied. "Success can be dangerous—you feel you know it all. I've learned a great deal from my failures." A similar point was made by Richard Brooks about his ambitious money loser, *Lord Jim*. Recalling the three years of his life that went into it, talking almost with elation about the troubles that befell his unit in Cambodia, Brooks told me that he learned more about his craft from this considerable failure than from his many earlier hits.

11.   It's a point, of course, that applies throughout the arts. Writers, playwrights, painters and composers work in the expectation of periodic defeat, but they wouldn't keep going back into the arena if they thought it was the end of the world. It isn't the end of the world. For an artist—and perhaps for anybody—it is the only way to grow.

12.   Today's younger generation seems to know that this is true, seems willing to take the risks in life that artists take in art. "Society," needless to say, still has the upper hand—it sets the goals and condemns as a failure everybody who won't play. But the dropouts and the hippies are not as afraid of failure as their parents and grandparents. This could mean, as their elders might say, that they are just plumb lazy, secure in the comforts of an affluent state. It could also mean, however, that they just don't buy the old standards of success and are rapidly writing new ones.

13.   Recently it was announced, for instance, that more than two hundred thousand Americans have inquired about service in VISTA

(the domestic Peace Corps) and that, according to a Gallup survey, "more than three million American college students would serve VISTA in some capacity if given the opportunity." This is hardly the road to riches or to an executive suite. Yet I have met many of these young volunteers, and they are not pining for traditional success. On the contrary, they appear more fulfilled than the average vice-president with a swimming pool.

14.   Who is to say, then, if there is any right path to the top, or even to say what the top consists of? Obviously the colleges don't have more than a partial answer—otherwise the young would not be so disaffected with an education that they consider vapid. Obviously business does not have the answer—otherwise the young would not be so scornful of its call to be an organization man.

15.   The fact is, nobody has the answer, and the dawning awareness of this fact seems to me one of the best things happening in America today. Success and failure are again becoming individual visions, as they were when the country was younger, not rigid categories. Maybe we are learning again to cherish this right of every person to succeed on his own terms and to fail as often as necessary along the way.

QUESTIONS

1. Zinsser develops his thesis in paragraphs 1–4. What is his thesis, and what sentence states it most fully?
2. Paragraphs 5–8 provide support for the thesis by *defending* the right to fail. What form does this defense take? What does Zinsser gain by citing the hero of *Catcher in the Rye?*
3. Paragraphs 9–12 *qualify* what has been said earlier: Zinsser tells us what he does not mean by "the right to fail." What does he not mean, and how does he qualify his idea of failure through discussion of success and failure in the arts, the film art specifically?
4. Paragraphs 13–15 provide additional supporting evidence that the maverick has a role to play in American society (Zinsser's point in paragraphs 6 and 7), and restate the thesis to conclude the essay. What is that evidence, and how is the thesis restated?
5. Do you agree with Zinsser that parents and society provide teenagers with rigid standards of success? Do you agree with his belief that failure is a means to growth?

WRITING ASSIGNMENTS

1. Discuss your agreement or disagreement with Zinsser about the demands made on teenagers today, drawing on your own experi-

ences and ideas of success and failure. Do not try to speak for all teenagers. Limit yourself to your experience and personal goals.
2. Discuss the value of two or three different courses you took in high school, with attention to the effect of these courses on your choice of a college or a college major, or the development of long-term goals (or all of these).
3. Write an essay on one of the following topics. Develop it as Zinsser develops his essay: state a thesis and explain it, defend it with supporting evidence, qualify it (explaining what you do not mean and limiting your generalizations), provide additional evidence for one or more of your supporting ideas, and restate your thesis in conclusion.
   a. unintended lessons taught in high school classes
   b. lessons that cannot be taught in school
   c. discovering the nature of prejudice
   d. friendships that endure
   e. "rules" that work at home or at school

Beginning and Ending

ELLEN GOODMAN

Inward Bound

1.   The sophomore had left college to "find herself," rather as if she were a set of misplaced keys. She had the notion that her mind was a collection of pockets and if she searched in each one of them long enough she would find the keys to unlock this self. Months later, she told her parents that she was deeply into the independent study called "Who Am I?" And by now, surely, she had become a professional introspector. A very private eye.
2.   The woman didn't know this sophomore very well; she was a friend of the parents. But she knew others her age who conducted their own missing persons bureau; others who had turned inward to see what they could find and had found self-discovery a totally absorbing sort of trip. The woman wasn't opposed in principle to interior travels. She knew too many people who went through life without even stopping to interview themselves. They were wind-up toys. They

did, therefore they were. Until they stopped. They never asked who or why.

3. Yet so many, so early, seemed so inward bound. They focused more energy on who they were than on who they might become. For every seventeen-year-old who actually "found" him or herself, there was another who simply lost experience. For every nineteen-year-old who got closer to his or her psyche, there was another who withdrew. There was a young man she knew who spent his junior year in a dorm room rummaging through his mental pockets and never finding anything except lint. There was a twenty-two-year-old in her neighborhood whose horizons were still limited to the first person.

4. She wondered if there wasn't an age at which our pockets are waiting to be filled rather than sorted. Prolonged psyche-tripping at eighteen or nineteen seemed rather like writing an autobiography at ten or eleven. Sooner or later, you ran out of material. There are people, more mystical than this woman, who believe that they were born with complete, coherent inner beings which only need to be uncovered and expressed. There are people, less mystical, who believe that they were born blank and then marked. Their selves are products of indelible chalk.

5. She had always figured that people were born with tendencies . . . potential . . . possibilities. But they "grew" selves. It wasn't the primal scene of birth that seemed most interesting, but the process of autobiography. Some of the most self-aware people had taken their chances first and their temperature second. They didn't put introspection as a barrier before experience. They knew themselves in retrospect, through their histories. As an old and understanding man had said once in Detroit, "My life has been on-the-job training."

6. It was odd, but those who always tried to get their act together before they acted sometimes got stuck at the beginning. Those who thought of themselves as constantly improving sometimes learned more about their own character. This sophomore was still on her own internal trip. But perhaps she, too, would soon go and make some new material. After all, most people don't find themselves; they become themselves. And life has a way of interrupting the most hypnotic private eye.

DISCUSSION: Beginning and Ending

If writers want to make their ideas convincing, they will want to capture the attention of their readers and hold it. Writers will lose this attention if they describe in too much detail how they intend to proceed.

Usually they will indicate a point of view and perhaps also the ways their subject is to be developed. There may be excellent reasons for beginning an essay with the thesis, but in most instances the thesis needs an introduction: writers will build to it by showing why the subject is worth discussing and why the thesis is worth the reader's attention. The following opening paragraphs effectively accomplish this purpose:

> The administration of criminal justice and the extent of individual moral responsibility are among the crucial problems of a civilized society. They are indissolubly linked, and together they involve our deepest personal emotions. We often find it hard to forgive ourselves for our own moral failures. All of us, at some time or other, have faced the painful dilemma of when to punish and when to forgive those we love—our children, our friends. How much harder it is, then, to deal with the stranger who transgresses.—David L. Bazelon, "The Awesome Decision"

> The aim of this book is to delineate two types of clever schoolboy: the converger and the diverger. The earlier chapters offer a fairly detailed description of the intellectual abilities, attitudes and personalities of a few hundred such boys. In the later chapters, this description is then used as the basis for a more speculative discussion—of the nature of intelligence and originality and of the ways in which intellectual and personal qualities interact. Although the first half of the book rests heavily on the results of psychological tests, and the last two chapters involve psychoanalytic theory, I have done my best to be intelligible, and, wherever possible, interesting to everyone interested in clever schoolboys: parents, schoolteachers, dons, psychologists, administrators, clever schoolboys.—Liam Hudson, *Contrary Imaginations*

In the first of these paragraphs, readers are eased into the subject: their interest is aroused by the personal consideration—their attitude toward themselves, their children, their friends. The author assumes that this interest needs to be aroused. In the second opening paragraph, interest is challenged: no easing into the subject here, for the opening sentence announces both the subject of the book and a key distinction. The bonus is the wit of the author—and the promise of more.

An effective ending will not let the discussion drop; the reader should not have a sense of loose ends, of lines of thought left uncompleted. In the formal essay, the ending may be used for a restatement of the thesis or perhaps a full statement of it—if the writer has chosen to build to it. One of the most effective conclusions is the reference back to ideas that opened the essay.

QUESTIONS

1. The Goodman captures the attention of the reader quickly and establishes the thesis without much buildup or elaboration of detail. How does Goodman seek to capture the attention of her reader? How does she establish her thesis?
2. How many restatements of the thesis do you find in the essay? Does the final restatement—in the concluding paragraph—add new understanding of the thesis? What is the meaning of the final sentence?
3. Is Goodman taking sides in the debate between the "more mystical" people and the "less mystical"? Or is she examining possibilities of finding oneself, without taking a definite stand?
4. What is gained by writing from the point of view of a friend of the parents? Would the tone of the essay be different if it were written in the first person?

WRITING ASSIGNMENTS

1. Discuss the extent to which Zinsser would agree with Goodman's ideas, comparing statements from the two essays to support your ideas.
2. Discuss the extent to which Goodman would agree with Zinsser on "the right to fail" and his ideas on success and failure. Compare statements of them both to support your interpretation.
3. Discuss the extent of your agreement with Goodman on one of the matters she discusses, perhaps the statement that "people don't find themselves; they become themselves."

SHIRLEY JACKSON

My Life with R. H. Macy

1. And the first thing they did was segregate me. They segregated me from the only person in the place I had even a speaking acquaintance with; that was a girl I had met going down the hall who said to me: "Are you as scared as I am?" And when I said, "Yes," she said, "I'm in lingerie, what are you in?" and I thought for a while and then

said, "Spun glass," which was as good an answer as I could think of, and she said, "Oh. Well, I'll meet you here in a sec." And she went away and was segregated and I never saw her again.

2. Then they kept calling my name and I kept trotting over to wherever they called it and they would say ("They" all this time being startlingly beautiful young women in tailored suits and with short-clipped hair), "Go with Miss Cooper, here. She'll tell you what to do." All the women I met my first day were named Miss Cooper. And Miss Cooper would say to me: "What are you in?" and I had learned by that time to say, "Books," and she would say, "Oh, well, then, you belong with Miss Cooper here," and then she would call "Miss Cooper?" and another young woman would come and the first one would say, "13-3138 here belongs with you," and Miss Cooper would say, "What is she in?" and Miss Cooper would answer, "Books," and I would go away and be segregated again.

3. Then they taught me. They finally got me segregated into a classroom, and I sat there for a while all by myself (that's how far segregated I was) and then a few other girls came in, all wearing tailored suits (I was wearing a red velvet afternoon frock) and we sat down and they taught us. They gave us each a big book with R. H. Macy written on it, and inside this book were pads of little sheets saying (from left to right): "Comp. keep for ref. cust. d.a. no. or c.t. no. salesbook no. salescheck no. clerk no. dept. date M." After M there was a long line for Mr. or Mrs. and the name, and then it began again with "No. item. class. at price, total." And down at the bottom was written ORIGINAL and then again, "Comp. keep for ref.," and "Paste yellow gift stamp here." I read all this very carefully. Pretty soon a Miss Cooper came, who talked for a little while on the advantages we had in working at Macy's, and she talked about the salesbooks, which it seems came apart into a sort of road map and carbons and things. I listened for a while, and when Miss Cooper wanted us to write on the little pieces of paper, I copied from the girl next to me. That was training.

4. Finally someone said we were going on the floor, and we descended from the sixteenth floor to the first. We were in groups of six by then, all following Miss Cooper doggedly and wearing little tags saying BOOK INFORMATION. I never did find out what that meant. Miss Cooper said I had to work on the special sale counter, and showed me a little book called *The Stage-Struck Seal*, which it seemed I would be selling. I had gotten about halfway through it before she came back to tell me I had to stay with my unit.

5.   I enjoyed meeting the time clock, and spent a pleasant half-hour punching various cards standing around, and then someone came in and said I couldn't punch the clock with my hat on. So I had to leave, bowing timidly at the time clock and its prophet, and I went and found out my locker number, which was 1773, and my time-clock number, which was 712, and my cash-box number, which was 1336, and my cash-register number, which was 253, and my cash-register-drawer number, which was K, and my cash-register-drawer-key number, which was 872, and my department number, which was 13. I wrote all these numbers down. And that was my first day.

6.   My second day was better. I was officially on the floor. I stood in a corner of a counter, with one hand possessively on *The Stage-Struck Seal,* waiting for customers. The counter head was named 13-2246, and she was very kind to me. She sent me to lunch three times, because she got me confused with 13-6454 and 13-3141. It was after lunch that a customer came. She came over and took one of my stage-struck seals, and said "How much is this?" I opened my mouth and the customer said "I have a D.A. and I will have this sent to my aunt in Ohio. Part of that D.A. I will pay for with a book dividend of 32 cents, and the rest of course will be on my account. Is this book price-fixed?" That's as near as I can remember what she said. I smiled confidently, and said "Certainly; will you wait just one moment?" I found a little piece of paper in a drawer under the counter: it had "Duplicate Triplicate" printed across the front in big letters. I took down the customer's name and address, her aunt's name and address, and wrote carefully across the front of the duplicate triplicate "1 Stg. Strk. Sl." Then I smiled at the customer again and said carelessly: "That will be seventy-five cents." She said "But I have a D.A." I told her that all D.A.'s were suspended for the Christmas rush, and she gave me seventy-five cents, which I kept. Then I rang up a "No Sale" on the cash register and I tore up the duplicate triplicate because I didn't know what else to do with it.

7.   Later on another customer came and said "Where would I find a copy of Ann Rutherford Gwynn's *He Came Like Thunder?*" and I said "In medical books, right across the way," but 13-2246 came and said "That's philosophy, isn't it?" and the customer said it was, and 13-2246 said "Right down this aisle, in dictionaries." The customer went away, and I said to 13-2246 that her guess was as good as mine, anyway, and she stared at me and explained that philosophy, social sciences and Bertrand Russell were all kept in dictionaries.

8.   So far I haven't been back to Macy's for my third day, because

that night when I started to leave the store, I fell down the stairs and tore my stockings and the doorman said that if I went to my department head Macy's would give me a new pair of stockings and I went back and I found Miss Cooper and she said, "Go to the adjuster on the seventh floor and give him this," and she handed me a little slip of pink paper and on the bottom of it was printed "Comp. keep for ref. cust. d.a. no. or c.t. no. salesbook no. salescheck no. clerk no. dept. date M." And after M, instead of a name, she had written 13-3138. I took the little pink slip and threw it away and went up to the fourth floor and bought myself a pair of stockings for $.69 and then I came down and went out the customers' entrance.

9. I wrote Macy's a long letter, and I signed it with all my numbers added together and divided by 11,700, which is the number of employees in Macy's. I wonder if they miss me.

QUESTIONS

1. What information does Jackson provide about herself and her job, in her opening paragraph? What information does she not provide? How does this selection of detail establish a focus of interest?
2. What is gained by the abrupt opening sentence? What do you think happened earlier that connects with the opening "and"?
3. What is her thesis, and where does she first state it? How does she keep this thesis before the reader throughout the essay?
4. In what order does she present her experiences at Macy's?
5. How is the concluding paragraph related to the opening one? Do you find it an effective conclusion?
6. What is the overall tone of the essay, and how is it established?

WRITING ASSIGNMENTS

1. Describe your first day on a new job. Use your opening paragraph to suggest a thesis, and state it fully toward the end of your essay, or in your concluding paragraph. Keep in mind that your reader knows nothing about you or your place of work. Select your details carefully; don't tell the reader everything.
2. Rewrite one or two paragraphs of Jackson's essay from the point of view of a customer or another salesperson who is observing the speaker of the essay. Decide before you write what tone you wish to establish.

Analysis

JOHN CIARDI

Is Everybody Happy?

1. The right to pursue happiness is issued to Americans with their birth certificates, but no one seems quite sure which way it ran. It may be we are issued a hunting license but offered no game. Jonathan Swift seemed to think so when he attacked the idea of happiness as "the possession of being well-deceived," the felicity of being "a fool among knaves." For Swift saw society as Vanity Fair, the land of false goals.

2. It is, of course, un-American to think in terms of fools and knaves. We do, however, seem to be dedicated to the idea of buying our way to happiness. We shall all have made it to Heaven when we possess enough.

3. And at the same time the forces of American commercialism are hugely dedicated to making us deliberately unhappy. Advertising is one of our major industries, and advertising exists not to satisfy desires but to create them—and to create them faster than any man's budget can satisfy them. For that matter, our whole economy is based on a dedicated insatiability. We are taught that to possess is to be happy, and then we are made to want. We are even told it is our duty to want. It was only a few years ago, to cite a single example, that car dealers across the country were flying banners that read "You Auto Buy Now." They were calling upon Americans, as an act approaching patriotism, to buy at once with money they did not have, automobiles they did not really need, and which they would be required to grow tired of by the time the next year's models were released.

4. Or look at any of the women's magazines. There, as Bernard DeVoto once pointed out, advertising begins as poetry in the front pages and ends as pharmacopoeia and therapy in the back pages. The poetry of the front matter is the dream of perfect beauty. This is the baby skin that must be hers. These, the flawless teeth. This, the perfumed breath she must exhale. This, the sixteen-year-old figure she must display at forty, at fifty, at sixty, and forever.

5. Once past the vaguely uplifting fiction and feature articles, the reader finds the other face of the dream in the back matter. This is the harness into which Mother must strap herself in order to display that perfect figure. These, the chin straps she must sleep in. This is the salve that restores all, this is her laxative, these are the tablets that melt away fat, these are the hormones of perpetual youth, these are the stockings that hide varicose veins.

6. Obviously no half-sane person can be completely persuaded either by such poetry or by such pharmacopoeia and orthopedics. Yet someone is obviously trying to buy the dream as offered and spending billions every year in the attempt. Clearly the happiness market is not running out of customers, but what are we trying to buy?

7. The idea "happiness," to be sure, will not sit still for easy definition: the best one can do is to try to set some extremes to the idea and then work in toward the middle. To think of happiness as acquisitive and competitive will do to set the materialistic extreme. To think of it as the idea one senses in, say, a holy man of India will do to set the spiritual extreme. That holy man's ideal of happiness is in needing nothing from outside himself. In wanting nothing, he lacks nothing. He sits immobile, rapt in contemplation, free even of his own body. Or nearly free of it. If devout admirers bring him food he eats it; if not, he starves indifferently. Why be concerned? What is physical is an illusion to him. Contemplation is his joy and he achieves it through a fantastically demanding discipline, the accomplishment of which is itself a joy within him.

8. Is he a happy man? Perhaps his happiness is only another sort of illusion. But who can take it from him? And who will dare say it is more illusory than happiness on the installment plan?

9. But, perhaps because I am Western, I doubt such catatonic happiness, as I doubt the dreams of the happiness market. What is certain is that his way of happiness would be torture to almost any Western man. Yet these extremes will still serve to frame the area within which all of us must find some sort of balance. Thoreau—a creature of both Eastern and Western thought—had his own firm sense of that balance. His aim was to save on the low levels in order to spend on the high.

10. Possession for its own sake or in competition with the rest of the neighborhood would have been Thoreau's idea of the low levels. The active discipline of heightening one's perception of what is enduring in nature would have been his idea of the high. What he saved from the low was time and effort he could spend on the high. Thoreau certainly disapproved of starvation, but he would put into feeding himself only

as much effort as would keep him functioning for more important efforts.

11.   Effort is the gist of it. There is no happiness except as we take on life-engaging difficulties. Short of the impossible, as Yeats put it, the satisfactions we get from a lifetime depend on how high we choose our difficulties. Robert Frost was thinking in something like the same terms when he spoke of "the pleasure of taking pains." The mortal flaw in the advertised version of happiness is in the fact that it purports to be effortless.

12.   We demand difficulty even in our games. We demand it because without difficulty there can be no game. A game is a way of making something hard for the fun of it. The rules of the game are an arbitrary imposition of difficulty. When the spoilsport ruins the fun, he always does so by refusing to play by the rules. It is easier to win at chess if you are free, at your pleasure, to change the wholly arbitrary rules, but the fun is in winning within the rules. No difficulty, no fun.

13.   The buyers and sellers at the happiness market seem too often to have lost their sense of the pleasure of difficulty. Heaven knows what they are playing, but it seems a dull game. The Indian holy man seems dull to us, I suppose, because he seems to be refusing to play anything at all. The Western weakness may be in the illustration that happiness can be bought. Perhaps the Eastern weakness is in the idea that there is such a thing as perfect (and therefore static) happiness.

14.   Happiness is never more than partial. There are no pure states of mankind. Whatever else happiness may be, it is neither in having nor in being, but in becoming. What the Founding Fathers declared for us as an inherent right, we should do well to remember, was not happiness but the *pursuit* of happiness. What they might have underlined, could they have foreseen the happiness market, is the cardinal fact that happiness is in the pursuit itself, in the meaningful pursuit of what is life-engaging and life-revealing, which is to say, in the idea of *becoming*. A nation is not measured by what it possesses or wants to possess, but by what it wants to become.

15.   By all means let the happiness market sell us minor satisfactions and even minor follies so long as we keep them in scale and buy them out of spiritual change. I am no customer for either puritanism or asceticism. But drop any real spiritual capital at those bazaars, and what you come home to will be your own poorhouse.

DISCUSSION: Analysis

The methods of paragraph development—definition, division, comparison and contrast, and the like—are the methods we find in complete essays, and, as in most paragraphs, they do not occur alone. They are the means of analysis basic to exposition and also to argument. The reader of an essay should understand at every point why a particular method of analysis is being used, and how each method helps to develop the thesis, regardless of whether the thesis is stated or implied. Often transitional sentences are needed to make these relations clear. Writers must keep in mind that they know more about their subject than their readers do: they are illustrating ideas for their readers, and the kind and number of examples they provide depend on how much help is needed in understanding the thesis. No matter how logically developed the writer's ideas may be, if they are not explained clearly or illustrated, the essay will communicate nothing; it will convince no one except the writer.

QUESTIONS

1. Ciardi organizes his discussion of happiness as an extended definition. What kind of definition of happiness does he employ—denotative, connotative, stipulative, or theoretical?
2. Ciardi builds to his full definition of happiness through a consideration of advertising and the Eastern holy man. Given his opening comments on Swift and the American way of thinking, why does he delay his definition until late in the essay? How do his comments on advertising and the Eastern holy man help to establish his definition?
3. Where, finally does Ciardi state his definition?
4. "The pursuit of happiness" is so familiar a phrase that we are likely not to examine its full implications. Is Ciardi defining this phrase according to what he believes the founding fathers meant by it, or is he proposing his own definition?
5. Given what he says about this pursuit, would Ciardi agree with Goodman's thesis?

WRITING ASSIGNMENTS

1. Ciardi deals with an abstract idea through everyday experiences. Select another phrase in common use and define it as Ciardi does. Examine its implications fully.
2. Discuss the statment "We demand difficulty even in our games" through two different games that you enjoy playing. Indicate the extent of your agreement with Ciardi.

3. Develop the following statement through your personal observations: "Whatever else happiness may be, it is neither in having nor in being, but in becoming."
4. Ciardi analyzes women's magazines in light of the idea of happiness they purvey. Analyze a man's magazine in the same way, giving attention to the articles and the advertisements.

JAMES THURBER

What a Lovely Generalization!

1. I have collected, in my time, derringers, snowstorm paperweights, and china and porcelain dogs, and perhaps I should explain what happened to these old collections before I go on to my newest hobby, which is the true subject of this monograph. My derringer collection may be regarded as having been discontinued, since I collected only two, the second and last item as long ago as 1935. There were originally seventeen snowstorm paperweights, but only four or five are left. This kind of collection is known to the expert as a "diminished collection," and it is not considered cricket to list it in your *Who's Who* biography. The snowstorm paperweight suffers from its easy appeal to the eye and the hand. House guests like to play with paperweights and to slip them into their luggage while packing up to leave. As for my china and porcelain dogs, I disposed of that collection some two years ago. I had decided that the collection of actual objects, of any kind, was too much of a strain, and I determined to devote myself, instead, to the impalpable and the intangible.
2. Nothing in my new collection can be broken or stolen or juggled or thrown at cats. What I collect now is a certain kind of Broad Generalization, or Sweeping Statement. You will see what I mean when I bring out some of my rare and cherished pieces. All you need to start a collection of generalizations like mine is an attentive ear. Listen in particular to women, whose average generalization is from three to five times as broad as a man's. Generalizations, male or female, may be true ("Women don't sleep very well"), untrue ("There are no pianos in Japan"), half true ("People would rather drink than go to the theater"), debatable ("Architects have the wrong idea"), libelous ("Doctors don't know what they're doing"), ridiculous ("You never see foreigners fishing"), fascinating but undemonstrable ("People who

break into houses don't drink wine"), or idiosyncratic ("Peach ice cream is never as good as you think it's going to be").

3. "There are no pianos in Japan" was the first item in my collection. I picked it up at a reception while discussing an old movie called "The Battle," or "Thunder in the East," which starred Charles Boyer, Merle Oberon, and John Loder, some twenty years ago. In one scene, Boyer, as a Japanese naval captain, comes upon Miss Oberon, as his wife, Matsuko, playing an Old Japanese air on the piano for the entertainment of Loder, a British naval officer with a dimple, who has forgotten more about fire control, range finding, marksmanship, and lovemaking than the Japanese commander is ever going to know. "Matsuko," says the latter, "why do you play that silly little song? It may be tedious for our fran." Their fran, John Loder, says, "No, it is, as a matter of—" But I don't know why I have to go into the whole plot. The lady with whom I was discussing the movie, at the reception, said that the detail about Matsuko and the piano was absurd, since "there are no pianos in Japan." It seems that this lady was an authority on the musical setup in Japan because her great-uncle had married a singsong girl in Tokyo in 1912.

4. Now, I might have accepted the declarations that there are no saxophones in Bessarabia, no banjo-mandolins in Mozambique, no double basses in Zanzibar, no jews's-harps in Rhodesia, no zithers in Madagascar, and no dulcimers in Milwaukee, but I could not believe that Japan, made out in the movie as a great imitator of Western culture, would not have any pianos. Some months after the reception, I picked up an old copy of the *Saturday Evening Post* and, in an article on Japan, read that there were, before the war, some fifteen thousand pianos in Japan. It just happened to say that, right there in the article.

5. You may wonder where I heard some of the other Sweeping Statements I have mentioned above. Well, the one about peach ice cream was contributed to my collection by a fifteen-year-old girl. I am a chocolate man myself, but the few times I have eaten peach ice cream it tasted exactly the way I figured it was going to taste, which is why I classify this statement as idiosyncratic; that is, peculiar to one individual. The item about foreigners never fishing, or, at any rate, never fishing where you can see them, was given to me last summer by a lady who had just returned from a motor trip through New England. The charming generalization about people who break into houses popped out of a conversation I overheard between two women, one of whom said it was not safe to leave rye, Scotch or bourbon in your summer house when you closed it for the winter, but it was perfectly

all right to leave your wine, since intruders are notoriously men of insensitive palate, who cannot tell the difference between Nuits-St.-Georges and saddle polish. I would not repose too much confidence in this theory if I were you, however. It is one of those Comfortable Conclusions that can cost you a whole case of Château Lafite.

6. I haven't got space here to go through my entire collection, but there is room to examine a few more items. I'm not sure where I got hold of "Gamblers hate women"—possibly at Bleeck's—but, like "Sopranos drive men crazy," it has an authentic ring. This is not true, I'm afraid, of "You can't trust an electrician" or "Cops off duty always shoot somebody." There may be something in "Dogs know when you're despondent" and "Sick people hear everything," but I sharply question the validity of "Nobody taps his fingers if he's all right" and "People who like birds are queer."

7. Some twenty years ago, a Pittsburgh city editor came out with the generalization that "Rewrite men go crazy when the moon is full," but this is perhaps a little too special for the layman, who probably doesn't know what a rewrite man is. Besides, it is the abusive type of Sweeping Statement and should not be dignified by analysis or classification.

8. In conclusion, let us briefly explore "Generals are afraid of their daughters," vouchsafed by a lady after I had told her my General Wavell anecdote. It happens, for the sake of our present record, that the late General Wavell, of His Britannic Majesty's forces, discussed his three daughters during an interview a few years ago. He said that whereas he had millions of men under his command who leaped at his every order, he couldn't get his daughters down to breakfast on time when he was home on leave, in spite of stern directives issued the night before. As I have imagined it, his ordeal went something like this. It would get to be 7 A.M., and then 7:05, and General Wavell would shout up the stairs demanding to know where everybody was, and why the girls were not at table. Presently, one of them would call back sharply, as a girl has to when her father gets out of hand, "For heaven's sake, Daddy, will you be quiet! Do you want to wake the neighbors?" The General, his flanks rashly exposed, so to speak, would fall back in orderly retreat and eat his kippers by himself. Now, I submit that there is nothing in this to prove that the General was afraid of his daughters. The story merely establishes the fact that his daughters were not afraid of him.

9. If you are going to start collecting Sweeping Statements on your own, I must warn you that certain drawbacks are involved. You will be inclined to miss the meaning of conversations while lying in wait

for generalizations. Your mouth will hang open slightly, your posture will grow rigid, and your eyes will take on the rapt expression of a person listening for the faint sound of distant sleigh bells. People will avoid your company and whisper that you are probably an old rewrite man yourself or, at best, a finger tapper who is a long way from being all right. But your collection will be a source of comfort in your declining years, when you can sit in the chimney corner cackling the evening away over some such gems, let us say, as my own two latest acquisitions: "Jewelers never go anywhere" and "Intellectual women dress funny."

10. Good hunting.

QUESTIONS

1. Is Thurber's statement that a woman's "average generalization is from three to five times as broad as a man's" any better founded than other generalizations he cites? How do you think he wants the reader to take this statement?
2. How does each of the examples in paragraph 2 illustrate the labels Thurber gives them? Why is the statement that "People would rather drink than go to the theater" half true?
3. What is the overall tone of the essay, and how is it established? How is this tone related to Thurber's purpose in writing the essay?

WRITING ASSIGNMENTS

1. Collect examples of generalizations like those in paragraph 2, classifying them, and build your examples to a conclusion about the purpose such generalizations serve.
2. Write a characterization of Thurber from the way he talks about himself and talks to the reader of the essay. Consider his qualities as a humorist.

VERONICA GENG

Quote Commitment Unquote

An awful lot of worrying was done in the Fifties about whether people were able To Love or not. . . . all that talk about "commitment" and "permanent relationships" . . .

—Philip Roth, "Marriage à la Mode," *American Review #18*

1. Roth's way with the capital letter and the quotation mark suggests that he writes with an amused backward glance, as if the terms *able to love, commitment,* and *permanent relationships* were artifacts as remote as the series of Hogarth paintings from which he has drawn his story's title. This cool posture is a little démodé. The language Roth calls Fifties-feminese is back in style—for both sexes—and sneer at your own risk.

2. The term *commitment* is the operative one, for it is widely supposed to be the key to the other two: *Love without commitment is just fooling around; love with commitment is (or inexorably leads to) a permanent relationship.* A lot of people find it hard to think in any other way about love or permanent relationships. A mystique of committedness has taken hold and grabs everybody by the lapels to inform them of its imperatives.

3. I am irritated by the number of times per day this word breathes on me. I have begun to shrink from it, to view it with suspicion, as though it were propaganda for some unnamed special interest. I am wondering if people know what they mean by it, or if they are dupes.

4. "I believe in being able to commit myself to another person." What does that mean? A contract? Why not say so? My friend the speaker allows that *commitment* and *contract* have in common certain implications of the long haul and of voluntary giving over—"but, uh, it's more than that." It would have to be more than that to have the power it does, but an explanation of the more is hard to elicit. As far as I can tell, my friend's primary attachment to *commitment* is that it has become a value-loaded word and *contract* hasn't. A contract is something one either does or does not enter into, as suits one's purpose; as yet, no halo radiates from the brow of the person "able" to sign papers for auto insurance payments. But ah, *commitment:* it carries with it the virtue of committedness, the so-called ability to commit oneself. In fact, like other virtues on which people preen themselves, committedness, despite its literal meaning, is often found to exist without an object. ("I'm a very committed person.")

5. "Sorry, but I don't want any heavy commitments right now"—a familiar male (and maybe increasingly female) kiss-off. The kissed-off is thrown into a hell of excruciating vagueness: what exactly is it that is not wanted? The burdens feared by Paul, the Prince Charming figure in Donald Barthelme's *Snow White* ("her responsibilities of various sorts . . . teeth . . . piano lessons. . . .")? Then why not break up with clarity? ("Sorry, but I don't want to have to: pay your bills/talk to you/make love to you every night/ever see you again/other.")

6.   But mystiques do not thrive on clarity. The entire point of a word like *commitment* is its maddening vagueness. One is simply supposed to have a "sense" of what it signifies. That vagueness serves to reinforce the mental and emotional laziness of those who succumb to the mystique ("Commitment—or togetherness or masculinity, etc.—is just a natural thing, it doesn't need to be taken apart and analyzed") and to discomfit those who reject it ("How can I reject something so nebulous? What am I rejecting? Maybe they're right—maybe there's something to it").

7.   It was this sort of discomfort that sent me to my dictionaries. Commitment has been used in English since the 1400s, mostly with reference to such loveless matters as war and politics, prisons and madhouses, storage and burial ("to engage as opponents; to charge with a duty or office; to consign officially to confinement; to consign for safekeeping or disposal"). The definition nearest the sense of the commitment cant one hears around is this: "to give in trust; to put into charge or keeping." *Webster's Second New International Dictionary* points out that the word used this way "may express merely the general idea of delivering into another's charge . . . or may have the special sense of an absolute transfer to a superior power or final custody." But nowhere is it suggested that such delivery or transfer is a virtue.

8.   The Latin *committere* makes current usage seem downright deformed. None of the Latin definitions implies virtue, and some are negative ("to incur a punishment; to sin"). Most of the others do not even suggest permanence, stability, or duration, but something very nearly the opposite: "to begin; to set on foot; to venture; to risk oneself." These do not imply contracts, custodies, or eternities, but, in Noel Coward's phrase, "something a little less binding": beginnings, chances, first steps.

9.   Obviously our words acquire the meanings we need them for. Why did a word once used for venture and risk come to imply that there is virtue in handing oneself over to a future decided in advance? Perhaps because "commitment" makes life easy. It relieves you of the difficult businesses of venture and risk, autonomy and choice. It protects you from trusting or testing yourself by providing a handy external coercion to make you do right. It absolves you of responsibility for your actions—you were, after all, only following through on a "commitment." Without this prop, there would be troublesome evaluations to be made at every turn and you would be forced to reconcile conflicting feelings and beliefs (hard work ahead there), or even live with the fact of the irreconcilable. Easier to give yourself over to *another's*

charge, to *a superior power,* to *custody,* for *confinement, storage,* or *disposal.*

10. A "commitment" also provides you with many convenient excuses. Your failures can be explained in comfortingly global terms. (Your love affair did not collapse because you were a liar or ate with your feet on the table but because you were "unable to commit yourself.") You can use your "commitment" to justify your fears. ("Sorry, I can't take up this offer because I have another commitment.") You can use it to rationalize your promiscuities. ("I deserve some fun because of this dreary commitment I've gotten myself tied to.") You can even use it to get power over other people. ("We've committed ourselves to each other, so I have a weapon to hit you with when you don't do what I want.")

11. One of the more practical aspects of "commitment" is The Rule That Dare Not Speak Its Name. No one will admit this, but you do not actually have to abide by a "commitment" unless you feel like it. Although people who use "lack of commitment" as an excuse for passivity like to pretend that a "commitment" is as difficult to extricate oneself from as a military engagement or a mental ward, that is not true. A "commitment" applies until it no longer applies. Of course, bolting for this exit involves a massive exercise in bad faith, but many people find that a small price to pay for the advantage: taking the dread out of permanence.

12. "Commitment" is especially useful to institutionalized power, which cannot afford to trust anyone. A group of "committed" citizens is less threatening than a group of citizens who have not abdicated their ability to make judgments. The witnesses before the Senate Watergate Committee were the most "committed" individuals in recent history. "Commitments" keep your toe to the line; without them, a madman like you might do most anything—blow a whistle, change direction, take a chance.

13. Perhaps we are afraid to trust ourselves. And so we agree that "commitments" are natural and good and hand ourselves over to them like washing machines whose futures are set by the inflexible terms of a contract. Till death or the Department of Consumer Affairs do us part.

QUESTIONS

1. One job of the writer concerned with a current issue is, first, to acquaint the reader with its details—including its background— and, second, to explain why the issue is important enough to write

about. How does Geng identify the issue, and show the reader why the issue is important to her?

2. How does she keep before the reader the importance she attaches to attitudes connected with commitment? What are these attitudes?

3. What is the purpose of the dictionary meanings of *commitment,* given in paragraphs 7 and 8? In general, what attitude toward language do you find implied in these pargraphs? Does the author make her attitude explicit later in the essay?

4. In paragraphs 9–13, what conclusions does she draw from the use of the word *commitment?* What is the principle of order in these paragraphs?

5. How does she conclude the essay—by stating or restating her thesis, by reviewing her main evidence for it, by suggesting an application of it, or by drawing a final conclusion about the use of the word today?

6. Do you agree with the author's conclusions about the use of the word? Do you have a different explanation for its widespread use? Do you use the word in a way other than the author specifies?

WRITING ASSIGNMENT

Discuss the meanings you attach, and hear attached, to one of the following words:

a. sincere   c. cool
b. viable   d. tough

EDWARD T. HALL

The English and the Americans

1. It has been said that the English and the Americans are two great people separated by one language. The differences for which language gets blamed may not be due so much to words as to communications on other levels beginning with English intonation (which sounds affected to many Americans) and continuing to ego-linked ways of handling time, space, and materials. If there ever were two cultures in which differences of the proxemic details are marked it is in the educated (public school) English and the middle-class Americans. One of the basic reasons for this wide disparity is that in the United States we

use space as a way of classifying people and activities, whereas in England it is the social system that determines who you are. In the United States, your address is an important cue to status (this applies not only to one's home but to the business address as well). The Joneses from Brooklyn and Miami are not as "in" as the Joneses from Newport and Palm Beach. Greenwich and Cape Cod are worlds apart from Newark and Miami. Businesses located on Madison and Park avenues have more tone than those on Seventh and Eighth avenues. A corner office is more prestigious than one next to the elevator or at the end of a long hall. The Englishman, however, is born and brought up in a social system. He is still Lord—— no matter where you find him, even if it is behind the counter in a fishmonger's stall. In addition to class distinctions, there are differences between the English and ourselves in how space is allotted.

2.   The middle-class American growing up in the United States feels he has a right to have his own room, or at least part of a room. My American subjects, when asked to draw an ideal room or office, invariably drew it for themselves and no one else. When asked to draw their present room or office, they drew only their own part of a shared room and then drew a line down the middle. Both male and female subjects identified the kitchen and the master bedroom as belonging to the mother or the wife, whereas Father's territory was a study or a den, if one was available; otherwise, it was "the shop," "the basement," or sometimes only a workbench or the garage. American women who want to be alone can go to the bedroom and close the door. The closed door is the sign meaning "Do not disturb" or "I'm angry." An American is available if his door is open at home or at his office. He is expected not to shut himself off but to maintain himself in a state of constant readiness to answer the demands of others. Closed doors are for conferences, private conversations, and business, work that requires concentration, study, resting, sleeping, dressing, and sex.

3.   The middle- and upper-class Englishman, on the other hand, is brought up in a nursery shared with brothers and sisters. The oldest occupies a room by himself which he vacates when he leaves for boarding school, possibly even at the age of nine or ten. The difference between a room of one's own and early conditioning to shared space, while seeming inconsequential, has an important effect on the Englishman's attitude toward his own space. He may never have a permanent "room of his own" and seldom expects one or feels he is entitled to one. Even Members of Parliament have no offices and often

conduct their business on the terrace overlooking the Thames. As a consequence, the English are puzzled by the American need for a secure place in which to work, an office. Americans working in England may become annoyed if they are not provided with what they consider appropriate enclosed work space. In regard to the need for walls as a screen for the ego, this places the Americans somewhere between the Germans and the English.

4.   The contrasting English and American patterns have some remarkable implications, particularly if we assume that man, like other animals, has a built-in need to shut himself off from others from time to time. An English student in one of my seminars typified what happens when hidden patterns clash. He was quite obviously experiencing strain in his relationships with Americans. Nothing seemed to go right and it was quite clear from his remarks that we did not know how to behave. An analysis of his complaints showed that a major source of irritation was that no American seemed to be able to pick up the subtle clues that there were times when he didn't want his thoughts intruded on. As he stated it, "I'm walking around the apartment and it seems that whenever I want to be alone my roommate starts talking to me. Pretty soon he's asking 'What's the matter?' and wants to know if I'm angry. By then I am angry and say something."

5.   It took some time but finally we were able to identify most of the contrasting features of the American and British problems that were in conflict in this case. When the American wants to be alone he goes into a room and shuts the door—he depends on architectural features for screening. For an American to refuse to talk to someone else present in the same room, to give them the "silent treatment," is the ultimate form of rejection and a sure sign of great displeasure. The English, on the other hand, lacking rooms of their own since childhood, never developed the practice of using space as a refuge from others. They have in effect internalized a set of barriers, which they erect and which others are supposed to recognize. Therefore, the more the Englishman shuts himself off when he is with an American the more likely the American is to break in to assure himself that all is well. Tension lasts until the two get to know each other. The important point is that the spatial and architectural needs of each are not the same at all.

QUESTIONS

1. What is Hall's thesis, and where is it first stated? Where does he restate it later in the essay?

2. How is the contrast between the English and the Americans organized? Does Hall contrast the English and American patterns point by point, or instead deal with one set of patterns first, another set afterwards? Or does he mix these methods of organization?
3. How does he illustrate these patterns? Does he illustrate all of them?
4. Hall traces cause-and-effect relations through contrast of living patterns. What are the chief relations he traces?
5. How do the examples explain the phrase *internalized a set of barriers,* in the concluding paragraph? What does Hall mean by *screening?*
6. What use does Hall make of classification in the whole essay? On what basis does he divide the English and the Americans?

WRITING ASSIGNMENTS

1. Discuss the extent to which your study habits fit the English or the American pattern. Use your analysis to comment on the accuracy of Hall's thesis.
2. Contrast two of your friends or relatives on the basis of their attitude toward space and architecture or toward privacy. State the similarities before commenting on the differences. Notice that the differences may be slight ones, and even slight differences may be revealing of people.

Order of Ideas

BEN MARSH

A Rose-Colored Map

1. Country music presents two images of life—life as it should be, and life as it should not be. The conflict between these two themes is the force that drives country music; it is this dialectic of right and wrong that makes country music exciting to the millions who listen to it. Perhaps the melodies are formulaic, but it is the lyrics that sell the songs, the descriptions of everyday people facing problems and making right or wrong decisions about them. The right decision is the one that lets people be honest, faithful, moral, and therefore happy.

2.   Right and wrong in country music are not distributed randomly across the American landscape. Goodness is concentrated in the South and in the countryside, while badness is far more common in cities and in the North. If the lyrics of country songs were all someone knew about America, he would think that everything of value was in the rural South. Country music contains a clear, if incidental, regional geography of the South, describing its terrain, its climate, its agriculture, and its natural resources. Everybody in country songs grew up on a farm in the South, where their parents still live. The normal city in country music is Nashville, the normal river is the Mississippi, the normal beer is Lone Star, the normal crop is cotton, the normal dog is a hound, and the normal food is black-eyed peas. And if the directions given in various songs are treated like a road map, that map says it is "up" to Chicago and Cincinnati, "down" to New Orleans and Georgia, "over" or "across" to the Carolinas, and "out" to Texas or California, while it is "back" to Tennessee or Kentucky, "back" to the mountains, and "back" to the farm. The center of country music's map of America is clearly the rural South, especially the mountain states.

3.   The South, as it is presented in country music, is the best possible place to live, the standard for comparing all other places, especially the Northern city. The North, in general, is a cold, gray, hazy area at the periphery of country music's map, as far from home as one can get. Listen to one song or a hundred, the pattern is the same. If a song is about someone being unfaithful, drunken, jobless, or lonely, it will be in a city, probably in the North. If a song is about family, security, childhood, love, or other pleasant things, it will be in the South, probably on a farm. Texas usually appears as a land of heroic men and romantic women. Canada and Alaska show up as our new frontiers, important places for individualists. And California is an ambiguous place with both Southern and Northern characteristics, perhaps a reflection of the conflict between the agricultural and urban parts of that state.

4.   There are obvious advantages for the writers of allegorical tales like country music's to have a conventionalized geography to reinforce the message. But why does country music use *this* image of America? Why is country music so pleased with the South and so upset with the North? The answer to this question lies not in the actual geography of the United States, but in how country music's audience perceives the geography of the United States. It is not a question of what America is, but of what America means to these people. As a result, the ques-

tion has to do with far more than just a style of singing, it has to do with the attitudes of the millions of Americans who listen to country music—attitudes about regional differences in American society, about the role of the media as part of the American power structure, and about the value of progress in general.

5. One attractive explanation of the geography *in* country music is that it is a reflection of the geography *of* country music. This argument holds that country music views the world from the South because most of the performers, or most of the audience, live in the South. However, this is untrue. Country music is not exclusively Southern in any sense but its history and its perspective. True, most of the older performers came from the South, but many were from Northern states like Illinois and Pennsylvania, or even from Canada. And modern country music stars are from all over the English-speaking world.

6. Country music's audience is even less Southern than its performers. The music is indisputably popular in the South, but the evidence—from the distribution of country music radio stations, from performers' itineraries, and from the regional circulation of fan magazines—indicates that country music has more listeners outside the South than in it. Some suggest that this is because a large part of country music's audience is homesick expatriate Southerners living in Northern cities, but the data does not support this. For example, country music is not, as one would expect, especially popular in industrial cities such as Detroit, which traditionally has been a pole of South-North migration.

7. Country music's Southern perspective on the world must be treated as symbolism, not reporting. Perhaps country music once glorified the South because it was parochial music about local places, but it is now popular nearly everywhere. In the United States country music is the typical music on stage at small-town high schools and county fairs all across America, and on the radio in machine shops and beauty parlors, on truckers' tape decks, and on jukeboxes in ten thousand little bars.

8. To understand how the vision of America in country music is appropriate to this audience, it is necessary to look carefully at how country music functions in American culture. Country music comes to its audience through the media and must be viewed in that context. Country music's morality plays appear on records, in movies, in magazines, on syndicated television shows, and especially over the radio. The history of early country music is inseparable from the history of

early radio, and there are now over 1,700 radio stations in the U.S. that play country music every day. Country music is a radio ministry, and the gospel it preaches—that we should all be moral, righteous, and Southern—makes sense when it is seen in this context.

9. Country music's view of America must be compared with another view, as distinctive as country music's but offering a different perspective—the image projected by network television, the wire services, and mass-circulation magazines. In these media virtually all the decisions about content are made in New York, Washington, Chicago, and Los Angeles. Accordingly, the brightest, most exciting, most memorable spots on these, our most frequently reinforced pictures of our land, are the big cities. Compared to them, the South and the rest of the country seem almost featureless, perhaps a little sinister, or maybe just boring.

10. Country music's image of America contradicts that of the "main-stream" American media—and that is its appeal. The South is presented as a virtuous place to country music fans all over America not for what it is, but for what it is not. Unlike the North, the seat of the media, the South is not responsible for the shape we are in. According to the media's own reporting, the South has had nothing to do with inflation, taxes, shortages, abuses of federal power, Supreme Court rulings, and so forth. The same innocence of the sins of power that let Jimmy Carter go from ex-governor of Georgia to President in twenty-two months lets country music paint the South as a haven from the sins of the nation.

11. The South has escaped bad press mostly because it is under-reported, and this is why country music has been free to impose whatever meaning it chooses on the South. When the South has appeared in the national media, it has been portrayed as backward, ignorant, and reactionary. But country music can transform these attributes into virtues: backward easily becomes rustic, ignorant becomes simple and uncomplicated, and reactionary becomes old-fashioned.

12. The ability to see a region which is nearly ignored in the media as the best part of America, and to see the centers of media power as the worst part, reflects deep displeasure by millions of Americans with the content of those media. Country music's gloomy image of the North is a reflection of what the audience feels about what is happening to America in general. The South, in contrast, is a picture of how the nation would be if it had not gone astray.

13. What country music's audience seeks to escape by vicarious life in the rural South is, in a word, progress. Country music's South is

above all old-fashioned. Life in the South means old-fashioned family, old-fashioned religion, old-fashioned values. Life in the South is life in the past, a laundered past without smallpox and without lynchings. This is what country music's rural Southern perspective is all about— the South has none of the problems of the North, and the country has none of the problems of the city, because the past has none of the problems of the present. Country music's South provides escape from modern America.

14. It seems extreme to suggest that millions of Americans feel the need to escape from the land they live in, yet that is the clear message of country music's picture of the world. Escape is certainly a common enough theme in the rest of country music. Drinking, divorce, traveling, prison, and death can all be considered kinds of escape, and all are quite common in country music. To Freud the countryside itself symbolized escape. The rural South is just another kind of escape; it is a place where one avoids the problems of the modern world and lives the simple, friendly, old-fashioned country life.

15. Who are the people who feel they need country music's exit and haven from the world we all live in? It is possible to construct a picture of an average country music listener from various kinds of television, radio, and magazine marketing data. The picture of this average person is entirely consonant with his expressed desire to avoid the wrongs of modern American life. Quite simply, the person who needs to escape into the mythically old-fashioned South is the one who is losing something as America progresses. It is not the rural-urban migrant, it is not the second- or third-generation European-American, it is not the Black. All these people have gained as America industrializes, urbanizes, progresses. None of them fear the future and cherish the past. None of them could be as nostalgic as the country music fan for a South that never was.

16. Country music is for the small-town American. Country music and its image of America pleases those millions of quiet people in traditional, socially conservative communities who daily face erosion of the values that make their lives meaningful. America is moving from the nineteenth century into mass society not in a smooth glide, but in a series of painful little shocks, and the person most likely to appreciate country music is the person for whom those shocks hurt most. Country music's function is to replenish the system of values that we seem to be losing.

17. The image of America in country music may seem extreme and one-sided, but it is in answer to what its audience perceives as an ex-

treme and one-sided world. It is important to these threatened Americans everywhere to know that there is still a region in this land where life is lived as they know it should be, and where there is relief from the changes they fear. The fiction of the rural South in country music is that place.

18. By glorifying the South, country music departs radically from nearly every other popular geography of the United States. But country music's message that America is taking drastically wrong directions is radical, too. Country music seems to have almost Marxian overtones in its treatment of the injuries of class. Poverty is ennobling, for example, while wealth imprisons its owners. And some recent songs have been surprisingly militant in their calls for greater social justice through rejection of illegitimate authority and through greater economic equity. Johnny Cash has produced several successful songs in the past few years about men's attempts to get more control on their jobs. In one an auto worker steals a Cadillac "one piece at a time" in his lunchbox; in another a hungry farmworker steals a strawberry cake from a fancy hotel, after spending weeks picking strawberries; and in a third song a machinist plots that on the day he retires he will punch out his boss as he leaves. The songs are meant to be ironic, yet they are portrayals of what would be acts of revolution if they occurred en masse. In content and even in style, these songs are reminiscent of Woody Guthrie's songs during the Depression.

19. Partly because of this radicalness, an odd convergence has taken place between country music and the music descended from the folk/protest tradition of the Sixties, sometimes called "folk-rock." Both are displeased with modern urban America and each uses instrumentation and arrangements derived from their common Appalachian folk origins. The result is that the themes and the performances in the two genres are similar enough that performers like Kris Kristofferson or Commander Cody, who are virtually antithetical in politics, religion, and life-style to the average country fan, can compete in the same market with some performers so puritanical that they will not appear in clubs where liquor is served.

20. Country music shares its radically positive image of the South with two other recent national movements. Neither the election of Jimmy Carter to the Presidency, nor those southward migrations of population, industry, and political power to the so-called Sun Belt, would have been possible in the face of strong anti-Southern sentiment. There are obvious differences between the motivations that determine how people vote, where they move to, and what kind of

music they listen to, but perhaps all these events are best thought of as manifestations of a single change in attitude. In years to come we can only expect to see more reaction to the old alignment of power in America, power expressed through the government and the major media.

21.   America was settled by immigrants, and we have never stopped moving. From Plymouth Rock to the Cumberland Gap to the Oregon Trail, if a man did not like life where he was, he could move down the road and it would be different. But we have run out of frontiers. Today, if a new place is needed, an old place must be redefined. Country music is showing us this process in action, as a major American region acquires a new image. However, allegiance to this new South takes place at the expense of allegiance to the country as a whole. The irony of country music's audience considering itself to be an especially patriotic group is that it is loyal to a mythical earlier America as symbolized by the sunny, old-fashioned South of country music, not to America as it now exists.

DISCUSSION: Order of Ideas

As in the paragraph, the order of ideas in an essay may be determined by the audience. Thus, if the audience is able to understand the thesis without explanation, it may be stated toward the beginning. But if explanation is required, writers may build to the thesis. It may also appear later if they assume their audience will be hostile to it or easier to convince, once the evidence has been considered.

Certain patterns of organization have become traditional in the essay, mainly because they reflect the natural processes of explanation and argument. The essay of ideas has been strongly influenced by the oration of the law courts and legislature of ancient Greece and Rome. The parts of this oration correspond to the essay as written today and can be summarized as follows:

exordium, or introduction, which shapes the mood of the audience, appeals to its interest and good will, and states the subject of the oration or essay.

division of proofs, which summarizes the kinds of evidence to be presented, and states the thesis partially or fully

narration, or background, which states the facts of the case

confirmation, or proof, which argues the thesis

refutation, which answers opponents

peration, or conclusion, which reinforces the original appeal to the audience, makes new appeals, and perhaps summarizes the proofs of the argument

The expository essay omits one or more of these parts, for example, the refutation; and the confirmation, or proof, consists usually of a presentation of details in support of the main point or thesis. The parts may also be arranged in a different way, the narration, or background, perhaps coming before the confirmation or combined with it. This procedure has the advantage of unifying the essay in accord with traditional approaches to the audience. In other words, the writer is able to exploit a familiar ordering of ideas.

The essay of personal experience may be as carefully organized as the essay of ideas, but the division of parts usually is less rigorous. For example, Orwell's "Shooting an Elephant" makes important comments on the relationship between imperialist ruler and those ruled through an episode that defines their relationship. These same comments could be made in a formal discussion of the problem, without illustration.

The ordering of ideas may reveal a characteristic way of thinking—one that we find in other essays by the same writer. We sometimes use the word *style* to describe this feature. In the larger sense of the word, *style* is the sum of choices we make—in diction and sentence construction as well as organization. One writer may favor long, heavily coordinated sentences, as in the speech of a non-stop talker. Another writer, used to speaking in short clipped sentences, may write in the same way. The preference for short or long paragraphs may reflect this same personal characteristic.

If choice is essential to style in writing, we might assume that only writing reflects style, since we usually do not plan how we talk. But we clearly do make choices in speaking—if only in our choice of vocabulary. In writing, our choices may be more deliberate—and usually *are* deliberate when we have a particular audience in mind. Choice and habit are hard to distinguish. The sentences we write depend on the shape and rhythm of the sentences we speak: we speak before we write. In the course of growing up, the influence of conventional usage affects our ways of expressing ourselves. Gradually we learn to fit these ways to various situations. Most of the time we depend on familiar phrases, and we usually do not depart from familiar sentence patterns. In formal situations our choices are increasingly selective: we are more sensitive to the appropriateness of words, and we may take care with our sentences and diction in ways we do not in ordinary conversation. Ultimately personal style is shaped not only by acquired habits of thought and feeling but by personality. Thought and expression in the literate person are inseparable processes. The order of ideas in our writing reflects how we think and also how we feel.

QUESTIONS

1. Marsh moves from the background and definition of country music (narration) to an explanation of its characteristics. What characteristics does he emphasize, and how are these related to his thesis, stated in his opening sentence?
2. As part of his explanation, Marsh refutes a common view of country music (paragraphs 5–6). What is that view, and how does he refute it?
3. What is the purpose of the comparison with the view of the media (paragraphs 9–10), and the history of early radio (paragraph 8)?
4. What attitudes explain the popularity of country music? Why does Marsh consider these attitudes after his discussion of the view of the media?
5. Why does Marsh conclude with a discussion of the radicalness of country music? Could he have discussed this radicalness before explaining the attitudes that make country music popular?
6. How does he restate his thesis in the concluding paragraph? How does he keep his thesis before the reader in the course of his discussion?

WRITING ASSIGNMENTS

1. Illustrate the attitudes Marsh discusses in country music you are familiar with. Discuss other attitudes that you find, and state whether these support Marsh's analysis.
2. Analyze the attitudes implied in rock lyrics or those of musical comedy written in a certain period—for example, the Rodgers and Hammerstein musicals of the 1940s.

JOAN DIDION

Marrying Absurd

1. To be married in Las Vegas, Clark County, Nevada, a bride must swear that she is eighteen or has parental permission and a bridegroom that he is twenty-one or has parental permission. Someone must put up five dollars for the license. (On Sundays and holidays, fifteen dollars. The Clark County Courthouse issues marriage licenses at any time of the day or night except between noon and one in the afternoon, between eight and nine in the evening, and between four and five in the morning.) Nothing else is required. The State of Nevada,

alone among these United States, demands neither a premarital blood test nor a waiting period before or after the issuance of a marriage license. Driving in across the Mojave from Los Angeles, one sees the signs way out on the desert, looming up from that moonscape of rattlesnakes and mesquite, even before the Las Vegas lights appear like a mirage on the horizon: "GETTING MARRIED? Free License Information First Strip Exit." Perhaps the Las Vegas wedding industry achieved its peak operational efficiency between 9:00 p.m. and midnight of August 26, 1965, an otherwise unremarkable Thursday which happened to be, by Presidential order, the last day on which anyone could improve his draft status merely by getting married. One hundred and seventy-one couples were pronounced man and wife in the name of Clark County and the State of Nevada that night, sixty-seven of them by a single justice of the peace, Mr. James A. Brennan. Mr. Brennan did one wedding at the Dunes and the other sixty-six in his office, and charged each couple eight dollars. One bride lent her veil to six others. "I got it down from five to three minutes," Mr. Brennan said later of his feat. "I could've married them *en masse,* but they're people, not cattle. People expect more when they get married."

2. What people who get married in Las Vegas actually do expect— what, in the largest sense, their "expectations" are—strikes one as a curious and self-contradictory business. Las Vegas is the most extreme and allegorical of American settlements, bizarre and beautiful in its venality and in its devotion to immediate gratification, a place the tone of which is set by mobsters and call girls and ladies' room attendants with amyl nitrite poppers in their uniform pockets. Almost everyone notes that there is no "time" in Las Vegas, no night and no day and no past and no future (no Las Vegas casino, however, has taken the obliteration of the ordinary time sense quite so far as Harold's Club in Reno, for which for a while issued, at odd intervals in the day and night, mimeographed "bulletins" carrying news from the world outside); neither is there any logical sense of where one is. One is standing on a highway in the middle of a vast hostile desert looking at an eighty-foot sign which blinks "STARDUST" or "CAESAR'S PALACE." Yes, but what does that explain? This geographical implausibility reinforces the sense that what happens there has no connection with "real" life; Nevada cities like Reno and Carson are ranch towns, Western towns, places behind which there is some historical imperative. But Las Vegas seems to exist only in the eye of the beholder. All of which makes it an extraordinarily stimulating and interesting place, but an odd one in which to want to wear a candlelight satin Priscilla of

Boston wedding dress with Chantilly lace insets, tapered sleeves and a detachable modified train.

3.   And yet the Las Vegas wedding business seems to appeal to precisely that impulse. "Sincere and Dignified Since 1954," one wedding chapel advertises. There are nineteen such wedding chapels in Las Vegas, intensely competitive, each offering better, faster, and, by implication, more sincere services than the next: Our Photos Best Anywhere, Your Wedding on A Phonograph Record, Candlelight with Your Ceremony, Honeymoon Accommodations, Free Transportation from Your Motel to Courthouse to Chapel and Return to Motel, Religious or Civil Ceremonies, Dressing Rooms, Flowers, Rings, Announcements, Witnesses Available, and Ample Parking. All of these services, like most others in Las Vegas (sauna baths, payroll-check cashing, chinchilla coats for sale or rent) are offered twenty-four hours a day, seven days a week, presumably on the premise that marriage, like craps, is a game to be played when the table seems hot.

4.   But what strikes one most about the Strip chapels, with their wishing wells and stained-glass paper windows and their artificial bouvardia, is that so much of their business is by no means a matter of simple convenience, of late-night liaisons between show girls and baby Crosbys. Of course there is some of that. (One night about eleven o'clock in Las Vegas I watched a bride in an orange minidress and masses of flame-colored hair stumble from a Strip chapel on the arm of her bridegroom, who looked the part of the expendable nephew in movies like *Miami Syndicate*. "I gotta get the kids," the bride whimpered. "I gotta pick up the sitter, I gotta get to the midnight show." "What you gotta get," the bridegroom said, opening the door of a Cadillac Coupe de Ville and watching her crumple on the seat, "is sober.") But Las Vegas seems to offer something other than "convenience"; it is merchandising "niceness," the facsimile of proper ritual, to children who do not know how else to find it, how to make the arrangements, how to do it "right." All day and evening long on the Strip, one sees actual wedding parties, waiting under the harsh lights at a crosswalk, standing uneasily in the parking lot of the Frontier while the photographer hired by The Little Church of the West ("Wedding Place of the Stars") certifies the occasion, takes the picture: the bride in a veil and white satin pumps, the bridegroom usually in a white dinner jacket, and even an attendant or two, a sister or a best friend in hot-pink *peau de soie*, a flirtation veil, a carnation nosegay. "When I Fall in Love It Will Be Forever," the organist plays, and then a few bars of Lohengrin. The mother cries; the stepfa-

ther, awkward in his role, invites the chapel hostess to join them for a drink at the Sands. The hostess declines with a professional smile; she has already transferred her interest to the group waiting outside. One bride out, another in, and again the sign goes up on the chapel door: "One moment please—Wedding."

5.   I sat next to one such wedding party in a Strip restaurant the last time I was in Las Vegas. The marriage had just taken place; the bride still wore her dress, the mother her corsage. A bored waiter poured out a few swallows of pink champagne ("on the house") for everyone but the bride, who was too young to be served. "You'll need something with more kick than that," the bride's father said with heavy jocularity to his new son-in-law; the ritual jokes about the wedding night had a certain Panglossian character, since the bride was clearly several months pregnant. Another round of pink champagne, this time not on the house, and the bride began to cry. "It was just as nice," she sobbed, "as I hoped and dreamed it would be."

QUESTIONS

1. One principle of order in the Didion is spatial: we see Las Vegas as a visitor would see it from the highway. How does this spatial view change as the essay progresses?
2. The essay at the same time moves to increasingly bizarre episodes, culminating in the wedding party of the final paragraph. What is bizarre about this episode? How do the transitional sentences that open some of the paragraphs indicate this principle of order?
3. Is Didion concerned mainly with characterizing Las Vegas through the weddings performed there, or is the city a backdrop for a comment she wishes to make about wedding customs or about American values in the late 1960s?
4. In Voltaire's *Candide* the philosopher Pangloss says, "All is for the best in this best of all possible worlds." How does the wedding described in the final paragraph reflect this attitude?
5. What is the dominant tone of the essay, and how is it established?
6. Where is the thesis stated? How do the details of the essay develop it? What ideas or attitudes does Didion imply rather than state?

WRITING ASSIGNMENTS

1. Discuss the extent to which the details of the essay support the view of the American wedding developed by Marcia Seligson (see page 38).
2. Characterize a city you have visited through an activity associated

with it that typifies its way of life and values. Let your details reveal this way of life and these values.

RALPH ELLISON
Living with Music

1.   In those days it was either live with music or die with noise, and we chose rather desperately to live. In the process our apartment—what with its booby-trappings of audio equipment, wires, discs and tapes—came to resemble the Collier mansion, but that was later. First there was the neighborhood, assorted drunks and a singer.

2.   We were living at the time in a tiny ground-floor-rear apartment in which I was also trying to write. I say "trying" advisedly. To our right, separated by a thin wall, was a small restaurant with a juke box the size of the Roxy. To our left, a night-employed swing enthusiast who took his lullaby music so loud that every morning promptly at nine Basie's brasses started blasting my typewriter off its stand. Our living room looked out across a small back yard to a rough stone wall to an apartment building which, towering above, caught every passing thoroughfare sound and rifled it straight down to me. There were also howling cats and barking dogs, none capable of music worth living with, so we'll pass them by.

3.   But the court behind the wall, which on the far side came knee-high to a short Iroquois, was a forum for various singing and/or preaching drunks who wandered back from the corner bar. From these you sometimes heard a fair barbershop style "Bill Bailey," free-wheeling versions of "The Bastard King of England," the saga of Uncle Bud, or a deeply felt rendition of Leroy Carr's "How Long Blues." The preaching drunks took on any topic that came to mind: current events, the fate of the long-sunk *Titanic* or the relative merits of the Giants and the Dodgers. Naturally there was great argument and occasional fighting—none of it fatal but all of it loud.

4.   I shouldn't complain, however, for these were rather entertaining drunks, who like the birds appeared in the spring and left with the first fall cold. A more dedicated fellow was there all the time, day and night, come rain, come shine. Up on the corner lived a drunk of legend, a true phenomenon, who could surely have qualified as the king of all the world's winos—not excluding the French. He was neither poetic like the others nor ambitious like the singer (to whom we'll

presently come) but his drinking bouts were truly awe-inspiring and he was not without his sensitivity. In the throes of his passion he would shout to the whole wide world one concise command, "Shut up!" Which was disconcerting enough to all who heard (except, perhaps, the singer), but such were the labyrinthine acoustics of courtyards and areaways that he seemed to direct his command at me. The writer's block which this produced is indescribable. On one heroic occasion he yelled his obsessive command without one interruption longer than necessary to take another drink (and with no appreciable loss of volume, penetration or authority) for three long summer days and nights, and shortly afterwards he died. Just how many lines of agitated prose he cost me I'll never know, but in all that chaos of sound I sympathized with his obsession, for I, too, hungered and thirsted for quiet. Nor did he inspire me to a painful identification, and for that I was thankful. Identification, after all, involves feelings of guilt and responsibility, and since I could hardly hear my own typewriter keys I felt in no way accountable for his condition. We were simply fellow victims of the madding crowd. May he rest in peace.

5.   No, these more involved feelings were aroused by a more intimate source of noise, one that got beneath the skin and worked into the very structure of one's consciousness—like the "fate" motif in Beethoven's Fifth or the knocking-at-the-gates scene in *Macbeth*. For at the top of our pyramid of noise there was a singer who lived directly above us; you might say we had a singer on our ceiling.

6.   Now, I had learned from the jazz musicians I had known as a boy in Oklahoma City something of the discipline and devotion to his art required of the artist. Hence I knew something of what the singer faced. These jazzmen, many of them now world-famous, lived for and with music intensely. Their driving motivation was neither money nor fame, but the will to achieve the most eloquent expression of idea-emotions through the technical mastery of their instruments (which, incidentally, some of them wore as a priest wears the cross) and the give and take, the subtle rhythmical shaping and blending of idea, tone and imagination demanded of group improvisation. The delicate balance struck between strong individual personality and the group during those early jam sessions was a marvel of social organization. I had learned too that the end of all this discipline and technical mastery was the desire to express an affirmative way of life through its musical tradition and that this tradition insisted that each artist achieve his creativity within its frame. He must learn the best of the past, and add to it his personal vision. Life could be harsh, loud and wrong if it

wished, but they lived it fully, and when they expressed their attitude toward the world it was with a fluid style that reduced the chaos of living to form.

7.   The objectives of these jazzmen were not at all those of the singer on our ceiling, but though a purist committed to the mastery of the *bel canto* style, German *lieder,* modern French art songs and a few American slave songs sung as if *bel canto,* she was intensely devoted to her art. From morning to night she vocalized, regardless of the condition of her voice, the weather or my screaming nerves. There were times when her notes, sifting through her floor and my ceiling, bouncing down the walls and ricocheting off the building in the rear, whistled like tenpenny nails, buzzed like a saw, wheezed like the asthma of a Hercules, trumpeted like an enraged African elephant—and the squeaky pedal of her piano rested plumb center above my typing chair. After a year of non-co-operation from the neighbor on my left I became desperate enough to cool down the hot blast of his phonograph by calling the cops, but the singer presented a serious ethical problem: Could I, an aspiring artist, complain against the hard work and devotion to craft of another aspiring artist?

8.   Then there was my sense of guilt. Each time I prepared to shatter the ceiling in protest I was restrained by the knowledge that I, too, during my boyhood, had tried to master a musical instrument and to the great distress of my neighbors—perhaps even greater than that which I now suffered. For while our singer was concerned basically with a single tradition and style, I had been caught actively between two: that of the Negro folk music, both sacred and profane, slave song and jazz, and that of Western classical music. It was most confusing; the folk tradition demanded that I play what I heard and felt around me, while those who were seeking to teach the classical tradition in the schools insisted that I play strictly accordng to the book and express that which I was *supposed* to feel. This sometimes led to heated clashes of wills. Once during a third-grade music appreciation class a friend of mine insisted that it was a large green snake he saw swimming down a quiet brook instead of the snowy bird the teacher felt that Saint-Saëns' *Carnival of the Animals* should evoke. The rest of us sat there and lied like little black, brown and yellow Trojans about that swan, but our stalwart classmate held firm to his snake. In the end he got himself spanked and reduced the teacher to tears, but truth, reality and our environment were redeemed. For we were all familiar with snakes, while a swan was simply something the Ugly Duckling of the story grew up to be. Fortunately some of us grew up with a genuine appre-

ciation of classical music *despite* such teaching methods. But as an aspiring trumpeter I was to wallow in sin for years before being awakened to guilt by our singer.

9.   Caught mid-range between my two traditions, where one attitude often clashed with the other and one technique of playing was by the other opposed, I caused whole blocks of people to suffer.

10.   Indeed, I terrorized a good part of an entire city section. During summer vacation I blew sustained tones out of the window for hours, usually starting—especially on Sunday mornings—before breakfast. I sputtered whole days through M. Arban's (he's the great authority on the instrument) double- and triple-tonguing exercises—with an effect like that of a jackass hiccupping off a big meal of briars. During school-term mornings I practiced a truly exhibitionist "Reveille" before leaving for school, and in the evening I generously gave the ever-listening world a long, slow version of "Taps," ineptly played but throbbing with what I in my adolescent vagueness felt was a romantic sadness. For it was farewell to day and a love song to life and a peace-be-with-you to all the dead and dying.

11.   On hot summer afternoons I tormented the ears of all not blessedly deaf with imitations of the latest hot solos of Hot Lips Paige (then a local hero), the leaping right hand of Earl "Fatha" Hines, or the rowdy poetic flights of Louis Armstrong. Naturally I rehearsed also such school-band standbys as the *Light Cavalry* Overture, Sousa's "Stars and Stripes Forever," the *William Tell* Overture, and "Tiger Rag." (Not even an after-school job as office boy to a dentist could stop my efforts. Frequently, by way of encouraging my development in the proper cultural direction, the dentist asked me proudly to render Schubert's *Serenade* for some poor devil with his jaw propped open in the dental chair. When the drill got going, or the forceps bit deep, I blew real strong.)

12.   Sometimes, inspired by the even then considerable virtuosity of the late Charlie Christian (who during our school days played marvelous riffs on a cigar box banjo), I'd give whole summer afternoons and the evening hours after heavy suppers of black-eyed peas and turnip greens, cracklin' bread and buttermilk, lemonade and sweet potato cobbler, to practicing hard-driving blues. Such food oversupplied me with bursting energy, and from listening to Ma Rainey, Ida Cox and Clara Smith, who made regular appearances in our town, I knew exactly how I wanted my horn to sound. But in the effort to make it do so (I was no embryo Joe Smith or Tricky Sam Nanton) I sustained the curses of both Christian and infidel—along with the encouragement of

those more sympathetic citizens who understood the profound satisfaction to be found in expressing oneself in the blues.

13. Despite those who complained and cried to heaven for Gabriel to blow a chorus so heavenly sweet and so hellishly hot that I'd forever put down my horn, there were more tolerant ones who were willing to pay in present pain for future pride.

14. For who knew what skinny kid with his chops wrapped around a trumpet mouthpiece and a faraway look in his eyes might become the next Armstrong? Yes, and send you, at some big dance a few years hence, into an ecstasy of rhythm and memory and brassy affirmation of the goodness of being alive and part of the community? Someone had to; for it was part of the group tradition—though that was not how they said it.

15. "Let that boy blow," they'd say to the protesting ones. "He's got to talk baby talk on that thing before he can preach on it. Next thing you know he's liable to be up there with Duke Ellington. Sure, plenty Oklahoma boys are up there with the big bands. Son, let's hear you try those 'Trouble in Mind Blues.' Now try and make it sound like old Ida Cox sings it."

16. And I'd draw in my breath and do Miss Cox great violence.

17. Thus the crimes and aspirations of my youth. It had been years since I had played the trumpet or irritated a single ear with other than the spoken or written word, but as far as my singing neighbor was concerned I had to hold my peace. I was forced to listen, and in listening I soon became involved to the point of identification. If she sang badly I'd hear my own futility in the windy sound; if well, I'd stare at my typewriter and despair that I should ever make my prose so sing. She left me neither night nor day, this singer on our ceiling, and as my writing languished I became more and more upset. Thus one desperate morning I decided that since I seemed doomed to live within a shrieking chaos I might as well contribute my share; perhaps if I fought noise with noise I'd attain some small peace. Then a miracle: I turned on my radio (an old Philco AM set connected to a small Pilot FM tuner) and I heard the words

Art thou troubled?
Music will calm thee . . .

I stopped as though struck by the voice of an angel. It was Kathleen Ferrier, that loveliest of singers, giving voice to the aria from Handel's *Rodelinda*. The voice was so completely expressive of words and music that I accepted it without question—what lover of the vocal art could resist her?

18.   Yet it was ironic, for after giving up my trumpet for the typewriter I had avoided too close a contact with the very art which she recommended as balm. For I had started music early and lived with it daily, and when I broke I tried to break clean. Now in this magical moment all the old love, the old fascination with music superbly rendered, flooded back. When she finished I realized that with such music in my own apartment, the chaotic sounds from without and above had sunk, if not into silence, then well below the level where they mattered. Here was a way out. If I was to live and write in that apartment, it would be only through the grace of music. I had tuned in a Ferrier recital, and when it ended I rushed out for several of her records, certain that now deliverance was mine.

19.   But not yet. Between the hi-fi record and the ear, I learned, there was a new electronic world. In that realization our apartment was well on its way toward becoming an audio booby trap. It was 1949 and I rushed to the Audio Fair. I have, I confess, as much gadget-resistance as the next American of my age, weight and slight income; but little did I dream of the test to which it would be put. I had hardly entered the fair before I heard David Sarser's and Mel Sprinkle's Musician's Amplifier, took a look at its schematic and, recalling a boyhood acquaintance with such matters, decided that I could build one. I did, several times before it measured within specifications. And still our system was lacking. Fortunately my wife shared my passion for music, so we went on to buy, piece by piece, a fine speaker system, a first-rate AM-FM tuner, a transcription turntable and a speaker cabinet. I built half a dozen or more preamplifiers and record compensators before finding a commercial one that satisfied my ear, and, finally, we acquired an arm, a magnetic cartridge and—glory of the house—a tape recorder. All this plunge into electronics, mind you, had as its simple end the enjoyment of recorded music as it was intended to be heard. I was obsessed with the idea of reproducing sound with such fidelity that even when using music as a defense behind which I could write, it would reach the unconscious levels of the mind with the least distortion. And it didn't come easily. There were wires and pieces of equipment all over the tiny apartment (I became a compulsive experimenter) and it was worth your life to move about without first taking careful bearings. Once we were almost crushed in our sleep by the tape machine, for which there was space only on a shelf at the head of our bed. But it was worth it.

20.   For now when we played a recording on our system even the drunks on the wall could recognize its quality. I'm ashamed to admit, however, that I did not always restrict its use to the demands of pleasure or defense. Indeed, with such marvels of science at my control I lost my humility. My ethical consideration for the singer up above shriveled like a plant in too much sunlight. For instead of soothing, music seemed to release the beast in me. Now when jarred from my writer's reveries by some especially enthusiatic flourish of our singer, I'd rush to my music system with blood in my eyes and burst a few decibels in her direction. If she defied me with a few more pounds of pressure against her diaphragm, then a war of decibels was declared.

21.   If, let us say, she were singing *"Depuis le Jour"* from *Louise*, I'd put on a tape of Bidu Sayão performing the same aria, and let the rafters ring. If it was some song by Mahler, I'd match her spitefully with Marian Anderson or Kathleen Ferrier; if she offended with something from *Der Rosenkavalier*, I'd attack her flank with Lotte Lehmann. If she brought me up from my desk with art songs by Ravel or Rachmaninoff, I'd defend myself with Maggie Teyte or Jennie Tourel. If she polished a spiritual to a meaningless artiness I'd play Bessie Smith to remind her of the earth out of which we came. Once in a while I'd forget completely that I was supposed to be a gentleman and blast her with Strauss' *Zarathustra*, Bartók's *Concerto for Orchestra*, Ellington's "Flaming Sword," the famous crescendo from *The Pines of Rome*, or Satchmo scatting, "I'll be Glad When You're Dead" (you rascal you!). Oh, I was living with music with a sweet vengeance.

22.   One might think that all this would have made me her most hated enemy, but not at all. When I met her on the stoop a few weeks after my rebellion, expecting her fully to slap my face, she astonished me by complimenting our music system. She even questioned me concerning the artists I had used against her. After that, on days when the acoustics were right, she'd stop singing until the piece was finished and then applaud—not always, I guessed, without a justifiable touch of sarcasm. And although I was now getting on with my writing, the unfairness of this business bore in upon me. Aware that I could not have withstood a similar comparison with literary artists of like caliber, I grew remorseful. I also came to admire the singer's courage and control, for she was neither intimidated into silence nor goaded into undisciplined screaming; she persevered, she marked the phrasing of the great singers I sent her way, she improved her style.

23. Better still, she vocalized more softly, and I, in turn, used music less and less as a weapon and more for its magic with mood and memory. After a while a simple twirl of the volume control up a few decibels and down again would bring a live-and-let-live reduction of her volume. We have long since moved from that apartment and that most interesting neighborhood and now the floors and walls of our present apartment are adequately thick and there is even a closet large enough to house the audio system; the only wire visible is that leading from the closet to the corner speaker system. Still we are indebted to the singer and the old environment for forcing us to discover one of the most deeply satisfying aspects of our living. Perhaps the enjoyment of music is always suffused with past experience; for me, at least, this is true.

24. It seems a long way and a long time from the glorious days of Oklahoma jazz dances, the jam sessions at Halley Richardson's place on Deep Second, from the phonographs shouting the blues in the back alleys I knew as a delivery boy, and from the days when watermelon men with voices like mellow bugles shouted their wares in time with the rhythm of their horses' hoofs and farther still from the washerwomen singing slave songs as they stirred sooty tubs in sunny yards; and a long time, too, from those intense, conflicting days when the school music program of Oklahoma City was tuning our earthy young ears to classical accents—with music appreciation classes and free musical instruments and basic instruction for any child who cared to learn and uniforms for all who made the band. There was a mistaken notion on the part of some of the teachers that classical music had nothing to do with the rhythms, relaxed or hectic, of daily living, and that one should crook the little finger when listening to such refined strains. And the blues and the spirituals—jazz—? they would have destroyed them and scattered the pieces. Nevertheless, we learned some of it all, for in the United States when traditions are juxtaposed they tend, regardless of what we do to prevent it, irresistibly to merge. Thus musically at least each child in our town was an heir of all the ages. One learns by moving from the familiar to the unfamiliar, and while it might sound incongruous at first, the step from the spirituality of the spirituals to that of the Beethoven of the symphonies or the Bach of the chorales is not as vast as it seems. Nor is the romanticism of a Brahms or Chopin completely unrelated to that of Louis Armstrong. Those who know their native culture and love it unchauvinistically are never lost when encountering the unfamiliar.

25. Living with music today we find Mozart and Ellington, Kirsten

Flagstad and Chippie Hill, William L. Dawson and Carl Orff all forming part of our regular fare. For all exalt life in rhythm and melody;
all add to its significance. Perhaps in the swift change of American society in which the meanings of one's origin are so quickly lost, one of
the chief values of living with music lies in its power to give us an ori-
entation in time. In doing so, it gives significance to all those indefin-
able aspects of experience which nevertheless help to make us what we
are. In the swift whirl of time music is a constant, reminding us of
what we were and of that toward which we aspired. Art thou troubled? Music will not only calm, it will ennoble thee.

QUESTIONS

1. How do the opening four paragraphs of the Ellison establish a tone
   and suggest a theme or line of thought to be pursued in the whole
   essay? How do these paragraphs prepare the reader for the more
   serious consideration of "a more intimate source of noise" in paragraph 5 and the paragraphs that follow, in particular the reference
   to "the chaos of living" at the end of paragraph 6?
2. What do the details of the opening seven paragraphs reveal about
   the background and character of the writer?
3. Ellison states an important idea in paragraph 8: "For while our
   singer was concerned basically with a single tradition and style, I
   had been caught actively between two: that of the Negro folk
   music, both sacred and profane, slave song and jazz, and that of
   Western classical music." Have paragraphs 1–7 anticipated this
   theme in any way? Is the conflict they deal with of the same kind?
4. How do the two kinds of music represent two cultural ideals and
   worlds in the whole essay? How does Ellison use his personal experience to keep the focus of the essay on these differences?
5. Ellison builds to a series of statements about music and about life
   in the United States. Could one of these be considered the thesis of
   the essay—a statement that explains the organization and accounts
   for the various details and considerations? Or are paragraphs 24
   and 25 afterthoughts or reflections? Might the essay have ended
   with paragraph 23 without seeming incomplete?

WRITING ASSIGNMENTS

1. Characterize the author of the essay on the basis of the details he
   provides about himself and his interests. Build your characterization to a statement of the quality you believe stands out most in
   the essay.

2. First describe your musical preferences, distinguishing them carefully. Then account for them and indicate the extent to which they
have produced a conflict in your life comparable to the conflict
Ellison portrays in paragraph 8.

Interpretation of Evidence

ROBERT A. HECHT

The Right to Remain Indian

1. American Indians are on the warpath again. Unlike the centuries
preceding 1900, however, this warpath is more subtle and less violent
(although some violence has occurred) than the older, traditional warpath that led directly to the enemy camp, and whose purpose was to
take something from the enemy, either his horses, his scalp, his life,
or all three. Today's warpath employs public relations campaigns,
protest marches, court actions, pressures on legislators, national Indian organizations, the support of Hollywood personalities, and other
special interest devices that other special interest groups have used in
American politics since Jamestown and Plymouth. And today's warpath aims not at stealing property or committing bloody deeds, but at
preserving Indian rights, especially the right to remain Indian. For
four centuries the American Indian fought for his life; now he is fighting for his way of life. And at the moment he is not doing badly, as a
catalogue of recent Indian legal and legislative victories demonstrates.
2. The non-Indian world generally expresses sympathy for the
American Indian whenever the subject of his affairs and history comes
up. Most Americans seem aware, however dimly and imprecisely, that
the Indian has been a major victim in history, and that something is
owed to him in restitution. Few Americans know, however, what the
Indian wants from the rest of us. Indeed, the Indians themselves are
not clear or united on most of their goals. But they are generally
agreed upon these: they want to hold onto their land bases called reservations, maintain tribal self-rule, and keep in force the treaties origi-

nally drawn up with the American government, all of which have helped to establish the Indians as a unique people with unique rights and privileges within American society.

3.   The reservation system as a way of providing self-contained, self-governing areas for the Indians, and the treaty system as a way of obtaining agreements with the various tribes, go back to the early days of English settlement in America. While the English did not recognize Indian sovereignty over the lands the Indians occupied, they did generally acknowledge a special political status for the tribes, a status that placed them outside the larger body politic. Within certain limitations, which varied from time to time and from colony to colony, Indian tribes controlled their own lands and ruled themselves.

4.   The treaty system of negotiating with the Indians was continued by the American government in 1776, until being abruptly ended by Congress in 1871. By that time hundreds of treaties had been drawn up and ratified, treaties dealing with all kinds of problems, but whose main purpose in nearly every case was to secure land from the tribes. An interesting and perplexing legal question had been raised by the treaty system, however—since treaties were traditionally drawn up only between sovereign bodies, did this not mean that the American government recognized the tribes as sovereign nations?

5.   It did not. The United States used the treaty system for nearly a century as a convenient method of buying land from the Indians. At no time was Indian sovereignty ever explicitly acknowledged by the American government. It dealt with the tribes *as if* they were sovereign, and *as if* their chiefs could act for their people the way an American president or a European monarch could act for his; but this was merely a device, a handy way of making deals with the Indians. The Indians were considered subject to the national sovereignty and to acts of Congress pertaining to them.

6.   Despite the denial of Indian sovereignty by the American government, however, the federal courts have handed down decisions over the years whose total effect has been to grant the tribes a measure of sovereignty within the larger sovereignty of the United States, if such a condition is conceivable. Chief Justice John Marshall in the early 1830s, for example, in struggling to find a way of defining the legal and political status of the tribes, called them "domestic dependent nations." By this he meant that they were within the United States (domestic), needful of American aid and protection (dependent), and yet had certain powers of self-governance (nations). Marshall never denied that Congress had ultimate authority over the Indians. But his

decision, and others that have followed since then, clearly set the tribes apart both politically and legally from the rest of the American people.

7. In addition to court decisions defining a unique status for the tribes, Congress itself, beginning in 1790, has passed laws contributing to that same end. In that year it enacted the Indian Non-Intercourse Act, which provided that no state could obtain land from the Indians without Congressional approval. Any sales of land within the states had to be ratified by Congress. This law, for many years ignored, but never repealed, is the basis for some gigantic Indian land claims that are presently working their way through the courts. The largest of these claims, lodged against the state of Maine by the Penobscot and Passamaquoddy tribes, was settled out of court last October. Originally claiming some two-thirds of Maine, or about 12½ million acres of land, these tribes accepted instead $37 million in cash, and 100,000 acres to be added to their present reservations. A number of other eastern states are also being subjected to Indian lawsuits seeking restoration of illegally sold lands. New York, for instance, negotiated 55 land purchases from the Indians after 1790, none of which was approved by Congress. Massachusetts, Connecticut, and Rhode Island are facing similar legal actions from tribes within their borders.

8. Other Congressional legislation since 1790 has continued to acknowledge, either implicitly or explicitly, the separate status of the tribes in America. Not all this legislation, of course, has worked in favor of the Indians, which should not surprise us, since in the nineteenth century Congress was invariably motivated in its Indian dealings by demands from white Americans to secure Indian lands for white settlement. The long and grim history of the Indians during that century is abundantly illustrated by the conflicts between them and the American military, consistently called in to defend whites infringing upon Indian lands, and the harvest of land cessions, embodied in the form of treaties, that inevitably followed these conflicts. By 1887 the total Indian land base, nearly all of it west of the Mississippi River, had shrunk to under 140,000,000 acres. The treaty system as applied to the American Indians had led to disastrous consequences for them. Their chiefs, through a combination of ignorance and despair on their part, and bribery and threats by American officials, had disposed of nearly all their people's lands by putting their marks on pieces of paper that few of them could read or understand. It had been a great price to pay for the semisovereign status that Congress and the courts had conferred upon them.

9.   Between 1887 and 1934 their land base declined even more. Thanks to passage of the Dawes Severalty Act of 1887, which provided for breaking up the reservations (and along with them the tribes) by allotting the land in individual plots to individual Indians, and the selling of the rest to the general public, the Indians lost the bulk of their holdings. By 1934 they were down to 48,000,000 acres (almost half of that barren and unusable), and the future of tribal existence seemed bleak and uncertain.

10.   In the 1920's, however, a number of liberal white Americans, including the anthropologist and future Bureau of Indian Affairs Commissioner John Collier, joining with some prominent Indian leaders, began an extensive crusade for Indian reform. In general the goals of this crusade were to halt the further sale of Indian lands, to improve the condition of Indians in general, and to enlarge and reinforce tribal authority on the reservations that remained. The crusade culminated in the Indian Reform Act of 1934, which produced at least the partial accomplishment of these goals.

11.   Despite a number of termination bills in the 1950's, severing the government relationship with some specific tribes, which led to the reduction of some tribal holdings and the disappearance of some reservations altogether (the Klamaths of Oregon sold their entire reservation), the Indians have generally managed to remain in business as tribes, and the tribes have continued to exercise considerable authority, through their elected councils, over their reservations. Indeed, one recent complaint from the non-Indian world, and from some Indians, has been that the tribal councils exercise too much authority, to the detriment of the civil rights of many individual Indians.

12.   This is one of the interesting peculiarities of the reservation system. In the past two decades both Congress and the courts, and even some state authorities, have moved to the position that the American Constitution does not apply to Indian reservations. In several recent cases the federal courts have concluded that the enactments of tribal councils supersede the Constitution, unless Congress specifies otherwise. This has led to some outrageous violations of individual Indians' civil rights, all sanctioned by the courts, which have refused to assume jurisdiction in these disputes. In some cases the courts have argued that the goal of tribal self-government is more important than protecting the rights of individual Indians under the Constitution. In others, judicial jurisdiction has been denied on the grounds that reservations are not states, but rather self-governing entities within states. The

Fourteenth Amendment, which begins, "No *State* shall . . . deprive any person of life, liberty, or property without due process of law," does not apply to reservations since they are not states or parts of states.

13.   A few of these court cases have involved freedom of religion. In *Toledo et al v. Pueblo de Jemez et al*, tried in the United States District Court for New Mexico, six Protestant Indians of this predominantly Catholic reservation charged that the Pueblo tribal council had denied them the right to bury their dead in the tribal cemetery, to build their own church or hold services in their own homes, to allow Protestant missionaries onto the reservation, or to use machinery owned by the tribe in common. A clearer instance of religious discrimination could hardly be found. The court, however, did not make a judgment; it dismissed the case on the grounds that it lacked jurisdiction.

14.   In another case, this one involving the Native American Church, which uses the hallucinogenic drug peyote in its ritual, it was claimed that the Navaho tribal council was denying freedom of religion to the members of this federally recognized religion by prohibiting the use of peyote on the Navaho reservation. The members of this church sued for their right to worship freely under the First and Fourteenth Amendments. In 1959 the Tenth Circuit Court of Appeals, all three justices concurring, found that it did not have jurisdiction.

15.   Some states have also refused to intervene in Indian civil rights disputes. In 1974 the Onondaga tribal council in New York passed a law which ordered eviction from the reservation of any mixed-blood families, where either the husband or wife was not of Indian ancestry. Their properties, including their homes, were to be turned over to the council. Some two dozen families were involved. When they refused to move, as some of them did, they were driven from their homes by tribal policemen. Appeals for help to local state authorities went unheeded. The state police turned the calls over to the sheriff's office. The sheriff's office termed it a "hot potato," and refused to intercede. The evacuations proceeded, with some of the evacuees burning their own houses rather than see them fall into the hands of the council members.

16.   The most recent publicized case involving tribal authority versus an individual Indian's civil rights was decided in May, 1978 by the Supreme Court. This case, stemming from the Indian Civil Rights Act passed by Congress in 1968, which generally applied the civil rights of other Americans to Indian reservations, seemed to fall into a different category from those brought under the federal Constitution. Here was

a case, after all, arising under a Congressional enactment. The plaintiff, Mrs. Julia Martinez, a Santa Clara Pueblo Indian, was suing the tribal council because it was denying her children the right to vote in tribal elections, to a share of federal funds granted to the tribe, or to inherit her property when she died. The council had passed a law in 1939 prohibiting tribal membership, or rights of inheritance, to the children of any female Santa Clara Indians who married outside the tribe. Male members would not be penalized if they did the same thing. Mrs. Martinez had married a Navaho. The children of their marriage were not considered members of the tribe, and therefore not entitled to any tribal benefits. Under the Indian Civil Rights Act of 1968, which ordered tribal governments to implement the due process clause of the Fourteenth Amendment, Mrs. Martinez was suing for equal treatment with male Santa Clara Indians.

17. Mrs. Martinez seemed to have a good case, but she lost. The Supreme Court, only Byron White dissenting, denied that it had jurisdiction, since Congress had not specifically granted it jurisdiction when it passed the bill. In writing the majority opinion Thurgood Marshall said that to allow such suits as that of Mrs. Martinez, "would be at odds with the Congressional goal of protecting tribal self-government." The Indian Civil Rights Act of 1968, therefore, seems to depend on the good will and cooperation of the tribal councils if it is to be effective.

18. In general, reservation Indians clearly approve these decisions. There have been no significant Indian voices raised in favor of outside interference on reservations to protect the civil rights of Indians. On the contrary, tribal members have been fighting harder than ever to maintain the unique Indian position within the United States, a position enjoyed by no other religious, ethnic, or racial group in the country. Only the Indians, on their reservations, have such special rights of self-government. They may not be true nations, but they have come closer to that status than any other group in American society.

19. At the moment, however, there are a number of bills before Congress that would, if passed, reduce Indian control over their reservations. One would restrict tribal rights to waters flowing through their reservations. Another would take away the extraordinary fishing rights of Indians in the state of Washington, granted to them under nineteenth-century treaties, and confirmed more recently by the courts. Another would terminate the federal connection with the reservations. These bills inspired the recent "Longest Walk," a five-month trek by several hundred Indians, joined by hundreds of others

NATIVE AMERICANS

• About half of all Indians live in urban areas, 28 percent live on reservations, the remainder live in rural areas.

• The ten states with the largest Indian populations:

Oklahoma	98,468
Arizona	95,812
California	91,018
New Mexico	72,788
North Carolina	44,406
Washington	33,386
So. Dakota	32,365
New York	28,355
Montana	27,130
Minnesota	23,128

• Total Indian population, 1970 census: 792,730

• There are about 115 Indian reservations in the United States, the great bulk of them west of the Mississippi River. The biggest reservation is that of the Navahos in Arizona, Utah and New Mexico which exceeds 25,000 square miles (slightly larger than the state of West Virginia) and contains nearly 60,000 inhabitants. One of the smallest reservations belongs to the Pajoaque Pueblos in New Mexico, the population of which in 1970 numbered 33.

• Suicide rate: 32 per 100,000 as compared with the rate for the general population of 16.

• Unemployment rate: an estimated 45 percent compared with about 6 percent for the general population.

• Median family income for 1971: $4,000 as compared with $9,867.

• Infant mortality rate: 30.9 per 1000 live births as compared with 21.8 per 1000 live births.

• Percent entering college in 1971: 18 percent as compared with 50 percent.

• Median years of schooling (1970): 9.8 as compared with 12.1.   R.A.H.

---

along the way, from San Francisco to Washington, D.C. One of the objectives of this walk was to protest and defeat these bills. The Indians met with Vice President Mondale, who greeted them cordially, alternately booed and cheered Senator Kennedy, and almost conferred with President Carter.

20. Even without the effort of the Longest Walk, however, it seems highly unlikely that any of these bills will ever come to a vote, much less pass. Congress, like the courts and states, is wary of arousing the Indian world and the non-Indian supporters of that world. Indian reservations, with all their unique characteristics, with their good things and their bad, will continue on into the indefinite future. Despite some anti-Indian "backlash" against some of the violent Indian actions in recent years, such as the occupation of Alcatraz, the storming and pillaging of the B.I.A. office in Washington, and the siege at Wounded Knee in South Dakota, there are no serious threats to Indian self-determination appearing at this time.

21. The "vanishing Indian," the stereotype of the late nineteenth-century, is far from vanishing. Reservation home rule is more solidly established than ever, Indian self-esteem is on the rise, and the Indian world is in ferment. Where this will lead is anybody's guess, but at

this writing the Indian's future, if not bright, certainly seems brightening. Alexander Pope's "poor Indian! whose untutor'd mind/Sees God in clouds, or hears him in the wind" has become a sophisticated and successful practitioner of the art of survival in the modern world.

DISCUSSION: Interpretation of Evidence

Narratives, which provide background, are indispensable to exposition, and also to argument, to be considered next. Whether in an exposition of our ideas or in a debate, they tell the audience that the past facts give importance to one issue rather than another. Some matters of fact are of concern to most if not all Americans today. We can take for granted that most Americans accept the need of energy conservation: the issue in the current debate over nuclear power plants is not whether we should seek new and efficient energy sources but whether nuclear energy is both efficient and safe. A narrative of the history of nuclear power plants in the United States is essential not only as a source of evidence in an exposition of our ideas on nuclear energy but also, in arguments, as a means of persuading people that the issue is a crucial one today.

No evidence is as neutral or objective as many wish to believe, nor does all evidence have the same weight of importance. In choosing evidence it is important to distinguish between *primary* sources—firsthand accounts by participants or observers—and *secondary* sources—later reports and interpretations by those who were not present. Primary evidence must be sifted for differing versions of an event and for distinctive viewpoints that color the reporting. Almost twenty years after the assassination of President Kennedy, authorities disagree on what to consider evidence and on what alleged eyewitnesses heard or saw. In 1979 a special Congressional committee reopened the question of evidence bearing on the Kennedy assassination and that of Martin Luther King, Jr.

Determining the reliability of eyewitness accounts is only one of the writer's concerns. The motives of witnesses can obviously affect the reports of events and their interpretation. A German general's account of the Normandy invasion, in a dispatch to Hitler, is certain to be different from the account of an American general witnessing the same events. Secondary sources may help the writer determine what is factual and accurate in primary sources, but these also must be used with caution, since later writers often shape evidence to fit a particular view of people or history. Indeed, all interpretations are shaped by personal and cultural attitudes that the writer may or may not be aware of. Primary and secondary sources supplement each other as means to arriving at the truth about a subject.

QUESTIONS

1. Hecht divides his narrative between the older and the recent history of issues bearing on the rights of American Indians. What aspects of the older history does he focus on in paragraphs 3–11?
2. What light does this older history shed on current issues? What do such recent events as the Martinez case and the Longest Walk tell us about issues of most concern to American Indians today? What issues are of less concern, or perhaps of little or no concern?
3. What is Hecht's purpose in writing? Is he providing an exposition of the present situation, or is he seeking to persuade the reader of some particular idea?
4. Does Hecht remain neutral in his presentation of the facts, or does he express or imply agreement or disagreement with people on either side of any of the issues discussed?

WRITING ASSIGNMENT

Examine an article or book concerned with one of the issues discussed in the essay to describe the following:

a. the use of primary sources
b. the use of secondary sources
c. interpretations of these various sources
d. stated or implied attitudes that shape or color these interpretations
e. the writer's position on the issue—stated or implied

BARBARA EHRENREICH AND DEIRDRE ENGLISH

The Rise of the Single Girl

1. In 1955, or even 1960, no one looking for a likely new culture heroine would have thought of the single woman. For one thing, she was hard to find, appearing in the women's media only as a short-lived premarital phase, or, in her later years (twenty-five plus) as a vexing problem for hostesses. She was the odd woman in a couple-oriented culture, an object of pity to her married sisters, something of a freak to the medical profession. She might be brilliant, famous, visibly pleased with herself, successful in every way—but the judgment hung over her that she had "failed as a woman." The woman who remained

single long enough for the condition to appear to be chronic was writ-ten off as a sexual cripple, a biological anomaly.

2.   The "single girl" who burst out into the media in the early sixties corresponded to a new social reality: the single woman, divorced or never married, who lived alone and supported herself. In the early six-ties, a trend-setting minority of single women had begun to crowd into the "singles ghettos" of New York, San Francisco, Washington, D.C., and Seattle. They were secretaries, stewardesses, social work-ers, "gal fridays," and "assistants" of various kinds in publishing houses, banks, departments stores, etc. They wanted to get married sometime, but not to be "just a housewife." They went to bars (the first "singles bar" opened in 1964 on New York's Upper East Side) to meet men. They saved for ski weekends. They skipped meals so they could afford (and fit) the latest clothes. They had "relationships."

3.   For many real-life "single girls," the new sexual freedom that went with life in the big city was not exactly a libidinal romp. In the sixties most clerical jobs *required* women to look sexy—as if women's entry into the marketplace had to be masked with an ever-more deter-mined facade of "femininity." And it took a certain desperation for women to thrust themselves into the after-hours social scene: the suc-cessful singles bars soon became known cynically as "meat markets." But from a distance it all looked glamorous enough: the big-city single girl wore the latest fashions from the pages of *Cosmo* or *Glam-our*. She took the pill and lived in an apartment with a double bed. She spent her money on herself and men spent attention on her. She was the old feminist ideal of the independent woman with a new twist—she was sexy.

4.   It was Helen Gurley Brown, more than anyone else, who was responsible for the transformation of the "spinster" of the forties and fifties into "the newest glamour girl of our times." Her book *Sex and the Single Girl* announced the new woman in 1962; her magazine, *Cos-mopolitan*, has promoted the single-girl image since Brown's takeover as editor in 1965. An ex-single girl herself, who worked her way up from clerical jobs to the top of the publishing industry, Brown knew from personal experience what it took to create—and hold onto—a sexy image. "When I got married," she confides in *Sex and the Single Girl*, I moved in with six-pound dumb-bells, slant board, an electronic device for erasing wrinkles . . . and enough high-powered vitamins to generate life in a statue." "I'm sure of this," she exhorted her readers. "You're not too fat, too thin, too tall, too small, too dumb, or too myopic to have married women gazing at you wistfully." [1]

5. Brown's message was more than a pep talk for insecure singles. She grasped the appalling fact that "magazines never deal with, that single women are too brainwashed to figure out, that married women know but won't admit. . . ." namely, that men *didn't like* the suburban housewives of the romantic ideal. Expert ideology had so thoroughly knitted sex to reproduction that there was supposed to be one continuous blur of female regression linking sexual intercourse, childbirth, and Jimmy's first Little League game. Brown understood how tenuous the links really were: who wanted to embrace a woman who had baby drool on her shoulder and chocolate fingerprints all over her blouse? Sex could be peeled away from the home and family scene as easily as clingy sweaters could be peeled off the willing starlets in James Bond movies. When the single girl walked away with female sexuality, then the housewife would indeed have nothing to do but gaze wistfully after her.

6. Brown, perhaps even more than feminist Betty Friedan, whose *Feminine Mystique* followed *Sex and the Single Girl* in 1963, sensed the profound misogyny which was spreading under the suburban "dream houses" like seepage from a leaky septic tank. Men resented their domestication, and hated the company of sexless "Moms." Brown advised her single girls to avoid the Formica practicality of the suburbs and transform their apartments into lairs of erotic fascination. But the new single girl was not using her sexiness simply to drag a man down into a world of female "trivia." Her world, like his, was the world of the Market:

. . . a single woman, even if she is a file clerk, moves in the world of men. She knows their language, the language of retailing, advertising, motion pictures, exporting, shipbuilding. Her world is a far more colorful world than the one of P.T.A., Dr. Spock and the jammed clothes dryer.[2]

The single girl had the pizazz which came from facing the real world on the same terms as a man (though for only a fraction of the pay):

She is engaging because she lives by her wits. She supports herself. . . . She is not a parasite, a dependent, a scrounger, a sponger or a bum. She is a giver, not a taker, a winner and not a loser.[3]

7. The housewife, by implication *was* a parasite, a dependent, a "bum." While the single girl braved the rigors of the business world, the housewife lived a life of sheltered ease. To Brown, the wife deserved no quarter; the worst that could happen to her was that she too

would get a taste of the single life. "I'm afraid I have a rather cavalier attitude about wives," Brown wrote. Husbands were fair game for the single girl, who after all, had no desire to take the wife's place behind a vacuum cleaner in Levittown. The new single girl was not just a sexy object; she needed male attention and she went after it—wives, children, mortgages, and the *Ladies' Home Journal* notwithstanding.

8.   The triumph of the single girl was complete by the late sixties and early seventies. *Cosmopolitan,* which reached a circulation of about two and a half million, was followed by *Viva* and *Playgirl,* while the hard-core propagandists of domesticity—*Woman's Day* and *Family Circle*—held on only at the supermarket checkout stands (where they remain leading sellers). Debbie Reynolds, Doris Day, and Lucille Ball vanished into the canyons of Beverly Hills to make way for tough new heroines like Faye Dunaway and Angie Dickinson, and at last the single working girl burst into family viewing time in the engaging persona of Mary Tyler Moore.

9.   Meanwhile, in the popular media, the full-time housewife had sunk to approximately the level of prestige once occupied by single women. She was more and more likely to be portrayed as the object of pity—an infantile neurotic who got through the day with the aid of "mother's little helper" (tranquilizers) and three-hour doses of soap operas. *Diary of a Mad Housewife* showed her pacing in the confinement of her family; in *A Woman Under the Influence,* she breaks out—to a mental hospital. TV's favorite housewife in the mid-seventies was Mary Hartman—who has a neurotic relationship with her daughter, an affair with a policeman, a dramatic mental breakdown—all the while remaining distracted by the details of housekeeping, like the "waxy yellow build-up" on the kitchen floor. Eventually the housewife's reputation got so bad that even the *Ladies' Home Journal* dropped her, preferring to be known henceforth as "LHJ," and telling its advertisers:

LHJ stands for Ladies' Home Journal.

And Ladies' Home Journal stands for the woman who never stands still. . . .

One moment, she's off to the mountains for some skiing. The next moment, she's off to the islands for some tennis. And in between, she's a growing family [sic], an exciting career and creative way of life that's hers and hers alone.[4]

10.   American capitalism crossed the culture gap from *LHJ* to *Cosmo,* from the shopping mall to the discothèque, with barely a

tremor of discomfort. To be sure, presidential proclamations on the importance of the family to the American way of life have become a bipartisan tradition, and there are continuing right-wing attempts to revive a romantic ideal of femininity. But the marketing men were, on the whole, delighted with the new singles lifestyle. First of all, in just a physical sense, the singles lifestyle meant more demand for the basic necessities like appliances and furniture. In a suburban home, four or more people might use one TV set; in a singles apartment, one person used one set. If everyone could be induced to live alone (including children, for the sake of the argument), the demand for TV sets would increase fourfold or more, with no increase in population. The director of market research for a major U.S.-based multinational corporation (who asked that neither he nor the corporation be identified) explained this principle to us in a 1974 interview. Asked what he thought of the trend toward women delaying marriage and living alone, he said:

There's nothing in this that business would be opposed to. People living alone need the same things as people living in families. The difference is there's no sharing. So really this trend is good because it means you sell more products. The only trend in living arrangements that I think business does not look favorably on is this thing of communes, because here you have a number of people using the same products.*

11.   In addition to expanding the market for familiar products like TVs, blenders, and vacuum cleaners, the singles lifestyle represented a new *kind* of market, centered on travel, liquor, hi fi and sports equipment, clothing, and cosmetics. The theme was instant gratification. American families spent their best years *saving*—for the kids' college education or for a larger house someday, or they channeled it into home improvements and durable goods. But there was nothing to stop the single from enjoying her (or his) money now. For example, an ad for *Psychology Today* magazine, directed at potential advertisers, shows what is supposed to be a typical reader: A young woman, sitting on her living room floor, wearing a scuba mask and flippers, holding ski poles, with a tennis racket tucked under one arm. The caption says in bold lettering, **"I love me."** "I'm not conceited," the ad goes on:

---

* He went on to explain that the way "business" dealt with the commune threat was by keeping them out of the media. Thus there are no situation comedies about life in a commune, no ads, etc. The glamour of singleness, however, is continually extolled.

I'm just a good friend to myself.

And I like to do whatever makes me feel good.

Me, myself and I used to sit around, putting things off until tomorrow.

Tomorrow we'll buy new ski equipment, and look at the new compact cars. And pick up that new camera.

The only trouble is that tomorrow always turned into the next tomorrow.

And I never had a good time "today" . . .

[But now] **I live my dreams today, not tomorrow.**[5]

12.   It had to happen. Ever since the first warm winds of "permissiveness" swept America in the twenties, something like this had been in the air. In the thirties, forties, and fifties women were told to "express themselves," to follow their "instincts," by all means to have fun. Then the experts and the admen told them that "fun" meant a house and babies, that it in fact meant hard work and sacrifice. Sooner or later someone had to discover that there was desperately little pleasure to be gotten out of new aluminum siding, or a fifteen-hundred-dollar living room set which is kept under plastic until company comes. The media which reflected—and promoted—the new singles lifestyle spoke in a subversive whisper to a generation of young women: "Why wait? Why sacrifice? You don't need any excuses to indulge yourself. It's OK to have fun right now—for yourself." No one denied that a woman should fulfill herself even though "fulfillment" might mean masochistic suffering. But if fulfillment meant casual sex and new cameras, instead of freckled kids and a lawn free of crab grass—what was wrong with that?

13.   A clear-headed capitalist could only rejoice at the new self-indulgent mood of young women. Sexual romanticism had sustained a market for single-family homes, for large cars, heavy appliances, and fruit-flavored breakfast cereals. But it was now becoming clear that one sybaritic single could outconsume a family of four. Spending no longer had to be justified in terms of the house, the kids, the future. For example, an advertisement for ad space in *Mademoiselle* magazine shows a relaxed and elegant young woman above the headline, "I could be happy with less, but I prefer being happy with more," with the text:

Mademoiselle readers don't live beyond their means. But they see no reason to live below them.

They are young women who have acquired a taste for the better things in life, and have earned the means to acquire them.

Mademoiselle has the highest index of readers of all young women's magazines who own audio components . . .

And, as you might expect, the highest index of successfully employed young women.[6]

To keep up with the times, an intelligent corporation had only to rewrite its ad copy, scale down its products to singles' size (e.g., the single-serving can of Campbell's soup, the one-hamburger frying pan, the compact car instead of the station wagon, etc.) and if possible, acquire a subsidiary in the booming "leisure industry."

Notes

1. Helen Gurley Brown, *Sex and the Single Girl* (New York: Giant Cardinal Edition, Pocket Books, 1963), pp. 7–8.
2. Brown, p. 4.
3. Brown, p. 3.
4. The New York *Times*, January 19, 1977.
5. The New York *Times*, October 24, 1975.
6. The New York *Times Magazine*, June 5, 1977, p. 85.

QUESTIONS

1. How various is the evidence on which the writers draw to support their statements? Is there evidence primary or secondary or both?
2. Is their purpose merely to trace the changes in the life of "the single girl" and attitudes toward her, or are they arguing that these changes have been for the better?
3. In describing efforts to revive the romantic ideal of womanhood as "right-wing" (paragraph 11), are they merely describing the politics of those seeking a revival, or are they passing judgment on them? Are they passing judgment on the attitudes and practices of advertisers?
4. How persuasive do you find the evidence for the conclusions drawn from them?

WRITING ASSIGNMENTS

1. Compare advertisements in issues of a magazine published at least twenty years apart to draw conclusions on one of the following:
   a. the image of the housewife
   b. the image of the father

   c. the image of teenage boys or girls

   d. the image of children

2. Compare advertisements in several recent magazines to determine how various the images are of any class of people (mothers, fathers, teenagers, people at work) portrayed in advertisements.

3. Analyze how you discover the attitude of Ehrenreich and English toward those who promoted the rise of the single girl and toward the advertising discussed.

ARGUMENT AND PERSUASION

Deductive Reasoning

H. L. MENCKEN
Reflections on War

1. The thing constantly overlooked by those hopefuls who talk of abolishing war is that it is by no means an evidence of decay but rather a proof of health and vigor. To fight seems to be as natural to man as to eat. Civilization limits and wars upon the impulse but it can never quite eliminate it. Whenever the effort seems to be most successful—that is, whenever man seems to be submitting most willingly to discipline, the spark is nearest to the powder barrel. Here repression achieves its inevitable work. The most warlike people under civilization are precisely those who submit most docilely to the rigid inhibitions of peace. Once they break through the bounds of their repressed but steadily accumulating pugnacity, their destructiveness runs to great lengths. Throwing off the chains of order, they leap into the air and kick their legs. Of all the nations engaged in the two World Wars the Germans, who were the most rigidly girded by conceptions of renunciation and duty, showed the most gusto for war for its own sake.

2. The powerful emotional stimulus of war, its evocation of motives and ideals which, whatever their error, are at least more stimulating than those which impel a man to get and keep a safe job—this is too obvious to need laboring. The effect on the individual soldier of its

very horror, filling him with a sense of the heroic, increases enormously his self-respect. This increase in self-respect reacts upon the nation, and tends to save it from the deteriorating effects of industrial discipline. In the main, soldiers are men of humble position and talents—laborers, petty mechanics, young fellows without definite occupation. Yet no one can deny that the veteran shows a certain superiority in dignity to the average man of his age and experience. He has played his part in significant events; he has been a citizen in a far more profound sense than any mere workman can ever be. The effects of all this are plainly seen in his bearing and his whole attitude of mind. War may make a fool of man, but it by no means degrades him; on the contrary, it tends to exalt him, and its net effects are much like those of motherhood on women.

3. That war is a natural revolt against the necessary but extremely irksome discipline of civilization is shown by the difficulty with which men on returning from it re-adapt themselves to a round of petty duties and responsibilities. This was notably apparent after the Civil War. It took three or four years for the young men engaged in that conflict to steel themselves to the depressing routine of everyday endeavor. Many of them, in fact, found it quite impossible. They could not go back to shovelling coal or tending a machine without intolerable pain. Such men flocked to the West, where adventure still awaited them and discipline was still slack. In the same way, after the Franco-Prussian War, thousands of young German veterans came to the United States, which seemed to them one vast Wild West. True enough, they soon found that discipline was necessary here as well as at home, but it was a slacker discipline and they themselves exaggerated its slackness in their imagination. At all events, it had the charm of the unaccustomed.

4. We commonly look upon the discipline of war as vastly more rigid than any discipline necessary in time of peace, but this is an error. The strictest military discipline imaginable is still looser than that prevailing in the average assembly-line. The soldier, at worst, is still able to exercise the highest conceivable functions of freedom—that is, he is permitted to steal and to kill. No discipline prevailing in peace gives him anything even remotely resembling this. He is, in war, in the position of a free adult; in peace he is almost always in the position of a child. In war all things are excused by success, even violations of discipline. In peace, speaking generally, success is inconceivable except as a function of discipline.

. . .

5. The hope of abolishing war is largely based upon the fact that men have long since abandoned the appeal to arms in their private disputes and submitted themselves to the jurisdiction of courts. Starting from this fact, it is contended that disputes between nations should be settled in the same manner, and that the adoption of the reform would greatly promote the happiness of the world.

6. Unluckily, there are three flaws in the argument. The first, which is obvious, lies in the circumstances that a system of legal remedies is of no value if it is not backed by sufficient force to impose its decisions upon even the most powerful litigants—a sheer impossibility in international affairs, for even if one powerful litigant might be coerced, it would be plainly impossible to coerce a combination, and it is precisely a combination of the powerful that is most to be feared. The second lies in the fact that any legal system, to be worthy of credit, must be administered by judges who have no personal interest in the litigation before them—another impossibility, for all the judges in the international court, in the case of disputes between first-class powers, would either be appointees of those powers, or appointees of inferior powers that were under their direct influence, or obliged to consider the effects of their enmity. The third objection lies in the fact, frequently forgotten, that the courts of justice which now exist do not actually dispense justice, but only law, and that this law is frequently in direct conflict, not only with what one litigant honestly believes to be his rights, but also with what he believes to be his honor. Practically every litigation, in truth, ends with either one litigant or the other nursing what appears to him as an outrage upon him. For both litigants to go away satisfied that justice has been done is almost unheard of.

7. In disputes between man and man this dissatisfaction is not of serious consequence. The aggrieved party has no feasible remedy; if he doesn't like it, he must lump it. In particular, he has no feasible remedy against a judge or a juryman who, in his view, has treated him ill; if he essayed vengeance, the whole strength of the unbiased masses of men would be exerted to destroy him, and that strength is so enormous, compared to his own puny might, that it would swiftly and certainly overwhelm him. But in the case of first-class nations there would be no such overwhelming force in restraint. In a few cases the general opinion of the world might be so largely against them that it would force them to acquiesce in the judgment rendered, but in perhaps a majority of important cases there would be sharply divided sympathies, and it would constantly encourage resistance. Against that

resistance there would be nothing save the counter-resistance of the opposition—*i.e.*, the judge against the aggrieved litigant, the twelve jurymen against the aggrieved litigant's friends, with no vast and impersonal force of neutral public opinion behind the former.

DISCUSSION: Deductive Reasoning

Deduction, in the simplest sense, is reasoning from a general truth to a particular instance:

> Since learning depends on constant study and practice (*general truth*), I failed to learn algebra because I did not study the equations or do the practice problems (*particular instance*).

Induction, in the simplest sense, is reasoning from particular instances to a general conclusion or truth:

> I did not study the equations or do the practice problems, and I failed algebra. I did not study my French grammar and I did not do the exercises in the language lab, and I failed French. I did study the chemical formulas and I did perform the chemistry experiments, and I passed chemistry (three *particular instances*). Therefore, learning must depend on constant study and practice (*general truth*).

These are everyday types of reasoning, and they are closely related. From our past experiences we draw various conclusions, and then apply these conclusions to new situations and experiences.

Deductive arguments can be stated formally in what is called a *syllogism:*

> An act of learning depends on constant study and practice.
>
> The mastery of algebra is an act of learning.
>
> Therefore, the mastery of algebra is an act that depends on constant study and practice.

In ordinary conversation we state such reasoning informally: "I didn't learn algebra because I failed to study and do the practice problems." Notice that the first two statements of the syllogism—statements called the *major* and *minor* premises respectively—were not stated, but only implied. But sometimes we do state and develop one or both of our premises or assumptions, because we wish to stress them:

> The child needs to acquire fundamental skills in com-
> munication—to learn to read, write, and express himself flexibly
> and clearly—in order to function as a social creature [*major
> premise*]. The television experience does not further his verbal
> development [*conclusion*] because it does not require any verbal
> participation on his part, merely passive intake [*minor
> premise*].—Marie Winn, *The Plug-In Drug*

The foremost characteristic of deductive argument is that its
premises provide the sole evidence for its conclusion; in other words,
the premises are accepted as true, and since they are true, the conclusions drawn from them must be true also. If it is true that learning
depends on constant study and practice, and if it is also true that the
mastery of algebra is learning, then it *must* follow that mastering algebra depends on constant study and practice. No other evidence need
be provided though if my audience may have trouble understanding
one of my premises, I may wish to illustrate it. A true statement is not
always obvious to everyone.

Where do these truths or assumptions come from? Some of them
begin as conclusions drawn inductively from repeated observation
and experience; these may become so well established that they can
serve as premises in deductive arguments. Many common adages and
proverbs are in this class of statements. People may later dispute
these premises on the basis of new observations and experiences—new experiments in learning may at some time challenge the
assumption that constant study and practice are essential to
learning—but in the absence of challenges they are held as true.

Other premises are thought to be "self-evident" or true by definition:

> We hold these truths to be self-evident: that all men are created
> equal; that they are endowed by their creator with certain una-
> lienable rights; that among these are life, liberty, and the pursuit
> of happiness.—*Declaration of Independence*

> The desire to devote oneself to another person or persons seems to
> be as innate as the desire for personal liberty. If the two desires
> could combine, the menace to freedom from within, the fundamen-
> tal menace, might disappear, and the political evils now filling all the
> foreground of our lives would be deprived of the poison which
> nourishes them.—E. M. Forster, *Two Cheers for Democracy*

Like the axioms of geometry, the premises of deductive arguments
may be established by definition or common consent. The proposition
that all squares have four sides is a premise of this kind: a figure with
five sides would not be called a square. In the same way, people in a

particular age and in a particular society agree to consider true a group of propositions like those of the Declaration of Independence. Many British politicians did not agree, nor did Jefferson and other American colonists believe that they all would. Often (as Mencken's reflections on war show) discussion centers on the premises themselves—defending and illustrating them, even though the writer holds them to be true and capable of providing decisive evidence for the conclusions drawn from them.

Let us consider briefly some of the technical points logicians make about deductive arguments. The first of these is that the assumptions or beliefs we have been discussing can be stated as propositions—statements that can be affirmed or denied, asserted as true or false. And, second, the whole deductive argument is either *valid* or *invalid*—that is, correct or incorrect—in the way it reasons from premises to conclusion.

Note that valid does not mean true: a valid argument may be false in its premises and conclusion. The term *valid* refers only to the process by which the conclusion was reached—the formal structure of an argument. If all terms mentioned in the conclusion are mentioned in the premises, and if the terms are properly arranged, then whether or not the premises are true in fact, the argument is considered valid. Thus the premises of the following argument are obviously false, yet the argument is valid in form:

All Americans speak French.

All waiters in French restaurants are Americans.

Therefore, all waiters in French restaurants speak French.

A valid deductive argument whose premises are true is called a sound argument. These arguments are most desirable and are particularly powerful in winning disputes.

Invalid arguments are not easy to analyze, and logicians have complex procedures for testing the validity of the many kinds of syllogism. We will note only a few of the elementary tests for validity and soundness:

First, the middle term of the syllogism must be distributed in at least one of the premises; that is, it must refer to all members of the class named:

All *property owners* are taxpayers.

My neighbors are *property owners.*

Therefore, my neighbors are taxpayers.

The middle term is *property owners,* and it is distributed in the first premise because it refers to all of the members of the class "property owners." The conclusion follows from the premises because we can be sure that what is true of all property owners must be true of neighbors included in that class. But if the syllogism is written

All property owners are *taxpayers.*

My neighbors are *taxpayers.*

Therefore, my neighbors are property owners.

the middle term is *taxpayers* and is undistributed in both premises: it refers only to *some* of the class of taxpayers. The major premise does not say that all taxpayers are property owners; only some may be. And though all my neighbors are taxpayers, they may belong to the class of taxpayers who are not property owners. The premises allow the certainty only that some of my neighbors are property owners, not that all are. Therefore, the syllogism is invalid because the conclusion does not follow from the premises.

A syllogism is also invalid if the middle term is ambiguous:

Whoever thrusts a knife into a person is a murderer.

A surgeon is someone *who thrusts a knife into a person.*

Therefore, a surgeon is a murderer.

Finally, both premises of a syllogism must be affirmative if the conclusion is affirmative; if one of the premises is negative, the conclusion must be negative too. Therefore, the following syllogism is invalid:

No dogs are allowed in the store.

Tigers are not dogs.

Therefore, tigers are allowed in the store.

If both premises are negative, no conclusion whatsoever can be drawn, and the argument is considered invalid.

In summary, disagreement over deductive reasoning does not arise only over the way conclusions are derived from premises; disagreement may arise over the truth of the premises and the soundness of the argument. An argument may seem "logical" because the process of reasoning is valid, but still be unsound because its premises are questionable or false.

QUESTIONS

1. In paragraphs 1–4, Mencken argues that war will not be easily abolished, and he states his major premise explicitly: "To fight seems to be as natural to man as to eat." How does the wording of this

statement and the wording of others in these paragraphs show that Mencken regards these premises as certain and decisive evidence for his conclusions? What conclusions does he reach, based on these premises?

2. Though he regards his premises as certain, Mencken explains and illustrates them. What examples does he present? Does he discuss one civilization, or instead generalize about "warlike people" on the basis of observations made over a period of time?

3. Paragraph 1 of the Mencken contains the makings of several syllogisms; in the first of these, the major premise may be stated in these words: "The expression of a natural instinct is evidence of health and vigor." What are the minor premise and conclusion?

4. In paragraph 1 Mencken argues that repression of a natural instinct leads to increased destructiveness. What are the minor premise and conclusion?

5. L. A. White, in *Science of Culture,* argues that the need for military conscription refutes the assumption that people are naturally warlike. Given his assumptions and evidence, how might Mencken answer this objection? What do paragraphs 5–7 suggest?

6. In paragraphs 5–7 Mencken challenges "the hope of abolishing war," a hope based on the assumption that people have long since "submitted themselves to the jurisdiction of courts." What flaws does Mencken find in the argument, and what kind of evidence does he present in refutation? Does he deal with particular instances or instead generalize from observations made over a period of time?

7. Decide whether the following arguments are valid or invalid. It may be necessary to reword the premises:
   a. Since all voters are citizens and I am a voter, I am a citizen.
   b. Since all voters are citizens and I am a citizen, I am a voter.
   c. Since the Irish are vegetarians and Bernard Shaw was Irish, Shaw was a vegetarian.
   d. Those who made 93 or better on the exam will receive an A in the course. Seven of us received an A in the course and therefore must have made 93 or better on the exam.
   e. Since beneficent acts are virtuous and losing at poker benefits others, losing at poker is virtuous.

8. An *enthymeme* is a condensed syllogism, one of whose premises is implied: Because I did not study the equations, I failed algebra. In the following enthymemes, reconstruct the original syllogism by supplying the missing premise, and evaluate the argument. The premises and conclusion may need rewording:
   a. John F. Kennedy was a good President because he supported the space program and other kinds of scientific research.
   b. Capital punishment protects society from depraved individuals.

c. I am a successful businessman because I once had a paper route.

d. I am an independent voter, just as my father and grandfather were.

WRITING ASSIGNMENT

Write an argument for or against one of the following. In an additional paragraph identify one or more assumptions that underlie your argument, and explain why you hold these assumptions:

a. nuclear power plants
b. a ban on smoking in public transportation
c. the 55-mile-per-hour speed limit
d. periodic examination of licensed drivers
e. required attendance in college classes
f. compulsory gun registration

KENNETH B. CLARK

The Limits of Relevance

1.   As one who began himself to use the term "relevant" and to insist on its primacy years ago, I feel an obligation to protest the limits of relevance or to propose a redefinition of it to embrace wider terms.

2.   Definitions of education that depend on immediate relevance ignore a small but critical percentage of human beings, the individuals who for some perverse reason are in search of an education that is not dominated by the important, socially and economically required pragmatic needs of a capitalist or a communist or a socialist society. Such an individual is not certain what he wants to be; he may not even be sure that he wants to be successful. He may be burdened with that perverse intelligence that finds the excitement of life in a continuous involvement with ideas.

3.   For this student, education may be a lonely and tortuous process not definable in terms of the limits of course requirements or of departmental boundaries, or the four- or six-year span of time required for the bachelor's or graduate degree. This student seems unable to seek or to define or to discuss relevance in terms of externals. He seems somehow trapped by the need to seek the dimensions of rele-

vance in relation to an examination and re-examination of his own internal values. He may have no choice but to assume the burden of seeking to define the relevance of the human experience as a reflection of the validity of his own existence as a value-seeking, socially sensitive, and responsive human being. He is required to deny himself the protective, supporting crutch of accepting and clutching uncritically the prevailing dogmatisms, slogans, and intellectual fashions.

4. If such a human being is to survive the inherent and probably inevitable aloneness of intellectual integrity, he must balance it by the courage to face and accept the risks of his individuality; by compassion and empathetic identification with the frailties of his fellow human beings as a reflection of his own; by an intellectual and personal discipline which prevents him from wallowing in introspective amorphousness and childlike self-indulgence. And, certainly, he must demonstrate the breadth of perspective and human sensitivity and depth of affirmation inherent in the sense of humor which does not laugh at others but laughs with man and with the God of Paradox who inflicted upon man the perpetual practical joke of the human predicament.

5. American colleges, with few notable exceptions, provide little room for this type of student, just as American society provides little room for such citizens. Perhaps it is enough to see that institutions of higher education do not destroy such potential. One could hope wistfully that our colleges and even our multiuniversities could spare space and facilities to serve and to protect those students who want to experiment without being required to be practical, pragmatic, or even relevant.

6. Is it still possible within the complexity and cacophony of our dynamic, power-related, and tentatively socially sensitive institutions for some few to have the opportunity to look within, to read, to think critically, to communicate, to make mistakes, to seek validity, and to accept and enjoy this process as valid in itself? Is there still some place where relevance can be defined in terms of the quest—where respect for self and others can be taken for granted as one admits not knowing and is therefore challenged to seek?

7. May one dare to hope for a definition of education which makes it possible for man to accept the totality of his humanity without embarrassment? This would be valuable for its own sake, but it might also paradoxically be the most pragmatic form of education—because it is from these perverse, alone-educated persons that a practical society receives antidotes to a terrifying sense of inner emptiness and despair.

They are the font of the continued quest for meaning in the face of the mocking chorus of meaninglessness. They offer the saving reaffirmation of stabilizing values in place of the acceptance of the disintegration inherent in valuelessness. They provide the basis for faith in humanity and life rather than surrender to dehumanization and destruction. From these impracticals come our poets, our artists, our novelists, our satirists, our humorists. They are our models of the positives, the potentials, the awe and wonder of man. They make the life of the thinking human being more endurable and the thought of a future tolerable.

QUESTIONS

1. How does Clark explain the meanings of the term *relevant?* Why does he briefly review these meanings?
2. What assumptions does Clark make about the educational needs of people?
3. What conclusions does Clark derive from his assumptions?
4. Do you agree that American colleges have little room for the kind of student described in paragraph 4? What is your answer to the questions Clark asks in paragraph 6?
5. Does Clark seek to refute those who argue the "pragmatic needs" of education? Or does he present confirming arguments only?

WRITING ASSIGNMENT

Evaluate one of the following statements on the basis of your experience and observation:

a. "American colleges, with few notable exceptions, provide little room for this type of student, just as American society provides little room for such citizens.

b. ". . . it is from these perverse, alone-educated persons that a practical society receives antidotes to a terrifying sense of inner emptiness and despair."

JOHN HOLT

The Right to Control One's Learning

1. Young people should have the right to control and direct their own learning, that is, to decide what they want to learn, and when, where, how, how much, how fast, and with what help they want to

learn it. To be still more specific, I want them to have the right to decide if, when, how much, and by whom they want to be *taught* and the right to decide whether they want to learn in a school and if so which one and for how much of the time.

2.   No human right, except the right to life itself, is more fundamental than this. A person's freedom of learning is part of his freedom of thought, even more basic than his freedom of speech. If we take from someone his right to decide what he will be curious about, we destroy his freedom of thought. We say, in effect, you must think not about what interests and concerns *you*, but about what interests and concerns *us*.

3.   We might call this the right of curiosity, the right to ask whatever questions are most important to us. As adults, we assume that we have the right to decide what does or does not interest us, what we will look into and what we will leave alone. We take this right for granted, cannot imagine that it might be taken away from us. Indeed, as far as I know, it has never been written into any body of law. Even the writers of our Constitution did not mention it. They thought it was enough to guarantee citizens the freedom of speech and the freedom to spread their ideas as widely as they wished and could. It did not occur to them that even the most tyrannical government would try to control people's minds, what they thought and knew. That idea was to come later, under the benevolent guise of compulsory universal education.

4.   This right of each of us to control our own learning is now in danger. When we put into our laws the highly authoritarian notion that someone should and could decide what all young people were to learn and, beyond that, could do whatever might seem necessary (which now includes dosing them with drugs) to compel them to learn it, we took a long step down a very steep and dangerous path. The requirement that a child go to school, for about six hours a day, 180 days a year, for about ten years, whether or not he learns anything there, whether or not he already knows it or could learn it faster or better somewhere else, is such a gross violation of civil liberties that few adults would stand for it. But the child who resists is treated as a criminal. With this requirement we created an industry, an army of people whose whole work was to tell young people what they had to learn and to try to make them learn it. Some of these people, wanting to exercise even more power over others, to be even more "helpful," or simply because the industry is not growing fast enough to hold all the people who want to get into it, are now beginning to say, "If it is good for children for us to decide what they shall learn and to make

them learn it, why wouldn't it be good for everyone? If compulsory education is a good thing, how can there be too much of it? Why should we allow anyone, of any age, to decide that he has had enough of it? Why should we allow older people, any more than young, not to know what we know when their ignorance may have bad consequences for all of us? Why should we not *make* them know what they *ought* to know?"

5. They are beginning to talk, as one man did on a nationwide TV show, about "womb-to-tomb" schooling. If hours of homework every night are good for the young, why wouldn't they be good for us all— they would keep us away from the TV set and other frivolous pursuits. Some group of experts, somewhere, would be glad to decide what we all ought to know and then every so often check up on us to make sure we knew it—with, of course, appropriate penalties if we did not.

6. I am very serious in saying that I think this is coming unless we prepare against it and take steps to prevent it. The right I ask for the young is a right that I want to preserve for the rest of us, the right *to decide what goes into our minds*. This is much more than the right to decide whether or when or how much to go to school or what school you want to go to. That right is important, but it is only part of a much larger and more fundamental right, which I might call the right to Learn, as opposed to being Educated, *i.e.*, made to learn what someone else thinks would be good for you. It is not just compulsory schooling but compulsory Education that I oppose and want to do away with.

7. That children might have the control of their own learning, including the right to decide if, when, how much, and where they wanted to go to school, frightens and angers many people. They ask me, "Are you saying that if the parents wanted the child to go to school, and the child didn't want to go, that he wouldn't have to go? Are you saying that if the parents wanted the child to go to one school, and the child wanted to go to another, that the child would have the right to decide?" Yes, that is what I say. Some people ask, "If school wasn't compulsory, wouldn't many parents take their children out of school to exploit their labor in one way or another?" Such questions are often both snobbish and hypocritical. The questioner assumes and implies (though rarely says) that these bad parents are people poorer and less schooled than he. Also, though he appears to be defending the right of children to go to school, what he really is defending is the right of the state to compel them to go whether they

want to or not. What he wants, in short, is that children should be in school, not that they should have any choice about going.

8.   But saying that children should have the right to choose to go or not to go to school does not mean that the ideas and wishes of the parents would have no weight. Unless he is estranged from his parents and rebelling against them, a child cares very much about what they think and want. Most of the time, he doesn't want to anger or worry or disappoint them. Right now, in families where the parents feel that they have some choice about their children's schooling, there is much bargaining about schools. Such parents, when their children are little, often ask them whether they want to go to nursery school or kindergarten. Or they may take them to school for a while to try it out. Or, if they have a choice of schools, they may take them to several to see which they think they will like the best. Later, they care whether the child likes his school. If he does not, they try to do something about it, get him out of it, find a school he will like.

9.   I know some parents who for years had a running bargain with their children, "If on a given day you just can't stand the thought of school, you don't feel well, you are afraid of something that may happen, you have something of your own that you very much want to do—well, you can stay home." Needless to say, the schools, with their supporting experts, fight it with all their might—Don't Give in to Your Child, Make Him Go to School, He's Got to Learn. Some parents, when their own plans make it possible for them to take an interesting trip, take their children with them. They don't ask the school's permission, they just go. If the child doesn't want to make the trip and would rather stay in school, they work out a way for him to do that. Some parents, when their child is frightened, unhappy, and suffering in school, as many children are, just take him out. Hal Bennett, in his excellent book *No More Public School*, talks about ways to do this.

10.   A friend of mine told me that when her boy was in third grade, he had a bad teacher, bullying, contemptuous, sarcastic, cruel. Many of the class switched to another section, but this eight-year-old, being tough, defiant, and stubborn, hung on. One day—his parents did not learn this until about two years later—having had enough of the teacher's meanness, he just got up from his desk and without saying a word, walked out of the room and went home. But for all his toughness and resiliency of spirit, the experience was hard on him. He grew more timid and quarrelsome, less outgoing and confident. He lost his ordinary good humor. Even his handwriting began to go to

pieces—was much worse in the spring of the school year than in the previous fall. One spring day he sat at breakfast, eating his cereal. After a while he stopped eating and sat silently thinking about the day ahead. His eyes filled up with tears, and two big ones slowly rolled down his cheeks. His mother, who ordinarily stays out of the school life of her children, saw this and knew what it was about. "Listen," she said to him, "we don't have to go on with this. If you've had enough of that teacher, if she's making school so bad for you that you don't want to go any more, I'll be perfectly happy just to pull you right out. We can manage it. Just say the word." He was horrified and indignant. "No!" he said, "I couldn't do that." "Okay," she said, "whatever you want is fine. Just let me know." And so they left it. He had decided that he was going to tough it out, and he did. But I am sure knowing that he had the support of his mother and the chance to give it up if it got too much for him gave him the strength he needed to go on.

11. To say that children should have the right to control and direct their own learning, to go to school or not as they chose, does not mean that the law would forbid the parents to express an opinion or wish or strong desire on the matter. It only means that if their natural authority is not strong enough the parents can't call in the cops to make the child do what they are not able to persuade him to do. And the law may say that there is a limit to the amount of pressure or coercion the parents can apply to the child to deny him a choice that he has a legal right to make.

12. When I urge that children should control their learning there is one argument that people bring up so often that I feel I must anticipate and meet it here. It says that schools are a place where children can for a while be protected against the bad influences of the world outside, particularly from its greed, dishonesty, and commercialism. It says that in school children may have a glimpse of a higher way of life, of people acting from other and better motives than greed and fear. People say, "We know that society is bad enough as it is and that children will be exposed to it and corrupted by it soon enough. But if we let children go out into the larger world as soon as they wanted, they would be tempted and corrupted just that much sooner."

13. They seem to believe that schools are better, more honorable places than the world outside—what a friend of mine at Harvard once called "museums of virtue." Or that people in school, both children and adults, act from higher and better motives than people outside. In this they are mistaken. There are, of course, some good schools. But on the whole, far from being the opposite of, or an antidote to, the

world outside, with all its envy, fear, greed, and obsessive competitiveness, the schools are very much like it. If anything, they are worse, a terrible, abstract, simplified caricature of it. In the world outside the school, some work, at least, is done honestly and well, for its own sake, not just to get ahead of others; people are not everywhere and always being set in competition against each other; people are not (or not yet) in every minute of their lives subject to the arbitrary, irrevocable orders and judgment of others. But in most schools, a student is every minute doing what others tell him, subject to their judgment, in situations in which he can only win at the expense of other students.

14.   This is a harsh judgement. Let me say again, as I have before, that schools are worse than most of the people in them and that many of these people do many harmful things they would rather not do, and a great many other harmful things that they do not even see as harmful. The whole of school is much worse than the sum of its parts. There are very few people in the U.S. today (or perhaps anywhere, any time) in *any* occupation, who could be trusted with the kind of power that schools give most teachers over their students. Schools seem to me among the most anti-democratic, most authoritarian, most destructive, and most dangerous institutions of modern society. No other institution does more harm or more lasting harm to more people or destroys so much of their curiosity, independence, trust, dignity, and sense of identity and worth. Even quite kindly schools are inhibited and corrupted by the knowledge of children and teachers alike that they are *performing* for the judgement and approval of others—the children for the teachers; the teachers for the parents, supervisors, school board, or the state. No one is ever free from feeling that he is being judged all the time, or soon may be. Even after the best class experiences teachers must ask themselves, "Were we right to do that? Can we prove we were right? Will it get us in trouble?"

15.   What corrupts the school, and makes it so much worse than most of the people in it, or than they would like it to be, is its power—just as their powerlessness corrupts the students. The school is corrupted by the endless anxious demand of the parents to know how their child is doing—meaning is he ahead of the other kids—and their demand that he be kept ahead. Schools do not protect children from the badness of the world outside. They are at least as bad as the world outside, and the harm they do to the children in their power creates much of the badness of the world outside. The sickness of the modern world is in many ways a school-induced sickness. It is in school that most people learn to expect and accept that some expert

can always place them in some sort of rank or hierarchy. It is in school that we meet, become used to, and learn to believe in the totally controlled society. We do not learn much science, but we learn to worship "scientists" and to believe that anything we might conceivably need or want can only come, and someday will come, from them. The school is the closest we have yet been able to come to Huxley's *Brave New World*, with its alphas and betas, deltas and epsilons—and now it even has its soma. Everyone, including children, should have the right to say "No!" to it.

QUESTIONS

1. Holt states his major premise in paragraphs 1 and 2: young people have the right to "control and direct their own learning." In paragraph 3 he explains why the Constitution does not mention this right. What words in these opening paragraphs show that Holt holds the premise to be true without question?

2. What conclusions does he draw from the premise in paragraph 4? What conclusions does he show can be draw from different premises in paragraphs 4 and 5?

3. What is the larger premise that Holt introduces in paragraph 6? Why do you think he did not begin his essay with it?

4. What further deductions does Holt draw from his premises in paragraph 7, and how does he answer objections to these ideas?

5. In paragraph 8, Holt now *qualifies* his ideas; that is, he states what his premises do *not* entail. What qualifications does he make in this and later paragraphs?

6. In paragraph 9, Holt shows that his proposal is feasible; in paragraph 10, that enforced schooling can have dire effects on children. How does he show that the proposal is feasible, and what are the dire effects?

7. Paragraphs 4–11 form the *confirmation* of the argument. What in the wording of paragraph 12 shows that Holt is turning now to his main *refutation*? What objection does Holt introduce to his argument, and how does he answer it in paragraphs 13–15?

8. Where in the concluding paragraph does he restate his major premise (actually the thesis of the essay)?

9. With what aspects of the argument do you agree or disagree? Do you agree with Holt's major premise and with his estimate of schools today, or do you disagree with one or both of these?

WRITING ASSIGNMENTS

1. Using Holt's major premise, draw conclusions from it relating to the rights of children in the family. If young people have the right to "control and direct their own learning," what rights and privileges

with respect to money and the use of such property as the family automobile should be theirs? When you have finished your discussion of these rights, state whether you agree with Holt's premises, and discuss the feasibility of such rights and privileges that the premise entails.

2. Write an estimate of your school, and use it to test the soundness of Holt's charges in paragraphs 13–15. If you believe his conclusions need to be qualified, explain why and how they should be.

NORMAN COUSINS
Cop-out Realism

1.   On all sides, one sees evidence today of cop-out realism—ostensible efforts to be sensible in dealing with things as they are but that turn out to be a shucking of responsibility.

2.   Example: Until fairly recently, off-track betting was illegal in New York State. Gambling on horses was regarded as a disguised form of stealing, run by professional gamblers who preyed upon people who could least afford to lose. Also outlawed was the numbers game, in which people could bet small amounts of money on numbers drawn from the outcome of the day's horse races.

3.   Attempts by government to drive out the gambling syndicates had only indifferent results. Finally, state officials decided that, since people were going to throw their money away despite anything the law might do to protect them, the state ought to take over off-track betting and the numbers racket.

4.   It is now possible to assess the effect of that legalization. The first thing that is obvious is that New York State itself has become a predator in a way that the Mafia could never hope to match. What was intended as a plan to control gambling has become a high-powered device to promote it. The people who can least afford to take chances with their money are not only not dissuaded from gambling but are actually being cajoled into it by the state. Millions of dollars are being spent by New York State on lavish advertising on television, on radio, in buses, and on billboards. At least the Mafia was never able publicly to glorify and extol gambling with taxpayer money. And the number of poor people who were hurt by gambling under the Mafia is miniscule compared to the number who now lose money on horses with the urgent blessings of New York State.

5.   A second example of cop-out realism is the way some communities are dealing with cigarette-smoking by teenagers and pre-teenagers. Special rooms are now being set aside for students who want to smoke. No age restrictions are set; freshmen have the same lighting-up privileges as seniors.

6.   The thinking behind the new school policy is similar to the "realism" behind New York's decision to legalize off-track betting and the numbers game. It is felt that since the youngsters are going to smoke anyway, the school might just as well make it possible for them to do it in the open rather than feel compelled to do it furtively in back corridors and washrooms.

7.   Parents and teachers may pride themselves on their "realism" in such approaches. What they are actually doing is finding a convenient rationalization for failing to uphold their responsibility. The effect of their supposedly "realistic" policy is to convert a ban into a benediction. By sanctioning that which they deplore, they become part of the problem they had the obligation to meet. What they regard as common sense turns out to be capitulation.

8.   Pursuing the same reasoning, why not set aside a corner for a bar where students can buy alcoholic beverages? After all, teenage drinking is a national problem, and it is far better to have the youngsters drink out in the open than to have them feel guilty about stealing drinks from the cupboard at home or contriving to snatch their liquor outside the home. Moreover, surveillance can be exercised. Just as most public bars will not serve liquor to people who are hopelessly drunk, so the school bartender could withhold alcohol from students who can hardly stand on their feet.

9.   It is not far-fetched to extend the same "reasoning" to marijuana. If the youngsters are going to be able to put their hands on the stuff anyway, why shouldn't they be able to buy it legally and smoke it openly, perhaps in the same schoolroom that has been converted into a smoking den?

10.   We are not reducing the argument to an absurdity; we are asking that parents and teachers face up to the implications of what they are doing.

11.   The school has no right to jettison standards just because of difficulties in enforcing them. The school's proper response is not to abdicate but to extend its efforts in other directions. It ought to require regular lung examinations for its youngsters. It ought to schedule regular sessions with parents and youngsters at which reports on these examinations can be considered. It ought to bring in cancer researchers who can run films for students showing the difference between the

brackish, pulpy lungs caused by cigarette smoking and the smooth pink tissue of healthy lungs. The schools should schedule visits to hospital wards for lung cancer patients. In short, educators should take the U.S. Surgeon-General's report on cigarettes seriously.

12.   In all the discussion and debate over cigarette smoking by children, one important fact is generally overlooked. That fact is that a great many children *do not* smoke. The school cannot ignore its obligation to these youngsters just because it cannot persuade the others not to smoke. It must not give the nonsmokers the impression that their needs are secondary or that the school has placed a seal of approval on a practice that is condemning millions of human beings to a fatal disease.

13.   Still another example of cop-out realism is the policy of many colleges and universities of providing common dormitories and common washrooms for both sexes. The general idea seems to be that it is unrealistic to expect young people not to sleep together. Besides, it is probably reasoned, if people are old enough to vote they are old enough to superintend their own sex habits. So, the thinking goes, the school might just as well allow them to share the same sleeping and toilet facilities.

14.   The trouble with such policies is that they put the school in the position of lending itself to the breakdown of that which is most important in healthy relations between the sexes—a respect for privacy and dignity. No one ever need feel ashamed of the human body. But that doesn't mean that the human body is to be displayed or handled like a slab of raw meat. Sex is one of the higher manifestations of human sensitivity and response, not an impersonal sport devoid of genuine feeling. The divorce courts are filled to overflowing with cases in which casual, mechanistic attitudes toward sex have figured in marital collapses. For the school to foster that casualness is for it to become an agent of de-sensitization in a monstrous default.

15.   The function of standards is not to serve as the basis for mindless repressive measures but to give emphasis to the realities of human experience. Such experience helps to identify the causes of unnecessary pain and disintegration. Any society that ignores the lessons of that experience may be in a bad way.

QUESTIONS

1. Cousins states his major premise in paragraph 1. How does he illustrate this premise in paragraphs 2–6?
2. In paragraphs 2–6 Cousins confirms his premise by showing cer-

tain consequences of "cop-out realism." In paragraphs 7–10 he shows that if we adopt such a policy, certain consequences follow—consequences that he considers obvious absurdities. What are these absurd consequences?

3. In stating in paragraphs 11–14 what the schools should be doing, Cousins draws further conclusions from the policy of "cop-out realism." What are these conclusions? Do you agree with them?

4. In the concluding paragraphs, what basic premises or assumptions concerning human responsibility and dignity emerge? How does Cousins use these premises to summarize his basic argument?

WRITING ASSIGNMENTS

1. Cousins combines confirmation and refutation, in showing that "cop-out realism" entails absurd consequences, and joins narration to these, in presenting the background on gambling and schools in New York State. Write an argumentative essay in which you combine narration with confirmation or refutation in the same way. Your refutation need not take the same form as Cousins'. You may prefer to answer objections to your basic premise and proposals directly.

2. Discuss the extent to which, in your view, Cousins would disagree with Holt's premise and basic proposals on education. Support your discussion with comparison of their premises and reasoning.

LEONARD GROSS

Is Less More?

1. The following superlative is offered after considerable thought: Americans are, or will shortly be, in the process of making the most fundamental adjustment they have ever had to make. If this adjustment concerned solely their standard of living, the superlative would not be valid. What makes it so is that this is the first time Americans have ever had to change the *assumptions* about the manner in which they live.

2. There have been times of sacrifice before, particularly during wars, but the assumption was that times would be "good" again when the emergency ended. Today, however, economic factors are such that

the prudent American must adjust to the likelihood that material life may never be the same again.

3.   This country is in the process of discovering that it can no longer afford the big life. That is the downstream meaning of our present economic turmoil. From whatever area you approach the problem, be it resources, inflation, population or politics, the prospect remains the same. Solutions will necessarily require permanent alterations in the size and scope of our activities, possessions and dreams.

4.   Already, the broadly shared dream of upper-middle-class affluence has passed the average dreamer by. He figured that if he ever earned $20,000 a year, he'd have it made. Today, he's got the salary, but he's also got hobbling debts. Gains in real income for the middle class have been tiny; there's almost no upward mobility any longer. Aspirations to send children to college have been tempered by the immense cost and inability of degree holders to find employment.

5.   Call it "middle-class discontent." It's demonstrably higher now than at any time in recent history. It will not lessen in our lifetime, not, at least, as a consequence of improved conditions. The cost of land will not diminish. The cost of money may diminish somewhat, but not to the levels that enabled millions of Americans to build their own homes in the years after the second world war. The value of the dollar will not increase. The cost of goods and services will not diminish, if only because the cost of fuel, a major production factor in every economic sector, will never return to previous levels. Populations will increase here and abroad, compounding problems of employment, education and maintenance.

6.   It all sounds pretty bleak. And yet, and yet. Inherent in the problem is a stunning resolution—nothing less than a change in the values by which we measure life. Because there *is* one variable in all this picture: the individual. He can diminish his discontent by reordering his priorities.

7.   What happens to a society when its members have less purchasing power is already beginning to be apparent. There will be practical changes in the way people live: smaller, less elaborate houses, fewer single-family dwellings, more cluster zoning, more condominiums, better use of land so as to provide more recreation near the home. Because travel will be so expensive, the environment near the home will receive greater attention.

8.   With the price of food so high, discretionary income will be diverted to supplement food budgets. That means less money for entertainment and an increasing reliance on the home as the family enter-

tainment center. Such vacations as will be possible will change their nature. Vacation clubs, little known in the United States but enormously successful in Europe, will come into vogue. The Club Méditerranée, originator of the concept and prototype for other clubs, has already developed an American market.

9.   Railroads work in Europe because Europeans use railroads. And because they work. Europeans can board a train in the evening and be at their skiing station early the next morning after an inexpensive and acceptable night in a couchette. When Americans can no longer afford long trips in automobiles or airplanes, they will return to the railroads, the least expensive and the least environment-punishing form of mass transportation.

10.   A subtle strain runs through these eventualities. Without neglecting the individual, we address ourselves to the common good. Everyone isn't vying for first cabin any longer; we're content to get there more modestly—and happy in the knowledge that our arrival is assured. The new American dream will esteem "small" more than "big." The trend to smaller cars, recently made concrete by the General Motors announcement that its new models will be an average of 700 pounds lighter, is thus not simply a response to the fuel shortage. Eventually, it becomes an expression of taste.

11.   "Less is more" is a phrase attributed to Mies van der Rohe, the German architect, a leader of the Bauhaus group and pivotal force in the field of modern design. That single statement crystallized the philosophy of contemporary architecture and design—to do away with frilly styles. Would a life-style that did away with unnecessary baggage achieve the same simplicity and purity? Every week, it seems, I hear of one more American who thinks so. All were successful. All had made it to the top and then decided that the prize hadn't been worth the trip. "Can you imagine spending your life getting to a place and then finding you didn't want to be there?" one of them asked rhetorically.

12.   Economic necessity will do more to change styles of life than any previous factor. Moral imperatives don't embody an imperative for change. But when you can no longer afford the life you're living, or the life you can buy for what you earn becomes unacceptable, *then* you're motivated to change.

13.   Since our inception, the American Premise has stated that happiness lay ahead, in the bigger job, the bigger home, the bigger life. The larger implication of our new economic reality is nothing less than a rejection of that premise, with profound consequences in terms of

social objectives and how they're expressed commercially. That many Americans will continue to grab for the brass ring while others are letting go in no way invalidates the premise. Facts in apparent contradiction can be simultaneously true.

QUESTIONS

1. Gross organizes his essay in the argumentative form discussed earlier:

   introduction (paragraph 1)
   division of proofs: partial statement of thesis (paragraphs 2–3)
   narration (paragraphs 4–6)
   confirmation (paragraphs 7–11)
   refutation (paragraphs 12–13)
   conclusion (paragraph 13)

   Where in the confirmation does Gross state his thesis fully? How does he restate his thesis in the concluding paragraph?
2. What information does he provide in the narration, and for what purpose? Is he writing to a special or a general audience, and how do you know?
3. Gross is writing a special kind of essay that refutes assumptions held by a large number of Americans. What are these assumptions, and how does Gross challenge them? What assumptions of his own does he make explicitly and implicitly?
4. Gross supports his own ideas from experience: he is thus showing that new assumptions can and do find support in the world today. What are these experiences?

WRITING ASSIGNMENTS

1. Discuss how an experience like the gas shortage of 1979 forced you to change your standard of living and perhaps your thinking. Use this discussion to support or challenge one of Gross's ideas.
2. Challenge an assumption held by people your age, or perhaps your teachers or parents. Do so by showing how this assumption is contradicted by your experiences and observations. Follow the pattern of the argumentative essay shown above. Vary this pattern as you find necessary.

LEWIS THOMAS

On Cloning a Human Being

1.   It is now theoretically possible to recreate an identical creature from any animal or plant, from the DNA contained in the nucleus of any somatic cell. A single plant root-tip cell can be teased and seduced into conceiving a perfect copy of the whole plant; a frog's intestinal epithelial cell possesses the complete instructions needed for a new, same frog. If the technology were further advanced, you could do this with a human being, and there are now startled predictions all over the place that this will in fact be done, someday, in order to provide a version of immortality for carefully selected, especially valuable people.

2.   The cloning of humans is on most of the lists of things to worry about from Science, along with behavior control, genetic engineering, transplanted heads, computer poetry, and the unrestrained growth of plastic flowers.

3.   Cloning is the most dismaying of prospects, mandating as it does the elimination of sex with only a metaphoric elimination of death as compensation. It is almost no comfort to know that one's cloned, identical surrogate lives on, especially when the living will very likely involve edging one's real, now aging self off to the side, sooner or later. It is hard to imagine anything like filial affection or respect for a single, unmated nucleus; harder still to think of one's new, self-generated self as anything but an absolute, desolate orphan. Not to mention the complex interpersonal relationship involved in raising one's self from infancy, teaching the language, enforcing discipline, instilling good manners, and the like. How would you feel if you became an incorrigible juvenile delinquent by proxy, at the age of fifty-five?

4.   The public questions are obvious. Who is to be selected, and on what qualifications? How to handle the risks of misused technology, such as self-determined cloning by the rich and powerful but socially objectionable, or the cloning by governments of dumb, docile masses for the world's work? What will be the effect on all the uncloned rest of us of human sameness? After all, we've accustomed ourselves through hundreds of millennia to the continual exhilaration of uniqueness; each of us is totally different, in a fundamental sense, from all the other four billion. Selfness is an essential fact of life. The

thought of human nonselfness, precise sameness, is terrifying, when
you think about it.

5. Well, don't think about it, because it isn't a probable possibility,
not even as a long shot for the distant future, in my opinion. I agree
that you might clone some people who would look amazingly like their
parental cell donors, but the odds are that they'd be almost as different as you or me, and certainly more different than any of today's
identical twins.

6. The time required for the experiment is only one of the problems,
but a formidable one. Suppose you wanted to clone a prominent, spectacularly successful diplomat, to look after the Middle East problems
of the distant future. You'd have to catch him and persuade him,
probably not very hard to do, and extirpate a cell. But then you'd
have to wait for him to grow up through embryonic life and then for
at least forty years more, and you'd have to be sure all observers
remained patient and unmeddlesome through his unpromising, ambiguous childhood and adolescence.

7. Moreover, you'd have to be sure of recreating his environment,
perhaps down to the last detail. "Environment" is a word which really
means people, so you'd have to do a lot more cloning than just the
diplomat himself.

8. This is a very important part of the cloning problem, largely
overlooked in our excitement about the cloned individual himself.
You don't have to agree all the way with B. F. Skinner to acknowledge that the environment does make a difference, and when you examine what we really mean by the word "environment" it comes
down to other human beings. We use euphemisms and jargon for this,
like "social forces," "cultural influences," even Skinner's "verbal
community," but what is meant is the dense crowd of nearby people
who talk to, listen to, smile or frown at, give to, withhold from,
nudge, push, caress, or flail out at the individual. No matter what the
genome says, these people have a lot to do with shaping a character.
Indeed, if all you had was the genome, and no people around, you'd
grow a sort of vertebrate plant, nothing more.

9. So, to start with, you will undoubtedly need to clone the parents.
No question about this. This means the diplomat is out, even in
theory, since you couldn't have gotten cells from both his parents at
the time when he was himself just recognizable as an early social
treasure. You'd have to limit the list of clones to people already certified as sufficiently valuable for the effort, with both parents still
alive. The parents would need cloning and, for consistency, their

parents as well. I suppose you'd also need the usual informed-consent forms, filled out and signed, not easy to get if I know parents, even harder for grandparents.

10.   But this is only the beginning. It is the whole family that really influences the way a person turns out, not just the parents, according to current psychiatric thinking. Clone the family.

11.   Then what? The way each member of the family develops has already been determined by the environment set around him, and this environment is more people, people outside the family, schoolmates, acquaintances, lovers, enemies, car-pool partners, even, in special circumstances, peculiar strangers across the aisle on the subway. Find them, and clone them.

12.   But there is no end to the protocol. Each of the outer contacts has his own surrounding family, and his and their outer contacts. Clone them all.

13.   To do the thing properly, with any hope of ending up with a genuine duplicate of a single person, you really have no choice. You must clone the world, no less.

14.   We are not ready for an experiment of this size, nor, I should think, are we willing. For one thing, it would mean replacing today's world by an entirely identical world to follow immediately, and this means no new, natural, spontaneous, random, chancy children. No children at all, except for the manufactured doubles of those now on the scene. Plus all those identical adults, including all of today's politicians, all seen double. It is too much to contemplate.

15.   Moreover, when the whole experiment is finally finished, fifty years or so from now, how could you get a responsible scientific reading on the outcome? Somewhere in there would be the original clonee, probably lost and overlooked, now well into middle age, but everyone around him would be precise duplicates of today's everyone. It would be today's same world, filled to overflowing with duplicates of today's people and their same, duplicated problems, probably all resentful at having had to go through our whole thing all over, sore enough at the clonee to make endless trouble for him, if they found him.

16.   And obviously, if the whole thing were done precisely right, they would still be casting about for ways to solve the problem of universal dissatisfaction, and sooner or later they'd surely begin to look around at each other, wondering who should be cloned for his special value to society, to get us out of all this. And so it would go, in regular cycles, perhaps forever.

17.   I once lived through a period when I wondered what Hell could

be like, and I stretched my imagination to try to think of a perpetual sort of damnation. I have to confess, I never thought of anything like this.

18. I have an alternative suggestion, if you're looking for a way out. Set cloning aside, and don't try it. Instead, go in the other direction. Look for ways to get mutations more quickly, new variety, different songs. Fiddle around, if you must fiddle, but never with ways to keep things the same, no matter who, not even yourself. Heaven, somewhere ahead, has got to be a change.

QUESTIONS

1. Thomas introduces his subject and provides a narrative in paragraphs 1–4, and this introduction and narrative lead into his thesis statement in paragraph 5. What background does the narrative present? What is gained by building to the thesis instead of beginning the essay with it?

2. In paragraphs 6–13, Thomas shows what cloning would entail; his reasoning is therefore deductive, because he is showing what certain premises necessarily imply. What does cloning entail, according to Thomas, and how do these implications show the difficulty, even the absurdity, of the premise?

3. In paragraphs 14–18, Thomas draws conclusions from his refutation: he looks at underlying attitudes and proposes an alternative course. What are these attitudes that underlie the wish to clone human beings, and what alternative does he propose? How does this concluding discussion enlarge the thesis developed earlier?

4. What is the tone of the essay, and how is it established? Is Thomas amused, sarcastic, ironic, or even jocular about cloning, or is he writing in a deeply serious tone?

WRITING ASSIGNMENT

Write an essay on what would happen if one of the following were possible. Use your deductive analysis to state whether such a course or happening would be desirable.

a. providing cheap public transportation in your city
b. drafting women for the armed forces
c. providing a free college education to all high school graduates
d. eliminating attendance requirements in college courses
e. making television the only means of watching movies, plays, and sports

Inductive Reasoning

R. KEITH MILLER

The Idea of Children

1. I know it's the International Year of the Child, and we should all be busy paying homage to the little tykes. But I've had enough. Not that I have anything much against children per se—after all, who could blame children for being children? It is, as the saying goes, only a stage that they're going through, and sooner or later most of them will manage to grow up. But I do have something against adults, for it is adults who have sentimentalized children and fostered a variety of misconceptions about childhood—misconceptions that have had serious consequences in both our homes and our schools.

2. Foremost among these misconceptions is the idea that children are imaginative and creative. Given the state of modern art, it's easy to see how many a proud parent can confuse finger painting with the latest excess at the local museum. But can anyone who has taken the trouble to think about it really believe that children are imaginative? They certainly have little respect for diversity, the average child being as desperate as any executive at IBM to conform to the ways of his peers. And most children are hopelessly dependent upon adults for direction: their most common complaint—and believe me, they have plenty of complaints—is, "I don't know what to do."

3. What we rush to label as "imagination" is at best a degree of spontaneity. Prolonged conversation with a nine-year-old is unlikely to be very stimulating. The truth of the matter is that children are relatively predictable. And anyone who says, "You never know what the little devil will be up to next," knows, at least, that it probably will be something rotten.

4. Despite much evidence to the contrary, we also like to believe that children are sensitive. Never mind the idiotic television programs that engage them for hours. Or their fascination with violence and all the paraphernalia of violence from water pistols to BB guns. Never mind the shrieks of delight that are likely to accompany the magic cinematic moment when a car goes tumbling over a California cliff, and the adults inside (who look suspiciously like parents) are presum-

ably burned to a crisp. Never mind all that. I'm sure that you could always dig up a child psychologist somewhere or other who would carefully explain that children don't really *enjoy* this sort of thing—it only *looks* that way.

5. Another myth has it that children are somehow "purer" than you or I. Few advocates of "children's rights" would go so far as to demand sexual rights for children. Nearly everyone agrees that children deserve the protection of law, since they are vulnerable to abuse.

6. But is it wise to assume that if you protect children from adults, you need not worry about protecting them from other children? Children may indeed be "born innocent," but complete innocence is seldom likely to survive the first grade. The realization that children are interested in their own bodies and that they are not beyond sexual experimentation makes many adults extremely uncomfortable. Apparently, we prefer to think of our children as Victorian gentlemen thought of their wives: attractively ornamental but blissfully sexless. The alternative is disturbing. It is to recognize that while not necessarily more sensitive or more creative than adults, children can be every bit as complex.

7. But what has happened to our memories? Children can be appallingly cruel to one another. Spend a few days on a public playground and try to reconcile all this sensitivity business with the taunts, the name-calling, the betrayals and—worst of all—the systematic victimization of any child who is weak or just plain different. We knew this when we were young, and we were constantly on guard lest some other kid got to us before we got to him. But somehow or other we manage to forget all this when we have children of our own—it's so much more satisfying to believe that children are happier than we are.

8. I suspect that many adults are not so much interested in children, as in the *idea* of children—children as individuals hold less value for them than children as the mythic representation of all they feel is lacking in their own lives. The unhappier they are with themselves, the more desperately they try to believe their children are somehow different. This results in a curiously contradictory attitude: many of the same people who affirm the importance of children effectively undermine that importance by turning young people into something far more ethereal than real flesh and blood.

9. We need to recognize that ideas have consequences. By granting a special status to children, we go far toward ensuring that they will be self-occupied and, all too often, irresponsible. If children are fundamentally different from you and me, how could we possibly expect

them even to begin to measure up to the same standards? How can you discipline them when, by definition, they are supposed to be creative, natural and free? And so we find ourselves prone to make excuses where excuses are uncalled for—producing children that increasingly become sullen, spoiled and altogether unpleasant adolescents. We have forgotten that today's angry teen-ager was yesterday's celebrated child.

10.   Consider also the dubious results of progressive education, which is based in part on the idea that children are intrinsically good and that if they are free to be themselves, they will respond by learning and growing. I've always thought that a positively lovely notion— but it's hard to believe in its practicality when we look at the serious decline in reading and math abilities over the last ten years.

11.   Meanwhile, teachers in our cities increasingly find themselves victimized by knife-wielding seventh graders—who are, in turn, protected by a penal code that is so heavily imbued with the idea that children are special that twelve-year-old murderers get off with probation.

12.   Of course, I am speaking here of an extreme. And it is only fair to admit that there are many delightful children who represent everything that we like to believe is the norm—imagination, sensitivity and honor. On the other hand, many adults have precisely the same virtues. I do not wish to argue that children are any worse than adults, only to assert that they are not fundamentally better simply by virtue of being children. It's time that we recognized that children are not some marvelously enlightened minority group from which we all need to learn. Children can be clever, but they can also be dull—and a callous child is no more extraordinary than a callous adult. Children are, in short, only human. We should see them as they are, not as we wish we were.

DISCUSSION: Inductive Reasoning

Induction means deriving generalizations from particular instances— for example, parents and teenagers seldom like the same kind of music. I draw this conclusion from my own family and other families I have observed. Inductive arguments are neither valid nor invalid; they are characterized instead as more or less *probable* depending on the strength of the evidence in relation to the conclusion. The more parents and teenagers whose musical tastes I survey in a random sample of families representing a cross section of backgrounds, incomes, and education, the stronger my conclusion will be.

Perfect inductions or generalizations are possible when the group surveyed is small: the teenagers in my family like the same kind of music as the adults. But most inductions deal with groups or classes containing a very large number of members—a number much too great to survey. It would be impossible to find out whether all teenagers past and present have liked the same kind of music as their parents: it would be hard to find out whether all living teenagers do. The problem in induction is to choose particular instances that we can say are truly representative of the group or class about which the generalization is made.

"Hasty generalization" is a judgment on the basis of insufficient evidence or special cases—arguing that people over seventy should be denied licenses to drive because an extraordinary number of old people were involved in traffic accidents during a particular winter. The argument might be worth considering if the behavior of the old people involved in accidents could be shown to be typical. But other relevant evidence must be considered: an extraordinary number of drivers of *all* ages might have been involved in accidents that winter. Judgments and generalizations should be tested by exceptions that we can think of or that are brought to our attention; the statement "the exception proves the rule" means the generalization must explain *all* apparent exceptions to it, not that the rule must have an exception.

We often make statements in the form of generalizations that do not seem preposterous to us, though they may to other people, as James Thurber humorously shows (see page 229). Some people assume without question that small towns are safer to live in than cities; that Irishmen have short tempers; that New Yorkers are rude; that children who watch television more than two hours a day are fast (or slow) learners. To establish these generalizations we must show that the small towns we have lived in or the New Yorkers we have encountered are typical of all small towns or all New Yorkers—that there are no special circumstances that would account for the quality cited. The New Yorkers who prompted the generalization about rudeness may have been observed on a crowded, stalled bus on the hottest day of the year. Showing that these particular instances are indeed representative is exceedingly difficult: this is why generalizations must be carefully limited and qualified.

An inductive argument is considered probable only—never certain—because of the difficulty of guaranteeing a representative sample. A special kind of inductive argument—argument by analogy, in which similar objects or situations are taken to imply other similarities—is probable for other reasons. If identical twins are both English majors, wear the same clothes, enjoy the same films and music, play the same sports, and have the same hobbies, it may be argued that their respective friends will have a lot in common. As a rule, the greater the number of points of similarity, the stronger the probability of this conclusion. But these points of similarity—particulars in the process of generalization—must be relevant to the conclusion and lend strength to it. They do not, for example, establish that the twins have the same friends or always will have the same kind.

The points of dissimilarity must not weaken the conclusion. If, in seeking a job as a shoe salesman, I argue that my three years as an army drill sergeant fit me for the job, I will have to show that certain indispensable skills are common to both jobs and that certain differences in situation or dissimilarities are relatively insignificant. It is significant, for example, that customers can walk out of the store, but recruits cannot walk off the parade ground. Dissimilarities may increase the strength of an argument, too. If I argue that fifty former army drill sergeants are now successful shoe salesmen and that I should be hired for this reason, my argument will be strengthened if the sergeants *differ* in age, background, experience in selling—any relevant characteristics other than being a drill sergeant.

In general a limited conclusion may be drawn from a limited analogy if the points of similarity are clearly specified (or at least agreed on), if there is agreement on the relevance of the points considered, and if inferences are drawn from these points only. If these limits are not observed, the analogy may be considered false. Many people will accept the notion that "anything goes" in advertising because, they are told, the world of buying and selling is a jungle in which only the "fit" survive. The shoe salesman who accepts this analogy and thinks of himself as a "tiger" may discover its falseness: deceived buyers (unlike the tiger's dinner) are permitted to learn from their mistakes.

Cause-and-effect reasoning, on which analogy often depends and which is common in both science and everyday life, is also capable of reaching probable—sometimes highly probable—but not absolutely certain conclusions. We may think (on the basis of repeated efforts) that we know the conditions sufficient to produce a perfect soufflé—until we try to make one in a city at a high elevation, and the soufflé fails to rise. This limitation on cause-and-effect reasoning applies to the various kinds considered earlier (see pages 73–74).

Here, briefly described, are a few common errors in reasoning:

Post hoc, ergo propter hoc ("after this, therefore because of this"): the mistaken assumption that one event is the cause of a second merely because it precedes it. If nuclear explosions precede a sudden increase in tornado activity, they cannot be blamed for the increase in tornados unless a direct relationship can be established. One way to do this is to show that *every* such increase in tornado activity since 1945 was preceded by one or more nuclear explosions. However, that would establish a probable causal relationship only; further investigation might disclose the why of this relationship.

Begging the question: If I argue that "the useless custom of tipping should be abolished because it no longer has a purpose," I have assumed that the custom is useless before I have shown it to be. A close relative is

Arguing in a circle: "Nice girls don't chew gum because that is something no nice girl would do." I have not given a reason; I have merely restated my opening assertion.

Non sequitur ("it does not follow"): If I assert that I am against capital punishment because my father is, I am assuming without saying so that fathers know best. Since this premise has not been made explicit, the second part of the statement "does not follow" from the first part. The hidden premise may have been suppressed because, once stated, it shows the statement to be questionable or absurd.

Irrelevant conclusion: If the point-at-issue is whether private insurance companies or the federal government should operate a national health insurance plan, the argument that national health insurance is needed *now* is an irrelevant argument.

Ad hominem argument ("to the person"): an attack on the individual rather than the issue—for example, arguing that a proposal for national health insurance is unsound because its proponents are employees of insurance companies. In other circumstances (as in an election campaign), the individual may be the specific issue.

Ad populum argument ("to the people"): an appeal to such things as popular prejudice and patriotic feeling to gain support for or to attack an issue—Abraham Lincoln would have favored (or opposed) national health insurance; therefore, national health insurance is good (or bad).

Either-or hypothesis: the setting up of two alternatives—for example, national health insurance *or* private insurance plans—and not allowing for other plans or other solutions to the problem.

QUESTIONS

1. Miller exposes various misconceptions about children by presenting contrary evidence, drawn from observation and personal experience. What evidence contradicts "the idea that children are imaginative and creative"? And what evidence contradicts the views that children are "sensitive" and are "purer" than adults?

2. Miller builds to a discussion in paragraph 8 of why many adults hold these misconceptions. What is his explanation, and how does he support it?

3. In paragraphs 9–12, Miller shows the consequences of these misconceptions. What evidence does he present for these consequences?

4. To what conclusion does Miller build his argument inductively?

What statements throughout the essay show that he regards his argument as a probable one, and that he is not generalizing about all children and adults?

5. What fallacious kind of reasoning is he attacking in paragraph 12, and why does he reserve this attack for his final paragraph?

6. Do your own observations and personal experience give support to Miller, or can you cite evidence contrary to his?

WRITING ASSIGNMENTS

1. Defend or attack one of the following statements, drawing on your observation and personal experience for support. Remember that the probability of your argument depends on the strength of your evidence:

   a. "They certainly have little respect for diversity, the average child being as desperate as any executive at IBM to conform to the ways of his peers."

   b. "Children can be appallingly cruel to one another."

   c. "Children can be clever, but they can also be dull—and a callous child is no more extraordinary than a callous adult."

2. Miller states that "we need to recognize that ideas have consequences." Choose a misconception about a class of people other than children, and present evidence that exposes this misconception. Build your essay to a discussion of its consequences, as Miller does. In your concluding paragraph, draw conclusions from the evidence you have presented.

BARRY COMMONER

Nature Knows Best

1. In my experience this principle is likely to encounter considerable resistance, for it appears to contradict a deeply held idea about the unique competence of human beings. One of the most pervasive features of modern technology is the notion that it is intended to "improve on nature"—to provide food, clothing, shelter, and means of communication and expression which are superior to those available to man in nature. Stated baldly, the third law of ecology holds that any major man-made change in a natural system is likely to be *detrimental* to that system. This is a rather extreme claim; nevertheless I believe it has a good deal of merit if understood in a properly defined context.

2. I have found it useful to explain this principle by means of an analogy. Suppose you were to open the back of your watch, close your eyes, and poke a pencil into the exposed works. The almost certain result would be damage to the watch. Nevertheless, this result is not *absolutely* certain. There is some finite possibility that the watch was out of adjustment and that the random thrust of the pencil happened to make the precise change needed to improve it. However, this outcome is exceedingly improbable. The question at issue is: why? The answer is self-evident: there is a very considerable amount of what technologists now call "research and development" (or, more familiarly, "R & D") behind the watch. This means that over the years numerous watchmakers, each taught by a predecessor, have tried out a huge variety of detailed arrangements of watch works, have discarded those that are not compatible with the over-all operation of the system and retained the better features. In effect, the watch mechanism, as it now exists, represents a very restricted selection, from among an enormous variety of possible arrangements of component parts, of a singular organization of the watch works. Any random change made in the watch is likely to fall into the very large class of inconsistent, or harmful, arrangements which have been tried out in past watch-making experience and discarded. One might say, as a law of watches, that "the watchmaker knows best."

3. There is a close, and very meaningful, analogy in biological systems. It is possible to induce a certain range of random, inherited changes in a living thing by treating it with an agent, such as x-irradiation, that increases the frequency of mutations. Generally, exposure to x-rays increases the frequency of all mutations which have been observed, albeit very infrequently, in nature and can therefore be regarded as *possible* changes. What is significant, for our purpose, is the universal observation that when mutation frequency is enhanced by x-rays or other means, nearly all the mutations are harmful to the organisms and the great majority so damaging as to kill the organism before it is fully formed.

4. In other words, like the watch, a living organism that is forced to sustain a random change in its organization is almost certain to be damaged rather than improved. And in both cases, the explanation is the same—a great deal of "R & D." In effect there are some two to three billion years of "R & D" behind every living thing. In that time, a staggering number of new individual living things have been produced, affording in each case the opportunity to try out the suitability of some random genetic change. If the change damages the viability of the organism, it is likely to kill it before the change can be passed on

to future generations. In this way, living things accumulate a complex organization of compatible parts; those possible arrangements that are not compatible with the whole are screened out over the long course of evolution. Thus, the structure of a present living thing or the organization of a current natural ecosystem is likely to be "best" in the sense that it has been so heavily screened for disadvantageous components that any new one is very likely to be worse than the present ones.

5. This principle is particularly relevant to the field of organic chemistry. Living things are composed of many thousands of different organic compounds, and it is sometimes imagined that at least some of these might be improved upon if they were replaced by some man-made variant of the natural substance. The third law of ecology suggests that the artificial introduction of an organic compound that does not occur in nature, but is man-made and is nevertheless active in a living system, is very likely to be harmful.

6. This is due to the fact that the varieties of chemical substances actually found in living things are vastly more restricted than the *possible* varieties. A striking illustration is that if one molecule each of all the possible types of proteins were made, they would together weigh more than the observable universe. Obviously there are a fantastically large number of protein types that are *not* made by living cells. And on the basis of the foregoing, one would reason that many of these possible protein types were once formed in some particular living things, found to be harmful, and rejected through the death of the experiment. In the same way, living cells synthesize fatty acids (a type of organic molecule that contains carbon chains of various lengths) with even-numbered carbon chain lengths (i.e., 4, 6, 8, etc., carbons), but no fatty acids with odd-numbered carbon chain lengths. This suggests that the latter have once been tried out and found wanting. Simiarly, organic compounds that contain attached nitrogen and oxygen atoms are singularly rare in living things. This should warn us that the artificial introduction of substances of this type would be dangerous. This is indeed the case, for such substances are usually toxic and frequently carcinogenic. And, I would suppose from the fact that DDT is nowhere found in nature, that somewhere, at some time in the past, some unfortunate cell synthesized this molecule—and died.

7. One of the striking facts about the chemistry of living systems is that for every organic substance produced by a living organism, there exists, somewhere in nature, an enzyme capable of breaking that substance down. In effect, no organic substance is synthesized unless there is provision for its degradation; recycling is thus enforced. Thus, when a new man-made organic substance is synthesized with a molec-

ular structure that departs significantly from the types which occur in nature, it is probable that no degradative enzyme exists, and the material tends to accumulate.

8.   Given these considerations, it would be prudent, I believe, to regard every man-made organic chemical *not* found in nature which has a strong action on any one organism as potentially dangerous to other forms of life. Operationally, this view means that all man-made organic compounds that are at all active biologically ought to be treated as we do drugs, or rather as we *should* treat them—prudently, cautiously. Such caution or prudence is, of course, impossible when billions of pounds of the substance are produced and broadly disseminated into the ecosystem where it can reach and affect numerous organisms not under our observation. Yet this is precisely what we have done with detergents, insecticides, and herbicides. The often catastrophic results lend considerable force to the view that "Nature knows best."

QUESTIONS

1. What are the points of similarity between poking a pencil into the back of the watch and introducing man-made changes into nature? Does the fact that the watch is man-made, unlike nature, weaken the analogy?
2. What other analogy might Commoner have chosen? What would have been gained or lost had he employed this analogy?
3. What knowledge and assumptions does Commoner assume in his audience, and how do you know?

WRITING ASSIGNMENT

Explain a phenomenon you are familiar with—stereophonic or quadraphonic sound, or condensation, or the "knuckler" or "spitball" in baseball—through a familiar analogy. Write to a general audience that needs an explanation of basic terms.

BROOKS ATKINSON

The Warfare in the Forest Is Not Wanton

1.   After thirty-five years the forest in Spruce Notch is tall and sturdy. It began during the Depression when work gangs planted thousands of tiny seedlings in abandoned pastures on Richmond Peak

in the northern Catskills. Nothing spectacular has happened there since; the forest has been left undisturbed.

2. But now we have a large spread of Norway spruces a foot thick at the butt and 40 or 50 feet high. Their crowns look like thousands of dark crosses reaching into the sky.

3. The forest is a good place in which to prowl in search of wildlife. But also in search of ideas. For the inescapable fact is that the world of civilized America does not have such a clean record. Since the seedlings were planted the nation has fought three catastrophic wars, in one of which the killing of combatants and the innocent continues. During the lifetime of the forest 350,000 Americans have died on foreign battlefields.

4. Inside America civilized life is no finer. A President, a Senator, a man of God have been assassinated. Citizens are murdered in the streets. Riots, armed assaults, looting, burning, outbursts of hatred have increased to the point where they have become commonplace.

5. Life in civilized America is out of control. Nothing is out of control in the forest. Everything complies with the instinct for survival— which is the law and order of the woods.

6. Although the forest looks peaceful it supports incessant warfare, most of which is hidden and silent. For thirty-five years the strong have been subduing the weak. The blueberries that once flourished on the mountain have been destroyed. All the trees are individuals, as all human beings are individuals; and every tree poses a threat to every other tree. The competition is so fierce that you can hardly penetrate some of the thickets where the lower branches of neighboring trees are interlocked in a blind competition for survival.

7. Nor is the wildlife benign. A red-tailed hawk lived there last summer—slowly circling in the sky and occasionally drawing attention to himself by screaming. He survived on mice, squirrels, chipmunks and small birds. A barred owl lives somewhere in the depth of the woods. He hoots in midmorning as well as at sunrise to register his authority. He also is a killer. Killing is a fundamental part of the process. The nuthatches kill insects in the bark. The woodpeckers dig insects out. The thrushes eat beetles and caterpillars.

8. But in the forest, killing is not wanton or malicious. It is for survival. Among birds of equal size most of the warfare consists of sham battles in which they go through the motions of warfare until one withdraws. Usually neither bird gets hurt.

9. Nor is the warfare between trees vindictive. Although the spruces

predominate they do not practice segregation. On both sides of Lost Lane, which used to be a dirt road, maples, beeches, ashes, aspens and a few red oaks live, and green curtains of wild grapes cover the wild cherry trees. In the depths of the forest there are a few glades where the spruces stand aside and birches stretch and grow. The forest is a web of intangible tensions. But they are never out of control. Although they are wild they are not savage as they are in civilized life.

10.   For the tensions are absorbed in the process of growth, and the clusters of large cones on the Norway spruces are certificates to a good future. The forest gives an external impression of discipline and pleasure. Occasionally the pleasure is rapturously stated. Soon after sunrise one morning last summer when the period of bird song was nearly over, a solitary rose-breasted grosbeak sat on the top of a tall spruce and sang with great resonance and beauty. He flew a few rods to another tree and continued singing: then to another tree where he poured out his matin again, and so on for a half hour. There was no practical motive that I was aware of.

11.   After thirty-five uneventful years the spruces have created an environment in which a grosbeak is content, and this one said so gloriously. It was a better sound than the explosion of bombs, the scream of the wounded, the crash of broken glass, the crackle of burning buildings, the shriek of the police siren.

12.   The forest conducts its affairs with less rancor and malevolence than civilized America.

QUESTIONS

1. One sometimes hears the argument that violence is natural to human beings, since we are a part of a warring natural world. How does Atkinson implicitly reject this analogy? More specifically, what are the points of dissimilarity between the world of the forest and the world of humans?

2. How might the world of the forest be used to argue that competition in the world of humans need not be destructive of some of those competing—as the argument that only the "fit" survive in the world of business implies?

3. How does Atkinson increase the probability of his argument through the details he marshals in support of it?

4. How similar is Atkinson's view of nature to Commoner's?

Each of the following statements suggests an analogy. Write on one of them, discussing points of similarity and dissimilarity and using this discussion to argue a thesis.

a. The family is a small nation.
b. The nation is a large family.
c. College examinations are sporting events.
d. Choosing a college is like buying a car.

NORMAN COUSINS

Who Killed Benny Paret?

1. Sometime about 1935 or 1936 I had an interview with Mike Jacobs, the prize-fight promoter. I was a fledgling newspaper reporter at that time; my beat was education, but during the vacation season I found myself on varied assignments, all the way from ship news to sports reporting. In this way I found myself sitting opposite the most powerful figure in the boxing world.

2. There was nothing spectacular in Mr. Jacobs's manner or appearance; but when he spoke about prize fights, he was no longer a bland little man but a colossus who sounded the way Napoleon must have sounded when he reviewed a battle. You knew you were listening to Number One. His saying something made it true.

3. We discussed what to him was the only important element in successful promoting—how to please the crowd. So far as he was concerned, there was no mystery to it. You put killers in the ring and the people filled your arena. You hire boxing artists—men who are adroit at feinting, parrying, weaving, jabbing, and dancing, but who don't pack dynamite in their fists—and you wind up counting your empty seats. So you searched for the killers and sluggers and maulers—fellows who could hit with the force of a baseball bat.

4. I asked Mr. Jacobs if he was speaking literally when he said people came out to see the killer.

5. "They don't come out to see a tea party," he said evenly. "They come out to see the knockout. They come out to see a man hurt. If they think anything else, they're kidding themselves."

6. Recently a young man by the name of Benny Paret was killed in

the ring. The killing was seen by millions; it was on television. In the twelfth round he was hit hard in the head several times, went down, was counted out, and never came out of the coma.

7.   The Paret fight produced a flurry of investigations. Governor Rockefeller was shocked by what happened and appointed a committee to assess the responsibility. The New York State Boxing Commission decided to find out what was wrong. The District Attorney's office expressed its concern. One question that was solemnly studied in all three probes concerned the action of the referee. Did he act in time to stop the fight? Another question had to do with the role of the examining doctors who certified the physical fitness of the fighters before the bout. Still another question involved Mr. Paret's manager; did he rush his boy into the fight without adequate time to recuperate from the previous one?

8.   In short, the investigators looked into every possible cause except the real one. Benny Paret was killed because the human fist delivers enough impact, when directed against the head, to produce a massive hemorrhage in the brain. The human brain is the most delicate and complex mechanism in all creation. It has a lacework of millions of highly fragile nerve connections. Nature attempts to protect this exquisitely intricate machinery by encasing it in a hard shell. Fortunately, the shell is thick enough to withstand a great deal of pounding. Nature, however, can protect man against everything except man himself. Not every blow to the head will kill a man—but there is always the risk of concussion and damage to the brain. A prize fighter may be able to survive even repeated brain concussions and go on fighting, but the damage to his brain may be permanent.

9.   In any event, it is futile to investigate the referee's role and seek to determine whether he should have intervened to stop the fight earlier. This is not where the primary responsibility lies. The primary responsibility lies with the people who pay to see a man hurt. The referee who stops a fight too soon from the crowd's viewpoint can expect to be booed. The crowd wants the knockout; it wants to see a man stretched out on the canvas. This is the supreme moment in boxing. It is nonsense to talk about prize fighting as a test of boxing skills. No crowd was ever brought to its feet screaming and cheering at the sight of two men beautifully dodging and weaving out of each other's jabs. The time the crowd comes alive is when a man is hit hard over the heart or the head, when his mouthpiece flies out, when blood squirts out of his nose or eyes, when he wobbles under the attack and his pursuer continues to smash at him with poleax impact.

10. Don't blame it on the referee. Don't even blame it on the fight managers. Put the blame where it belongs—on the prevailing mores that regard prize fighting as a perfectly proper enterprise and vehicle of entertainment. No one doubts that many people enjoy prize fighting and will miss it if it should be thrown out. And that is precisely the point.

QUESTIONS

1. Cousins distinguishes between the immediate and the remote causes of Paret's death. What does he show to be the immediate cause, and why can this cause be stated with near certainty?
2. Cousins is concerned chiefly with the remote cause of Paret's death. How is this concern basic to his purpose in writing the essay? What are the chief indications of that purpose?
3. How would a different purpose have required Cousins to focus instead on the immediate cause?
4. How does Cousins establish the remote cause? Is his evidence statistical—based on a sample of statements of boxing fans? Is it theoretical—based on a discussion of "human nature"? Is he concerned with the psychology of the crowd or the sociology of boxing? Is his analysis of the event intended to offer a complete explanation?

WRITING ASSIGNMENTS

1. Analyze a mass sport like pro football or hockey to determine the extent of its appeal to violent emotions.
2. Contrast Cousins' view of the causes of Paret's death with Mailer's view in "The Death of Benny Paret."

HERBERT HENDIN
Students and Drugs

1. No more dramatic expression of the dissatisfaction students feel with themselves can be found than students abusing drugs. Students often become drug abusers, that is, heavy and habitual users, in an attempt to alter their emotional lives, to transform themselves into the

people they wish they could be, but feel they never could be without drugs. What they crave is to restructure their own emotions, not to be themselves, but to live as some "other." What this "other" is like and how it can be achieved cut to the center of the changing American psyche.

2. The turmoil over performance, achievement, and success, the increasing terror of becoming "too" involved with anyone; the attempt to find in fragmentation the means of effecting a pervasive change in one's total relation to life—all these are everywhere prevalent on campus. Students abusing drugs are often attempting to cure themselves of the malaise they see everywhere around them and in themselves.

3. Why do some students take LSD or heroin while others take marijuana or amphetamines? Why do still others take anything and everything? Students who are intrigued by drugs can learn through trial and error and from other students to find and favor the drugs which most satisfy their particular emotional needs. They rapidly become expert psychopharmacologists, able to locate the specific drug cure for what disturbs them. One student who by seventeen had tried just about everything and had become a daily, intravenous heroin user, had rejected LSD early in his drug career, explaining, "I can't see what anyone gets out of it. It just sort of makes you schizy—quiet one minute and freaked out the next."

4. Some students were initially drawn to the "cops-and-robbers" quality of drug abuse. While they were clearly out to defy their parents and the whole structure of authority, they were often unaware that their abuse had anything to do with their families, so profoundly had they pushed their rage at them out of their consciousness. Such students were invariably unable to deal with their parents directly and were bound in a need to defy them and a simultaneous need to punish themselves for their rebellion.

5. Drugs provided these students with both crime and punishment, while removing their defiance out of the direct presence of their parents. One student would "let his mind float away" and concentrate on music he liked whenever his father berated him. Afterward he went out and took whatever drugs he could buy. While he never connected his drug abuse with his anger toward his father, he often dreamed of it as a crime for which he would be punished. He had a dream in which a riot was going on in another part of town while he was shooting heroin. He was afraid that somehow he would be arrested along with the rioters. Drugs were clearly his way of rioting, of diverting the crime of rebellion to the crime of drug abuse and focus-

ing his destructive potential on himself. The expectation this student had that he would be arrested was typical, and revelatory of the appeal of drugs for him. Jail signified to such students a concrete way of locking up their rage. Drugs permitted them to both contain their rage and to express it in a way that gave them a sense of defiance, however self-damaging that defiance may be. Often, students who are most in trouble with the police over drugs are those for whom the need for crime and punishment was more significant than the need for drugs.

6. For most of the students who abused them, drugs also provided the illusion of pleasurable connection to other people while serving to detach them from the emotions real involvement would arouse. Drugs were, for these students, the best available means of social relations. Heroin abusers found in the junkie underworld a sense of security, belonging, and acceptance derived from the acknowledgment and the shared need for heroin. LSD abusers felt their most intimate experiences involved tripping with another person. Marijuana abusers felt that drugs "took the edge off their personality" enough to permit them to be gentle and to empathize with other people. Amphetamine abusers were pushed into the social round on amphetamine energy, often being enabled to go through sexual experience they would otherwise have found unendurable.

7. For many students drug abuse is the means to a life without drugs. Such students take drugs to support the adaptation they are struggling to make. Once it is established, they are often able to maintain it without drugs. The period of heavy drug abuse often marks the crisis in their lives when they are trying to establish a tolerable relation to the world and themselves. Appealing, tumultuous, sometimes frighteningly empty, the lives of students who turn to drugs are an intense, dramatic revelation of the way students feel today, what they are forced to grapple with not only in the culture, but in themselves.

QUESTIONS

1. Does Hendin single out a cause of drug use among students, or instead identify a number of related (or unrelated) causes?
2. Does he distinguish psychological from social causes, or does he assume these are one and the same?
3. Is Hendin generalizing about all students today—even those who do not use drugs—or is he commenting merely on student drug users?
4. How does drug use foster "fragmentation" in the drug user? How

can "fragmentation" provide a solution to the problems Hendin identifies in paragraph 2?
5. What does Hendin mean by the statement, "For many students drug abuse is the means to a life without drugs"?

WRITING ASSIGNMENT

Describe the tensions you have observed in yourself or in fellow students, and discuss the extent to which these tensions resemble those that Hendin identifies. Suggest some of the causes for those you have experienced or observed.

ALAN WERTHEIMER
[Statistical] Lives

1. Suppose the following were true:
2. At least some money spent on open-heart surgery could be used to prevent heart disease. True, patients in need of such surgery might die, but many more lives would be saved.
3. Some money spent treating tooth decay among low-income children might be used on fluoridation and dental hygiene. True, some decay would go untreated, but fewer children would ever need such treatment.
4. We could prohibit ransom payments to kidnappers. True, kidnapped children might die, but by lowering the incentive to kidnap, fewer children would be taken.
5. We could drastically reduce unemployment compensation. True, the unemployed would suffer, but by converting the money saved to private investment and by lowering the incentive to stay jobless, there would be substantially less unemployment.
6. These cases exhibit a similar structure. All involve choosing between a policy designed to help specific persons and one that seeks to prevent the need for such help. These choices are especially difficult because we know who needs help. The patient requiring open-heart surgery, the kidnapped child, the unemployed auto worker—they have names and faces; they are "identifiable" lives. On the other hand, we do not know whose lives will be saved or who will benefit from the prevention of heart disease, tooth decay, kidnappings, or cre-

ation of new jobs. Some people will, and we may be able to estimate their numbers with precision. These are real lives, but they are only "statistical" lives.

7. We might say we do not have to choose between helping those in need and preventing future needs. After all, we could do both. But resources are scarce, and even when resources are not at issue (as in the kidnapping case), we often must choose between competing persons or goals. We cannot do everything we might like to the extent we might like. We must often choose between helping identifiable lives and saving statistical lives.

8. I wish to make three points about these dilemmas. First, we do seem to favor the interests of identifiable lives (saving the kidnapped child) and it may not be irrational to do so. Second, we nevertheless do see the need to attend to the interests of statistical lives, even if this injures identifiable lives. Thus it is now common to hear people advocating directing more medical resources to primary prevention of disease and fewer to treatment. Israel's policy of refusing to negotiate with terrorists may risk the lives of some hostages, but we do see the point. Third, welfare-state policies focus on identifiable lives, whereas conservative economists prefer to focus on statistical lives.

9. Monetary theory and other technical issues aside, the new Adam Smiths tell us that however well-intentioned, welfare-state policies have not (always) worked—on the policies' own terms. Minimum-wage laws, unemployment compensation, consumer protection, occupational safety, Medicaid, Social Security—by interfering with market efficiency, by discouraging individual initiative, by impeding private-capital formation, by incurring large-scale expenditures on governmental bureaucracies—all these policies (and others) have been self-defeating. They argue that liberal economics, filled with concern for the genuine needs of identifiable lives, has swelled the future ranks of statistical lives in need. Welfare-state humanitarianism is short-sighted, they say, and is thus less humanitarian than we may believe.

10. We need not dwell on the accuracy of this account. Conservative economists may be wrong about the facts. We certainly need not assume that market choices and private-capital formation always serve the interests of all social groups, that regulation always does more harm than good. But suppose conservative economists are (sometimes) right about the facts. Suppose that attempts to serve the needs of identifiable lives do end up harming future statistical lives. Should we turn our back on the needs that we see in order to prevent those that we cannot see? Regrettably, the answer may sometimes be yes.

QUESTIONS

1. Wertheimer's argument is in part inductive: he shows that well-established facts and expert testimony make the dilemma real, not fictitious. What are these facts and testimony? What in the wording of paragraphs 9–10 show that Wertheimer considers this evidence highly probable, and not certain?
2. The argument is in part deductive: Wertheimer shows what each policy would entail if adopted. If we choose to save specific persons, what would be the consequences? What would they be if we choose to save "statistical" lives?
3. One way of refuting a dilemma is to "grasp the horns" and show that at least one of the alternatives is false or would not lead to the alleged consequences. Another way is to "go between the horns" and show that a third alternative exists—a policy that would save specific persons and "statistical" lives both. In paragraphs 7–8, Wertheimer anticipates refutation of the dilemma, and answers it. What kind of refutation might be presented, and how does he answer it?
4. Do you agree with Wertheimer's response to the dilemma, in paragraph 10? On what evidence do you base your agreement or disagreement—facts, expert testimony, or assumptions that you regard as self-evident?

WRITING ASSIGNMENTS

1. Present examples of your own of the dilemma Wertheimer presents, and use them to explore their implications for the policies discussed. Build your discussion to a statement of your own beliefs and conclusions.
2. Present a dilemma that you believe should concern Americans today. Introduce facts or expert testimony to show that the dilemma is a real one, anticipate a refutation of your dilemma and answer it, and state your own views on what can or should be done.

Controversy

GEORGE BERNARD SHAW

Capital Punishment and Imprisonment

1.   Some of the popular objections to [capital punishment] may be considered for a moment. Death, it is said, is irrevocable; and after all, they may turn out to be innocent. But really you cannot handle criminals on the assumption that they may be innocent. You are not supposed to handle them at all until you have convinced yourself by an elaborate trial that they are guilty. Besides, imprisonment is as irrevocable as hanging. Each is a method of taking a criminal's life; and when he prefers hanging or suicide to imprisonment for life, as he sometimes does, he says, in effect, that he had rather you took his life all at once painlessly, than minute by minute in long-drawn-out torture. You can give a prisoner a pardon; but you cannot give him back a moment of his imprisonment. He may accept a reprieve willingly in the hope of a pardon or an escape or a revolution or an earthquake or what not; but as you do not mean him to evade his sentence in any way whatever, it is not for you to take such clutchings at straws into account.

2.   Another argument against the death penalty for anything short of murder is the practical one of the policeman and the householder, who plead that if you hang burglars they will shoot to avoid capture on the ground that they may as well be hanged for a sheep as for a lamb. But this can be disposed of by pointing out, first, that even under existing circumstances the burglar occasionally shoots, and, second, that acquittals, recommendations to mercy, verdicts of manslaughter, successful pleas of insanity and so forth, already make the death penalty so uncertain that even red-handed murderers shoot no oftener than burglars—less often, in fact. This uncertainty would be actually increased if the death sentence were, as it should be, made applicable to other criminals than those convicted of wilful murder, and no longer made compulsory in any case.

3.   Then comes the plea for the sacredness of human life. The State should not set the example of killing, or of clubbing a rioter with a po-

liceman's baton, or of dropping bombs on a sleeping city, or of doing many things that States nevertheless have to do. But let us take the plea on its own ground, which is, fundamentally, that life is the most precious of all things, and its waste the worst of crimes. We have already seen that imprisonment does not spare the life of the criminal: it takes it and wastes it in the most cruel way. But there are others to be considered beside the criminal and the citizens who fear him so much that they cannot sleep in peace unless he is locked up. There are the people who have to lock him up, and fetch him his food, and watch him. Why are their lives to be wasted? Warders, and especially wardresses, are almost as much tied to the prison by their occupation, and by their pensions, which they dare not forfeit by seeking other employment, as the criminals are. If I had to choose between a spell under preventive detention among hardened criminals in Camp Hill and one as warder in an ordinary prison, I think I should vote for Camp Hill. Warders suffer in body and mind from their employment; and if it be true, as our examination seems to prove, that they are doing no good to society, but very active harm, their lives are wasted more completely than those of the criminals; for most criminals are discharged after a few weeks or months; but the warder never escapes until he is superannuated, by which time he is an older jailbird than any Lifer in the cells.

4. How then does the case stand with your incurable pathological case of crime? If you treat the life of the criminal as sacred, you find yourself not only taking his life but sacrificing the lives of innocent men and women to keep him locked up. There is no sort of sense or humanity in such a course. The moment we face it frankly we are driven to the conclusion that the community has a right to put a price on the right to live in it. That price must be sufficient self-control to live without wasting and destroying the lives of others, whether by direct attack like a tiger, parasitic exploitation like a leech, or having to be held in a leash with another person at the end of it. Persons lacking such self-control have been thrust out into the sage-brush to wander there until they die of thirst, a cruel and cowardly way of killing them. The dread of clean and wilful killing often leads to evasions of the commandment "Thou shalt not kill" which are far more cruel than its frank violation. [. . .]

5. Modern imprisonment: that is, imprisonment practised as a punishment as well as a means of detention, is extremely cruel and mischievous, and therefore extremely wicked. The word extremely is used advisedly because the system has been pushed to a degree at

which prison mortality and prison insanity forced it back to the point at which it is barely endurable, which point may therefore be regarded as the practicable extreme.

6. Although public vindictiveness and public dread are largely responsible for this wickedness, some of the most cruel features of the prison system are not understood by the public, and have not been deliberately invented and contrived for the purpose of increasing the prisoner's torment. The worst of these are (a) unsuccessful attempts at reform, (b) successful attempts to make the working of the prison cheaper for the State and easier for the officials, and (c) accidents of the evolution of the old privately owned detention prison into the new punitive State prison.

7. The prison authorities profess three objects (a) Retribution (a euphemism for vengeance), (b) Deterrence (a euphemism for Terrorism), and (c) Reform of the prisoner. They achieve the first by simple atrocity. They fail in the second through lack of the necessary certainty of detection, prosecution, and conviction; partly because their methods are too cruel and mischievous to secure the co-operation of the public; partly because the prosecutor is put to serious inconvenience and loss of time; partly because most people desire to avoid an unquestionable family disgrace much more than to secure a very questionable justice; and partly because the proportion of avowedly undetected crimes is high enough to hold out reasonable hopes to the criminal that he will never be called to account. The third (Reform) is irreconcilable with the first (Retribution); for the figures of recidivism, and the discovery that the so-called Criminal Type is really a prison type, prove that the retributive process is one of uncompensated deterioration.

8. The cardinal vice of the system is the anti-Christian vice of vengeance, or the intentional duplication of malicious injuries partly in pure spite, partly in compliance with the expiatory superstition that two blacks make a white. The criminal accepts this, but claims that punishment absolves him if the injuries are equivalent, and still more if he has the worse of the bargain, as he almost always has. Consequently, when absolution on his release is necessarily denied him, and he is forced back into crime by the refusal to employ him, he feels that he is entitled to revenge this injustice by becoming an enemy of Society. No beneficial reform of our treatment of criminals is possible unless and until this superstition of expiation and this essentially sentimental vice of vengeance are unconditionally eradicated.

9. Society has a right of self-defence, extending to the destruction or

restraint of lawbreakers. This right is separable from the right to revenge or punish: it need have no more to do with punishment or revenge than the caging or shooting of a man-eating tiger. It arises from the existence of (A) intolerably mischievous human beings, and (B) persons defective in the self-control needed for free life in modern society, but well behaved and at their ease under tutelage and discipline. Class A can be painlessly killed or permanently restrained. The requisite tutelage and discipline can be provided for Class B without rancor or insult. The rest can be treated not as criminals but as civil defendants, and made to pay for their depredations in the same manner. At present many persons guilty of conduct much viler than that for which poor men are sent to prison suffer nothing worse than civil actions for damages when they do not (unhappily) enjoy complete immunity.

10.   The principle to be kept before the minds of all citizens is that as civilized society is a very costly arrangement necessary to their subsistence and security they must justify their enjoyment of it by contributing their share to its cost, and giving no more than their share of trouble, subject to every possible provision by insurance against innocent disability. This is a condition precedent to freedom, and justifies us in removing cases of incurable noxious disability by simply putting an end to their existence.

11.   An unconquerable repugnance to judicial killing having led to the abolition of capital punishment in several countries, and to its reservation for specially dangerous or abhorrent crimes in all the others, it is possible that the right to kill may be renounced by all civilized States. This repugnance may be intensified as we cease to distinguish between sin and infirmity, or, in prison language, between crime and disease, because of our fear of being led to the extirpation of the incurable invalid who is excessively troublesome as well as to that of the incurable criminal.

12.   On the other hand, the opposite temperament, which is not squeamish about making short work of hard cases, and which is revolted by the daily sacrifice of the lives of prison officials, and of relatives and nurses, to incurable criminals and invalids, may be reinforced by the abandonment of ethical pretentiousness, vengeance, malice, and all uncharitableness in the matter, and may become less scrupulous than at present in advocating euthanasia for all incurables.

13.   Whichever party may prevail, punishment as such is likely to disappear, and with it the ear-marking of certain offences as calling for specially deterrent severities. But it does not follow that lethal treat-

ment of extreme cases will be barred. On the contrary, it may be extended from murder to social incompatibility of all sorts. If it be absolutely barred, sufficient restraint must be effected, not as a punishment but as a necessity for public safety. But there will be no excuse for making it more unpleasant than it need be.

14. When detention and restraint are necessary, the criminal's right to contact with all the spiritual influences of his day should be respected, and its exercise encouraged and facilitated. Conversation, access to books and pictures and music, unfettered scientific, philosophic, and religious activity, change of scene and occupation, the free formation of friendships and acquaintances, marriage and parentage: in short, all the normal methods of creation and recreation, must be available for criminals as for other persons, partly because deprivation of these things is severely punitive, and partly because it is destructive to the victim, and produces what we call the criminal type, making a cure impossible. Any specific liberty which the criminal's specific defects lead him to abuse will, no doubt, be taken from him; but if his life is spared his right to live must be accepted in the fullest sense, and not, as at present, merely as a right to breathe and circulate his blood. In short, a criminal should be treated, not as a man who has forfeited all normal rights and liberties by the breaking of a single law, but as one who, through some specific weakness or weaknesses, is incapable of exercising some specific liberty or liberties.

15. The main difficulty in applying this concept of individual freedom to the criminal arises from the fact that the concept itself is as yet unformed. We do not apply it to children, at home or at school, nor to employees, nor to persons of any class or age who are in the power of other persons. Like Queen Victoria, we conceive Man as being either in authority or subject to authority, each person doing only what he is expressly permitted to do, or what the example of the rest of his class encourages him to consider as tacitly permitted. The concept of the evolving free man in an evolving society, making all sorts of experiments in conduct, and therefore doing everything he likes as far as he can unless there are express prohibitions to which he is politically a consenting party, is still unusual, and consequently terrifying, in spite of all the individualist pamphlets of the eighteenth and nineteenth centuries. It will be found that those who are most scandalized by the liberties I am claiming for the convict would be equally scandalized if I claimed them for their own sons, or even for themselves.

16. The conclusion is that imprisonment cannot be fully understood by those who do not understand freedom. But it can be understood

quite well enough to have it made a much less horrible, wicked, and wasteful thing than it is at present.

DISCUSSION: Controversy

A single argument may involve both inductive and deductive reasoning. In debates over current issues like capital punishment and nuclear power, the kind of reasoning employed depends on what is taken to be the *point-at-issue.* The proponents of nuclear power plants may insist that the economic welfare of a particular region is the point-at-issue in locating a nuclear plant in the vicinity. Opponents may argue that the potential danger of these plants (compared to coal-fueled power plants) or the difficulty of disposing of nuclear wastes is the point-at-issue. Much of the debate may be devoted to establishing this point.

The arguments employed in such a debate probably will be inductive: statistical information on productivity and electrical fuels, eyewitness accounts of nuclear operations, scientific reports on waste disposal, accident reports, and the like. The parties to the dispute may agree on certain assumptions: that a high standard of living is a desirable goal for Americans; that the rights of society must be compatible with the rights of the individual citizen; that world peace depends on continuing high productivity in industrial nations like the United States. From these assumptions certain conclusions may be drawn directly, but used to different advantage by each party in the debate. Or these assumptions may underlie—and determine the outcome of—the debate without being identified and argued. Each party may direct the argument to specific opponents, or may direct it to the general public. The kind of evidence chosen will depend in part on the audience and in part on the needs of the argument.

QUESTIONS

1. The Shaw passages are taken from his *Crude Criminology,* written in 1921–22. The second passage (paragraphs 5–16) is the concluding summary of the main argument in the whole book. In an earlier passage Shaw argues that some criminals cannot be changed and when released from prison continue to torture and murder people:

Now you cannot get rid of these nuisances and monsters by simply cataloguing them as subthyroidics and superadrenals or the like. At present you torment them for a fixed period, at the end of which they are set free to resume their operations with a savage grudge against the community which has tormented them. That is stupid. Nothing is gained by punishing people who cannot help themselves and on whom deterrence is thrown away. Releasing them is like releasing the tigers from the Zoo to find their next meal in the nearest children's playing ground.

In the passages printed here, what other arguments does Shaw present in favor of capital punishment? What assumptions is he making about society and the individual in these arguments?
2. How does Shaw answer the objections to capital punishment he presents?
3. Why does he reject life imprisonment as an alternative to capital punishment? What does he believe the purpose of imprisonment should be?

WRITING ASSIGNMENT

Shaw distinguishes three attitudes toward imprisonment. Discuss which of these attitudes represents your own, and defend your reasons for holding one of them and rejecting another. Compare your assumptions about society and the individual with Shaw's.

AMERICA
The Injustice of the Death Penalty

1. Future annalists of our nation's Bicentennial year will probably note that it marked the revival of capital punishment in the United States. As we go to press, Gary Mark Gilmore faces imminent execution by a Utah firing squad. Even if something happens at the last minute to defer his execution, there are 422 other inmates in the death rows of our prisons. Some of them are scheduled for execution before Christmas. Unless there is a radical change in public sentiment, the nation will soon see its first public execution since 1967.
2. Mr. Gilmore stunned the nation by proclaiming the justice of his death sentence and demanding his immediate execution. But it does not really matter whether the first prisoner executed is Mr. Gilmore or someone else who does not want to die. What matters is that capital punishment is being revived when there is no justification for it.
3. Despite the fact that 35 state legislatures have revised their death penalty laws since the Supreme Court declared the pre-1972 laws unconstitutional, the American public is still profoundly confused about

the morality and utility of capital punishment. This confusion is the natural result of the conflict between the traditional lawfulness of the death penalty and the absence of any solid evidence to justify its continuation. Many Americans who favor the death penalty in the abstract for certain types of crimes are against it in the concrete for almost every type of individual.

4. Indeed, Mr. Gilmore touched a raw nerve in the public conscience when he announced his desire to die. Suddenly the public executioner looked like an accomplice in suicide. But it is patently absurd to argue that the death penalty is moral when the prisoner does not want to die but immoral when he wishes to do so. The only possible justifications for capital punishment are that it "fits the crime" and that it serves to deter the rest of the population from committing a similar crime.

5. Americans have long since rejected the morality of the "eye for an eye, tooth for a tooth" approach to criminal punishment. Experience has taught them that the appropriateness of a punishment depends upon the restitution it makes to the social order, its efficiency as a deterrent against similar criminal conduct and the contribution it makes to the rehabilitation of the criminal. The death penalty fails on all three counts. It does not restore the life of the murderer's victim. It does not seek to rehabilitate the murderer himself. It stands, for its justification, solely on its potential for deterrence.

6. Because the death penalty has long since ceased to be either certain or swift in the United States, the deterrent effect argument in support of the death penalty has lost its force. The death penalty has become uncertain because Americans rightly insist on tailoring the punishment not just to the crime but to the individual criminal. And the death penalty has become slow because Americans rightly insist that the full panoply of legal appeals be available to those condemned to die. What Americans must now recognize is that their commendable passion for justice has made the death penalty irretrievably unjust.

7. Moreover, the careful studies that have been made of the actual correlation between the death penalty and the commission of heinous crimes have resulted in a total failure of proof, positive or negative, that the death penalty has any deterent effect. Faced with this fact, supporters of the death penalty have resorted to a "common sense" argument. But common sense is not an argument when it is based on hunches rather than facts.

8. Most supporters of capital punishment concede that it can be justified only as a last resort. But given the lack of any empirical proof

that the death penalty works as a deterrent, the religious, philosophical and practical arguments against capital punishment become overwhelming. When the state deliberately executes one of its members in cold blood and as an act of sovereign justice, the state acts with an insupportable claim of total lordship and with irreversible finality. Moreover, no one has yet devised a "humane" method of capital punishment, and the very grisliness of an execution dramatizes its inherent inhumanity.

9.   The abolition of capital punishment would leave, of course, the problem of the proper confinement of heinous criminals unresolved. Anyone familiar with our prison system knows that there are some inmates who behave little better than brute beasts. But the very fact that these prisoners exist is itself a telling argument against the efficacy of capital punishment as a deterrent. If the death penalty had been truly effective as a deterrent, such prisoners would long ago have vanished. The incorrigible criminal is precisely that, and no number of executions will rehabilitate him. And as long as we have faith in the dignity of man and convictions about the limited sovereignty of the state, it is better to suffer the incorrigibility of a few than for the nation to revert to the barbarism of capital punishment.

QUESTIONS

1. Paragraphs 1–5 provide the narrative or background of the situation that prompted the *America* editorial, and lead into a statement of the point-at-issue in the argument about capital punishment. What background is provided? How does the editorial establish the point-at-issue?

2. What values and arguments relating to capital punishment does the editorial assume are evident to the readers of *America* and need not be stated or argued? What is gained by not doing so?

3. Paragraphs 6–8 present the chief argument against capital punishment. What is that argument?

4. Paragraph 9 concedes that the abolition of capital punishment creates a serious problem. What is that problem, and how does the editorial use it to reinforce the chief argument against capital punishment?

5. What form does refutation take in paragraphs 5–9?

WRITING ASSIGNMENTS

1. Shaw wrote his defense of capital punishment in 1921–22; the *America* editorial was published on December 11, 1976. Discuss the

extent to which the issues of capital punishment changed in the intervening years, given the evidence of these two arguments.
2. Discuss the extent to which you agree with the views attributed to
Americans today, including the attitude toward "eye for an eye,
tooth for a tooth" morality and toward capital punishment in the
abstract and in the concrete.

ANTHONY LEWIS

Let's Do It

1. In the early morning of Nov. 13, 1849, Charles Dickens came
upon a crowd outside Horsemonger Lane Jail in London. People were
waiting to see a Mr. and Mrs. Manning hanged for the murder of their
lodger. Dickens watched through the hours until sunrise, as the crowd
screamed and laughed and sang "Oh Mrs. Manning" to the tune of
"Oh Susannah." Later that day he wrote a letter to The Times of
London.
2. "A sight so inconceivably awful as the wickedness and levity of
the immense crowd collected at that execution could be imagined by
no man . . ." he wrote. "I am solemnly convinced that nothing that
ingenuity could devise to be done in this city, in the same compass of
time, could work such ruin as one public execution."
3. Three days later, after some other comment, Dickens wrote a second letter to the editor. He said executions attracted as spectators "the
lowest, the most depraved, the most abandoned of mankind." And he
said steps should be taken to limit titillation of the public by stories
about a condemned person.
4. "I would allow no curious visitors to hold any communication
with him," Dickens said. "I would place every obstacle in the way of
his sayings and doings being served up in print on Sunday mornings
for the perusal of families."
5. Not even Dickens, with his sense of the grotesque, could have
imagined the spectacle enacted last week in the United States. The last
sayings and doings of a murderer were retailed by the press. His picture graced the weekly journals. And the grossest details of his execution were reproduced on television, to be savored by millions of families in their homes.

6. Most people I know who have been physically present when the state killed a human being—prison wardens, priests, newspaper reporters—have thereafter been opposed to capital punishment. Twenty years ago, on assignment as a reporter, I watched an electrocution in the District of Columbia jail. When it was over, the room smelled of roasted flesh.

7. But to experience such scenes vicariously removes, for many, the nausea factor. Television drama has made blood and violence as acceptable as cherry pie. It was only a small additional step to restage an actual execution. And so we had the scene of Gary Gilmore's death on the evening news programs, and sketches of his last moment in sober newspapers.

8. Some press agencies wanted to hire helicopters to circle over the prison yard, but the Federal Aviation Agency vetoed that idea. Reporters were forced to rely on hourly bulletins from the prison authorities, which some complained were dull.

9. The great innovation in the Gilmore case was an execution literary agent. A movie producer named Lawrence Schiller signed the condemned man and his relatives to an exclusive contract for a film to be shown on television. Schiller was allowed to interview Gilmore for many hours in prison, and then to attend the execution.

10. The agent gave the press the juicy details of the end. When the execution order was read out by an official, Schiller said, "Gary looked at him, holding his own, not quivering." It was Schiller who said he "believed" Gilmore's last words were "Let's do it"—a phrase that the press flashed across the land.

11. Later, the press learned that Gilmore in his last days had had an intense correspondence with an 11-year-old girl named Amber Hunt. Miss Hunt was interviewed, and a week later her voice was still being heard on the radio.

12. The slaughter of gladiators and Christians in the Circus Maximus is generally regarded as a symptom of the decadence of Rome. What does it say about a country when punishment for crime becomes a circus, to be reenacted in every home? Can a society savor such spectacles without being coarsened?

13. Murderers do not usually deserve sympathy. But the objection to having the state kill them in turn is not sentimental. Using the apparatus of official power to extinguish a life has corrupting consequences—the more so when capital punishment is, as it has become in this country, a spectacular occasion: an event cruel and unusual.

14. In the absence of convincing evidence that executions deter mur-

derers, there must be a suspicion that the practice goes on to satisfy an atavistic public desire for dramatized vengeance. Revival of the death penalty in the United States may in fact encourage murder by persons such as Gary Gilmore—a man with suicidal impulses, who could have seen a way to assure his own spectacular death.

15. Dickens saw that point. In 1845, in a letter to a friend, he argued among other grounds for opposing capital punishment: "I believe it to have a horrible fascination for many of those persons who render themselves liable to it, impelling them onward to the acquisition of a frightful notoriety."

QUESTIONS

1. What is Lewis's purpose in writing—to show what Americans have become, or to warn them about what they may become? Does he generalize about all Americans?
2. How strong is the argument of deterrence for Lewis?
3. How do you think Lewis would answer Shaw's defense of capital punishment?

WRITING ASSIGNMENT

Analyze newspaper and magazine reports of the Gary Gilmore legal proceedings in November and December, 1976 or those of his execution on January 17, 1977. Discuss the prominence given certain features of the case—for example, Gilmore's statements concerning the proceedings and his behavior, and his "last words." Or analyze the reporting of a similar event.

FRANCES FITZGERALD
This Man's Army

1. President Carter's call for the registration of women for the draft cannot fail to stir some passionate debate in the United States armed forces as well as in Congress. For the possibility exists that the drafting of women, even for noncombat roles, will bring a radical change to the armed forces and to society at large.

2.   Of course there are many reasons to suppose that the drafting of women will make as little difference to the military system as women's suffrage made to the political system in the United States. Those who will predict a decline of morale or discipline may well be wrong.

3.   In the first place, there are already 150,000 women in the services, and while it could be argued that these are volunteers and that draftees would be another matter, the counter-argument is the result of universal conscription in Israel. Women in Israel have long served the armed forces in almost every capacity, including the manning (or womanning) of tanks along the Golan Heights. Demonstrably the morale and discipline of that extraordinary fighting force has not suffered.

4.   Then, too, women usually fight in guerrilla wars. In Vietnam, for example, women constituted an important part of the guerrilla (as against the regular military) forces. For some years, a woman commanded all the Vietcong forces in a major military region of the South. On the basis of their experience with women spies, saboteurs and assault troops among the enemy, United States commanders in Vietnam would have been hard put to argue that women lacked anything in skill, courage or the killer instinct.

5.   But in the Vietnamese guerrilla army, as in Israel, the decision to conscript women was based on sheer necessity: at stake was the very survival of an army and a people fighting on their own home ground. In the United States, the decision to draft women would be— uniquely, as far as I know—a matter of principle: to fulfill a conception of equal rights and equal obligations. As such, the decision would surely raise the hackles of military men who harbor other views of women and, more important, other views of soldiers.

6.   As correspondents in Vietnam in 1966, I and my women colleagues used to encounter a kind of hostility from American military officers and enlisted men that male journalists were spared. At the time I could understand why soldiers would refuse to take a woman into combat—when they would take an equally unarmed and untrained man. But what puzzled me for a long time was the hostility of soldiers in the rear areas or on the fringes of the combat zones, particularly when in the same situation American civilians and Vietnamese military men accommodated us with a fair amount of grace. Finally after spending a week in one military outpost town (where I was interviewing Vietnamese civilians, male and female) I figured out the reason for this hostility.

7.   The main emotion of the officers in that place was boredom—hor-

rendous boredom tinged with anxiety. Apart from the knowledge that they were serving their country, the one compensation the soldiers had was their sense of superior masculinity.

8. Watching combat movies every night, they conjured up a vision of themselves as heroes facing constant danger with courage and fortitude. My presence there was an affront, for it kept reminding them that there was very little danger there and that just about anyone could put up with it. The presence of a woman dispelled all the glamor of war.

9. The world has changed somewhat since then. The women's movement began in the middle of the Vietnam War, and my colleagues who worked in Vietnam from 1969 to 1971 reported feeling like Rip Van Winkle when they returned home. In the last two or three years of the war, many more women journalists went to Vietnam. They had a much easier time of it not because of a change in military attitudes but only because most of the United States forces had pulled out and the remaining American military advisers had come to dislike all correspondents equally.

10. Military attitudes toward women have changed far more slowly than civilian attitudes. There are many reasons for this, but one I have a certain sympathy with. One purpose of military training is to reduce individual differences and to make men as nearly as possible into replaceable units. A soldier's compensation for his loss of individuality is in participating in a group identity—and the more specific that identity, the more compelling. To draft women is necessarily to diffuse this collective identity—to change the very idea of what a soldier is. In the absence of a national emergency that would bind soldiers and civilians, men and women, together in a common purpose, the drafting of women takes away whatever fun there is in being a soldier.

QUESTIONS

1. What is the difference between the drafting of women in Israel and North Vietnam and the drafting of women in the United States? Why does the writer introduce this distinction?

2. What is the purpose of the discussion in paragraphs 6–10? Is FitzGerald reviewing her experiences in Vietnam to show that drafting women will be an exercise of their rights and obligations, or is there another point-at-issue? To state this question in another way, does she argue the issue of "equal rights and equal obligations," taking this to be the point-at-issue and worth discussing?

3. How does the writer establish her authority on the issue? Does she

claim that her explanation of male hostility toward women in the military is true?

WRITING ASSIGNMENTS

1. Write an argumentative essay in favor of or opposing the registration of women as well as men in the United States.
2. Write an argumentative essay on a current issue with which you have had personal experience. In the course of your argument, state what that experience is and how much authority it grants you in analyzing motives and events and stating what should be done.

GEORGE F. WILL

Armies Should Win Wars

1. Conscription is an issue that stimulates campus rebels whose lives are frustratingly barren of things to rebel about. It does reach a fundamental philosophic issue, the allocation of civic responsibilities. But it is, first, a question of military calculations.
2. Harold Brown, the Secretary of Defense, prefaces his annual report with words Lincoln wrote in April 1861: "I think the necessity of being *ready* increases. Look to it." There is so much the U.S. is not ready to do (such as enforce the "Carter Doctrine"), it is hard to say what should be looked to first. Not all readiness shortcomings involve manpower. (The U.S. is supposed to have 90 days' worth of war stocks in Europe but has less than 30 days' worth.) And conscription cannot cure the gravest manpower problems. Draft registration is a sound idea because it would expedite any emergency expansion of the broad training base of the military pyramid. But the gravest problems are higher up the pyramid.
3. Brown quotes Churchill: "You cannot ask us to take sides against arithmetic." The services just had their worst recruiting year, falling 24,000 short. But a draft of that number would touch only twelve of every 1,000 18-year-old males, six of every 1,000 18-year-olds. That would neither instill a "service ethic" nor leaven the military by significantly altering the racial or intellectual mix. Assuming the services are not substantially enlarged, the choice is between an all-volunteer and an almost all-volunteer force. If political leaders would lead a re-

vival of respect for military careers and would express society's respect through pay commensurate with that for comparable private-sector employment, there would be no shortage of first-term enlistees.

4. But the most critical shortages (2,400 Air Force pilots, 45,000 Army noncommissioned officers, 20,000 senior Navy petty officers) are retention problems. The manning of Navy ships and aircraft squadrons is significantly below combat readiness. People with vital skills sought by the civilian economy are being asked to make severe financial and family sacrifices to stay in the Navy. In Pascagoula, Miss., there are two completed and two partially built destroyers that Iran was going to buy. They should be heading for sea under the U.S. flag. But the Navy lacks the skilled personnel to man them. The fewer ships the Navy can rotate, the worse its retention problems become. When, on Feb. 25, the U.S.S. Kitty Hawk returns to San Diego, its home port, it will have been away for nine months.

5. Because conscription touches so many of society's moral dimensions, the case for or against it cannot be made merely by arithmetic. Gen. Maxwell Taylor, whose career has earned him the nation's continuing attention as well as lasting gratitude, says conscription is needed not only to provide "the reserves essential for sustained combat" but also "to demonstrate our seriousness of purpose." Certainly U.S. reserves are alarmingly weak on paper and are even weaker in reality. (Low-cost incentives, such as educational benefits, might rectify this more efficiently than conscription would.) And the strongest case for conscription is, indeed, that it would demonstrate, to the American people as well as the Soviet Government, U.S. seriousness.

6. But the Soviet Government might be more impressed by increased U.S. investment in other military assets, such as the high-technology weapons that are America's strength and that can be the basis of a war-fighting strategy that does not rest on maximum expenditure of manpower. Soviet strategy stresses massed armor attacking behind rolling barrages by artillery, so the U.S. needs an abundance of high-density assault-breaking munitions. The Soviet Union has 20 million trained reservists. U.S. forces should be configured for a strategy of avoiding, not winning, a Battle of the Somme, a battle of attrition.

7. The intricate debate about conscription is being muddied by the extraneous issue of sexual equality. Let us begin with basics. Douglas MacArthur to West Point's class of 1962: "Your mission remains fixed, determined, inviolable—it is to win wars. Everything else in your professional career is but corollary to this vital dedication. All

other public purposes . . . will find others for their accomplishment; but you are the ones who are trained to fight . . ."

8. So that open societies can survive in an inhospitable world, they maintain military establishments embodying values (authority, hierarchy, sacrifice, discipline) sharply at variance with those of the civilian populations. That is one reason why a relaxed democracy tends to disdain its military (until there is some dying to be done). The military mission is not to replicate the civilian society's evolving notions of equity. The mission is to be good at sustained, controlled violence.

9. There is evidence that women will volunteer in numbers sufficient for the noncombat roles open to them. The military cannot be an equal-opportunity employer unless it assigns women to combat roles. Granted, there is an artificial clarity to the distinction. Were war to erupt many women, such as mechanics with the Third Armored Division in Germany, would be in combat. But the distinction is worth trying to preserve, and not merely because combat is stressful enough without the added tension inescapably attendant upon mixing young men and women in extreme situations. The question is not just, or even primarily, whether women are physically "tough" enough. The question, at bottom, is whether this society wants participation in war's brutality broadened to include women.

10. Society is a seamless web and cannot anticipate all the consequences of abandoning an ancient practice that is deeply felt and subtly related to some of our civilization's best expectations. The almost instinctive and universal exemption of women from combat draws a line against the encroachment of violence upon havens of gentleness. It confers upon women a privilege of decency. It has been inseparably involved in the organic growth of societies committed to such things as the sancity of the family, and civilian supremacy. Before a nation breaks that cake of custom, it should have a better reason than the presumption that the settled practice of civilization is, suddenly, anachronistic.

QUESTIONS

1. Will builds from the lesser argument for conscription (paragraphs 2–4) to the greater argument (paragraphs 5–6). What is the lesser argument, and how does he show that it is the lesser? What is the greater argument, and how does he show that it is the greater?

2. How does Will show that the issue of sexual equality is "extraneous" and not the point-at-issue? Why do you think he introduces

this discussion at the end of the essay, where the issue gains prominence?
3. Will's argument against the conscription of women is a deductive argument, based on stated truths. What are these truths, according to Will, and what deductions does he make from them?

WRITING ASSIGNMENT

Discuss the extent to which FitzGerald would disagree with Will on the matter of the conscription of women. State whether there is a basis in her essay to believe that she would agree or disagree with other opinions stated in Will's essay.

THE NEW YORKER
The Victim-Armies

1.   President Carter's proposal to register women as well as men for the draft, being opposed alike by many feminists, who are against any draft, and by many supporters of the draft, who believe that wars should be fought by men, has clouded the policy that inspired the revival of registration in the first place. Intending to demonstrate the county's unity and resolve to the Soviet Union in response to its invasion of Afghanistan, the Administration has instead become embroiled in a murky altercation about the influence of women on men in trench warfare and about ratification of the Equal Rights Amendment, all of it superimposed on a renewed protest movement against any draft and a swelling debate, greatly amplified by an exceptionally crowded and busy Presidential campaign, about just what the potential draftees, whether men or women, might have to do under the Carter policy. In the spreading confusion, a somber declaration of national purpose to the world has degenerated into a highly visible domestic quarrel, with every member of the family loudly putting in his or her word.
2.   So far, the argument about women and the draft has centered on reasonable-sounding questions like whether or not women are physically strong enough for combat, but intense passions, undoubtedly fed by apprehensions of a more primeval sort, are churning just beneath the surface. War, of course, got its foothold in human affairs long

before women launched their drive, now in full swing in most parts of the globe, for equality with men in the public realm. In the traditional order, as feminist thinkers have often pointed out, the assignment of men to the battlefield and that of women to the domestic household were closely related. The presence of a protected, even hidden, domestic sphere, presided over by women, in which new life was brought into the world and the community was sustained, was felt to give war an elemental justification. As the bearers of children, women were the symbols and substance of peace and life, and were to be spared the destruction and death of war—except in defeat. The exclusion of women from war held intact a part of life *for which* wars could be fought by men. In the logic of this scheme, just as the migration of women from home to office, if it were to be unaccompanied by any rush of men in the opposite direction, would leave the home deserted, and thus would undercut one of the original aims of work—namely, the support of life—so the dispatch of women to war would, in a manner of speaking, empty out the heart of the community and undercut any justification for fighting.

3.   But even to describe these traditional arrangements for domesticity and war, whether one looks on them fondly or with anger, is to reveal that they have broken down irreparably across the board. The most thorough transformation has taken place in war itself. Insofar as any nation's military forces ever had the ability to protect its people, they have lost it now. The invasion of the civilian realm by modern war began with universal male conscription and the bombing of cities, and was brought to completion with the advent of nuclear weapons, which assail life at its genetic foundations. War has now penetrated to the core of the domestic sphere—its capacity for the renewal of life. Nuclear weapons have overmatched the procreativity of nature, and it is now they that, in an appropriation of life's characteristics, monstrously "proliferate," and bring forth one "generation" after another, as though death itself had gained the power to give birth and multiply. In the new military strategy, the role of the civilian population, including its heretofore undrafted female half, is to be held hostage by the rival nuclear power. Indeed, it is now an essential element of global stability that each superpower in effect bare the breast of its people to a nuclear attack or counterattack by its adversary; otherwise, deterrence, which depends on the vulnerability of each side to a reprisal by the other, would break down. Our nation, in a proper display of reverence for life, has exerted itself as one man to secure the release of some fifty hostages in Iran, but, in the same period, when nuclear war

over Middle Eastern oil has been under discussion we have somehow managed to pass lightly over the fates of the tens of millions of hostages which are at stake in such a conflict. Once, military forces were deployed to protect the civilian population, but now the civilian population is deployed to protect the military forces. Across the oceans, two vast victim-armies face one another. No one was ever registered to serve in this force, but we have all been conscripted into it anyway. Women, who are certainly strong enough to push the button—should any of them aspire to that doubtful honor—just as they are weak enough to die in a holocaust, don't have to be sent to the front lines; they are already there.

QUESTIONS

1. Written at a time when the registration of women as well as men was being considered by the Carter administration and was being debated nationally, this editorial comment in an important magazine shows how narrative can be used to define broader issues that remain after a specific proposal is rejected or forgotten. What are these broader issues, according to paragraph 2?
2. The editorial also shows how the point-at-issue in the current national debate can be redefined and shown to be a less important or unimportant consideration. How does the editorial accomplish this redefinition?
3. Does the editorial take a stand on whether women should be drafted, or is this issue left unresolved?

WRITING ASSIGNMENT

Letters to the editor of a newspaper or newsmagazine are frequently concerned with redefining the point-at-issue in a national debate. Examine a series of letters on a current public issue, and identify the point-at-issue in each of them, giving particular attention to those that explicitly redefine the issue. Then discuss your own views on the issue, arguing what you believe the point-at-issue should be.

Persuasion

BARBARA WARD

"Triage"

1. Now that the House of Representatives has bravely passed its resolution on the "right to food"—the basic human right without which, indeed, all other rights are meaningless—it is perhaps a good moment to try to clear up one or two points of confusion that appear to have been troubling the American mind on the question of food supplies, hunger, and America's moral obligation, particularly to those who are not America's own citizens.

2. The United States, with Canada and marginal help from Australia, are the only producers of surplus grain. It follows that if any part of the world comes up short or approaches starvation, there is at present only one remedy and it is in Americans' hands. Either they do the emergency feeding or people starve.

3. It is a heavy moral responsibility. Is it one that has to be accepted?

4. This is where the moral confusions begin. A strong school of thought argues that it is the flood tide of babies, irresponsibly produced in Asia, Africa and Latin America, that is creating the certainty of malnutrition and risk of famine. If these countries insist on having babies, they must feed them themselves. If hard times set in, food aid from North America—if any—must go strictly to those who can prove they are reducing the baby flood. Otherwise, the responsible suffer. The poor go on increasing.

5. This is a distinctly Victorian replay of Malthus.* He first suggested that population would go on rising to absorb all available supplies and that the poor must be left to starve if they would be incontinent. The British Poor Law was based on this principle. It has now been given a new descriptive analogy in America. The planet is com-

---

* Thomas Malthus (1766–1834), in his *Essay on the Principle of Population* (1798), argued that population growth would have to be controlled, because population increases faster than the food supply. He opposed relief for the poor and higher wages on the ground that these encouraged idleness and early marriage. Ed.

pared to a battlefield. There are not enough medical skills and supplies to go round. So what must the doctors do? Obviously, concentrate on those who can hope to recover. The rest must die. This is the meaning of "triage."

6. Abandon the unsavable and by so doing concentrate the supplies—in the battlefield, medical skills; in the world at large, surplus food—on those who still have a chance to survive.

7. Thus the people with stable or stabilizing populations will be able to hold on. The human experiment will continue.

8. It is a very simple argument. It has been persuasively supported by noted business leaders, trade-unionists, academics and presumed Presidential advisers. But "triage" is, in fact, so shot through with half truths as to be almost a lie, and so irrelevant to real world issues as to be not much more than an aberration.

9. Take the half truths first. In the last ten years, at least one-third of the increased world demand for food has come from North Americans, Europeans and Russians eating steadily more high-protein food. Grain is fed to animals and poultry, and eaten as steak and eggs.

10. In real energy terms, this is about five times more wasteful than eating grain itself. The result is an average American diet of nearly 2,000 pounds of grain a year—and epidemics of cardiac trouble—and 400 pounds for the average Indian.

11. It follows that for those worrying about available supplies on the "Battlefield," one American equals five Indians in the claims on basic food. And this figure masks the fact that much of the North American eating—and drinking—is pure waste. For instance, the American Medical Association would like to see meat-eating cut by a third to produce a healthier nation.

12. The second distortion is to suggest that direct food aid is what the world is chiefly seeking from the United States. True, if there were a failed monsoon and the normal Soviet agricultural muddle next year, the need for an actual transfer of grain would have to be faced.

13. That is why the world food plan, worked out at Secretary of State Henry A. Kissinger's earlier prompting, asks for a modest reserve of grain to be set aside—on the old biblical plan of Joseph's "fat years" being used to prepare for the "lean."

14. But no conceivable American surplus could deal with the third world's food needs of the 1980's and 1990's. They can be met only by a sustained advance in food production where productivity is still so low that quadrupling and quintupling of crops is possible, provided investments begin now.

15. A recent Japanese study has shown that rice responds with copybook reliability to higher irrigation and improved seed. This is why the same world food plan is stressing a steady capital input of $30 billion a year in third-world farms, with perhaps $5 billion contributed by the old rich and the "oil" rich.

16. (What irony that this figure is barely a third of what West Germany has to spend each year to offset the health effects of overeating and overdrinking.)

17. To exclaim and complain about the impossibility of giving away enough American surplus grain (which could not be rice anyway), when the real issue is a sustained effort by all the nations in long-term agricultural investment, simply takes the citizens' minds off the real issue—where they can be of certain assistance—and impresses on them a nonissue that confuses them and helps nobody else.

18. Happily, the House's food resolution puts long-term international investment in food production firmly back into the center of the picture.

19. And this investment in the long run is the true answer to the stabilizing of family size. People do not learn restraint from "give-aways." (The arms industry's bribes are proof enough of that.) But the whole experience of the last century is that if parents are given work, responsibility, enough food and safe water, they have the sense to see they do not need endless children as insurance against calamity.

20. Because of food from the Great Plains and the reform of sanitation, Malthusian fears vanished as an issue in Europe and North America in the 1880's. China is below 2 percent population growth today on the basis of intensive agriculture and popular health measures.

21. Go to the root of the matter—investment in people, in food, in water—and the Malthus myth will fade in the third world as it has done already in many parts of it and entirely in the so-called first and second worlds.

22. It may be that this positive strategy of stabilizing population by sustained, skilled and well-directed investment in food production and in clean water suggests less drama than the hair-raising images of inexorably rising tides of children eating like locusts the core out of the whole world's food supplies.

23. But perhaps we should be wise to prefer relevance to drama. In "triage," there is, after all, a suggestion of the battlefield. If this is how we see the world, are we absolutely certain who deserves to win—the minority of guzzlers who eat 2,000 pounds of grain, or the majority of despairing men of hunger who eat 400 pounds?

24.   History gives uncomfortable answers. No doubt as they left their hot baths and massage parlors for the joys of dining, vomiting and redining, Roman senators must have muttered and complained about the "awkwardness of the barbarians." But the barbarians won. Is this the battlefield we want? And who will "triage" whom?

DISCUSSION: Persuasion

How we choose to present our ideas depends on our purpose in speaking or writing. The demands of exposition and persuasive argument are not the same. In exposition, we are guided by the need to make our ideas clear; in persuasive argument, we need to be clear but, in addition, we want to present our ideas in the most convincing way. In describing how to sharpen a knife, our concern is to make the process clear to those who want to understand how to do it; our main concern is not to persuade them to do so. In both exposition and persuasion, the order of ideas may be determined by the audience. Writing to a general one, we may begin an exposition of a new medical treatment with definitions that an audience of physicians and nurses would not require. Directing an argument to a hostile audience, we may begin with ideas we know are acceptable and build to controversial ones.

Persuasive arguments present additional challenges. We must use exposition in presenting the background of the argument, but we must also construct a sound argument, arouse the interest of the audience through a legitimate appeal to their emotions, and show that we are honest and well-informed enough to deserve a serious hearing. Though some writers and speakers seek to avoid all emotional appeals in the belief that the soundness of an argument guarantees its persuasiveness, few if any arguments are entirely free of emotion. We need, then, to be aware of the kind of appeals we are capable of making. Earlier we quoted this statement of E. M. Forster:

> The desire to devote oneself to another person or persons seems
> to be as innate as the desire for personal liberty.

If such desires are indeed innate, we should have little difficulty in arousing the sympathies of our readers for the plight of their fellow human beings. The difficulty would obviously be greater if our readers held a view like the following:

> Each of us has interests of great concern to himself, but not nor-
> mally or naturally of great concern to other people. A few may
> sympathize if they hear that my life or my job is in jeopardy, but
> they will not bestir themselves very much.—J. R. Lucas, *Democ-*
> *racy and Participation*

The consideration in persuasive arguments is not *whether* to appeal to emotions, but rather what emotions we want to arouse and how, as we make the soundest argument we can.

QUESTIONS

1. The general issue of Ward's essay is the feeding of the poor throughout the world: the point-at-issue is stated in paragraph 3: "It is a heavy responsibility. Is it one that has to be accepted?" What are the real issues that Ward identifies later, in dealing with the point-at-issue?
2. What background or narration does Ward provide? How does she use this narration to state the assumptions of those who argue for triage?
3. What assumptions does she present, in opposition to those she is criticizing? How does she explain these assumptions?
4. Notice that Ward has put a deductive argument to the use of persuasion: this is why she must explain and defend her own assumptions. In doing so, what appeal to experience does she make, particularly in the concluding paragraph?
5. In the course of the essay, Ward poses a dilemma: either we select certain people to feed, or we all eventually starve and die. How does she deal with this dilemma?

WRITING ASSIGNMENT

Discuss the extent of your agreement with Ward's assumptions and conclusions. If you agree with her conclusion for different reasons, explain what these are, and defend them.

JONATHAN SWIFT

A Modest Proposal

For Preventing the Children of Poor People in Ireland from Being a Burden to Their Parents or Country, and for Making Them Beneficial to the Public

1.   It is a melancholy object to those who walk through this great town, or travel in the country, when they see the streets, the roads,

and cabin-doors crowded with beggars of the female sex, followed by three, four, or six children, all in rags, and importuning every passenger for an alms. These mothers, instead of being able to work for their honest livelihood, are forced to employ all their time in strolling to beg sustenance for their helpless infants: who, as they grow up, either turn thieves for want of work, or leave their dear native country to fight for the Pretender in Spain, or sell themselves to the Barbadoes.

2.   I think it is agreed by all parties, that this prodigious number of children in the arms, or on the backs, or at the heels of their mothers, and frequently of their fathers, is in the present deplorable state of the kingdom, a very great additional grievance; and, therefore, whoever could find out a fair, cheap, and easy method of making these children sound and useful members of the commonwealth, would deserve so well of the public, as to have his statue set up for a preserver of the nation.

3.   But my intention is very far from being confined to provide only for the children of professed beggars; it is of a much greater extent, and shall take in the whole number of infants at a certain age, who are born of parents in effect as little able to support them as those who demand our charity in the streets.

4.   As to my own part, having turned my thoughts for many years upon this important subject, and maturely weighed the several schemes of other projectors, I have always found them grossly mistaken in their computation. It is true, a child, just dropped from its dam, may be supported by her milk for a solar year with little other nourishment; at most, not above the value of two shillings, which the mother may certainly get, or the value in scraps, by her lawful occupation of begging; and it is exactly at one year old that I propose to provide for them in such a manner, as, instead of being a charge upon their parents or the parish, or wanting food and raiment for the rest of their lives, they shall, on the contrary, contribute to the feeding, and partly to the clothing, of many thousands.

5.   There is likewise another great advantage in my scheme, that it will prevent those voluntary abortions, and that horrid practice of women murdering their bastard children, alas, too frequent among us, sacrificing the poor innocent babes, I doubt more to avoid the expense than the shame, which would move tears and pity in the most savage and inhuman breast.

6.   The number of souls in this kingdom being usually reckoned one million and a half, of these I calculate there may be about two hundred thousand couple whose wives are breeders; from which number I subtract thirty thousand couple, who are able to maintain

their own children (although I apprehend there cannot be so many, under the present distresses of the kingdom); but this being granted, there will remain an hundred and seventy thousand breeders. I again subtract fifty thousand for those women who miscarry, or whose children die by accident or disease within the year. There only remain a hundred and twenty thousand children of poor parents annually born. The question therefore is how this number shall be reared and provided for? which, as I have already said, under the present situation of affairs, is utterly impossible by all the methods hitherto proposed. For we can neither employ them in handicraft or agriculture; we neither build houses (I mean in the country) nor cultivate land: they can very seldom pick up a livelihood by stealing until they arrive at six years old, except where they are of towardly parts; although I confess they learn the rudiments much earlier; during which time they can, however, be properly looked upon only as probationers; as I have been informed by a principal gentleman in the county of Cavan, who protested to me, that he never knew above one or two instances under the age of six, even in a part of the kingdom so renowned for the quickest proficiency in that art.

7.　I am assured by our merchants that a boy or a girl before twelve years old is no salable commodity; and even when they come to this age they will not yield above three pounds or three pounds and half-a-crown at most, on the exchange; which cannot turn to account either to the parents or kingdom, the charge of nutriment and rags having been at least four times that value.

8.　I shall now, therefore, humbly propose my own thoughts, which I hope will not be liable to the least objection.

9.　I have been assured by a very knowing American of my acquaintance in London, that a young healthy child, well nursed, is, at a year old, a most delicious, nourishing, and wholesome food, whether stewed, roasted, baked, or boiled; and I make no doubt that it will equally serve in a fricassee or a ragout.

10.　I do therefore humbly offer it to public consideration, that of the hundred and twenty thousand children already computed, twenty thousand may be reserved for breed, whereof only one-fourth part to be males; which is more than we allow to sheep, black cattle, or swine; and my reason is, that these children are seldom the fruits of marriage, a circumstance not much regarded by our savages, therefore one male will be sufficient to serve four females. That the remaining hundred thousand may, at a year old, be offered in sale to the persons of quality and fortune through the kingdom; always advising the mother to let them suck plentifully in the last month, so as to render them plump and fat for a good table. A child will make two dishes at an entertainment for friends; and when the family dines alone, the fore or hind quarter will make a reasonable dish, and, seasoned with a little pepper or salt, will be very good boiled on the fourth day, especially in winter.

11.   I have reckoned, upon a medium, that a child just born will weigh twelve pounds, and in a solar year, if tolerably nursed, increaseth to twenty-eight pounds.

12.   I grant this food will be somewhat dear, and therefore very proper for landlords, who, as they have already devoured most of the parents, seem to have the best title to the children.

13.   Infants' flesh will be in season throughout the year, but more plentifully in March, and a little before and after: for we are told by a grave author, an eminent French physician, that fish being a prolific diet, there are more children born in Roman Catholic countries about nine months after Lent than at any other season; therefore, reckoning a year after Lent, the markets will be more glutted than usual, because the number of popish infants is at least three to one in this kingdom; and therefore it will have one other collateral advantage, by lessening the number of papists among us.

14.   I have already computed the charge of nursing a beggar's child (in which list I reckon all cottagers, labourers, and four-fifths of the farmers) to be about two shillings per annum, rags included; and I believe no gentleman would repine to give ten shillings for the carcass of a good fat child, which, as I have said, will make four dishes of excellent nutritive meat, when he has only some particular friend, or his own family, to dine with him. Thus the squire will learn to be a good landlord, and grow popular among his tenants; the mother will have eight shillings net profit, and be fit for work till she produces another child.

15.   Those who are more thrifty (as I must confess the times require) may flay the carcass; the skin of which, artificially dressed, will make admirable gloves for ladies, and summer-boots for fine gentlemen.

16.   As to our city of Dublin, shambles[1] may be appointed for this purpose in the most convenient parts of it, and butchers we may be assured will not be wanting; although I rather recommend buying the children alive, and dressing them hot from the knife, as we do roasting pigs.

17.   A very worthy person, a true lover of his country, and whose vir-

---

[1] Butcher shops. (All notes in this selection are the editor's.)

tues I highly esteem, was lately pleased, in discoursing on this matter, to offer a refinement upon my scheme. He said, that many gentlemen of this kingdom, having of late destroyed their deer, he conceived that the want of venison might be well supplied by the bodies of young lads and maidens, not exceeding fourteen years of age, nor under twelve; so great a number of both sexes in every country being now ready to starve for want of work and service; and these to be disposed of by their parents, if alive, or otherwise by their nearest relations. But, with due deference to so excellent a friend, and so deserving a patriot, I cannot be altogether in his sentiments; for as to the males, my American acquaintance assured me from frequent experience, that their flesh was generally tough and lean, like that of our schoolboys, by continual exercise, and their taste disagreeable; and to fatten them would not answer the charge. Then as to the females, it would, I think, with humble submission, be a loss to the public, because they soon would become breeders themselves: and besides, it is not improbable that some scrupulous people might be apt to censure such a practice (although indeed very unjustly) as a little bordering upon cruelty; which, I confess hath always been with me the strongest objection against any project, how well soever intended.

18.   But in order to justify my friend, he confessed that this expedient was put into his head by the famous Psalmanazar,[2] a native of the island Formosa, who came from thence to London above twenty years ago; and in conversation told my friend, that in his country, when any young person happened to be put to death, the executioner sold the carcass to persons of quality as a prime dainty; and that in his time the body of a plump girl of fifteen, who was crucified for an attempt to poison the emperor, was sold to his Imperial Majesty's prime minister of state, and other great mandarins of the court, in joints from the gibbet, at four hundred crowns. Neither indeed can I deny, that if the same use were made of several plump young girls in this town, who, without one single groat to their fortunes, cannot stir abroad without a chair, and appear at playhouse and assemblies in foreign fineries which they never will pay for, the kingdom would not be the worse.

19.   Some persons of a desponding spirit are in great concern about that vast number of poor people who are aged, diseased, or maimed; and I have been desired to employ my thoughts what course may be taken to ease the nation of so grievous an encumbrance. But I am not

---

[2] A French writer, George Psalmanazar, who posed as a native of Formosa in a fake book he published about that country in 1704, in England.

in the least pain upon that matter, because it is very well known, that they are every day dying, and rotting, by cold and famine, and filth and vermin, as fast as can be reasonably expected. And as to the younger labourers, they are now in almost as hopeful a condition: they cannot get work, and consequently pine away for want of nourishment, to a degree, that if at any time they are accidentally hired to common labour, they have not strength to perform it; and thus the country and themselves are happily delivered from the evils to come.

20.   I have too long digressed, and therefore shall return to my subject. I think the advantages by the proposal which I have made are obvious and many, as well as of the highest importance.

21.   For first, as I have already observed, it would greatly lessen the number of papists, with whom we are yearly overrun, being the principal breeders of the nation as well as our most dangerous enemies; and who stay at home on purpose with a design to deliver the kingdom to the Pretender, hoping to take their advantage by the absence of so many good Protestants, who have chosen rather to leave their country than stay at home and pay tithes against their conscience to an idolatrous Episcopal curate.[3]

22.   Secondly, the poorer tenants will have something valuable of their own, which by law may be made liable to distress, and help to pay their landlord's rent; their corn and cattle being already seized, and money a thing unknown.

23.   Thirdly, whereas the maintenance of an hundred thousand children, from two years old and upwards, cannot be computed at less than ten shillings a piece per annum, the nation's stock will be thereby increased fifty thousand pounds per annum; besides the profit of a new dish introduced to the tables of all gentlemen of fortune in the kingdom who have any refinement in taste. And the money will circulate among ourselves, the goods being entirely of our own growth and manufacture.

24.   Fourthly, the constant breeders, besides the gain of eight shillings sterling per annum by the sale of their children, will be rid of the charge of maintaining them after the first year.

25.   Fifthly, this food would otherwise bring great custom to taverns; where the vintners will certainly be so prudent as to procure the best receipts for dressing it to perfection, and, consequently, have their houses frequented by all the fine gentlemen, who justly value themselves upon their knowledge in good eating: and a skillful cook, who

---

[3] Swift is attacking the prejudice against Irish Catholics in his time, and also the motives of a number of Protestant dissenters from the Church of England.

understands how to oblige his guests, will contrive to make it as expensive as they please.

26. Sixthly, this would be a great inducement to marriage, which all wise nations have either encouraged by rewards, or enforced by laws and penalties. It would increase the care and tenderness of mothers towards their children, when they were sure of a settlement for life to the poor babes, provided in some sort by the public, to their annual profit instead of expense. We should soon see an honest emulation among the married women, which of them could bring the fattest child to the market. Men would become as fond of their wives during the time of their pregnancy, as they are now of their mares in foal, their cows in calf, or sows when they are ready to farrow; nor offer to beat or kick them (as is too frequent a practice) for fear of a miscarriage.

27. Many other advantages might be enumerated. For instance, the addition of some thousand carcasses in our exportation of barrelled beef; the propagation of swine's flesh, and improvement in the art of making good bacon, so much wanted among us by the great destruction of pigs, too frequent at our tables, which are no way comparable in taste or magnificence to a well-grown, fat yearling child, which, roasted whole, will make a considerable figure at a Lord Mayor's feast, or any other public entertainment. But this, and many others, I omit, being studious of brevity.

28. Supposing that one thousand families in this city would be constant customers for infants' flesh, besides others who might have it at merry meetings, particularly weddings and christenings, I compute that Dublin would take off annually about twenty thousand carcasses; and the rest of the kingdom (where probably they will be sold somewhat cheaper) the remaining eighty thousand.

29. I can think of no one objection that will possibly be raised against this proposal, unless it should be urged, that the number of people will be thereby much lessened in the kingdom. This I freely own, and it was indeed one principal design in offering it to the world. I desire the reader will observe that I calculate my remedy for this one individual kingdom of Ireland, and for no other that ever was, is, or I think ever can be, upon earth. Therefore let no man talk to me of other expedients: of taxing our absentees at five shillings a pound: of using neither clothes nor household-furniture except what is of our own growth and manufacture: of utterly rejecting the materials and instruments that promote foreign luxury: of curing the expensiveness of pride, vanity, idleness, and gaming in our women; of introducing a

vein of parsimony, prudence, and temperance: of learning to love our country, wherein we differ even from Laplanders, and the inhabitants of Topinamboo:[4] of quitting our animosities and factions, nor act any longer like the Jews, who were murdering one another at the very moment their city was taken:[5] of being a little cautious not to sell our country and consciences for nothing: of teaching landlords to have at least one degree of mercy towards their tenants: lastly, of putting a spirit of honesty, industry, and skill into our shopkeepers; who, if a resolution could now be taken to buy only our native goods, would immediately unite to cheat and exact upon us in the price, the measure, and the goodness, nor could ever yet be brought to make one fair proposal of just dealing, though often and earnestly invited to it.

30.　Therefore I repeat, let no man talk to me of these and the like expedients, till he hath at least some glimpse of hope that there will ever be some hearty and sincere attempt to put them in practice.

31.　But, as to myself, having been wearied out for many years with offering vain, idle, visionary thoughts, and at length utterly despairing of success, I fortunately fell upon this proposal; which, as it is wholly new, so it hath something solid and real, of no expense and little trouble, full in our own power, and whereby we can incur no danger in disobliging England. For this kind of commodity will not bear exportation, the flesh being of too tender a consistence to admit a long continuance in salt, although perhaps I could name a country which would be glad to eat up our whole nation without it.

32.　After all, I am not so violently bent upon my own opinion as to reject any offer proposed by wise men which shall be found equally innocent, cheap, easy, and effectual. But before something of that kind shall be advanced in contradiction to my scheme, and offering a better, I desire the author, or authors, will be pleased maturely to consider two points. First, as things now stand, how they will be able to find food and raiment for a hundred thousand useless mouths and backs? And, secondly, there being a round million of creatures in human figure throughout this kingdom, whose whole subsistence put into a common stock would leave them in debt two millions of pounds sterling, adding those who are beggars by profession, to the bulk of farmers, cottagers, and labourers, with the wives and children who are beggars in effect; I desire those politicians who dislike my overture, and may perhaps be so bold as to attempt an answer, that they will first ask the parents of these mortals, whether they would not at this

---

[4] A district of Brazil notorious for its barbarism and ignorance.
[5] Swift is referring to the fall of Jerusalem to the Babylonians.

day think it a great happiness to have been sold for food at a year old, in the manner I prescribe, and thereby have avoided such a perpetual scene of misfortunes as they have since gone through, by the oppression of landlords, the impossibility of paying rent without money or trade, the want of common sustenance, with neither house nor clothes to cover them from the inclemencies of weather, and the most inevitable prospect of entailing the like, or greater miseries, upon their breed for ever.

33. I profess, in the sincerity of my heart, that I have not the least personal interest in endeavouring to promote this necessary work, having no other motive than the public good of my country, by advancing our trade, providing for infants, relieving the poor, and giving some pleasure to the rich. I have no children by which I can propose to get a single penny; the youngest being nine years old, and my wife past child-bearing.

QUESTIONS

1. Jonathan Swift (1667–1745), the son of English Protestant parents, was born and educated in Ireland. He therefore witnessed early in his life the sufferings of the Irish poor, most of whom were Catholic. Swift left Ireland in 1688 to make a career for himself in England; he returned to Ireland permanently in 1714, as Dean of St. Patrick's Cathedral in Dublin. In the succeeding years Swift wrote widely on various questions bearing on Ireland and England; for Ireland was an occupied country, impoverished and incapable of remedies for evils created by English policies. The Irish, for example, were restricted in selling their goods and could not produce enough food for themselves. In 1729 Swift, writing as a disinterested observer, proposed a "modest" solution to the poverty of the Irish. How does he establish the basic character and motives of this observer in the opening paragraphs of the proposal?

2. How does Swift reveal his attitude toward the writer of the proposal? Is he in accord with his general views of English motives? Are those motives stated directly or instead implied?

3. Is the proposer—and perhaps Swift himself—critical of the Irish poor, or does he exonerate them entirely?

4. Short of adopting the actual "modest proposal," is there another way of remedying the evils exposed in the course of the essay? In other words, does Swift suggest other policies that would reduce poverty and starvation in Ireland?

5. In general, what strategy does Swift employ to deal with English policies and motives and perhaps Irish attitudes too?

6. How persuasive do you find the essay? Is it an essay of historical interest or literary interest only, or does it have something to say to people today?

WRITING ASSIGNMENTS

1. Write your own "modest proposal" for dealing with a current social or political evil. You may wish to write as yourself or, like Swift, impersonate someone who wishes to make a modest proposal. Maintain a consistent tone throughout your essay, or at least make any shifts in tone consistent with the character of your speaker and his or her motives in writing.
2. Contrast Swift's attack on the English with Ward's attack on the idea of "triage." Distinguish the various persuasive means that they employ.

BARBARA BROWN
All the Poor Patriots

1.   Never has it been so apparent that the poor bear the burden of the future. This past summer, President Carter invoked faith to combat the energy crisis and presented practical guidelines for living out that faith: consume less, conserve more, consider the good of the world community in all things. Where I live, at least, there has been no sign of cooperation, except on the part of the ever-visible poor.

2.   The poor do not seem particularly conscious of their patriotism. One old man has been pushing a grocery cart up and down Peachtree Street for years, collecting bottles and aluminum cans for the few dollars they will bring him at a recycling center. He lives off the trash of the city, and has never heard of ecology. He does not own an automobile and does not make unnecessary trips out of town. His only experience with an air conditioner is in the doughnut shop where he waits out the nights. He is a model conservationist. He has no choice.

3.   When Atlanta opened the first six miles of its new mass transit system in July, the stations were for a while crowded with curious citizens from every neighborhood in town. Now that almost everyone has enjoyed the ride at least once, the trains, like the city buses before them, serve a predominantly black and poor working class. These

people use public transportation, loyally—not because the president asked them to, but because it is how they get to work on time.

4. Those of us who continue our commutes to the office in automobiles we cannot yet give up lament an energy crisis that is in fact a crisis of life style, of individual privacy and freedom. For as long as I drive my own car, I go where I want when I want, without asking permission or waiting for anyone. I can even tune in some music or adjust the climate to my comfort. It is a small thing to visit friends across town, and if the city begins to wear me down, I can always throw a suitcase into the trunk and head for the lake.

5. Such freedom is beyond the experience of whole populations, and it is this freedom that the energy crisis threatens to repeal. Because we cannot talk about the price of the way we live our lives, we talk about the price of gasoline. Because we cannot face the global compromise that is our only real hope for the future, we turn our backs, turn into reactionaries, who appeal with sudden fervor to the constitutional promise of liberty for all, which we misunderstand as license for each.

6. Even the church disappoints. In a July pastoral letter, the bishops of the Episcopal Church outlined their concern for world hunger and proposed that September 14, Holy Cross Day, be a day of fasting and prayer. For this exercise in self-denial, they suggested that "two light meals are appropriate and one meal eliminated altogether." Two light meals? Since when did two meals constitute a fast? If this is the church's institutional response to the world's hunger, one can only blush and apologize. The peasants of Nicaragua have not seen two meals a day since May.

7. The crisis is not one of energy but one of mortality. Cash has always purchased a mighty bulwark against the inevitabilities of discomfort and death, but the national economy has robbed more than a few of that privileged defense. Retirement savings are worth less now than when they were socked away years ago, and careful investments have shriveled under the hot sun of inflation. The old defenses are not working any more, and our human limits are cropping up all around us—cropping up from where they have been rooted all along.

8. Despite increased security, Atlanta's murder rate is double what it was last year, but what most of Walter Cronkite's audience does not know is that the majority of the killings happen in the poor parts of town, in the black and transient neighborhoods where the future is beginning to happen. Death is no stranger there, and everyone knows that money only hastens its appearance, as blood attracts a shark. The idea is to keep to yourself, mind your own business, and stay away from the door after dark.

9.   But on those blocks where neighbors get together and make commitments to one another, where they agree to watch each other's houses and keep track of each other's kids, the murders decrease, move on to other sections of town where people are not yet talking, are not yet pooling their resources. Their crisis is the real energy crisis, because whether the current issue is fuel or food or air to breathe, the fundamental crisis is what energy it takes to be human, and to survive on the planet with other humans—and not merely to survive but to live together in a way that defines integrity once and for all.

10.   It is an ancient lesson. Why are we so slow to learn? We are one body. If any part of the body suffers or sickens, so will the whole, sooner or later. If I have more than enough, it is because someone else has less than enough, and that is no platitude but physics. Our lives impinge upon one another. It is no longer possible to pretend that we are not related, that we exist independent of one another. Our fortunes are linked at head, heart and gut—and the poor command the crystal ball.

11.   I do not wish to sentimentalize the poor. Poverty is no tonic for character; it may in fact murder character, but what it guarantees is a severe simplification, a forced distillation of what is necessary for life and what is damnable luxury. This knowledge of the essences is the wisdom of poverty, and with just such unelected clarity do the poor bear the future into the present.

12.   Consuming less, conserving more, they are the good citizens of this country, but not by their own choice. They are patriots by necessity, because the expensive choices have already been made, and those of us still naïve to the power of their witness would be well—would do mortally well—to fear their rebuke.

QUESTIONS

1. The tone of this essay changes as Brown moves from her response to President Carter's appeal to her final statement of what constitutes a good society. What is the tone of her comments in paragraphs 1–3?
2. How does her tone change as she turns to the situation of the privileged in American society and to the response of the bishops (paragraphs 4–5)? What is the tone of the paragraphs that follow?
3. What is Brown's thesis, and what strategy has she chosen to persuade her readers of it? What satirical devices of Swift's does she also use?
4. In her concluding paragraph she returns to the point of her open-

ing paragraphs. How effective do you find this return? How effective is the rhetoric of the whole essay?

WRITING ASSIGNMENT

Compare the rhetoric of "A Modest Proposal" with the rhetoric of "All the Poor Patriots," noting similarities and differences in strategy and devices of persuasion. Comment on the relative effectiveness of these devices.

BAYARD RUSTIN
The Premise of the Stereotype

1.   The resort to stereotype is the first refuge and chief strategy of the bigot. Though this is a matter that ought to concern everyone, it should be of particular concern to Negroes. For their lives, as far back as we can remember, have been made nightmares by one kind of bigotry or another.

2.   This urge to stereotype groups and deal with them accordingly is an evil urge. Its birthplace is in that sinister back room of the mind where plots and schemes are hatched for the persecution and oppression of other human beings.

3.   It comes out of many things, but chiefly out of a failure or refusal to do the kind of tough, patient thinking that is required of difficult problems of relationship. It comes, as well, out of a desire to establish one's own sense of humanity and worth upon the ruins of someone else's. Nobody knows this, or should know it, better than Negroes and Jews.

4.   Bigots have, for almost every day we have spent out of Africa or out of Palestine, invented a whole catalogue of Negro and Jewish characteristics, invested these characteristics with inferior or undesirable values, and, on the basis of these fantasies, have engaged in the most brutal and systematic persecution.

5.   It seems to me, therefore, that it would be one of the great tragedies of Negro and Jewish experience in a hostile civilization if the time should come when either group begins using against the other the same weapon which the white majorities of the West used for centuries to crush and deny them their sense of humanity.

6.   All of which is to say that we ought all to be disturbed by a climate of mutual hostility that is building up among certain segments of the Negro and Jewish communities in the ghettos.

7.   Jewish leaders know this and are speaking to the Jewish conscience about it. So far as Negroes are concerned, let me say that one of the more unprofitable strategies we could ever adopt is now to join in history's oldest and most shameful witch hunt, anti-Semitism. This attitude, though not typical of most Negro communities, is gaining considerable strength in the ghetto. It sees the Jew as the chief and only exploiter of the ghetto, blames the ghetto on him, and seems to suggest that anything Jews do is inherent in the idea of their Jewishness.

8.   I believe, though, that this attitude has two aspects—one entirely innocent of anti-Semitic animus. The first is that the Negro, in responding justifiably to bitterness and frustration, blames the plight of the ghetto on any visible reminder or representative of white America.

9.   Since in Harlem Jews happen to be the most immediate reminders of white American oppression, they naturally inherit the wrath of black frustration. And I don't believe that the Negroes who attack out of this attitude are interested in the subtleties of ethnic, cultural, and religious distinction, or that they would find any such distinction emotionally or intellectually useful.

10.   It is the other aspect of the attitude that is more dangerous, that is consciously anti-Semitic, and that mischievously separates Jews from other white Americans and uses against them the old stereotypes of anti-Semitic slander and persecution. It is outrageous to blame Harlem on Jewishness. Harlem is no more the product of Jewishness than was American slavery and the subsequent century of Negro oppression in this country.

11.   In the ghetto everybody gets a piece of the action: those who are Jews and those who are Christians; those who are white and those who are black; those who run the numbers and those who operate the churches; those—black and white—who own tenements and those—black and white—who own businesses.

12.   Harlem is exploited by American greed. Even those who are now stirring up militant anti-Semitic resentments are exploiting the ghetto—the ghetto's mentality, its frustration, and its need to believe anything that brings it a degree of psychological comfort.

13.   The Jews are no more angels than we are—there are some real grounds for conflict and contention between us as minority groups—

but it is nonsense to divert attention from who it is that really oppresses Negroes in the ghetto. Ultimately the real oppressor is white American immorality and indifference, and we will be letting off the real oppressor too easily if we now concentrate our fulminations against a few Jews in the ghetto.

14. The premise of the stereotype is that everything that a man does defines his particular racial and ethnic morality. The people who say that about Jews are the same people who say it about Negroes. If we are now willing to believe what that doctrine says about Jews, then are we not obligated to endorse what it says about us?

15. I agree with James Baldwin entirely. I agree with him that we should "do something unprecedented: to create ourselves without finding it necessary to create an enemy . . . the nature of the enemy is history; the nature of the enemy is power; and what every black man, boy, woman, girl is struggling to achieve is some sense of himself or herself which this history and this power have done everything conceivable to destroy."

16. To engage in anti-Semitism is to engage in self-destruction—man's most tragic state.

QUESTIONS

1. Rustin deals with a specific point-at-issue—the attitude of some Harlem blacks to the Jewish businessman and landlord—but he addresses certain larger issues also. What are these issues?
2. These larger issues are a means—a strategy—of persuasion. Rustin might have appealed to the sense of fair play—another strategy—but he does not. Is the strategy he adopts more effective, in your opinion, and would an appeal to fair play have been ineffective?
3. Has Rustin sought to shame his reader? Is his tone accusing or conciliatory? Could the issue be treated in a satirical manner?

WRITING ASSIGNMENT

Rustin states: "The premise of the stereotype is that everything that a man does defines his particular racial and ethnic morality." Show how the "premise of the stereotype" can be used to deal unfairly with another minority, social or ethnic: women in public life, women in business, college students, the Irish, the Italians, the Poles, and so forth.

Continued from page ii
permission of William Morrow & Company, Inc. Copyright © 1973 by Marcia Selig-son. Selection title by editor.   **40** THE MEANING OF "NORMAL" From *Human Nature and the Human Condition* by Joseph Wood Krutch. Copyright © 1959 by Joseph Wood Krutch. Reprinted by permission of Random House, Inc. Selection title by editor.   **43** THE NEWSPAPER From *Allan Nevins on History*, edited by Ray Allan Billington. Reprinted by permission of Charles Scribner's Sons. Copyright © 1975 by Columbia University. Selection title by editor.   **46** KINDS OF DISCIPLINE From *Freedom and Beyond* by John Holt. Copyright © 1972 by John Holt. Reprinted by permission of the publisher, E. P. Dutton & Co., Inc. Selection title by editor.   **50** QUEUE From *The Crowding Syndrome* by Caroline Bird, published by David McKay Company, Inc. Copyright © 1972 by Caroline Bird. Reprinted by permission of the publisher.   **53** READING AND TELEVISION From *The Plug-In Drug* by Marie Winn. Copyright © 1977 by Marie Winn. Reprinted by permission of Viking Penguin Inc. Selection title by editor.   **55** THE ATHLETE AND THE GAZELLE From *The Ascent of Man* by J. Bronowski. Copyright © 1973 by J. Bronowski. Reprinted by permission of Little, Brown and Company. Selection title by editor.   **57** THE CONCEN-TRATION-CAMP INMATE From *Origins of Totalitarianism*, new edition, by Hannah Arendt. Copyright 1951, © 1958, 1966 by Hannah Arendt. Reprinted by permission of Harcourt Brace Jovanovich, Inc. Selection title by editor.   **59** CIRCLING THE MOON From *Carrying the Fire* by Michael Collins. Excerpted and reprinted by permission of Farrar, Straus & Giroux, Inc. Copyright © 1974 by Michael Collins. Selection title by editor.   **62** PINBALL From "The Inner Game of Pinball" by J. Anthony Lukas. Copyright © 1979 by The Atlantic Monthly Company, Boston, Mass. Reprinted by permission of the author. Selection title by editor.   **64** NEW YORK From *Here Is New York* by E. B. White. Copyright 1949 by E. B. White. Reprinted by permission of Harper & Row, Publishers, Inc. Selection title by editor.   **66** THURSDAY MORNING IN A NEW YORK SUBWAY STATION From *The Kandy Kolored Tangerine Flake Streamline Baby* by Tom Wolfe. Copyright © 1964 by New York Herald Tribune, Inc. Reprinted by permission of Farrar, Straus & Giroux, Inc. Selection title by editor.   **68** HOW TO SHARPEN YOUR KNIFE From *How to Make Whirligigs and Whimmy Diddles* by Florence H. Pettit. Copyright © 1972 by Florence H. Pettit. Reprinted by permission of Thomas Y. Crowell Company, Inc., publisher. Selection title by editor.   **69** SNOW HOUSES From *American Indian Arts* by Julia M. Seton (Ronald Press, 1962). Reprinted by permission of the Estate of Julia M. Seton. Selection title by editor.   **72** THE TELEPHONE From *Telephone: The First Hundred Years* by John Brooks. Copyright © 1975, 1976 by John Brooks. Reprinted by permission of Harper & Row, Publishers, Inc. Selection title by editor.   **75** THE AMERICAN VIGILANTE From *Vigilante!*, copyright © 1976 by William E. Burrows. Reprinted by permission of Harcourt Brace Jovanovich, Inc. Selection title by editor.   **78** HUDSON STREET From *The Death and Life of Great American Cities* by Jane Jacobs. Copyright © 1961 by Jane Jacobs. Reprinted by permission of Random House, Inc. Selection title by editor.   **88** THE FUNERAL OF GENERAL GRANT From *Always the Young Strangers* by Carl Sandburg. Reprinted by permission of Harcourt Brace Jovanovich, Inc. Selection title by editor.   **89** THE DEATH OF BENNY PARET From *The Presidential Papers* by Norman Mailer. Reprinted by permission of G. P. Putnam's Sons. Copyright © 1960, 1961, 1962, 1963 by Norman Mailer. Selection title by editor.   **91** THE TURTLE From *The Grapes of Wrath* by John Steinbeck. Copyright 1939, copyright © renewed 1967 by John Steinbeck. Reprinted

THEMATIC TABLE OF CONTENTS

Index of Authors and Topics

A 0
B 1
C 2
D 3
E 4
F 5
G 6
H 7
I 8
J 9